D0912719

BISON
BOOKS

TEXTS & CONTEXTS

AVITAL RONELL

# FINITUDE'S SCORE

ESSAYS FOR THE END OF THE MILLENNIUM

UNIVERSITY OF NEBRASKA PRESS: LINCOLN & LONDON

Acknowledgments for permission to
reprint previously published essays appear on p.xv.

Manufactured in the United States of America
♾
First Bison Books printing: 1998
Most recent printing indicated by the last digit below:
10 9 8 7 6 5 4 3 2
Library of Congress Cataloging-in-Publication Data
Ronell, Avital.
Finitude's score : essays for the end of the millennium / Avital Ronell.
p. cm. – (Texts and contexts) Includes index.
ISBN 0-8032-3911-4 (cl: alk. paper). –
ISBN 0-8032-8949-9 (pa: alk. paper)
1. Popular culture – United States – History – 20th century. 2. Avant-garde (Aesthetics) – United States. 3. Literature, Modern – 20th century – History and criticism.
4. Violence – Social aspects – United States.
I. Title. II. Series.
E169.04R66 1994 306'.0973–dc20
93-11942 CIP

TO THE MEMORY

OF

Paul Gershon Ronell

# CONTENTS

# PREFACE

As the millennium comes to an end, and the twentieth century scarifies our fragile memory, very little will stand out in terms of epochal splendor. If anything, humanity will have exhausted the heroic mythemes on which so much has been staked. Humanity (a term which acquired the prestige of its contemporary usage at the Nuremberg trials) will certainly have to rethink the projects and projections that have, despite everything, traced out a history of indecency – a history which compromises the very possibility of a thinking of futurity. In its fading moments, even as it signals change, the last century will have been dominated in the end by a diction of deficit: deficiency, whether immuno or projected outwardly and marked by complementary economies, no longer carries the bounce of lack or the sure fire of nihilism but says, more simply, that we have been depleted. This depletion has to do with a relation to the outside – a *national* deficit, for example – but it also controls a low-energy intensity that involves everyone. It seems as though all accounts of savings and saviors are understood to be depleted. Exhausted with the failure of models, identities, leaders, promise, so-called breakthroughs, vampirized by figures of exigence or ecstasy, the last century sees itself as standing out, if only in the sense that there is an outstanding debt to be paid – but to whom? to what?

In case you're thinking, Well, Avital, fuck her, she just lives inside her own head, this work reveals a growing concern over the finite figures that comprise our shared experience. As long as there is something like experience, it is not entirely mine. Nonetheless, if there is a growing sense that the writer is inhabiting an inside that is out of it, this condition cannot simply be debited to the account of the solitary worker but is rather a symptom pointing to *the vanishing of the experienceability of the world* – assuming that, after all is said and done, one can still say 'world.' In my previous work, I have tried to show in a Heideggerian way the shattering of world and, correspondingly, the extent to which 'worldview' (*Weltanschauung*) has been obsolesced. In this work, taking into account the fact of an irredeemably fissured world, I try to consider remappings urged by literature and psychoanalysis but also by the logic of teletopical incursions that has supplanted ground and grounding. On another level, in a requiem for George Bush, I trace the phantasmic history that has led to the relegitimization of war. In order to explore the recodifications of war for which 'GeoBush' is responsible, it was necessary to take recourse to psychoanalytic writings on paranoiac aggression and to understand how the Persian Gulf War metonymized the compulsion of the Western logos to 'finish with.' In this case, GeoBush's personal trauma in World War II was found to coincide with a national crypt which we understand as unmournable Vietnam. More technologically defined, the Gulf War disclosed the essence of the test site and the crucial relatedness of technology to testing. Still, the drama of an unfinished world war, which left wide open the question of air space, was refitted to Iraq according to the strategic command system of a very personal obsession. GeoBush's obsession with air space, which led me to inquire why there are so many cowboys in cyburbia, continued into his last days in office: eerily marking to the day and to the minute the anniversary of his initial bombing of Iraq, Bush announces that 'the skies are safer now.' His final utterance upon reviewing the military in January 1993 was to assure himself and us that closure had been finally, in the final moments, achieved. But what are the terms of such a closure? And has the double history of traumatic repetition been brought to term? Whether or not war can be read any longer as a Hegelian pregnancy test for historical becoming, we have to come to terms with the possibility that we no longer know how to wage war – which is why one has the uncanny sense of riding the wave of a personal pathology when finding oneself engaged in 'war.'

But political events are shaped by parasitical utterances as well. These range from rumors that cut you down at the job or on the streets to the deadly contagion that often shares the unstoppable curriculum of a spreading rumor. From the consistency of polemics to daily mutations in what we call war (on the streets, at work, out of work, or in your body), these barely visible forces, whose temporal run is not at all secured, can end up terminating you before your time, in the comma of an unfinished narrative. The status of rumor as a problem for a general etiology, the coextensive qualities of rumor and disease, are part of the mutating phenomena to which I devote a considerable amount of space. Working overtime and underground, the dynamic of rumor *and* disease control links the names of Shakespeare, Rousseau, and Nietzsche with those of our friends who have fallen victim to AIDS. But who today remembers these names, that is, who (to echo Rilke) remembers Gaspara Stampa?

You may no longer recall the precise sense of distress with which the names of George Bush and Rodney King – or even Goethe, for that matter – have been associated. The very transitoriness in the stature of these names reveals something about our relationship to a history that supplants monumentality with the incessant movement of fading in which we live. It has become hard to name singularity without conceding effects of technology that we associate with rapid turnover, substitutional acceleration, seriality, and the erasures which these imply.

One of the motifs that runs through these essays concerns the omnitopology of the police. Strictly speaking, it is no longer possible to cordon off or even to limit the force of policing according to discourse, neighborhood, or concept. Maybe you live in areas where they are not really breathing down your neck or making you eat the pavement. Maybe, you think, they're not really threatening democratic institutions, at least not empirically. Yet the police, haunting everything, are everywhere, even where they are not; their mode of being present does not coincide with presence, which is why the pernicious effects of increased surveillance need to be studied beyond any simplistic notions of a subject's 'being present at the scene.' Tracking the way in which our being has been modalized by technologies that work according to different protocols of ethical attunements, this work maps a politics of contamination, running a continuous APB on the figure of the police, no matter how fugitive, disseminated, or otherwise morphed: there is police work in Freud, where the police punch in a different time clock than that of the solitary detective who, working in the name of Truth, sometimes turns in the badge; there is the transcendentally policed site of Kafka's castle; there is in Goethe the SWAT team of *Bildung* that moves in on the fevered poet. It would be futile to summarize the policing and self-policing that has emerged with AIDS, but this is something to which I have pledged a number of pages and which, I am convinced, has unconsciously spread to dominate the rhetoric of the 'bloodless' and safe war in the Persian Gulf. In this regard I try to show, according to different registers of analysis, how the Gulf War became a technological test site in which our national body scored HIV-negative. It is here that the relationship between testing and technology sets forth a paradox of considerable consequence: there is no technology that will not be tested; but once technology is tested it is no longer, as such, a test. The test has everything to do with the way policing takes place in our modernity – even though 'taking place' is what is thrown into question by the exigencies of testing.

The provisional logic of the test infiltrates the very core of the technological project, exceeding the range of any model or machine. The test site as protoreal marks out the primary atopos, therefore, producing a 'place' where the real is put on the line, awaiting confirmation. If it were the case that technology had a finite, computable task – efficiency, minimization of labor, domination of nature – it would have destined its own finitude or homeostatic completion. Instead, technology ensures its own evolving perpetuation by positing, as its purpose, an infinite Testing severed from any empirical function. In effect, this means that an elliptical circuit has been established between Testing and the Real; a circuit so radically installed cancels the difference between the test and 'the real thing.' At this point, ethical dilemmas of the present negotiate matters of life and death through indirect media and according to a question which has more to do with testing than with certainty: Whom do we expose to risk? This question, typically subject to probabilistic determinations, would not be particularly new or difficult if the machine had not imported, as its negative condition, a crisis in computability. The machine is able to facilitate the process of prodigious computation only because it is predicated, as in the case of computer design, on a thorough reconsideration of the *meaning of computability.* Accordingly, risk has been submitted to revaluation: no longer an object calculable on the linear scales of a metaphysical ethics, risk finds itself implicated in the very possibility of calculation. The question of experimental testing, which touches everything from the recent wars, urban planning, and police, to space, medical, and reproductive technologies, to the aporias in ethics, drug testing, and GRE scores, involves a thoroughgoing reconstitution of the subject of law. If it were up to me, I would urge universities to draw up plans for instituting departments of the Field Test.

*Finitude's Score* culminates in a reading of the technopolice in Los Angeles with their electronic tagging systems and state of the art helicopter surveillance – an area recognized by William Gibson and Mike Davis as extending beyond the imagination of cyberpunk, obsolescing even the decisive edge of *Blade Runner.* The last chapters analyze the mediatic and technological dimensions of foreign and domestic war policies, but also the ectopian promise of interactive phenomena such as virtual reality, where the possibility of community is zoned according to newly designed spaces. The political disruptions ascribed to the figure of Rodney King made it necessary to read not the history of a subject but the place in the media where testimonial video breaks through the more institutionalized forms of broadcast television. The final essay, concerned with racism and performative television, explores the collapse of functions of policing and of television. The video tape of the King beating required us to reopen the dossier of the effaced Gulf War. When TV had collapsed into a blank stare, whiting out the Gulf War, nomadic video in turn flashed a metonymy of police action perpetrated upon a black body. More generally, television's obsession with crime time, cointricating structures of serial murder and serial programming, requires us to rethink the premises of national and international politics which will evermore be linked to the referential assignments of television and future cybervisual electronic systems.

~

This work offers a discursive sampler that reveals, if it reveals anything at all, an obsessive meditation on . . . well, I was going to say the persecuted, the culpabilized, but it would have been equally true to say on music, dissimulation, pleasure, and then I realized that, all told, this work is simply an obsessive meditation. The obsessiveness with writing, the insomnia, have spanned a number of years, often difficult, jobless, and certainly anxious years. Much of the time I was exploring a history of atopicality or of that which resists presentation: those things that are nonsubstantial, tending to obliterate the originariness of site, such as drugs, telephone, and haunted writing. Electronic culture, like drugs, indicated, I thought, a type of prosthetic *écriture*. This had implications both for the materiality of what I was observing and for the nature itself of my observations. On one level, prosthetic *écriture* had appeared to put writing under erasure. Among other things, the work on the telephone and drugs tried to elaborate the fate of writing within the technological field. Electronic culture makes us ask (again) whether it is now obsolete or timely to write. It arrives on the scene after writing has lost some of its instructional character, utilitarian necessity, or auratic quality. Of course, writing has always been thought to be that which is belated, secondary, excremental, and it does not stop with but actually infiltrates electronics and all the programs that involve us. Still, there is a sense in which *writing* has been obsolesced, divested, leaving us with the question of what to do with the remainders of writing. In my case, I would not hesitate to assert that I am writing for writing because it died. This is why, at least in part, writing is necessarily bound up with mourning. Yet there are many ways to mourn and to encounter the spectral experience in which technology plays a considerable part.

One last word. It is possible that *we have gone too far.* This possibility needs to be considered if we, as a species, as a history, are going to get anywhere at all. It is not as if I can draw the line beyond which going too far takes place, though one could try to do so without succumbing to simple linearizations. Sometimes it is clearer to me than at other times: it is possible that *this time* we have gone too far. So far, in fact, that the forceful distinction between destruction and devastation can no longer be maintained. Destruction implies the work of clearing away, of decisively doing away with that which, already destroyed, is destructive in its continuance. To the extent that it is possible only on the basis of a new and more radical affirmation, destruction, moreover, has pledged itself to the future. Devastation holds no such contract with futurity but, on the contrary, has to do with fundamental shutdown, even if things should keep on replicating themselves with regional improvements. A thinking of the future can no longer be pumped up by the pathological high of a telic finality or fulfillment or the accomplishment, once and for all, of a Goal. It is possible, this time, that we terrestrials have gone too far. And yet we would be remiss in our task if we were to assert that what has happened and what has failed to happen could be come to terms with here and now, without delay, at the presumed end of the millennium. The desire to finish once and for all, or to be done with definitively, is a legacy of the Western logos, promising finite transcendence but also a new, infinitizing start; and while I feel that termination is as much a myth as origin, offering the narcissistic comfort that goes along with closure – who would not want to wrap it up? – I have to call it as I see it: it may be that this time we have gone too far.

This book, a collection of essays, could not have been brought into its current form without the scrupulous care and insightful readings of my research assistant and friend, Shireen R. K. Patell. I could hardly fail at this point to acknowledge the rescue missions, companionship and sustained brilliance of Peter Connor, Marie-Hélène Huet and Pierre Alféri.

# ACKNOWLEDGMENTS

Grateful acknowledgment is made for permission to reprint the following: The first part of 'Queens of the Night' was published in ZYZZYVA (Summer 1994). The second part of 'Queens of the Night' was published in *Genre* XVI (Winter 1983): 405–22. © University of Oklahoma. 'Hitting the Streets: *Ecce Fama*' was published in the *Stanford Italian Review* VI, no.1–2 (Fall 1986): 119–40. 'Street-Talk' was published in *Benjamin's Ground,* edited by Rainer Nägele, 119–45. © 1989 Wayne State University Press. 'The *Sujet Suppositaire:* Freud and Rat Man' appeared in *On Puns: The Foundation of Letters,* edited by Jonathan Culler. © 1988 Blackwell Publishers. 'Taking It Philosophically: *Torquato Tasso's* Women as Theorists' appeared in MLN 100, no.3 (April 1985): 599–631. 'Namely, Eckermann' appeared in *Looking after Nietzsche,* edited by Laurence A. Rickels. © 1990 State University of New York Press. 'Doing Kafka in *The Castle:* A Poetics of Desire' was published in *Kafka and the Contemporary Critical Performance,* edited by Alan Udoff. © 1987 Indiana University Press. 'Starting from Scratch: The Mastermix' was published in the *Socialist Review* 88, no.2 (1988): 73–85. 'The Worst Neighborhoods of the Real: Philosophy–Telephone–Contamination' appeared in *differences: A Journal of Feminist Cultural Studies* 1, no.1 (1989): 125–45. 'The Walking Switchboard' appeared in *Substance* 61 (1990): 75–94. Reprinted by permission of the University of Washington Press. 'The *Differences* of Man' appeared in *diacritics* 19, no.3–4 (Fall-Winter 1988): 63–75. The first Activist Supplement to 'Support Our Tropes' was published by City Lights in 1992. The second Activist Supplement to 'Support Our Tropes' was published in the *Yale Journal of Criticism* 5, no.2 (Spring 1992): 73–80 as 'Support Our Tropes II.' A different version of 'Support Our Tropes' appeared in *Rhetorical Republic: Governing Representations in American Politics,* edited by F. M. Dolan and T. L. Dumm (University of Massachusetts Press, 1993).

# INTRODUCTION

You have all heard – by now – the story of writing's ambiguity, its instabilities, the scission in address to which it is notoriously susceptible. Fragile and exposed, the work exposes something other than itself; and if you do not quite grasp this, then you have encountered the work's own relation to the unknowing hesitation in which it originated. I would like to think that I am writing to the community of those who have no community – to those who have known the infiniteness of abandonment. As for me, to the degree that I am writing this to you, I never simply pose my solitariness alone. The one for whom I-write: 'The one for whom I write is the one whom one cannot know.'[1] It is precisely the unknown and the relation to the unknown that exposes me to death or finitude.

Always basically finite, what I-write can never become absolute. Its inescapable temporal predicament means that no final definition will ever stabilize or settle this writing. If it befell the work to be called a score it is not because I want to settle things with you, once and for all, absolutely and without reserve. Nor because I am tabulating some sort of achievement on the scoreboard of a finite *Bildung*. There will be no final tabulation, if only because one has to account for the incalculable and for the unexpected granting through which writing comes to pass. If I am in the position of giving you anything – and this is not clear to me – I know that one cannot hope to give anything but the future. That which cannot be given, what I in any case failed to give you before, is the past. (My fatality: I was never able to give my father the past. Children of survivors and of the persecuted in general will understand the brutal aporias of this fact.) All that one can give is what is going to happen, which may have little to do with a present that you can grasp. Perhaps this is a gift of nothing or, offered another way, a present of that which remains to come.[2] One can only give something to come, something to be enjoyed *tomorrow*. You surpass my initiative. From my place, which is that of a limit, I understand only that for this to-come not to be nothing, the *offering* of the to-come must have taken place. That's all. As you accompany me to the nonplace of writing you will come to sense that there exists an exteriority beyond appropriation, the advent of something that can be neither fully predicted nor contained. Exposed simultaneously to relation and absence of relation you discover an ectopia of all 'proper' places – the place of literature, the place of music, the woman's place, the workplace – and, gradually, you give yourself over to the anonymity of the work. What does the asserted dislocation to an outside have to do with the community of those who have no community, even if they should be quietly connected as a community of readers? 'If it sees its fellow-being die,' Georges Bataille once wrote, 'a living being can subsist only *outside itself*.'

> Each one of us is driven out of the confines of his person and loses himself as much as possible in the community of his fellow creatures. It is for this reason that it is necessary for communal life to maintain itself at a level *equal to death*. The lot of a great number of private lives is pettiness. But a community cannot last except at the level of the intensity of death – it decomposes as soon as it falls shy of danger's peculiar grandeur. It must take upon it what is 'unappeasable' and 'unappeased,' and maintain a need that thirsts for glory.[3]

This covenant with deadly intensity forms the dangerous commitment of community, even if it should be maintained in the solitude of the I-write. Here, to lose oneself in the predicament of the other implies no mystical ascension toward the value of infinity; it is rather to abandon oneself to abandonment, which is 'a level equal to death.' The incursion of an outside or *ouverture* bears all the intrusiveness of the trauma of the experience of finitude, which Bataille understood as shaping the community without essence, without a substantial project (qualities which, for example, would underlie a fascist community), a community shattered and way past the mirror stage of self-recuperation.

There is no finitude in or of itself. Finitude can make itself known only through the other's mortality. That, in part, is why I have never stopped calling you, each time in another way, according to a different impulse. I did not initiate the calls, they were never from or about me (how many times have we rehearsed this?) – it was the call of Being, first figured as the call of conscience in *Being and Time*. How could you have heard this call unless it had come from another's exposition of the finitude of their being? 'Finitude's score' is another tracing or inscription of a thought of mortality. Imparted to you, it begins by acknowledging the partition, between us, among us, a community of readers and activists, infinitely divisible yet sharing. At times, according to your own tempo or the movement of your hands, you will want to accompany me, the infinitely abandoned. There will be other times when you no longer recognize me. You will want nothing more to do with me. And then, one day, you will be brought back to the nonplace of writing. You will set aside your work, ignore the empirical accidents that harass your being like imperatives of life. You will not answer your phone; this other call will summon you, softly and deliberately. You are being paged elsewhere. Endlessly. Yet when you come to accompany me, it will not be simply in order to encounter the ambiguity of appropriations, which you already knew. This, this ectopia, is where you affirm the finite experience of nonidentity to yourself as underivable interpellation because this time, in time, it comes from the other, from the trace of the other. Yes, you will come to seek the affirmation without closure. Even if all the odds are against you and you are pressed by the time of a persistent regime that wants only to close you down. Resist the numbing banality of the they, the dictatorship of nonreading. Resist me, too, but only a little – enough to get traction and the trace of the other.

Sometimes you experience the suspensive nothing. You feel your need for interruption – the hiatus that marks you. There is interruption by the other, or by the presentiment of death. Remember the examples or figures of interruption like the caesura or the syncope. Nevertheless: interruption may always be a sign of life. Yesterday, in Irvine, I interrupted Derrida: 'How do you recognize that you are speaking to a living person?' He responded: 'By the fact that they interrupt you.' That was yesterday. Today I have slipped into the quiet grief of the work, the continuity of which can only be simulated. But I am not interested in producing the discursivity of a genesis, a history, a trajectory, a closure of the work and the inevitable prestige of the anomalies it bears. If anything interests me anymore, it is the community of the question: a threatened community. What does it mean to ask oneself something? Or to ask something *of* oneself? Only a being able to die is able to ask questions. Says Heidegger. It is the proper place of a *Sein-zum-Tode* to ask questions of herself, of a self given to her as another in its finitude. Asking, she understands that every question contains a demand of herself coming from elsewhere. And even when the demand is not put in the form of a question, it always requires some sort of answer. According to Heidegger, an animal cannot ask questions because it does not experience death. Derrida, in response, has suggested that there are, however, acts of questioning which do not necessarily take recourse to discursivity.[4] The consequences of this assertion are not inconsiderable, for this would mean that acts of questioning are not necessarily uniquely human. Plants may be questioning, too. Every living being is equipped for receiving information. Every living being is capable of investigation, looking for something, one doesn't always know what. Vegetal beings show curiosity: a plant or a root probes. This supplement of indeterminacy says no more than that the human *inability* to question is radically different from animal inability. These observations, as peculiar as they may seem, widen the scope of what it means genuinely to question without taking refuge in the humanist arrogance of man which has effectively destroyed world. The thought that 'man' is the questioning animal has long been abandoned; what has to be faced now is a history of the human inability to question.

~

If I am unable to trace for you the genesis of these essays, even if they can be seen simply to underscore a certain allegorical understanding of finitude, this would be in part because a thinking of finitude compels us to designate the crucial multiplicity and nonresorption of signification (even of Being) that it implies.[5] To the extent that thought is always finite, one cannot suppose it to be outside this world, in a world of transcendence or immanence. So we can't point ourselves to some mystified Elsewhere, the otherside of the metaphysical fence where desire paradoxically ceases to be itself because it is fulfilled. No other side for you but only the persistent struggle with expropriation, alienation, and other forms of exteriority that exist tensely in the world to which we are abandoned. Kafka once noted that there is an infinity of hope – only not for us. It is not my intention to bring you down. (On the contrary.)

The thoughts assembled here were not necessarily intended to face each other under one cover. They are, however, not absolutely foreign to one another in terms of the anxiety that produced them. These essays do not, at any point, simply leave the pressure zones of material and social existence. They don't flee the exigencies of the here and now which, after all, is the mark of finitude; nor can they claim to appropriate the meaning of the here and now by which they were occasioned and to which they point, because finitude, in its 'essence,' stems from the inappropriated nature of meaning. There is always something that slips by, an excess that cannot be accounted for, and it is only where, historically, finitude has been *infinitized* that endless damage has been done: the frightful hubris of metaphysical man. The inappropriation of meaning may be in effect the question over which the end of the millennium will break. If finitude should be the opening, the welcoming of such a break (and not merely a dead end), then possibly there will come another type of demand for meaning, one that does not practice strategies of avoidance concerning the devastation that substantial meaning has wrought. Finitude means, here and now, that we still have to come to terms with the terms that have legitimated a real experience of destruction in this century. Hopefully finitude, as opening and breakthrough, offers the way to bring to term something surprising, new, resilient. But it could be the case – and this hypothesis needs to be drawn away from the consolations of denial – it really could be the case that the devastation *was* too great: de-finitively insurmountable.

It is not the case that infinity would be simply opposed to finitude.

Jean-Luc Nancy writes of the infinity that is inherent in finitude. It would be foolish to imagine that *finitude* designates an absolute limit, if only because the concept of limit often reverts to the simplicity of linearization. An absolute limit – if it were possible to imagine such a thing – would be a boundary without an outside, without a foreign, neighboring land, an edge without an outer dimension. *Finitude* is not another expression for this desired limit that denies contamination, invagination, depropriation. It is not equivalent to a 'line in the sand,' though the matter of such a line, and those that circumscribe ghettos and other deplorable sites of containment, will be treated with some gravity in the pages to come. Finitude is not about the end in terms of fulfillment or teleological accomplishment but about a suspension, a hiatus in meaning, reopened each time in the here and now, disappearing as it opens, exposing itself to something so unexpected and possibly *new* that it persistently eludes its own grasp.

The fragility of finitude, which begins at the moment of birth (henceforth, there will have been no going back, no recuperation of the intemporality prior to separation), counts on the finite here and now, which is not calibrated solely on the time infused with grandiose plans and decisive gestures of sovereignty. The fragility of finitude has everything to do with those moments of hijacked existence, the motionless time of destitution, or the waiting period when something is expected to happen. There is recovery time, there are dead zones, hollow times, times of futile effort, the empty interval and bad timing; there is leisure time, the musical tempo, the meanwhile, the time you went out for a walk – and these are not the hurried moments, the rush, of Heidegger's ec-static temporality. There is the time of the unconscious, which is not always our time, but the time of another scene. There is the time, between moments, undecidably given as trace, the modalities of time given as indeterminacy (archē, lapse, moment, eschaton, duration, present, past, future, suspension). There is the time clocked by the history of philosophy (history, telos, founding, continuity, succession, the archē, futuricity), which is zoned across spatial positings (boundaries, limits, fragments, breaks, totalities, bodies, ensembles). Without the consolation, the wish fulfillment of dialectical reappropriations, there is the serious untimeliness of *différance.* The appearance of infinite *différance* is itself finite. Thus, *différance,* which does not occur outside the relation, becomes the finitude of life understood as an essential relation with oneself and one's death.[6] Infinite *différance* is finite. These matters belong to a large corpus of critical thinking that you will have worked through and for which I admit to lacking the pedagogical patience necessary to repeat their lessons. What should be clearly brought out is the fact of finitude's *excessive* nature, not only because of the inappropriability of its meaning (human finitude: *factum est*) but, as the experience of sheer exposition, because of the way it refuses to disclose itself fully.

Human finitude resists any formal definition or any structure [*Gefüge*]. We could say that every work, or at least every artwork, each time anew, in the finite here and now, is also an allegory of human finitude. Working through the fine lines of this allegory, Christopher Fynsk refers his reader to a passage in Gérard Granel's 'Et Tu, qui es?' in which the fragility of the work touches what Fynsk calls 'the self-refusal of human finitude' – the trace of Dasein's self-reserving finitude, the effect of withdrawal that 'belongs to the work's self-delimitation as a tracing of the rift-design.'[7] Strangely excessive, finitude is related to the nothingness upon which the work, in its very relation to finitude, leans:

> Every human occupation conjures too soon its nothingness, and this in effect produces in it 'holes' – an ataxy, an amnesia, a strange beauty, a clumsiness, a dwarfism, a giantism, finally whatever form of the unexpected and the unheard that *happens* to this practice, and upon which it cannot turn back (which is therefore its history and its destiny at the same time).[8]

This history, diffused as it is by the experience of ataxy and amnesia, run through by figures – oversized or miniature – of a traumatizing dispersion of the cognitive effects of memory and language, offers a compelling way of naming a relation to finitude which these essays, in accordance with their particular inflections, tonalities, and urgencies, attempt to engage.

~

This morning, after an hour of writing, I ended up cutting out the part in which I explain myself and justify the sequencing of the textual episodes that make up this volume. Then I decided (this went back and forth several times but then I decided): No excuses, no explanations, no complaints. The one for whom I-write will understand why this elision of protocol was necessarily difficult for me. This time, if you are so inclined, and want some guidance, you may wish to treat this work as you would a television – don't hesitate to interrupt your reading (don't forget to eat) – you may switch the order of chapters at will, channel surfing through different programs, some of which may rerun by you echoes of what was unfinished before. Only there are no commercials and there was very little support for keeping these channels open. Which is the way it is, this being America. One has to read against so many grains, against, at times, the finite here and now of institutional ideologies and political presumptions about scholarship.

In the pages devoted to Oedipedagogy, teaching (how to read) remains elusive and blinding as it remains the promise of future illumination. But it is a future that will never have completed its task in the present. There was, for the one for whom I-write, a history consisting of many scenes of pedagogy. In fact, you learned far too many lessons. There was still never enough time to read. On the streets, in schools, reading. Piano lessons, cosmetics, reading. The runs in your stockings, Hegel, reading. B-ball, concert tickets, reading. This opens the dossier of another scene of finitude's score, the place of a reading that starts from scratch, or from a metaleptic scream, and from the silence of one who, refusing to respond, still dwells in language. The figure of the inscribing/cry, the *Schreiben/Schrei*, the *cri/écrit*, continues to haunt these pages. It reappears in the brief narrative of Marguerite Duras, *Moderato Cantabile*, where every object is detached from its place of substance so that music becomes the site of an original crime, the taking place of which can never be properly reconstituted.

The narrative unfolds around the discordant community of readers. They have all been marked, and one of them is still marking. She holds the pencil, and tries to hammer the piano lesson home to the boy who will not respond. Despite the sharp tonalities that contour their separate ways, you recognize the discipline, the resistance, and the refuge that seated figures together 'represent' (the score undermines this trope). You, however, are mobile; you identify-with each of the three characters in this tensed scene of reading. The institutional imperative, demanding that a title be presented, that substantial meaning be ascribed to it – how often have you responded to this demand, you who have been both the victim and transmitter of this exhortation to produce a meaningful title.

> 'Will you please read what's written above the score?' the lady asked.
> 'Moderato cantabile,' said the child.
> The lady punctuated his reply by striking the keyboard with a pencil.
> The child remained motionless, his head turned towards his score.[9]

It is not solely a matter of knowing what is written above the score as part of the score, if you are to understand the inaugural gesture that introduces and names the thing to be read. 'Moderato cantabile' (henceforth MC) changes valences according to the place in which it is read: in the musical text, within the frame of the story, it tells how to read, or even how to perform a reading. At the same time, citing as it does the legal title of the work, MC differs from the value of mere utterance when referring to effects of legality. As that which repeats and therefore initiates the title as a thing to be read, MC suggests not only how the notations are, in this place, to be read but also represents the law of reading itself. As law, it emits nothing more than a signal; it shows the way in which the score *should* be read. The interpretation of the score would be left to the reader. Would you please read what is written *above* what is written? The topography of the *meta* dominates the text, pointing constantly to an inscription which would supercede what is presented as readable. Already split, MC acts as synecdoche for the entire text, while it also functions as a directive for interpreting the musical score. As surtitle and notation, containing and contained by the score, it poses the double enigma of reading and its relation to law.

Somewhere between the graphic inscription and sound, sensation and perception, performance and meaning, the movements of the story lead us to a place where 'to insist on the musicality of every image is to see an image in its detachment from an object, that independence from the category of substance which the analysis of our textbooks ascribe to pure sensation not yet converted into perception (sensation as an adjective), which for empirical psychology remains a limit case, a purely hypothetical given.'[10] It is a narrative that hovers between its impulse to dissolve into music and its desire to observe the imperious claims made upon it by language. And while the articulation of music's refusal to mean threatens the sovereignty of assertions made by language, it is never the case that music and language would be separated definitively, each repairing to a domain of seclusion; they are made to meet repeatedly in the hybrid space of a musical score, where it is not clear which moment of phrasing dominates and structures the other. The impossible couple that desires its fusion as much as it must evade and renounce such a hope (a fusion that would, at the very least, semanticize music, giving it meaning, and soften language, letting it dream), is doubled by the polemical couple of the piano teacher and pupil.

The scene of the piano lesson, moored in the customary regulations that have required the pupil to leave home, amasses the sadomasochistic edges of learning, exposing the piano student to a moment of ontological syncope, a between-time nowhere, opening another way of transposing 'finitude's score.' The inscribing/cry transpierces this narrative where the tensional qualities of title and its meaning recur, introducing each time anew the question of how to read, a lesson that begins with the instability of reading the score. The rhetorical ambiance of the opening section (the *ouverture*) scores points made by the teacher only by splitting them into bits and pieces, imparting to all participants of the impossible concert their assigned parts. There is the teacher with her pointed pencil and the motionless pupil, petrified. Provisionally, the passively reassuring ear of the mother triangulates the scene into which the resistance to reading is set. The immobility of the pupil fixes that frozen moment which holds together what has been shattered, the rigidity of the breaking point or interval. The French word for score is *partition*. The one who is made to face the score is way past the mirror stage – im-mediately shattered, divided by the reading to which, in this case, he has been summoned. Way past the mirror stage means there will be no movement of the reflective gaze that can put together or ensure the *composure* of the one who is made to read the score. No ideology of gathering or self-collection where reading would mean looking past language. The score poses instead the locus of marking which, reflecting nothing back, marks the reader by exposing him to the material effects of its gaps, rendering the score nothing more than a scar in time.

There is the immobility of the child faced with the score. Motionless with the presentiment of death, he is infused by a dread that fills the interval. His gaze, a dead gaze, indicates what it means to be looking ahead of himself, to face the music in the space between reading and performance. The child is motionless because being asked to read always full-stops him, it stammers, it has him stammer and silences him. What silences him – a death that announces itself when the hiatus erupts in the form of a scream, a sudden crescendo that appears to come from elsewhere. Do you remember the rarefied atmosphere that surrounded your piano lessons? And what it was like not to have sufficiently prepared? The stifled silence, your numbed resistance to the piano teacher's instructions? And how time would stop so that the metronome could take over? The somnambular twilight of those sessions.

In French, as I was saying, it is not solely a matter of what is written above the score. In French (but what's the difference, *score* scans the same way in English) you are asked, by the woman, would you read what is written 'au dessus de ta partition' – above your 'partition'; you are asked to read that which cleaves you, your *apartition*.[11] The child, at this point, does not respond to the figural level of demand, not yet, which is why he responds at all. He understands the demand of reading only to require of him a recital, a repetition of what appears to be there, on the page. He is not disposed to being marked, not immediately, by the signifier, as Lacan might have said. (If Duras said it, Lacan said it, Lacan has said.)[12] There is a moment, or the possibility of an interval, before the effects of the signifier divide the reader who recognizes in the text 'ta partition.' But what can this be, to read into your partition? Read your part, your share, that part of you which can be 'yours' only in the vertiginous movement of depropriation to which you submit by what we call reading. It is imparted to you but never as a full-on totality in which you might recuperate yourself or accede to the certitude of knowing thyself. If reading asks you to read what is inscribed above your partition, as an inducement to facing your partition, it is small wonder that you resist the pressure of this demand. In the familiar unfamiliarity of this place where you will not find yourself, read your part, *do* your share – and, responding to the demand, the child gives title to the text. The woman with a pencil, the teacher, possibly a writer, occupies in this scene the provocative place of the paternal metaphor, teaching law by disciplining the child, threatening him, punctuating the little boy's reply with the metonymy of beating time: 'elle ponctua cette réponse d'un coup de crayon sur le clavier' (7).

The demonstration of the imperative to read shows the strongest figure, backed by institution and tradition, to be the more impressionistic and thematic reader, weak, though at any moment capable of flexing the muscle of received meaning.

> 'And what does moderato cantabile mean?'
> 'I don't know . . .'
> 'I told you the last time, I told you the time before that, I've told you a hundred times, are you sure you don't know what it means?'
> The child decided not to answer. The lady looked again at the object before her, her rage mounting . . .
> 'You're going to say it this minute,' the lady shouted.
> The child showed no surprise. He still didn't reply. Then the lady struck the keyboard a third time, so hard that the pencil broke. (63)

The child knows but he also does not know what it means to be asked the meaning of MC. His malaise is traced not so much to the conviction that what he is doing has no meaning as to the immoderateness of her demand for meaning. To repeat and amplify the sense of a nonpurity that traverses the scene of reading, there is random interference and a number of sonic intrusions which stray into the text. The most eventful of these is constituted by the quick modulations of the scream, which disrupts the text's desire to become music. The first instance of a scream, or cry, muffled as it is, occurs when the child withholds a response to the demand for meaning. What in English stresses the suppression of a groan ('The lady stifled an exasperated groan' [63]), in French emphasizes the hidden experience of impotence ('La dame poussa un cri d'impuissance étouffée' [7]). The teacher recognizes in the performance of pedagogy her end of the line, too.

It is not that the child does not know the answer (he has been told a hundred times) but that the question which will resonate from the field of another scene, an exteriority beyond appropriation, concerns the story of human finitude. In the primal scene of reading, which locates the impotence of the phallic function to teach meaning or stimulate memory (the child will not memorize but he will have later learned the text 'by heart'), the scenography of pedagogical torture places, in the background, seated ten feet away, a mother. Anne Desbaresdes. It is her task to witness the scene of her son's refusal to respond: 'A woman, seated ten feet away, gave a sigh . . . Anne Desbaresdes sighed again . . . The child decided not to answer' (63). Or more correctly still, it is her task to telepathize with her son, transmitting secrets of another, more remote and less literal reading. Anne Desbaresdes, unable to teach anyone anything but bound by the desire to know, fixes a limit of pedadogy which will prove to have opened another type of research facility. In the meantime,

> When the door was closed, the child stopped on the staircase.
> 'You saw how awful she was.'
> 'Do you do it deliberately?'
> The child gazed at the cluster of cranes, now motionless in the sky.
> 'I don't know,' the child said.
> 'I love you so much.'
> The child began slowly descending the stairs.
> 'I don't want to take any piano lessons.'
> 'I could never learn the scales,' Anne Desbaresdes said, 'but how else can you learn?' (98)

In any case, the primal scene of reading which comes about as a forgetting to read is interrupted one day by a scream, a cry, an expression of pain that comes from outside or below. It is a murder scene that will never be fully reconstituted but which breaks the frame of reading that has pushed aside the forgotten outside – an outer dimension that is never strictly outside the scene of reading, no matter how many police lines are securing the boundaries meant to contain the scene of the crime:

> 'Begin again,' the lady said.
> The child did not begin again.
> 'I said begin again.'
> The child still did not move. The sound of the sea filled the silence of his stubbornness. The pink sky exploded in a final burst of color.
> 'I don't want to learn how to play the piano,' the child said.
> In the street downstairs a woman screamed, a long, drawn-out scream so shrill it overwhelmed the sound of the sea. Then it stopped abruptly.
> 'What was that?' the child shouted.
> 'Something happened,' the lady said. (65)

We never know for sure if the constitution of an ectopian drama is an effect of reading or whether the unconscious of a refusal to read erupts in the form of a crime. This other scene, the one that has erupted from below, thematizing the unknowable meaning of the event that never ceases to demand a reading, more mysterious and elusive than the first scene, introduces the cadences and risks which accompany the necessity of reading and the fragile finity of its tentative outcome. Anne, who can only read tropically, in an atmosphere of sweltering heat that dissolves all literality, knows little about the literal dimension of the story that erupts, as a primal scene, into the room to create a tear in the fabric of a primal, if primitive, scene of reading. Anne knows only the death of the one with whom she comes nonetheless to identify – the death of the other to whom I am exposed.

This would be the split screen of finitude's score. In the second scene, arriving belatedly only to assert its primacy, the mother assumes the role of the child who wants to know but cannot respond to questions that refuse to pose or posit the question of my-death, an event that you can never come to know in experience and even less through speculation, just as you were not there for your birth. The double screams of the finity marked by death and by birth arrest the text without the solace of any language or cognition:

> Anne Desbaresdes made an effort to remember again.
> 'It was a long, high-pitched scream, that stopped when it was at its loudest,' she said.
> 'She was dying,' the man said. 'The scream must have stopped when she could no longer see him.'
> A customer came in, scarcely noticed them, and leaned on the bar.
> 'I think I must have screamed something like that once, yes, when I had the child.' (79)

There are identifications and dissolutions of identifications, the mutating screams that meet each other in a frozen zone where pain accumulates. There was the traumatic call from elsewhere that did and did not target you. In any case, you were always charged with figuring out the meaning.

In the second, irruptive scene, the lady with a pencil dissolves into the patronne of the bar downstairs, the place where 'something happened.' She is knitting, throughout the story she is knitting, and looping the red texture that grows in her hands; she watches, but, above all she listens. She listens for the scream down here, she listens for the music upstairs, she listens to the lovers' murmur, and hears the gossip cut through by factory sirens; she regulates the radiophonic decibels that dominate the noisy end of the narrative ('After she had left, the patronne turned the radio up louder. Some of the men complained that in their opinion it was too loud' [118].) Like the landlady in Kafka's *Castle*, the piano teacher/patronne acts as arche-interpreter, gathering the story as she gathers her yarn, ever setting things straight while stricturing the story as it proceeds. She commands a certain accredited knowledge in the space over which she presides, a space where she can interpret the subtle modulations of movement with a shrewd sense of anticipation and resolute déjà vu. The scream, the scream comes from elsewhere and can neither be divested of its excessive quality nor made to mean. It *is* the mark of finitude's excess par excellence: undecidably given between music and language, prior to signification, it also says, 'I've had enough!' It names the halting screech of the death drive, down there where traffic is stopped, at least for a moment of the finite here and now, the time of the suspensive nothing. As frozen syncope in signification, the scream *sees* what it cannot articulate, possibly because it comes from the future or, more poignantly still, from the unrecollected past. Someone has heard the scream. In fact the community shares the event of having been exposed to the scream. Paradoxically, its singularity generalizes itself without pause. The police and the inspector arrive in order to supply the scream with representation and closure. They write the report. But they, they are another story.

While intimately related to the couple that constitutes itself as readers of an unknowable story, the teacher/patronne enjoys a more assured, if diminished, sense of what has come to pass. You do not know what has happened, yet elsewhere, in your inward exteriority, you know the story that precedes and produces you. The couple, they speculate upon what has preceded their initiative and dissolve themselves in drink, blurring boundaries, forgetting the pitches that times their secret meetings; they cease to hear the sirens or radio broadcasts drowning out the silence of the bar, and, as they drink, they try to resurrect the memory of a story they will never have experienced but which they nonetheless repeat.

~

I have to return. If the child has resisted offering a response, this derives from the fact, in the earlier experience of reading, that something overwhelms the confusion introduced by the topology of what is to be read, or by the interlinear translation that is demanded of him. Above the score, as part of the score and yet also extraneous to it, parergonally situated, his task, surpassing the demand of the teacher, requires him to read *nonthematically*, in other words, to read music, the desemanticized field of notation always aspiring toward a language of which it must fall short. But precisely this interval between music and what it will not do and cannot say produces an allegory of the impossible place in which reading begins to take place. This exercise has consisted in nothing less than a reading of language that comes before or after music, telling you how to read the music but also naming the text in which music reads literature. Asked to read a pure dynamic, the young reader is at once asked (literally) to read for meaning and not to read for meaning, because reading for meaning on this score would already be a metonymic substitution for what was never meant in the first place. The child slows down the allegro of meaning which the teacher had prompted with her pointed pencil. He slows down the scene to the point where the pencil returns in the other scene, the contiguous yet ectopian drama, in the form of the lead bullets that riddle the body of the text, signaling the 'meaning' of violence which, precisely, is to have no meaning, to exceed our grasp, or to mark the absolute scandal of death, though it can be followed in certain cases by the symbolicity that grants it the veil of meaning and the ritual of stability.

In MC, the primary scene of simplified triangulation in effect shows that reading is never done alone or for oneself alone; even if the father is absent from the scene, or displaced to the phallic teacher, he seems to make his way back into it by the diffusion of a law that punctuates time and intervenes as noise. The oppressive and primary atmosphere in which reading is to take place, as a reading of law – 'What does it say' 'What does it mean?' 'You must separate from your mother who is now here with you.' (' "We might try having someone else come with him to his lessons," she said. "We could see if it did any good." "No," the child shouted. "I don't think I could bear that," Anne Desbaresdes said. "And yet I'm afraid that's what it will have to come to," said Mademoiselle Giraud' [96].) – opens the room to the paternal undercurrents striking the key points of the Lesson to be learned. Nor will reading take place without the effects of a technicity that marks the gaps or belies the transcendental silence that is supposed to envelope the work. As it turns out, there exists no purity of reading, but rather pressures are exerted that produce the ineluctably *multimediatic* scene of reading: the sirens, the radio, the random noise, the traffic that jams what was never in the first place silent. There is no thought of creation that is not accompanied by music or its corruption – a prior sounding that makes absolute silence resound. Yet, when facing the score the child at first is paralyzed by the possibility that the music will not come out. When he does manage to strike the keyboard, translating notations into sound, surpassing himself, we discover that each note returns as an echo through a different medium, resisting absolutely the specularity or self-reflection that reading, or playing, appears to offer to the inexperienced. Beyond the mirror stage, older than Narcissus, reading produces an interruption of relation to self, partitioning the one who reads, breaking the specular reflection of any reading. The piano lesson is also an organ lesson. The Diabelli sonatina, when it emerges, goes in one organ (the crowd in the bar becomes an ear that soaks up the sound) and out the other (a man in the crowd becomes stiff with desire for the receded mother of the child). But with the shattering of reflection and the dissolution of individuation, there comes on the scene as its double and extension the threat of frenzy, the Dionysian meltdown that occurs ectopically, but also inside, for the window remains open and the Apollonian dream is not opposed to Dionysus. Introducing the death of each instant into being, Dionysian violence endlessly reopens the possibility of reading finitude's score.

Once again the music crescendoed to its final chord. And the hour was up. The lady announced that the lesson was finished for today.

TRISTAN: Tristan du,
ich Isolde,
nicht mehr Tristan!

ISOLDE: Du Isolde,
Tristan ich,
nicht mehr Isolde!

Wagner *Tristan und Isolde*

# FINITUDE'S SCORE

.01 MIXED MEDIA: If he said it once, he said it twice. Friedrich Nietzsche understood opera to be the genre par excellence of contamination. In fact, it was not until he was a DJ that N. started working on a reel to reel, scratching and popping, going with the disjunctive flow of sampling. That's when he began to like what he saw. In the meantime, trouble was opera's middle name. It would be lodged as the irony of the eternal return, showing signs of negativity and disease. As if it still owed us something – if only an account of itself – opera has an outstanding debt. For the record, Nietzsche once felt that the choice of opera indicates a kind of vampirism, a depletion of musical purity's essential resources. Music used to be pure and strong, an accomplice to will. Where the *Genealogy of Morals* conceived music as the superior language, as the independent art as such, set apart from all other arts in that it does not offer up images of phenomenality but speaks rather the language of the will itself, directly out of the 'abyss' as its most authentic, elemental, nonderivative revelation – and where the musician 'became a kind of telephone from the beyond, a ventriloquist of God,' – the *Genealogy* argues that opera, which places music at the service of a text, is bad music. Of course, this means that Nietzsche must have suppressed the inscription of music, its status as text, in favor of a kind of demagnetized hookup which we shall have to consider.

In itself, music remains intelligible to the servant of Dionysus while opera merely offers a remedy against pessimism. Indeed, its side effects induce life-despising symptoms, for it marks the triumph of Socrates or Christ over Dionysus, of nihilism over life.[1] To the extent that it operates on the wrong side of the sound tracks, opera itself cannot, strictly speaking, be understood in Nietzschean terms, that is, under the conditions of affirmative action. Its form as artwork is inscribed in what Nietzsche calls the history of *ressentiment.*

This history unconsciously constitutes the discovery made by Catherine Clément in her provocative book on opera.[2] Opera somehow offers resentimental utterances against its own feminine figurations. But the case is possibly more difficult than Clément allows and, as Nietzsche has shown, resentment is not external or extraneous to opera; it cannot be regarded as a mere theme or detachable syntagm of the operatic desire. *Ressentiment* is the very articulation of the suffering, separation, and death machine that opera puts in gear.

Clément casts opera as the repression of the feminine without, however, reading the ideology of phantasms in which opera continues to be invested. By repeating the separation of which opera stands accused (male versus female, music versus text, in-house versus outdoors, and so on), and by trying to get even with the tradition through a mere reversal of priorities, her book is acting out the very symptoms of opera that Nietzsche had scrupulously reviewed. Where opera offers up the drama of self-severance, Clément presses a theoretical reinscription of the couple that comes to be asserted in an unreflected mode. Rather than handling the constitutive falling apart of the couple, Clément prefers to go steady and thus remains absorbed by the ressentimental structures that opera is constantly trying to throw up. The irreconcilable difference of the couple (Zorastro and the queen, Wotan and Brünhilde, Madame Butterfly and Mr. Pinkerton, Lucia and her brother, Moses and Aaron), the lack ensuing upon its breakup, and the fundamental untranslatability of its couples into sameness (music and language, music and drama) – this open wound of double or nothing – may well constitute opera's most serious legacy. Opera is the gathering place for a couple that relentlessly transmits its otherness to itself, teaching the nonappropriability of one term to the other within an economy of internal alterity or absolute difference. Indeed, if opera exhibits itself as divided species (or even as the difference of species: Papageno, and the proliferating zoomorphic signifiers of *Fledermaus*), this splitting is due in part to the property holdings of text and music, libretto and score, composer and author. Clément, however, typically reinscribes the unity of the couple responsible for producing the *petit a* opera, reminding us to recognize *Don Giovanni* as the offspring of Mozart and Da Ponte: 'yes, [Da Ponte] wrote the text of *Don Giovanni,* attributed eternally and to the end of time, to Mozart alone. Yes, the libretto of *Pelléas et Mélisande,* and Maeterlink's words, so naked and so sad, heard with such pure lucidity, are an essential part of the opera.' Regathering lost couples, Clément tries, moreover, to establish property rights for a body that has been usurped by the living: 'Opera's recent evolution produces yet another occultation. Now it is not even the musician who is the author. No, it is a third thief, who takes advantage of the other two: the director. I heard *Simon Boccanegra* called an opera by Giorgio Strehler. (This is so strange that I did not understand what was being said.) Pretty soon they will be saying that *Lulu* is an opera by Patrice Chéreau.'[3] This peculiar feminism that wants to establish proper paternity and legitimate authorship does nothing less than slide home into the precincts of the metaphysical male subject. Rehabilitating the rule of law and copyright, Clément exposes the true couple behind the couple, the classical paradigm for the transmission of knowledge: the one on one, which is to say, the man to man. Controlling and controlled, the seed may not spill over according to a logic of dissemination. It will never go to number two, in this case, to a director, or, for that matter, a woman.

Despite the theoretical discord which her book ineluctably provokes, Clément will have helped us locate the couple as the trauma zone in the being of opera. In this regard, the book opens up opera's pained readability. Opera will never get over itself as couple, one that practices s/m and domination rituals, constantly readjusting the terms of bond and bondage between the text and the music that sets it up. Yet, to the extent that music is said to dominate the text, it potentially reduces all language to the level of babelization, containing the language within it as a fall from the prelinguistic purity of sound. Opera stages the birth of language as a fall, a kind of 'thrownness' from the musical source. It would repeat the primordial shock in the splitting of sound into language and music. The question of accompaniment, or of priority of one over the other in the drama that severs language from music, bringing it together in the bastard form of opera, requires one to think the split and the transferential activity that opera engages. Unlike acts of translation – of one linguistic idiom into another, whose singular difficulties have been elaborated in the texts of Walter Benjamin, Paul de Man, and Jacques Derrida – opera has no original, but rather originarily happens as the work of translation without origin. Opera is not about the generation of one form into another; it cannot assert an organic totality, a kind of transcendental unity of its disparate forms. This is not to say that opera did not dream such a totality of its parts or desire an origin. You cannot establish with certainty whether the music precedes the text or whether it goes the other way around: which is why opera opens the great politics of contamination.

.02 BABEL ON TOUR: *Die Zauberflöte* (*The Magic Flute*) exemplarily thematizes the self-knowledge of opera as the contaminative genre. *La Voix humaine* (*The Human Voice*) deconstructs a certain reading of contamination by affirming it. The human voice comes to be supplemented by a prosthesis (a flute, a telephone) just as God has to be prosthetically reconstructed after Babel. Opera offers up a song of Babelian language, celebrating the divine union that is known to be missed. God, the promise of a universal idiom, is both the origin and victim of a crime that seeks to couple. Ever since the beginning, the couple has been made to answer for the crime (Adam and Eve, Abraham and Isaac, Moses and Aaron). I would like to make these somewhat dogmatic assertions clear.

Let us start with a sort of transfer that gives opera a peculiar status within the Babelian performance.

Opera is always lifting those words which enter its thematic body like a violent infectivity. As if to underscore the otherness of language to itself, its lingering proximity to a form of musicality, some composers seek their libretti in foreign tongues. This at once retains language in an aspect of alien otherness but also absorbs its semantic dimension to the musical code. Something of an altogether different order happened when Wagner refused the foreign tongue, preparing the stages of paranoiac opera within the dream of a totality of art forms, the *Gesamtkunstwerk.* The excess that we call 'Wagner' seeks to incorporate a totality which however places its essential bets on the exclusion of otherness. A totality without contamination is the Wagnerian dream. But something had to be sacrificed to the dream of a transparency, something had to go the way of repression. Surprisingly, the orchestra itself became the excluded negativity – the scriptural space that converts the score into sound was driven underground. The site of technicity, where music and instrument coincide, slipped into darkness. Stuff the orchestra in a darkened pit, Wagner said, under the stage, suffocate it the way you drive out the index of otherness. Collapse one of opera's lungs. The otherness of the orchestra to the living operatic body is something Wagner made explicit for us.[4] He was not the only one, but he marked off the trauma of the split. Mozart arranged the flute as magical otherness; Poulenc installed the telephone to amplify the orchestra as difference. But to the extent that all opera participates in the dream of pure transferability, of a transfer that would secure purity, it is perhaps not an accident that opera is also the phobic art form. *The Magic Flute,* like *Otello* or the Ring cycle, runs in part like an antipollution machine trying to clean up the toxic spill of Babel. Opera is at once occupied with the commensal of its first couple – the parasitic couple, music and language – and with trying to wipe out an internal difference. This first couple will have committed a crime which opera knows but can no longer name. It concerns the guilt of language that cannot bear music or create a genuine synthesis. In this respect, opera offers us a sidelong glance at the Babelian couple incarnate. Each calls out to the lack in the other. In the demand that their encounter make sense, opera figures the irreducible difference in language and music. Language, for its part, is left a little emptied by the encounter, for it discovers that it can never hear itself unless music plays the other of itself. This does not mean that music scores a victory over language. Music finds in language that it has been critically denied access to saying what it means. It is like Papageno: gagged. Not understanding what opera is about can therefore not be considered simply an accident that has befallen opera. Of course, we recognize the banal themes or familiar topoi. But this is beneath understanding or rather secondary to the 'aboutness' of opera. Not understanding opera is about the confusion that ensues from its disjunctive union, the impossible recuperation of the otherness that inhabits it. 'Confusion' is another name for Babel.[5]

To be sure, opera wears other masks, and hardly cares for theorizing its predicament. For the sake of appearances it is expected that opera expose its unity, somehow arranging a bridal party for two absolutely heterogeneous values. It is to follow the prescription made out by that opera of suture, *The Marriage of Figaro*. Divided, ambivalent, the ceremony nonetheless promises an effect of the universal idiom which is music's dowry. The marriage of these values reminds us that the bond or obligation implied by their accord does not pass between a donor and donee, a position of determinable strength and one of weakness, but rather between two texts. The ring that opera offers itself circles a circumscribed space of acknowledged difference which is then more or less effaced, depending on who's writing the inscription on the ring. But to the extent that opera constitutes itself within this double indebtedness of irreconcilable difference, it is also already establishing the grounds for a divorce court. It arranges the place where, within the continuum of a ceremony, the marriage will have turned to a failed institution, one that gives itself a hearing. How could opera not name this failure to couple?

This would be the broken record of opera. Forever and again, within the irony of the eternal return, the annulus does not close upon itself but keeps open a drama of nonrelations. In this sense, by formally and thematically posing the question of belonging and breaking out, opera comments on the aesthetics of closure.[6] The operatic embrace is open-ended, like the debt parceled out by the two values. The accounts are hardly closed but tell the story of a relation of affinity that stubbornly resists transferability. The broken contract between music and language does not imply that they are not in a desiring rapport to one another. On the contrary. The infatuation was so great that it had to come to this contract. They thought they had found something more originary in one another, a lost ground – the origin, for instance, of language in music. This, however, was before Babel. After Babel, they would need what Jacques Derrida has called a 'translation contract'; they needed to promise 'a kingdom to the reconciliation of languages. This promise, a properly symbolic event adjoining, coupling, marrying two languages,' offers to link two parts of a greater whole.[7] The symbolic complementarity or harmony between music and language is perhaps more fragile and indebted to the divine than language's scramble for comprehensibility.

.03 *THE MARRIAGE OF FIGARO*, DIVORCING THE QUEEN: In a crucial sense, Mozart's *Die Zauberflöte* stages its resistance to translation.

Mozart finally trips on the mother tongue. Of course, this will be *his* mother tongue, if such a thing there be, for opera cannot be said to command a truly native language. It is after Babel. In any event, Mozart at last produces an opera that in a sense dramatizes the loss of an originary, mother tongue. She is pressed for time and will literally go under, get pulled down from the sky. A mother brought down to earth, tumbling like the Tower of Babel, offered to systems of pollution and mutilation. This explains perhaps why Mozart had to begin with the apotropaic flute, a kind of dagger-flute that will turn against its original, female bearer. Let us start with this magic flute. Why is the flute magic, why must it enchant? It offers itself as a well-traveled maternal phallus on the road to exile. It sonically traces the borders of a divided realm where divorce reigns and the lunar realm of the feminine splits off from the rising regime of enlightenment. An opera whose formal levels thematize contamination and divorce, it charts the triumph of a *ressentiment* implemented by the priestly culture of Zorastro – indeed, a distant and divorced cousin of Zarathustra. Somewhat enigmatically, Mozart names his opera after an instrument he did not particularly like. This has something to do with the logic of inoculation deployed by Mozart's dying piece. Mozart was very ill and, as his letters to Constanze show, he identified with the sense of *Tod und Verzweiflung* [death and despair] expressed by the queen. Now, read in a Nietzschean light, the Queen of the Night can be seen to figure the embodiment of immediate and originary health. This health, which is to be understood at a level of symbolization and in terms of the valuation wars raging in the opera, is, for all its exemplariness, the most fragile of conditions. The magic wand or flute secures immunity, projects a safety zone within which the provisional owner is free of foreign agents. As it detaches itself from the queen, the flute points to the breakdown of originary health which, in fact, is shown to be the most vulnerable, the most exposed and 'immunodeficient.' Motifs of originary health, difference, cold independence fall before the spectacle of the daughter's marriage in the precincts of reason, in the paternal groundedness of the Enlightenment. Health has had to separate itself from itself in order to guarantee the victory of reason, that is, in Nietzsche's terms, of *ressentiment.* When it ceases to be the property of the original figure, the magic flute (health) becomes a mere *instrument* of increasingly failing strength. In another context I have tried to interpret the text of this opera in a way that would privilege a notion of impaired host defense within a movement marked by infectivity, parasitical inclusion, immunosuppression.[8] In a word, *The Magic Flute* would expose the drama of opera, an oeuvre knowingly caught up in syndromes of defenselessness and deficiency but, in the first place, it presents the misinterpretation of a foreign substance or disease-causing agent that enters the operatic body itself. The queen, Mozart's last antibody and guardian of the magic flute, will have had her forces steadily annulled. She gives away the gift of immunity to an exogenous invader who is headed straight for priesthood. He will become a monster of the Enlightenment and rather more pernicious than the worm by which he is pursued at the outset. The discourse of reason eventually assimilates the invader to its culture. Mozart calls this invader Tamino. I prefer to call him 'Contamino.'

*Die Zauberflöte,* as title of the opera and immunocompetent object, is Mozart's gift to himself. If such a claim for Mozart's *Gift* can be made in the mood of a Babelian conjugation of the English and German, it is in part because Mozart had little tolerance for the flute; he disliked the very instrument that was to name the remedy, the milieu of sonic shelter for his work. Thus the flute itself, the object and the name of the object, had to undergo an immunological treatment of sorts. It had to be de-demonized, disinfected, cleansed – made *Sauber* – or enchanted, *Zauber.* In short, it had to *become* the inoculating instrument, *die Zauberflöte,* the very stylus of immunization. (The monstrous quality of this shaft is reflected in the opera's other coded monster, the figure of Monostatos, whose name means single stemmed or single legged.) Handed the phallic syringe, Contamino becomes what he is. He eventually proves injurious to the noble host, nurse and nourisher, causing infection more by exploiting host susceptibility than by his own powers of pathogenicity. This, of course, strips the plot to the bare bones of an immunopathological action.

.04 THE ORCHESTRA PIT: Just as *Die Zauberflöte* was Mozart's last opera, *La Voix humaine* was to be Francis Poulenc's. Both operas can be said to perform the anguish of being cut down or cut off. They both singularize an instrument, the one ostensibly coming from the inside of an orchestral pit (the flute); the other belonging to a presumed outside of orchestrality (the telephone). But is this so? Are we absolutely secure in thinking that the telephone is not an instrument? Where can we locate it? The telephone hooks up with the conductor's baton as he operates the orchestra. It is not only a transmitter of musical signals but also a receiver. Entire orchestras have been heard to buzz within the labyrinthine cup of the telephone receiver. In *The Castle* Kafka alerts us to the *Gesang,* the children's chorus haunting the telephone. When they put you on hold, the telephone starts singing Muzak. In this way it is not only an instrument but an entire opera house which attends your ear. The telephone, then, cannot be asserted to exist in a simple relation of exteriority to music. It plays the position of an internal alterity. This brings us back to the trauma that Wagner introduced into music. When he wanted to incorporate the orchestra as exterior, when he rearranged the topography of production, Wagner himself turned the orchestra into a telephonic structure by driving it out of visibility's range, making it remote to the scene, in other words by changing the orchestra into a long-distance call.

As parasitical inclusion, the telephone engineers the noise that music suppresses, marking the disruption of musical closure or interiority. It is the locus par excellence where voice, language, and instrumentality share a common residence. The telephone marks the place where instrument and voice contaminate one another; it is the opera house of technology. Its click anticipates the curtain call.

In order to understand the politics of contamination practiced by Poulenc when he installed the telephone in the interstices between voice and instrument, thus conjuring a condensed doubling of operatic logic – the phantom of the opera – it is necessary to rewind to where Nietzsche names the purity of a music that would not yet be pulled into the districts of opera's hysterical inmixation.

A direct hit from the abyss, on the side of the most authentic, elemental, nonderivative revelation, the place most resistant to images of phenomenality, music is said to emerge as the language of the will itself. No problem so far. What seems particularly noteworthy, however, is that Nietzsche installs the telephone at a precontaminated site, prior to music's infection by opera. Telephone cables are set up in diaphanous heights, putting through calls that outdistance the Kantian aesthetic of castration. Kant is out of line, Nietzsche has decided, because he doesn't cut it with the figure of the artist. That is why Kant's take on art is stained with an essentially effeminate aesthetics. The other aesthetic, over the boundary of a marked masculinity, skips the gender gap altogether to technologize or at least to complicate the itinerary of the individual: the musician becomes a kind of telephone.

What this means essentially is that Nietzsche, anticipating Poulenc, scrambles the codes of what properly belongs to the precincts of musicality. The telephone, while extending a cord outside classical notions of musical closure, is the connection itself between music and a kind of transcendental touchtone of meaning: 'a kind of telephone from the beyond, a ventriloquist of God' (136). It is not clear whether God's requiem has yet been sung or if the telephone is all that is left, a delay call-forwarding system of the divine. Nonetheless, the emphasis is placed on the line to the beyond, the other end whose virtual presence is signaled by sheer instrumentality. As instrument, however, the musician, telephonically constellated, becomes the body through which an absent alterity – 'God,' the Other, the undead, you name it – speaks. Be that as it may, Nietzsche will have evoked the telephone as a transcendental Sprint to the beyond in the *Genealogy*. But already in the stages of foreplay that figure 'the seduction of the ear,' Nietzsche, in *The Birth of Tragedy*, starts wiring his texts telephonically. In the competition between phenomenal image and the sonic blaze, who would be so petty as to deny the possibility that Dionysus is a telephone? 'The Dionysian musician is, without any images, himself pure primordial pain and its primordial reechoing' (50).

The intersection between the imageless musician and God's mediated mode of absence, their relation to opera, rarely passes the scanner without pointing up Moses and Aaron, the telephonically structured couple. The ear of Moses is affixed to Aaron's transmitting mouth. There is something prompting the couple, a figure of thirdness, which is why Catherine Clément's gender gapping does not suffice to explain the genealogy of musical desire. Consider the difference between the way Nietzsche clears the abyss of gender while Clément spins her wheels in a peculiar heterosexist pit:

> Often the men are the musicians or the musicologists. One of them plays a piano. The piano has almost a physical attraction for him; he caresses it, makes it glow like a woman brought to climax. He shines its black frame and golden insides, he manhandles it. He represents all those for whom the music comes first, as the invincible giantess, the supreme mistress, love in the absolute. And for him opera is perversion itself. . . . This perfect musician is a Don Juan who has invested the enveloping nature of music with the fantasy of an ever elusive, inviolate woman. Impenetrable; that is why he loves and protects her.[9]

Clément is much more penetrating when she stops settling the sexist score. (Her sexism is no doubt inadvertent; still, why must so many forms of feminism be channeled through resentment? What would have happened if one considered this: 'Often the women are musicians or musicologists [Alicia de Larrocha, for instance, and Susan McClary, who introduced Clément's book]. One of them plays a piano. The piano has almost a physical attraction for her; she caresses it, makes it glow, like a woman brought to climax.' Well, she would possibly have to rethink the rest of the libretto to liberate it.)

When Clément leaps from one male fantasy to the other, she makes a surprise landing on the golden calf which, likened to opera, pits itself against Moses. 'Yes, the Golden Calf, something the people like, like opera. Yes, there is always some Moses to come down from his Sinai and destroy the idols. . . . Talk talk talk.' Now, Moses, the censor, essentially tries to supplant a televisual metaphysic with a telephonic logic; he wants to smash the image, even the phonetic image. He is in a restricted sense a servant of Dionysus, resisting the Apollonian mask. But more importantly, Moses is the partial headset of a speaking apparatus: receiving messages from the beyond, he requires another part, a transmitter. Aaron is the mouthpiece of the stutterer, Moses. Receiving and transmitting, the telephonic couple 'by a perfect coincidence' happens to figure 'one of the last operas in history (which) is called *Moses and Aaron.*' Clément names this a 'borderline opera.' Destabilizing the image and thematizing voice, speech and song, *Moses and Aaron* never reaches completion. It collapses as the impossibility of opera, an allegory of its deconstitution. 'Two characters engage in dialogue: Moses, who does not sing but speaks and Aaron, his brother, who does not speak and who gets the singing part. In other words, the best part in opera.'[10] Unfortunately, it makes little sense to cite Clément's discussion. She has shot her wad in fixing this opera as the last of a genre, but the unreflected opposition between singing and speaking and what constitutes the 'best part' do not contribute to theorizing opera. While locating the culmination of a certain history of opera in *Moses and Aaron* may not be original with Clément it nonetheless serves to emphasize a break-off point in the conceptualization of the art form, which is to say, the moment when opera confronts itself as its own double in vertiginous specularity: the meeting of language and its other, their union contracted by God, their break up and irreconcilable separation, all played out within the reflective narcissism and absolute synchrony of two brothers. Opera will have resolved itself into a stereophonic couple organized according to transmitting and receiving ends, cut off by the static on a singular line to the beyond-opera.

.05 THE SEVERED SILENCE: A few years prior to *The Undoing of Women,* Jean-François Lyotard devoted several pages in "Several Silences" to Schönberg's couple.[11] In a somewhat psychedelic admixture, Schönberg is made to signal both the position of Luther and the return of Judaism as device. To the extent that serialism was his Reformed church, Schönberg, asserts Lyotard, is the Luther of new music (Lyotard is the Luther of citation: 'just as Deleuze and Guattari say that Freud was the Luther of the unconscious; just as Engels says that Adam Smith was the Luther of modern political economy within the confines of private property' etc.)[12] At the same time, Schönberg, qua Luther, is truly Moses. This news seems to have been released by his press agent, Theodor Adorno:

> Schönberg, as Adorno rightly points out, wants to destroy appearances; Schönberg's exodus is far from musical Egypt, from continuous Wagnerian modulation, from expressionism, from *musica*

> *ficta,* in the direction of the desert: voluntary impoverishment of means, the series, the two operations – inversion and retrogradation, the four positions. (104)

The desert mapped out by Lyotard institutes the signifier to be shared by composer and analyst. Yet the desert maps a new mode of immobility, folding back upon its concept by denying the straying or drifting movement that titles Lyotard's book (*Driftworks*). The sounds emitted by the desert violate its concept, suspending the auditory mirage and repressing the labyrinthine structure of the ear: 'To extend the principle of dissonance universally is *to stop misleading the ear:* the principle of *Immobilization,* the same one that Cézanne's eye obeyed twenty-five years earlier in the Aix landscape and the one by means of which this Moses of new painting also wanted to stop misleading the eye.' It is extremely difficult to follow the trajectory of an unseduced ear; perhaps there is little to follow as the ear will stay fixed to one locus, frozen in the desert by the rule of the immobile. In this desired predicament of immobility, where stray shots of sonority are said to be quieted, music splits off from history and the salutary epiphany: 'Now one will stay in place,' writes Lyotard, 'there will be no resolution in the vanishing point, where the multiple gathers itself together, there will be no history, no salutary epiphany, there is a language without intention that requires not religion but faith.' Schönberg has taken music via this new route, offering a critique of 'music as an edifying recital,' and turned it into 'a *discourse,* produced by a language that is an arbitrary system, yet developed in all of its consequences [the language of Jehovah] and thus always experienced as unacceptable and tragic: something like the unconscious according to Lacan' (105; emphasis added).

Now, in order to establish the essentially tragic, unacceptable dimension of music, Lyotard must paradoxically deny the split. No longer as such 'edifying,' music gets swallowed up and neutralized, which is what I suppose its transformation into the effect of 'a language that is an arbitrary system' points up – something that is in turn reinforced by 'the unconscious according to Lacan,' which, we recall, is structured like a language. Music has abandoned its locus of otherness in regard to language and joins a procession of absorption into discourse. This is how Schönberg stops misleading the ear, in fact, by turning music out, exiling its crucial alterity. While music no longer survives Babel, losing as it does in this passage its edification, it nonetheless continues to be assimilated to a certain metaphysical desire, what Lyotard calls 'a new transcendence.' No seduction, no castration: music is shown at once to cut into the edifice while fortifying itself in a new transcendence, in other words, in a new coupling with language. Where opera, including that of Schönberg, continually remixes Babel, always reintroducing the trauma of separating off from itself, Lyotard tends to want to do a remake of the marriage ceremony. No running around, no being on the loose, cruising, or straying, the ear sticks to a singular position of following truly. Assimilated to a language that, no longer requiring religion, withdraws the promise of a salutary epiphany, music secularizes and institutionalizes itself. This may in part explain the insistence on the Reformed church in Lyotard's essay, the erection of an institution that has created static on the simultaneous line to Moses, breaker of institution. Opera is lodged on this borderline tracing institution and its breakup.

To a certain extent, Lyotard wants to deny the loss that opera continually reinscribes by situating Schönberg within a movement of tragic intensity. From this point to his essay titled *Heidegger and 'the jews,'*[13] a difficulty articulates itself around 'the Jews' for Lyotard. This will have to be taken up elsewhere but cannot be left simply unmarked here. Why would opera be thought to smash itself on the rock of Judaity? (Freud, Adorno, Schönberg . . . but one should resist repeating the lineup mentality.) This is an explicit issue for Clément as well. Let us limit our discussion to the understanding of Judaity as device, as that which introduces static and discontinuity, a certain rite of circumcision to which music submits.

### .06 SCHÖNBERG AND FREUD:

We are still driftworking.

> A new transcendence is introduced into sound material, all familiarity becomes impossible, the tragic triumphs, as in Freud. What the dodecaphonic and serial 'technique,' as well as analysis, seek is the tragic which in Freud's as in Schönberg's view is entirely lacking in the scientific or musical positivism of the nineteenth century. The tragic is intensity divested of signification, yet ascribed to the intention of an Other. (105)

In a crucial way, Lyotard starts jamming on technology when he turns Judaism into a 'device,' which, underlying both works, is also a figure of the unconscious. Citing Adorno on Schönberg, Lyotard engages a Judaism that introduces a critical function in relation to acritical society and ideology, 'but probably not where Adorno expected it.' Here's why:

> The desensitization of the material cannot be attributed to industrial society and its techniques of mechanical reproduction (which, as we know, can just as well produce the opposite, i.e., hypersensitization; just listen to the music of Kagel, Cage, Xenakis, Zappa, Hendrix). Neither can the Benjaminian concept of the destruction

> of *aura*, which also belongs to the negative thinking of the lost *chef d'oeuvre*, of modern technology as alienation, be of any use to us here. (105)

Desensitization arises rather from the field that Lyotard attributes to therapeutics, 'which haunts Schönberg's work as much as it does Freud's: therapeutics through a reinforcement of discourse, discontinuity, rationality, law, silence-law, negativity, not at all in the spirit of positivism but in that of tragic negativism, fate, the unconscious, dispossession' (105). We shall return to this assertion momentarily.

Returning to Freud, in particular to *Moses and Monotheism*, 'the ultimate text,' Lyotard outlines precisely in what tragic negativism consists:

> the mapping back of the cure apparatus, controlled transference, onto the primary process: reconstituting a critical theater in the doctor's office (after dismissal of the supposedly precritical theater of the parental chambers and the visual phantasy); blocking out the vertiginous discovery of libidinal displaceability of primary work, nomadism. And this mapping back, this restoration, go unrecognized by Freud himself, *ignored* in their arbitrary nature, in their unjustifiable madness as device. (106)

It is now becoming clear why Lyotard deploys Judaity as device, linking the Freudian project to Schönberg's innovation ('technique'), what he describes as the predominance of the written, the law, 'which destroys illusion: no apparent surface on which to inscribe a text, because no effect of depth, no background. Instead of idols, the Torah, a discourse without a third dimension' (107). Schönberg and Freud form a war-machine couple that attacks the visual fantasy, the realm of idols and Apollonian drawing power. Resisting illusion, deterring representation as ideology and fantasy, they align themselves with the signifier. 'No longer is there a resolution into surface chords, no more appearance, but there is a reserve in the silence of composition; like the analyst, the composer is on the side of the signifier' (107). In order to marry music off to psychoanalysis, Lyotard has slipped unobtrusively from 'music' to 'composition.' I have nothing against this collapse except that it is the price to be paid for denying and foreclosing the split between music and its other. Each term in the cited statement deserves careful scrutiny, including of course Lyotard's decision to couple analyst and composer in an economy that suspends the place of the musician. We shall restrict our observations here to the way Lyotard is forced to neutralize both music and language in order to squeeze them into the signifier. But why has psychoanalysis been called to the rescue? what about this marriage couch?

Psychoanalysis is credited with having severed the couple aural/visual, and this is where, according to Lyotard, it has been espoused by Schönberg. 'Psychoanalysis has carried out the critique of domination Italian-style, Egyptian-style, visual domination, the domination of phantasy, but from within a space that is still a space of Lutheran, Hebrew, auditory, sober domination' (107). What this passage to the ear canal tells us is that Lyotard anchors the Freudo-Schönbergian project within a kind of transmission system that canalizes the auditory libido. It is perhaps not entirely beside the point that the 'last opera in history,' *Moses and Aaron,* disconnects the whole operatic machine and lies there like a dead telephone surviving its memory of performance in silence, or even, to keep with Lyotard, in 'several silences.'

One of Lyotard's expressed purposes is to liberate music from a form of constraint that he understands in terms of tragic negativism. The music of anarchy hits the pages as Lyotard allows his text to theorize with a hammer ('No need for us to cry over that, we do not want more order, a music that is more tonal, more unified, or more rich and elegant. We want less order, more circulation by chance, by free wandering: the abolition of the law of value, which constitutes the body of *Kapital* as a surface to puncture, as appearance' [109]). Still, it seems to me that he gets sucked in by the very apparatus of restoration which he sees Freud ignoring. Freud has failed, he argues, to recognize the mapping back of the cure apparatus onto the primary process. Having more or less dismissed the 'precritical' theater of the parental scene, which Lyotard seems to want to restore through a certain value of primordiality, Freud has reconstituted a critical theater, primarily an aural space of representation, in the doctor's office. This aural space – which Freud explicitly structures according to a strict telephonic logic – is felt to displace the visual fantasy. The relation, therefore, which Freud promotes hooks up the analyst to the analysand, the receiver to the transmitter (in a multipath mode and not a simple recapitulation of the sender-receiver polarity) indicating a thinking of technology that supersedes, I would think, the orchestra pit of a parental chamber. The penis that the child saw disappear into the mother returns by other channels of transmission to the ear. But Lyotard seems to want to accord the 'supposedly precritical theater of the parental chambers and the visual phantasy' a higher status than it apparently enjoys in the switch from the visual to the aural, from the parental to the psychoanalytic precincts of attendance.

It is perhaps not an accident that Lyotard wishes to keep this fusion-bound (parental) couple intact where the analyst-analysand couple might be said to inhabit the scene of a nonrelation – or to stay with the metaphorology of Freud, the scene of disconnection. There is nothing more nomadically invested than the switchboard that Freud sets up at the base of his critical theater. This switchboard takes all sorts of calls, transfers others, while keeping still others on hold. It welcomes the arbitrary, linguistic pollutants or the free association which gave the access code to the talking cure. This is not to bill Freud as the one who relinquished the controls. But he routed the human subject through certain technological filters that complicate an understanding of simple repression.

Lyotard seems to know this when he writes of a cure *apparatus* or when he scans Freud's second setup for hysteria ('Freud constructs a second setup where the hysteric is an actress, and the analyst, the invisible listener: radio comes after theater, more precisely, a radio hooked up to the auditorium, the listener not seeing the stage himself, as in radio commentary of boxing matches, football games' [102]. Like almost everyone else, Lyotard opts for conjuring the radio over picking up the telephone. Why he chooses these somewhat macho programs for turning on the hysteric is another question.) His own restorative mood discloses itself in this essay when he attaches music and language to sameness and the signifier, absorbing music into discourse. The denial of the divorce court to which opera is summoned itself belongs to the registers of remapping and reconstitution. His motivation remains fully intelligible, however, and ought to be commented on.

The figure invisibly operating the essay was Adorno – he put Lyotard through to Schönberg. Or, if you prefer, it was to his radiophonic commentary that Lyotard was tuned when setting up the match of dissonance. Lyotard has approached the negative theology of Adorno in order to pluralize its silence, hence the pointed silence of his essay: several silences. To accomplish his goal without a penalty, Lyotard has had to make the transcendence of silence into music and language so that the object of music could become discourse. But the kind of pantheistic silence he establishes functions like (here I shift channels and games) a sacrifice bunt, which is to say that this movement of silence is bought at the price of reducing the silences of music. In this thinking Judaity would perhaps install a bar between noise and the phenomenological reduction of sound to sense.

.07 INTERRUPTION: *In the interruption something makes itself heard, namely, what remains after the interruption has taken place. . . . . . . . . . . . . . . . . . When a voice, or music, is suddenly interrupted, one hears just at that instant something else, a mixture or a betwixt of various silences and noises that had been covered over by the sound, but in this something else one hears again the voice or the music which have become in a way the voice or the music of their own interruption: a kind of echo, but one that does not repeat that of which it would be the reverberation.* . . . . . . . . . . . . . . . . . . . . . . . .[14]

.08 ANSWERING MACHINE: Returning to Nietzsche's insight, where the figure of the telephone and that of the musician form a singular couple: offering a new package deal of the invisible, both are seen to be inhabited by a rhetoric of the departed. The telephone, while not reducible to any level of brute instrumentality, is nonetheless instrumental in linking up with absence; it thereby marks a gap that tenuously joins what it separates. The telephone catches stray shots coming from any being of low visibility. It takes calls from street corners and bedrooms (something the Puritans tried to fight), from unidentified callers and from the voice within. The telephone comes at you to caress you, or it can be used like a weapon, an arm without traces, a gun pointed to your head. You can use its strangulating radius to measure your Oedipal leash ('call home'), or, like Joyce, to retap its umbilicus into your navel. There are perhaps other uses for the telephone.

Francis Poulenc always had a fascination for street noises. He developed a peculiar appreciation for Maurice Chevalier. His first choral piece rooted itself in the gutter of *Gerede;* it was a drinking song. Composed under the guidance of Charles Koechlin, *Chanson à boire* (1922) was written for the Harvard glee club. His anti-Wagnerian 'musideology,' his marked 'antisnobbism,' canonic defiance, and predilection for the atmosphere of the popular café earned Poulenc the title of 'guttersnipe.' He was on to random transmissions, cruising the streets, a telepath receptor of hard noise. At the intersection of Debussy, Mozart, and Stravinsky, he started revving his engine, getting ready to pick up the frequencies of sheer exteriority. He was a member of a gang, so to speak, Les Six, whose leaders ('guiding spirits') were Cocteau and Satie. They had a code of aesthetic politics, making him let go of Debussy, which he did between 1917 and 1922. Later he regretted this. Like I said, he was hitting the streets; he did not attend any of the established music schools – the Conservatoire, the École Normale, the École Niedermeyer or the Schola Cantorum. He hit the streets, but don't get me wrong: he was melancholic, anguished, and rich. Cocteau had had his eye on Poulenc. He liked him and Auric best of Les Nouveaux Jeunes, as they were also called, because they were the youngest, the most brash, and the most Parisian of the six. Les Six, it was said, brought music down to earth. But there were limits to Poulenc's tolerance. There were certain things he wouldn't put up with, for example, something that Satie and Milhaud had thrown together, some live background music they called *musique d'ameublement* [furniture music] intended to be ignored by the chatting, strolling audience. The show was set for 8 March 1920, and Poulenc would have no part of it. But he did go for *Les Mariés de la Tour Eiffel* which Cocteau and Les Six put together. It was narrated by two talking phonographs.

The technological support wasn't bad, considering that Poulenc eventually was to get backing from the Princess Edmond de Polignac. Her maiden name was Winaretta Singer of Singer Sewing Machine filament, under whose patronage he composed the *Concerto for Two Pianos* (1932) and the *Concerto for the Organ* (1932). Whatever in fact held his pieces together, Francis Poulenc created a kind of suturing factory for technology's music. Of course, putting *La Voix humaine* to music, or having phonographs talk and sewing machines pay the way does not necessarily supply the sonic blaze of high-tech mutation. As title, *La Voix humaine* appears to resist the technicity of its content. The cohabitation of the human voice with its technological filtering, its long-distance instrumentality, is set on the dividing line between opera and itself. The other, severed part of any duet expands into the noise machine and semantic shredding of the French telephone lines.

Poulenc offers opera a new chance for scoring on love and transference. The telephone qua instrument is by no means placed in a mimetic rapport with voice; while it is not identical with the human voice – something radically intervenes between voice and its transmission – it is also not a kind of mimetic xeroxing of the voice. The telephone says something about the rapport of music to language, instrument to voice, and the breakdown of easy identifications. Operating the quasi-dialectics of long-distance and the close call, the telephone is an instrument of transference par excellence. The wedding ceremony and divorce hearing collapsed into one ring, it attaches the severed umbilicus of the self to the other, the voice to its resonance in an unlocalizable beyond. Maintaining and joining, the telephone line holds together what it separates. It creates a space of asignifying breaks, producing an intersection where the lines of public diffusion cross into those of more private, inwardly turned harmonics. Isn't the telephone the place that opera, in its fundamental structure, always sought to occupy? The telephone communicates the difference between the street diffusion of the aria and the introspective echo of a great house. For Poulenc to pull the telephone line into the districts of operatic logic means that he is legislating zoning laws and boundaries, he is signifying the chains which keep the phantom of the opera restless.[15] Wagner's conspiracy, his burial plot for the orchestra, reemerges like a crack in a crypt of long-distance. How does the telephone in fact make itself the destination of opera? Follow the twisted cord of Poulenc's argument.

In the first place, Poulenc has slipped the operator into the logic of the opera, creating a theater of the invisible, linking all the ghosts of operatic history, the disruptors and masked voices of the beyond. From Lucia's phantom to the crackling interference run by the other side of Poulenc's switchboard, opera is hosting parasites, transmission bubbles, and a sort of scratch noise. There is no smooth transition or absolute translation that would be containable by this house. Now, what does it mean to run the question of transference by opera's switchboard? How does the telephone answer for the mixed media desire of the most contaminated of genres?

I need to consider *La Voix humaine* as a philosophical opera struggling with its own determinations. It is an opera that performs the textual allegorization of its predicament, and though we may want, as did Poulenc, to stick to the streets, it is perhaps justifiable to scuttle down the telephone wires that are holding together this opera. For the telephone is not a simple installation, not a transparent allegory of inclusion. There is something artificial about it, like the transplant of an artificial organ into the body of opera. It is an organ that functions both as an instrument and as a voice, simulating *la voix humaine* while staying resolutely on the side of artifice. First, let's rerecord the essential strains.

*La Voix humaine* was Poulenc's third and final opera. It comes at the end of the line, based on Cocteau's monodrama of 1930. The opera features one character who, though traditionally contoured as human subject, is attached to the telephone like an answering machine. This character, Elle, paces her bedroom like a caged animal. She materializes therefore somewhere between animal and machine. She is suffering the carceral silence of an enlarged telephone booth. We neither see nor hear the man on the other end, her lover. It has been said that the telephone receiver almost becomes the second onstage character. The opera is run through with interference, the intrusions brought about by the notorious hazards of the French telephone system. Elle is cut off twice, interrupted once, refers to the break-ins on five occasions and becomes the victim of a chronic wrong-number syndrome. Everything about the arrangement suggests that she is on a destinal call, about to be put on eternal hold. The story of a breakup, *La Voix humaine* dramatizes parasitical invasions on the abstract body of the couple. The couple is held together by a string instrument that is about to snap.

This is the last call; at the end of the opera Elle recognizes that she and her lover will have suspended relations after an impossible duet which, indeed, never manages to relate. The modulations of anguish do not follow any linear pattern, but suggest a subject that is wired, electrified by the shock of breaking off relations. On one level of phenomenal mobility, nothing happens. Still, this is Poulenc's most dramatic stage work. The drama bears upon the innovative techniques that Poulenc applied to the conversion of Cocteau's monodrama into opera. Of the 780 measures, 186 are for solo voice with no orchestral accompaniment whatsoever, a severing that Poulenc had introduced to a lesser degree in *Dialogues des Carmélites.* While Keith Daniel, for instance, feels that Poulenc is producing a vocal line imitative of proper or pure speech, it is always a speech structured by telephonic syncopation and disruption, not, I would submit, 'pure speech,' whatever that might be. Nonetheless, music is taking a return trip to the rhythmic constraints of speech:

> Unlike that in Poulenc's two previous operas, the vocal writing in *La Voix humaine* does not resemble that of his art songs – here he has deliberately rejected the lyricism of his solo vocal music. Poulenc's two major concerns here are to capture the proper rhythms of speech, and to mirror the normal inflections of speech with the subtle risings and fallings of the vocal line.[16]

The harmonic language of *La Voix humaine* tends to underscore the ambiguous light in which the opera sees itself. It produces a kind of demystified approach to a language with which it will never be joined but toward which it is always calling. Music places a call to language as if to affirm essential disconnection. Though tonality often emerges, there is more sustained tonal ambiguity in this opera than in any other Poulenc work of comparable length. Music begins by stammering, looking for itself, being deprived of stable tonality for the first eighteen measures. As the opera establishes a relation to language in a mood of immobile terror (*la donna* is not *mobile,* as we always knew, as Verdi radically showed us), it launches the following ambiguous harmonic characteristics with some regularity: nonfunctional harmonic progressions, unresolved dissonances, an extraordinary use of diminished structures, and progressions of chords used chromatically. Tonality makes itself heard only in the most lyrical passages, or by short orchestral motifs based upon functional harmonies. Yet these phrases are quickly cut off by a return to ambiguity.

Daniel's interpretation points to the exceptional quality of the opera, which is to say that it is situated on perceptibly unstable ground, about to fall apart:

> The overall structure of *La Voix humaine* is unusual in Poulenc's *oeuvre.* The choppy, fragmentary nature of the text, and Poulenc's declamatory setting of it (reminiscent of Satie's *Socrate*), would seem to place the opera in the danger of disintegrating. Poulenc's solution was to use the orchestra as a framework for holding the work together, by entrusting it with most of the lyricism. (34)

It is as if opera were in danger of suffering a 'schizonoiac' attack. At the point where opera is about to experience the disintegration of its parts, where music feels itself severed from the language that it had sought to enter, a prosthetic god perturbs the moment of narcissistic wounding and reinscribes the scene. The prosthetic god – the technicity of the jointure where music comes through to language – is how Freud describes the telephone. The thing that installs itself at the site of an absence, when something is experienced as lost or long-distance, removed. The orchestra responds to the distress signal sent out by a disintegrating operatic body by reemerging as a substitute for a lost object, that which we 'knew' before Babel, prior to the traumatic split of music from language. The role of the orchestra must not be underestimated, warns Daniel. In addition to assuming unifying and suturing functions, it portrays the ringing of the telephone 'with repeated notes on the xylophone; it expresses the singer's agitation and confusion while trying to reach her lover; it even suggests the jazz which she hears in the background through the phone. Most importantly, however, the orchestra fills in the voids created by the inherently dry, disjointed vocal line' (52).

Like the telephone, then, the orchestra is made to connect where there is little or no relation; it closes and unifies, suturing the performance like a wound. The orchestra tells time, its closural gesture opens the very wound that it is asked to conceal. This is because that which, according to Daniel, stalls disintegration renders it most visible – or in the truer language of psychosis, most *audible*. The mark of disintegration (for the 'schizonoiac') is always auditory – noise disaster hits the subject like an immense catastrophe, a sonic blaze. Poulenc allows the trauma of the split the temporal dimensions of the big bang, resonating a more originary sound-split in opera's survival of itself. This telephone rings after a felt obliteration – say, the one performed by *Moses and Aaron*.

On the somewhat less catastrophic register that links opera to noise disaster and to fantasies of language crashing into music, there is a synecdochic statement supplied by the supplemental instrument. The telephone, as member and dismembering of the orchestra, participates in the myths of organic unity where one discerns a shelter or defense against castration. We remember that the orchestra guaranteed organic totality with Wagner's dismemberment of it; or, prior to that traumatic action, the magic flute dedemonized the hideous contamination that occurred after successive splits in man and woman, day and night, man and bird, music and language, and so on. The orchestra and its parts, whether or not enchanted, act as metronome and mortality timer. When they emerge on the scene, as at the end of *Don Giovanni*, trouble is in the air, the death knell appears. In the great mystifications and denials of death, technology is seen as the corruption of being. Background music, drums in the distance, a telephone that keeps ringing, are announcements from finitude. The technology that accompanies the repetition compulsion and death drive, those instruments of being, vascillates between appearance and disappearance, marking the boundary between singing and speaking, music and its multiplicity of silences, several of which we gather under the heading of 'language.'

In any event, the telephone at once perverts the orchestra and amplifies its disconnective threat. It condenses being and time into a single ring that won't stop reverberating. Here's how *La Voix humaine* says it:

> Listen, dear, I'm suffering beyond words. This line is the last line which puts me in touch with you .......................... .............. The night before last? ............... I went to sleep. I took the telephone with me ................. No, in bed with me. ....... Yes, I know. I'm very silly, but I took the telephone to bed with me because, after all, we are connected by the telephone. It goes into your flat, and then there was this promise that you would give me a ring. So you can just imagine I counted the minutes and dreamt all manner of things. Then it became a different and dangerous kind of ring – a wring of the neck which strangles, a ring of a boxing match I couldn't get out of – the bell rang, you hit me and I was counted out. .....or I was at the bottom of the sea – it looked like the rooms in Wigmore Street – and I was connected with you by a diver's air tube, and I was begging you not to cut it – you know, dreams that are idiotic when told, but at the time terribly real ...................... .............. Because you're speaking to me .............. (. . .) Now, I can breathe again because you are speaking to me. But my dream's not foolish. If you break the connection, you snap the air tube I'm holding onto for dear life. ....................... ......

The telephone connects itself as artificial organ to the collapsed lung of the operatic body. Whether wind instrument or oxygen tent, voice box or atonal charm, the telephone taps back into a certain beginning where singing and language rose with the breath: 'Now I can breathe again,' sighs music, 'because you are speaking to me.' ('Maintenant, j'ai de l'air parce que tu me parles': now I have the air, the aria, because you are speaking to me.)

.09 PLAY IT AGAIN: And yet, Poulenc was a guttersnipe. His ears were open to the outside – he kept breaking out of the heavy walls of opera like a schizo safecracker. He hung out in music halls, cafés, and on street corners. This is why his last opera exposes itself to the street episteme of noise and dirt, avoiding the quarantined ghettos of transcendental music. Continually running interference with itself, his rendering of the human voice is accompanied by static. The telephone connection houses the improper. Hitting the streets, it welcomes linguistic pollutants and fakes music. Still, like opera, it stages the refusal to synthesize even as it switches on the contaminating blender. There's the mix, and there's even a match, but it will go no further.

Maybe I should add that the possibility of a telephone was never fully dissociated from musical strains. From Sir Charles Wheatstone, who called his string telephone (1819), a 'magic lyre,' to Kafka's *Castle*, on whose telephone angels sing, the telephone hollowed out an eerie symphony hall for departed spirits. Around 1874, Mr. Elisha Gray, Alexander Graham Bell's rival, was occupied with a system of musical telephone which he wished to apply to manifold telegraphic transmissions. The history of this phantasmic music hall has yet to be written. All I can say is that to this day the telephone still houses background music, as if to deaden the pain.[17]

.10 DISINTEGRATION: On 19 July 1960, Francis Poulenc wrote to the woman who sang the lead body part in *La Voix humaine*, Denise Duval. 'Mon Rossignol à larmes,' he began, 'J'aimais ta voix joyeuse au téléphone. Comme moi, tu n'es pas faite pour la solitude [My tearful nightingale, I loved your joyous voice on the telephone. Like me, you are not made for solitude].' Next paragraph, 'On ne parle que de toi et de *La Voix* à Aix. Le reste est un hors-d'oeuvre, dit-on. . . . À dimanche. Je t'adore. Fr. [At Aix, they talk only of you and *La Voix*. Everything else is just an appetizer, they say. Till Sunday. I adore you. Fr.].'[18] His biography reaches an end. I translate: 'Saturday, 26 January 1963, Francis Poulenc gave a concert in Maastricht, Holland, with Denise Duval. Francis returned to Paris the following Monday. On Tuesday, he telephoned Denise Duval to have lunch with her at her place the next day, but Wednesday morning, the 30th, he called her to say he was hoarse and could not go out. At one o'clock he died suddenly.'

.11 KIERKEGAARD RECITAL: quotequotequote 'But what follows from maintaining that wherever language ceases, I encounter the musical? This is probably the most perfect expression of the idea that music everywhere limits language' quotequotequotequotequoteBut what follows from maintaining that wherever language ceases, I encounter the musical? This is probably the most perfect expression of the idea that music everywhere limitsquotelanguagequotequotethat music everywhere limits language quotemusic everywhere limits languagequoteits language.

# QUEENS OF THE NIGHT

I. A NOTE ON THE FAILURE OF MAN'S CUSTODIANSHIP. Never felt to be a natural catastrophe, AIDS has from the start carried the traits of a *historical* event. If AIDS had been comprehensible only in terms of natural calamity, it would not have called for a critique: you cannot throw a critique at an earthquake, nor can you really complain about the pounding waves of the ocean, not even if you were inclined to view it through Bataille's pineal eye, as the earth's continual jerking off. But catastrophe, folded in by traits of historical if not conventional markings, calls for a critique; it demands a *reading*.

I started writing about the catastrophe at a time, now difficult to imagine, when the acronym AIDS was not acknowledged by the Reagan White House to exist, either in official or common language usage. The collapse of rumor and disease control was considerable; it was thought, in the obscure ages of the Reagan presidency, that to allow the word to circulate freely would in itself encourage the referential effects of naming to spread. There is nothing very new about language policies that try radically to abbreviate the itinerary of the rumor thought to be co-originary with the spreading velocities of disease. Defoe's *Journal of the Plague Year* would supply one among numerous examples of the way language is seen to be, as they now say, a virus. Ever since the original Reagan ban on the word (however repressed or forgotten this initial 'response' may be), a politics of containment and border patrol has dominated the way this culture looks at AIDS. On a level of far lesser consequence, AIDS had not yet acquired the status of an object worthy of scholarly solicitude. Looking back, we can understand why there was such resistance (evidenced by the political and linguistic behavior of straights and gays alike) to admitting the epidemic into the rarefied atmosphere of academic inquiry: AIDS *infected* the academy, dissolving boundaries that traditionally set the disciplines off from one another, if only to secure their sense of self-knowledge. It is small wonder that conservative literary critics, and those generally concerned by questions of history and reference, initially deplored the inclusion of this 'outside' referent, which by its very existence challenged the purity of institutional divisions. When it did come about, the study of AIDS encouraged the emergence of new, marginal, and 'deviant' areas of inquiry in the humanities: gender studies, gay studies, queer theory, mutant French theory, and even computer-based cyberpunk speculations.

My need to write about AIDS was originally motivated by a number of considerations, each felt by me to be as urgent as the next. My close friend, Marc Paszamant, was among the earliest victims that AIDS had claimed; an entire community was soon to follow. I was anxious over the ways in which the event of acquired immunodeficiency syndrome was being consistently put under erasure. The syndrome appeared to intensify the culpabilization of minorities and the social margin. Finally, those who were called upon to investigate the seemingly originary pathogenesis were being guided by uninterrogated metaphysical assumptions concerning its constitution. The first of the assumptions understood AIDS to derive from one cause, and this cause was reduced to a virus; secondly, the methodologies used to interpret the syndrome involved codes of research that depended upon the old news of a hidden matrix of signification and an absent center of meaning from which the truth was assumed to be pulsing in secrecy. Finally, those who had the funding and authority to study AIDS gave little consideration to the likelihood that the mutation of this virus – if it was a matter principally of virology – owes its existence to a multiplicity of factors, which locate it in our age of technological dominion, social inequity, and inwardly turned violence. The resistance to admitting the multifactoral aggregate which is responsible for AIDS, and the collective impulse to 'isolate' a single cause, seemed to lack a judicious construal of derivation. The sustained fabrication of autoimmune laboratories in our polity seemed worthy of consideration as well; that is, the protocols by which the United States was beginning systematically to turn weaker forces into contained spaces of internally discharged violence (of which the drug wars or, more locally, South Central Los Angeles are indisputable signs).

A genealogist – or anyone, for that matter, including the scientific 'community,' who knows something about the way science legitimates its procedures – must readily grant the possibility that the phenomenon submitted to study is routinely framed by theoretical assumptions, the reliability of which may be only partial. While we in the West are no longer restricted, in principle, in our thoughts by the divine monopoly that dominated medieval medicine (when doctors and theologians were one, and the plague, for example, was seen to originate in those carriers that were recognized, after much research, as Jews), I find it curious that AIDS, for all the discontinuities and anomalies it reflects, nonetheless leaves untouched the tradition by which epidemics come to be associated with minorities including, nowadays, the greater part of the so-called Third World. In fact, the culpabilization of minorities was 'grounded' once and for all in the twentieth century in the way we have permitted ourselves to think about the uncontrolled proliferation of AIDS. In one of his works, I can't remember which, Heidegger said that an error in thinking could mess us up for hundreds of years to come. I suspect that our inability to read AIDS constitutes such an error in an already overdrawn historical account. If this remark may seem excessive, it is so only to the degree that excess is constitutive of thinking; however, given the gravity of the subject, I consider these observations to be an exercise in understatement. In any case, I try to demonstrate in 'Support Our Tropes' (infra) how the inability to read AIDS has spread to the body politic, where the Persian Gulf War, as the phantasm of a safe and bloodless intervention, becomes the symptom par excellence for the uncontrolled translation of the syndrome into other bodies which feel the need to achieve, in a world historical operating theater for example, HIV-negative test results. But the failure to read AIDS is not reducible to a simple power failure or strategy of avoidance – it is bequeathed to us by the Western logos.

In the trajectory that my own work has tried to follow, therefore, the appearance of AIDS constitutes a crucial figure in the technological disclosure, while it also disarticulates any claim to subjective recuperation.[1] As it underscores the essential relationship between testing and technology, AIDS, for us, has made clear the notion that no technology exists that will not be tested; additionally, however, AIDS has shed light on the way our modernity has technologized the subject into a testable entity under state control. An effect of technology, AIDS is part of the radical destructuring of social bonds that will have been the legacy of the twentieth century. It is a bit of a platitude to observe that every epidemic is a product of its time; but the cofactors that have produced the destruction of internal self-defense capabilities still need to be studied in a mood of Nietzschean defiance toward the metaphysico-scientific establishment. For surely AIDS is in concert with the homologous aggression that is widely carried out against the weak within the ensemble of political, cultural, and medical procedures. It is not farfetched to observe that these procedures, today, take comparable measures to destroy any living, menacing reactivity, and thus have to be considered precisely in terms of the disconcerting reciprocity of their ensemble.

If AIDS appears to us as an event within history, or even as *historial* event, this means that it cannot be seen, as a misfortune, to come from elsewhere: it comes from man. Situated within the limits of a history gone bad, revealing its infirmity, AIDS for us does not come from God. But because it is not (yet) curable, it is perceived as a kind of self-destruction of a society abandoned to its own immanence.[2] The renewed experience of God's mute complicity or historical withdrawal ('God' is to be understood here as a promissory transcendence capable of forgiving debts and healing), explains in part why AIDS is a peculiarly *human* symptom, functioning as the locus of a suicidal impulse that increasingly determines our species. AIDS is the affair of man at the end of the millennium; it is 'about' man's self-annihilating toxic drive and his scorn for the figure of humanity as it has been disclosed until now. A sign of the failure of man's custodianship, AIDS is the end of the credit line humanity thought it could have with some form of transcendence.

While AIDS displays historial qualities, it should not be temporally confused with absolute emergence. 'The brutal appearance of an epidemic, within a set of multifactoral conditions that have evolved gradually, depends upon a quantitative threshold of emergence,' cautions Michel Bounan in his critically important work *Le Temps du sida.*[3] In effect, this epidemic should not be viewed as sudden, epochal appearance, but as a culmination in the history of a debilitating milieu of forces, the effects of which underscore the turning of a humanity rigorously set against itself. Dr. Bounan has written a treatise deploring life-despising medicine, or, in equally Nietzschean terms (though he does not himself articulate these terms), his scientific invective against the current state of AIDS research discloses the *medicalization of ressentiment* in our time. Indeed, it would be necessary to see the extent to which resentful medicine (for example, those branches of modern medicine that are servile to the dictatorship of pharmaceutical companies) is co-responsible, together with those effects of capital and technology to which we owe the degradation of the environment, for the increase in infectious and tumoral disease. The manifest inability to question the entire apparatus of theoretical presuppositions under which research has been conducted (cancer remains incomprehensible, AIDS confounds them absolutely), leads one to wonder whether this paralysis is not symptomatic of the paranoid condition typified in all epochs anticipating the end of civilization.

Medical science has been reluctant to ask the critical question: What are the multifactoral conditions for the possibility of this epidemic? The motivation behind the failure to ask is no doubt related to the narcissistically defended boundaries that scientific research has lacked the courage to cross. Though dominated by a logic of invasion and intervention, medical science halts its investigations on this side of a diagnostic ethics. Still bound by laws of causality and isolationist views of the phenomena to be studied, medicine is equally beholden to the idiom of limited polemological approach. There is probably nothing outrageous about mapping the body as an intensive conflictual site where war is continually being waged, for example, by one cell or another. And yet the strategies of attack that have been charted appear (despite high tech manipulation) to rely until now upon the premises of resentful medicine for their insight.

Still pre-Nietzschean in the strategic mapping of disease, medical science unfailingly favors 'conquering' symptoms by means of violent interventions. According to Bounan, medical science should seek to diminish pathogenic aggressions rather than adding to them; it should intensify defensive reaction rather than suppress it; and it should let disease follow its course rather than 'vanquishing' it – for the paradigms of absolute defeat are moored in phantasms of militaristic conquest. Diseases are not provoked *by* a pathogenic environment that would be merely destructive, but *against* it by a patient who is defending herself. These immunopathological actions directed *against* the pathogenic environment constitute efforts to *conserve* life. Illnesses are the 'natural defense' of the living, and not a message from the dead, which is in effect the only object of biological research. (Bounan demonstrates how biology, a misnomer, can interpret only what is dead and can never come to furnish, therefore, an understanding of the living.) Science has to ask itself what life is – a question, if not increasingly politicized, then at least problematized by technologies of reproduction and life extension – and what is foreign to life. The immunitary apparatus, the natural terminator of foreign formations, has itself become foreign. Modern medicine's principal pride consists of the antimicrobial war it has waged, which focuses on foreign productions. This war has mandated that vaccinations be globally deployed, an action that has contributed to massive resections affecting the living totality of *reactional coherency;* these interventions are coresponsible for ulterior pathologies. Is it a mere coincidence that the African AIDS epidemic followed a program of massive vaccination? Did not the introduction of vaccination in Africa, despite all good intentions, contribute to the destruction of the reactional coherency of indigenous communities, serving only to weaken their resolve to defend themselves within and outside their political bodies? In short, what sort of an aggression does mass inoculation imply, what kinds of shots are being administered to 'pacify' the West's other? 'A disease appears when an ensemble of 'homologous' aggressions, simultaneously physical and climatic, alimentary and toxic, microbial and emotional, self-induce a defensive mechanism, reaching a lesional threshold.'[4] Whether or not Western medicine was forcing upon Africans an internalization of *Ge-stell* (technological posure or framing), by injection, it is no exaggeration to say that Africa was *invaded* medically, just as doctors on the equally 'moral' side are assisting, via injection, in the administration of capital punishment in America – an absolute perversion of their responsibilities. On the one hand, medicine is answerable for its reluctance to *read* the decisive cuts it has made in understanding theoretical assumptions which support uninterrogated research habits; on the other hand, it must be made responsible for the effectivity, whether consciously or unconsciously conceived, of its own interventions. If diagnosis were truly to become what it is, it would have to respond to the reactional, if not revolutionary, exigency of discovery in relation to ever mutating conditions.

The censorship exercised by the medical community and the punitive measures taken by the National Institutes of Health against virologist Peter Duesberg is a case in point. When he proposed the theory that HIV is unrelated to AIDS, arguing that AZT (one of the few government-approved AIDS prevention and treatment drugs) constitutes a powerful poison which itself causes the body's immune system to collapse and can instigate full-blown AIDS, Duesberg was defunded – a fact which interests me only to the extent that it serves as an example of the insistence upon strict viral causality and the corresponding reluctance to explore the homologous aggressions to which AIDS must be linked. Just as etiological, lesional, or psychiatric treatments can be justly regarded as dubious interventions, so the 'precise cause' of a disease is to be understood as a trap.[5] It cannot be denied that a genuine treatment of AIDS would require us to risk overturning those pathological ideologies and metaphysical deceits which continue to dominate the world to this day. On the rise, suicide, anguish, poverty, and epidemics sign off the immanence of the one on one, humanity against itself – a humanity steadily abandoned by the promise of future or exteriority and barely able to read its multifactoral histories.

The problem with writing a timely or topical essay is that, as the surfaces of interpretability shift with time, adjustments come to be made in the research whose immobility one had deplored. This is a risk that accrues to such histories, one that I take knowing that it exposes my writing to the brutal exigency of a finite here-and-now. Perhaps tomorrow what I here understand as ressentimental medicine will have vindicated itself and transvaluated the meaning of its strategic interventions. If the effort to renew a commitment to the Nietzschean critique of science seems at once to reflect its own anachrony, lagging behind the event it seeks to understand, and to expose a symptom of excessive timeliness, my reading was also, from the start, untimely and even strangely cheerful. The example of Mozart read by Nietzsche – an example of scandalous achronicity regarding the imperious urgency of the present, for which AIDS is an unsubstitutable sign – implies that while AIDS is each time a singular event, its fundamental structures of defensive disintegration are also, as Mirko Grmek has subsequently argued, part of a much longer history. Understood solely in terms of its epidemiological dimensions, AIDS is an altogether new phenomenon. According to Grmek, moreover, the biological and social conditions of the past have prevented the full emergence of the particular circuitry to be followed by a retrovirus which would so relentlessly attack the immune system. An epidemic of such disastrous proportions could not have taken place, he argues, prior to the liberalization of morals combined with the control exercised in modern medicine by means of the technology of intravenous injections and blood transfusions; this is not intended to evaluate the so-called 'perversion of morals,' but rather to emphasize the critical level at which technology intervenes in contemporary pathology. 'But this epidemiological fact does not necessarily imply that the retrovirus in question is a newcomer in the absolute sense of the term – a mutant whose ancestors were never pathogenic.'[6] Our task, as genealogists, requires us to read how this syndrome, with its peculiar idiom of latency and invisibility, has activated autodestruct triggers to become the effect of what Grmek calls, perhaps too briefly, the consummate 'metaphor for our time,' linked as it is to drugs, sexuality, blood, high tech – and to the condition which allows for the recrudescence, once again comfortably couched in scientific language, of the culpabilization of minorities.

## II. NIETZSCHE'S ANTIBODIES

Would it be possible to engage a genealogical interpretation of a particular symbolic structure – that is, at this time, to gauge the reaction of a society against its own parasites in the terms set forth by Nietzsche? The dominant figures used to describe the defense and conservation, the immunity or decline of a body politic, or a given institutional body, derive primarily from physiology. On another register, the vocabulary of medicine, and in particular of immunology, tends to evoke valuations – and the emergence of new diseases produces powerful symbolic effects, for example by creating disturbances in a cultural rhetoric or new orders of phantasmata. Within this complex cultural interplay, where it is always a question of affirming or preserving real or phantasmic health, interpretations of illness and of remedies remain uncertain; there is nothing that would ensure or guarantee them, and all the incisive determinations of that which is healthy or diseased – be they biological, philosophical, or institutional – are in fact invalidated by the paradoxes of the symbolic structure. In a certain way, these paradoxes converge in the unsettling idea of immunodeficiency. As object of fascination and repression, immunodeficiency has become the occasion for interpretations of far-reaching consequence, the stakes of which are always high. Now, the Nietzschean psychology of reaction, preservation, and *ressentiment* also purports to be a physiology. Whatever its fragility or vulnerabilities, Nietzsche's psychology/physiology serves as a warning against all-too-hasty diagnostics while it confronts with persistence the idea and phenomenon of immunodeficiency. Perhaps it permits us to view with suspicion the translations and evaluations that have been made of this phenomenon thus far. But before considering the symbolic impact of a specific phenomenon, perhaps I ought first to back up, for backing up is of the essence here.

> *Of the putative viral agents posited . . . many researchers are inclined to place their bets on a human retrovirus. Retroviruses are so called because they replicate 'backwards,' using an enzyme called reverse transcriptase.*[7]

Back home, then, the American university will have entered a difficult yet irrevocable rapport to a certain type of French reading which, among other things, privileges the notions of parasitism and contamination. While the proper names linked to contemporary French thought have appeared most markedly to infest the disciplines of literary criticism, psychoanalysis, architecture, law and philosophy on this side of the Atlantic, it seems that another uneasy alliance which is taking shape in the medical sciences merits consideration as well. The academic community, and extraacademic research groups, have shown a demonstrable resistance to immunodeficiency or, in a word, to addressing an issue which has reached crisis proportions in this culture. The history of this resistance is yet to be written, and may be found to bear some essential relationship to a symbolically homosexual grounding of the very discourses that are bent on repressing the memory of an original effacement of otherness, sexual difference, and so on, in the transmission of knowledge. In other words, if academic discourse and its others cannot comfortably deal with cultures that are bound up with a problematics of contamination, and if these cultures are localized in an imagined exteriority to the community of researchers, this may be traceable to some primary repression but also to the compulsion to affirm a powerful yet mystified version of the ivory tower, itself a phallic temple, which would function to mark off the impregnable zone of a heteropluralistic liberalism. These would be the conditions of an affirmative *re*action.

At a time when the university in particular is beginning to acknowledge the dissolution of internal barriers which guaranteed the integrity of each discipline and in some sense assured the 'wholesomeness' of each part and the whole, at this time, when the raison d'être of the university and institutional modes of thinking are being seriously questioned, it hardly seems fortuitous if American researchers have felt the need to assert immunocompetence in the face of immunodeficiency.[8]

> *Dr. David Klatzmann, of the hospital La Pitié-Salpêtrière in Paris, has determined the* LAV *(Lymphadenopathy-Associated-Virus) specifically attacks helper T-cells – this property is called a 'tropism.'*[9]

Why the French, until now, have been more active than we in pursuing parasites inhabiting the fields of philosophy and science, infesting an entire community, is a question that I provisionally leave open to interpretation, to contaminative interpretation.

> *Precisely because of this concentration of world history, what resists analysis calls for another mode of thinking.*[10]

This takes us back to the voice that emerges in the *Genealogy of Morals*, a voice which bespeaks the confidence of power when it utters, 'What are parasites to me? . . . May they live and prosper: I am strong enough for that!'[11]

« 1 »

Since Nietzsche has sounded the alarm that enables us to recognize symptoms of a declining West, including those which determine the predicament of the last philosopher, and since Nietzsche has alerted us as well to the cognitive values of the anecdote, let me begin precisely in this vein by imparting one slight bio-graph before turning toward the biologic: California is my current institutional host; I have observed that on the West Coast one might feel inclined to read Nietzsche not only because of an originary and stringently instituted need for the catalytic converter – how often Nietzsche gasps for clean air in the *Genealogy!* – but also because we have become acutely sensitive to the rapport between parasitism and philosophy, to a revival, perhaps, of what Nietzsche calls 'the emergency conditions under which philosophy arose and survived.' As an example of this phenomenon, and as an introduction to the 'worms of vengefulness' that are the sovereign subjects to the negative trope he calls *ressentiment,* let me disclose the specific manner in which my host institution presents itself, its modes of transmission and its ordering of knowledge in the official communicating organ: the course catalog (see figure).

I hesitate to decide or name which thing is the worm in this context, what is being managed or mismanaged on any level of academic consciousness, nor which term might designate the foreign body – that thing which can be neither assimilated nor rejected, nor interiorized. And yet, as odd or unthinking as such an instance of academic reflection might appear, the host institution is not necessarily at odds with itself nor with the philosophical *or* for that matter, nematological grounding of itself. While no chair has been instituted for Zarathustra, as Nietzsche fantasized it would be, my host institution has gone even further – it has interpreted in irrefutably Nietzschean terms the vampiric activity or reactivity of philosophy. But this institutional text can also be read as a peculiarly Nietzschean injunction, as a late translation of Nietzsche's *Dawn* – the West Coast being the last to wake up in America – where it is written that 'no thinker, as yet, has had the courage to measure the health of a society and of individuals by the number of parasites they can

| COURSE | ID | | TITLE | UNITS | INSTRUCTOR | DAYS | TIMES | ROOM | BLDG | EX |
|---|---|---|---|---|---|---|---|---|---|---|
| NEMATOLOGY (NEM) (Continued) | | | | | | | | | | |
| NEM | 297 | DIRECTED RESEARCH | | | | | | | | |
| | | NEM-297-01 | RES | 1.0-6.0 | VAN GUNDY, SD | TBA | TBA | TBA | TBA | |
| | | | *SATISFACTORY/NO CREDIT (S/NC) GRADING* | | | | | | | |
| | | | *SEE DEPARTMENT FOR SECTION NUMBER* | | | | | | | |
| PEST MANAGEMENT (PST) | | | | | | | | | | |
| PST | 202 | PROP/USE PESTICIDES | | | | | | | | |
| | | PST-202-01 | LEC | 3.0 | THOMASON, JJ | M W F | 8:10 AM-9:00 AM | 217B | ENT | |
| PST | 250 | PEST MANAGEMENT | | | | | | | | |
| | | PST-250-01 | SEM | 1.0 | ERWIN, DC | T | 4:10 PM-5:00 PM | 1100 | GEOL | |
| | | | *SATISFACTORY/NO CREDIT (S/NC) GRADING* | | | | | | | |
| PST | 290 | DIRECTED STUDIES | | | | | | | | |
| | | PST-290-01 | FLD | 1.0-6.0 | THE STAFF | TBA | TBA | TBA | TBA | |
| | | | *SATISFACTORY/NO CREDIT (S/NC) GRADING* | | | | | | | |
| | | | *SEE DEPARTMENT FOR SECTION NUMBER* | | | | | | | |
| PST | 291 | INDIV STUDY-COORD | | | | | | | | |
| | | PST-291-01 | TUT | 1.0-6.0 | THE STAFF | TBA | TBA | TBA | TBA | |
| | | | *SATISFACTORY/NO CREDIT (S/NC) GRADING* | | | | | | | |
| | | | *SEE DEPARTMENT FOR SECTION NUMBER* | | | | | | | |
| PHILOSOPHY (PHL) | | | | | | | | | | |
| PHL | 1 | INTRO TO PHILOSOPHY | | | | | | | | |
| | | PHL-001-01 | LEC | 4.0 | JOHNSON, OA | MW | 10:10 AM-11:00 AM | 2340 | SPR | 4C |
| | | -21 | DIS | | | F | 10:10 AM-11:00 AM | 2340 | SPR | |
| | | -22 | DIS | | | F | 11:10 AM-12:00 AM | 3117 | LIBS | |
| | | -23 | DIS | | | F | 9:10 AM-11:00 AM | 1122 | HUM | |
| PHL | 2 | CONTMP MORAL ISSUES | | | | | | | | |
| | | PHL-002-01 | LEC | 4.0 | GORDON, C | MW | 11:10 AM-12:00 AM | 1340 | SPR | 2A |
| | | -21 | DIS | | | F | 10:10 AM-11:00 AM | 2351 | SPR | |
| | | -22 | DIS | | | F | 11:10 AM-12:00 AM | 1340 | SPR | |
| | | -23 | DIS | | | F | 12:10 AM- 1:00 PM | 2117 | LIBS | |

stand.' It would appear that quite a number of parasites are involved in a reading of Nietzsche, and one can easily enough imagine the risks he took in hosting them in his corpus.

> *As certain breeds of dog have become more beautiful, delicate and softer of fur, so have they begun to lose eyesight, suffer dislocation of the hip, and become subject to various other genetic diseases. . . . Much of the negative response to 'professing literature' in the* TLS *involved a fear that literary study was once again being perceived in foreign, mainly effete French, ways and that these were being taught to unsuspecting northeasterners by dangerous and insidious professors, all at Yale or trained there.*[12]

This essay addresses itself, then, to a state of emergency – my own as well as that of others. I would like to explore here the dream of 'the *great health*' which convulses Nietzsche in the *Genealogy of Morals,* his letters, and elsewhere; in other words, I ask that one open one's ears to a certain notion of autoimmunity, to the discordant condition, that is, in which a given body turns against itself because it has misunderstood or misinterpreted its systemic productions, having discerned something as foreign in the worst sense, as dangerously parasitical and inimical to its constitution. My point of departure is a footnote in the *Genealogy* to which we shall return in a moment. First let me suggest that my itinerary begins with this hypothesis: Nietzsche poses, the very questions that are being raised by contemporary immunopathologists. One such question regards the relationship of the body to what medical science calls the components of the 'nonself.' To put it simply and economically, why does a body – institutional, political, biological – not know that it is, under certain conditions, attacking itself, misconstruing a self as nonself or, very simply, misinterpreting the effects of friendly, fun-loving parasites? (That's putting it simply.) Or conversely, while attacking the friendly parasite, what are the conditions of the possibility for this body to remain passive, silent, nonresponsive and irresponsible in the face of compelling danger? Before I attempt to pose this question in different terms, I ought briefly to define the terms that will be circulating rather freely throughout the body of this presentation.

The antibody can be viewed, and is so viewed in medical texts, as a type of *reactive* warrior that comes riding in, or rather out, on a white blood cell to encounter or meet the call of an antigen. An antigen, normally, is a foreign substance in the blood stream. However, before the desired type of immediate reactivity on the part of the antibody can at all take place, the invading substance (be it endogenous or exogenous in origin), must in the first place be recognized and interpreted so that, for instance, the antibody-antigen complex can subsequently activate the rearguard action of phagocytes which then attack and devour foreign substances; or, more precisely, they attack and devour that which has been interpreted as foreign. Immunity, which in law means exemption or freedom from liability, was originally introduced into medicine to explain an organism's ability to resist or overcome microbial or parasitic (for example, helminthic) invasion; the concept has been expanded in the meantime to include the reaction of the body against any foreign substance (antigen) that invades or is introduced into its tissues. (An apology should be extended, no doubt, for injecting this vocabulary at a point where it might seem foreign to our purpose. However, this is a state of emergency and it may well be that we presently require a sizeable amount of foreign assistance.)

The point here is to demonstrate the extent to which Nietzsche's text is immunologically active. In this context one might recall his sensitivity to stench, his flair for sniffing out decay and degeneration in conjunction with what I smell as his nosophobia (derived from the Greek *nosos,* disease). Nietzsche, whom Deleuze justly calls a symptomatologist, appears primarily to be concerned of course with the general syndrome of *acquired* rather than congenital disease (man has *become* a sick animal; *ressentiment* is a blood-poisoning, he reminds us).[13] Indeed, Nietzsche's genealogical investigations take us back to an original sense of the 'good' and 'pure' as the immunocompetent, somewhat akin, ontogenetically, to the 'child who was born unbreakable, tensed, ready for new, harder, even remoter things' (44).

Before I interpret the host of problems that this raises, let me suggest that one type of genealogical question, perhaps the question par excellence, has been formulated in the *The Genealogy of Morals* precisely in these terms and determinations: 'Where does it come from, this sickliness?' (131). Let me suggest precipitously, too, that the strongest beings, in Nietzsche's conception, are essentially immunodeficient – an interpretation or diagnosis which, I believe, can be taken as the origin of Nietzsche's call, in a section treating disease, for a 'pathos of distance': a distance from herd diseases, slave morality, socialism, varieties of pharmakonic woman and man. And in particular, the ascetic priest. While we are all familiar by now with the arguments he launches against the culture of ascetic priests, we should bear in mind that they also deserve some credit. They are to be credited, he argues, for having at least rendered the sick harmless through the curative instinct of life; the ascetic priesthood has turned the sick into an autoimmune community, more or less tricking them into turning *ressentiment* against themselves, thus immunizing *to a certain extent* the healthy. These ascetic priests are to be commended, for they have instituted and sustained a chasm between the healthy and the sick, 'provisionally safeguarding the more healthily constituted.' 'That was much,' he adds, '*very much!*' So much for the credit accounting of this priestly caste. Nietzsche's objection, what he indeed calls 'our most fundamental objection,' comes down to the recognition that this priestly medication does not combat the cause of sickness, the real sickness, but merely administers consolation. Like Socrates, these priests only *seemed* to be physicians and saviors. In fact, however, they are failed etiologists who have 'only ruined health and taste.'

My point of destination here will have been a footnote, a swelling footnote on the edge of night and genealogy which has spread its singular effects throughout his corpus. I would like to ask that one take this passage in stride and examine its implication for him, and for them. In the first essay, section 17, Nietzsche appends to the body of his text this injunction: 'it is necessary to engage the interest of physiologists and doctors on these problems (of the *value* of existing valuations). . . . Indeed, every table of values,' he continues 'every "thou shalt" known to history or ethnology, requires first a *physiological* investigation and interpretation rather than a psychological one; and every one of them needs a critique on the part of medical science.' Two sections earlier he has conjectured that the 'physiological cause' of resentment 'remains hidden.' Parenthetically he proposes an etiology of resentment thus: '(It may perhaps lie in some disease of the *nervus sympathicus,* or in an excessive secretion of bile, or in a deficiency of potassium sulfate and phosphate in the blood, or in an obstruction in the abdomen which impedes the blood circulation, or in the degeneration of the ovaries and the like)' – it may require little speculation to divine what 'the like' means here.

Perhaps the night has become deep enough for us – for the ovaries and the like – to consider together patiently the physiology of *ressentiment* and the clever manner of pest management overseen by certain institutions. Pest management, by the way, is a relatively new science, born in the mid-sixties, basically designed to induce a species to destroy itself, to plant its own infectious parasites within itself, thus repelling the need for the intervention of an external police corps of sorts that would be charged with committing pesticide. As for Nietzsche, who is a pest manager of another genre, he is hopeful – still hopeful – of seeing a 'stronger type' develop in some figure that would have proceeded from an understanding of human preservation and adaptation, but that would exceed the mere premise of 'preservation.' In this resect, the so-called Nietzschean eschatology – while it may be pronounced by 'the last philosopher' – needs to be revaluated, I think, as essentially postapocalyptic in kind, breaking as it does with religious apocalyptic literature, with the book of hate, as he puts it, which Christianity signed. It projects instead a bridge held up by physiological and medical interpretive forces – by interpreting doctors, though not necessarily by doctors of philosophy. This bridge would extend from the last man to the overman. Man is over, man will be overman. The specificity of Nietzsche's scorn for the conservative, apocalyptic genre can be gleaned in the early sections of the *Genealogy.*

Nietzsche and his great epidemiologist, Zarathustra, are hardly conservative, and hardly on time for an apocalypse – now. Zarathustra, nurse to all convalescents, dances after his wards have regained a sense of (the) humoral, of the humoral immune system – that is, when they will have recovered their capacity to produce antibodies that can meet the immunologic challenge, becoming so many signs of the interpretive rigor that has known how to combat poisonous modes of infectivity, such as, to take one example, metaphysics. That the pathos or pathology of distance might be linked in Nietzsche to a problematics of infection seems to be borne out by the suggestion in the *Geneology* that the healthy – the immunodeficient – need to be put under quarantine. This in fact '*should surely be our supreme concern on earth,*' Nietzsche writes emphatically. 'That the sick should *not* make the healthy sick . . . but this requires above all that the healthy should be *segregated,* guarded even from the sight of the sick, that they may not confound themselves with the sick' (124). The healthy are so vulnerable, so susceptible to infection, that they must be placed in heavily immunized zones, in emergency wards for the healthy. They are so weak, or potentially so weak, these healthy ones, that they need to be protected from the sight of the sick; they are already subject to a form of visual contagion. Thus, whatever the physiological foundation of the psychology of *ressentiment* might be – and we have seen Nietzsche's prudence in the matter – the structure itself of Nietzschean health bars any one-to-one correspondence between a symptom of disease – whether physical or not – and a sign of decadence or weakness: the strongest and most active are also the most vulnerable; they are immunodeficient. The healthy are the healthy because they have not yet been seriously infected; we are speaking here of a condition that allows an infectious agent to enter and defeat the healthy – as the Romans were defeated. And so, when Nietzsche situates the highest caste in terms of 'purity' he insists upon the 'unsymbolical' mode, he prescribes diet and hygiene – he inscribes a kind of hygienealogy. Elsewhere, when he writes of the 'ennobling inoculation' – in *Human, All-too-Human* – Nietzsche does not want the wounds to be *dressed;* he wants them bared and resistant, held up in their stamina by gaiety. Thus even the wound, woman, need not be dressed according to his understanding of microbial resistance in the *Twilight of the Idols:* 'Contentment protects even against colds. Has a woman who knew herself to be well dressed ever caught cold? I am assuming she was barely dressed.'[14] Barely veiled, barely truthful, body and antibody, woman here, tête-à Medusian-tête with the contagion of frigidity, shakes the common cold in style. For a moment the woman in Nietzsche resembles the resentless man who 'shakes off with a single shrug much vermin that eats deep into others' (39).

« 2 »

As early as 1767 Mozart was saved from the disfigurement of smallpox. He sent as a token of his gratitude an arietta to his physician, Dr. Joseph Wolfe; it was entitled 'An die Freude.' The music was set to a Masonic text. I must ask you retain two apparently disjointed things. First the cure for smallpox gave birth to the discipline of immunology (or virology, immunopathology). The founding father of immunology, Edward Jenner, was, like many founding mothers and fathers, subjected to violent abuse and opposition, against which he was not entirely immunized – like many founding mothers and fathers. The scandal of his discovery grew out of his experimentation with inoculation, that is, out of his conviction that the offending agent must first contaminate a body – any body – before it can discharge itself of its poison. Jenner's discovery actually involved cowpox, and I would not hesitate to place Nietzsche's sensitivity to the cow in this context of ennobling inoculation. This is said half in jest – but only half. The second point, more to the point, concerns the circumstances under which Mozart wrote his first Masonic piece, as an ode to joy and recovery.

> *This anxious attention to his health accounts for the great interest which he attached to all new discoveries in medicine, or to new ways of theorising on the the old ones. . . . As to Dr. Jenner's discovery of vaccination, [Kant] was less favourably disposed to it; he apprehended dangerous consequences from the absorption of a brutal miasma into the human blood, or at least into the lymph; and at any rate he thought that, as a guarantee against the variolous infection, it required a much longer probation.*[15] *[Note: Kant, in his primary objections to the vaccine inoculation, will be confounded with Dr. Rowley, and other antivaccine fanatics. But this ought not to hide from us that, in his inclination to regard vaccination as no more than a temporary guarantee against smallpox, Kant's sagacity has been largely justified by the event.]*

I would like to speak tonight about the Queens of the Night, about the irreparable descent of a figure in Mozart's final piece. When *Die Zauberflöte* saw completion, Mozart began composing his *Requiem*, and died. We all know that his untimely, eternally untimely end gave rise to great speculation and countless thanatographies which sought to find the cause of death now in poisoning, now in heart failure and, recently, in a bizarre epidemic that spread through Vienna in 1791, but whose cause has not yet been determined.[16] British musicologist R. B. Moberly surmises that when he died Mozart 'was perhaps too poor, too weak, too exhausted to have any resistance to disease.'[17] Others link Mozart's sudden decline, or his consciousness of its inevitability, to his famous letter to his father 'On Death' written on 4 April 1787. But the only thing about his death that has been repeated with some sense of certainty concerns the moment of his passing away, when Mozart looked at his watch and murmured these words: 'At this moment, the Queen of the Night is coming onto the stage.' Her last aria, before her disappearance, announces the stage of *Tod und Verzweiflung.* And lest anyone suppose that Mozart is not himself the Queen passing over our horizon, let me refer to the letter he composed the morning he composed this aria, in which Mozart passes himself over to the third person. He is writing to his wife, Constanze: 'Death and despair [*Tod und Verzweiflung*] were all he earned,' he wrote of himself, to himself, posthumously. At this moment, at this untimely moment, then and now, the Queen of the Night is coming onto the stage.

If this opera is to be isolated for this stage and context, it is partially because death and despair are sounded by a 'woman with a dagger,' such as Nietzsche envisions woman precisely at a moment of imaginary vengeance – a moment which, were she to survive it, would render her the hysterical hyena of *ressentiment* that appears in the *Genealogy.* This woman with a dagger, on the edge of imaginary vengeance, is about to be put in her place; she's cooking: '*Der Hölle Rache kocht in meinem Herzen: Tod und Verzweiflung* [Hell's vengeance seethes in my heart].' The opera consists of a series of rescue operations and demands for help which are played out in terms of a relentless immunological drive. The triumphant institution that survives the queen's operation is a place of immunity, where vigilance is kept ('sorgsam gewacht') against *Fremdkörper.* The lunar realm of the feminine, the queen and her/his high F and nocturnal adagios are at stake, for the Mozartian body will produce no further antibodies. In Mozart's wake, there will be Nietzsche's Zarathustra to mourn this loss as the loss of that which was 'a help in my helplessness,' 'the sister soul to my insight;' 'you abyss of light,' he calls her. And as if to commemorate the queen's *Mutter Schwur* of vengeance, he quotes to her, 'whoever cannot bless should *learn* to curse.' All of this takes place in the passage entitled 'Before Sunrise.'

The *sternflammende Königin,* the flaming queen, is the mother inscribed by Mozart in the mother tongue, germinating in an opera that opts for a papagenealogy of sorts. Papageno himself, who knows not from where he stems, is not entirely man. Despite his Nietzschean stemlessness, he's not dynamite, really, nor overman; rather he is somewhat of a hybrid birdman. Biologically speaking, he as bird has evolved, together with man, the most complex immunological system, and it is perhaps noteworthy that he acts as the single figure to affirm, 'Mein Leben ist mir lieb [Most dear is life to me].' As such he remains a secondary figure, but no less vital to the unfolding dynamics of the rescue missions and transmissions.

While this is not the place to make sense of a libretto that has caused musicologists a good deal of trouble in terms of coherency, intelligibility, and intention, I would like to propose a reading of this text that would privilege a notion of impaired host defense in a movement whose stages are marked precisely by modes of infectivity, parasitical inclusion, and immunosuppression. In short, this would be the drama of drama, an oeuvre or opera knowingly caught up in syndromes of defenselessness and deficiency but, in the first place, in the misinterpretation of a foreign substance or disease-causing agent that enters the operatic body itself. Studies in immunopathology have established that the recognition of a substance as foreign or 'nonself' by the immune system is limited.[18] The queen, Mozart's great antibody, the female element that delivers the magic flute as the gift of immunity, is rendered finally but well before the finale, inoperant. Her rescue operation begins in the beginning, when Tamino arrives on stage from the Orient, defenseless, panic-stricken, having shot and therefore lost all his arrowheads. He is impotent. I would like to ask that one consider Nietzsche's assertion that 'it is because of their impotence that in them hatred grows to monstrous and uncanny proportions' (33). Tamino, of course, is headed straight for priesthood; he will become the monster of Enlightenment and rather more steadily pernicious than the worm which pursues him at the outset. The opening words of the opera demand aid: 'Zu Hilfe!' As for Tamino, he faints in the face of a monstrous apparition. This opera is convulsed with pleas for help, with moments of weakness and degenerescence. After three women, activated by the queen, attack the endogenous monster, saving the exogenous invader, Tamino affirms himself too weak to offer Papageno help ['Weil ich zu schwach zu helfen bin'], and the queen will admit having been too weak to save her daughter ['meine Hilfe war zu schwach']. An opera concerned with aid and general generic difference (Papageno and the daughter will produce a hymn that rather deliriously reproduces *Mann und Weib und Mann und Weib,* and so on). The nocturnal queen who saves and wants to save – she is the majestic version of Ms. Nightingale, that genre of women redeemers who belong to or in some sense have been exiled to the night, not, *nichts* – the queen who grants immunity both to Tamino and Papageno is to be eliminated by a discourse of reason and *Grund,* by a figure curiously called Zarathustra (Zorastro), who, having founded the religion of Parsiism, eventually assimilates 'Contamino' to his Bactrian culture.

Let me interrupt this narrative to recall that Nietzsche was himself a nurse, a nightingale, and he discloses his position and predicament as Queen of the Night to – Wagner, of course. His appointment as Extraordinary Professor in 1870 appears to have led him to volunteer his services, his *munis*, to the military corps (*immunis* means free from service). He writes this to the composer: 'I had to nurse six of the poor wretches myself . . . unmistakeable symptoms of disease appeared in me as well. . . . But we advanced on both of these contagious devils with the greatest possible vigor.' Soon, however, his health will be 'too shattered,' and 'Dear Friend: it's going *very* badly. My health,' and so on, 'What a life. And I'm the great affirmer of life!'[19] Nietzsche the nurse, the delicate nightingale, communicates to the operatic genius unmistakable symptoms of his disease. To put it most succinctly, we are dealing here, in the cases of Nietzsche and Mozart, with a type of physiophantasmic transaction whose scenario initially focuses on a passive, maternal immunity granted to an exogenous invader who will in turn prove injurious to the noble host, nurse and nourisher, perhaps, indeed, causing infection more by exploiting host susceptibility than by its own powers of pathogenicity.[20] For they are weak, they are wretched and wretching; they need help, the strong.

*Die Zauberflöte,* as title of the opera and immunocompetent object, is Mozart's gift to himself. If a claim can be made that the magic flute was Mozart's *Gift* to himself in the German and English senses of the word, it is in the first place because Mozart had little tolerance for the flute; he disliked the very instrument that was to name the remedy, the *Unterstützung,* of his work. Thus the flute itself, the object and the name of the object, had to undergo an immunological treatment of sorts; it had to be dedemonized, disinfected, cleansed – made *sauber* – or enchanted, *zauber.* In sum, it had to *become* the inoculating instrument, *die Zauberflöte,* the very stylus of immunization (the monstrous quality of this shaft is reflected in the opera's other monster, in the figure of Monostatos whose name means single-stemmed or legged). While Tamino is given the phallic syringe containing the poisonous remedy, Papageno's original flute is supplanted with a box of invaginated bells, which leave him wondering: 'Was drinnen sein mag? [What's inside?].'

On opening night, Mozart himself would play the bells, shortly before the death knell sounded for him, for the Queen of the Night. I, too, have to allow the Queen of the Night to perish at this stage, but it is with the hope of seeing her restored to life again, maybe tonight.

For our purposes – and our purposes must at times be crude, I'm afraid and I apologize, since we are in a marketplace – the choice of an opera, and in this case, one that renders the antibody inoperant and impotent, one that thematizes a type of vampirism and the turning of the dagger-flute against oneself, already involves, according to Nietzschean conviction, a discourse of immunodeficiency. Music is viewed in the *Genealogy* as the 'superior language,' as the independent art as such. It is set apart from all other arts in that it does not offer up images of phenomenality but speaks rather the language of the will itself, directly out of the 'abyss' as its most authentic, elemental nonderivative revelation. The musician 'became a kind of telephone from the beyond, a ventriloquist of God' (103) – opera, which places music at the service of a text (in this case, a text derived from a narrative entitled 'The Philosopher's Stone'), is bad music. Opera *is* the genre of contamination. Whereas music in itself remains intelligible to the servant of Dionysus, opera is merely a remedy against pessimism; as such, it is not aesthetic in nature, but moral and theoretical. Opera marks the triumph of Socrates or Christ over Dionysus, of nihilism over life, of slave over master or queen.

In this respect, the opera itself cannot as such be understood in Nietzschean terms; its form as artwork is inscribed in what Nietzsche calls the history of *ressentiment.* Above all, its resolution does not come with the triumph of Zarathustra, but with that of Zorastro, a figure of the Enlightenment. Nonetheless, the figure of identification for Mozart, the queen, is an embodiment of immediate and originary health, which is shown to be the most vulnerable, the immunodeficient, and which has to separate itself from itself in order to guarantee the victory of reason, that is, in Nietzsche's terms, of resentment. When it is no longer a property of the originary figure, the magic flute, that is, health, becomes a mere *instrument* of increasingly *failing* health. From this point onward, the entire process is nothing more than a proliferating complication within a condition of general breakdown.

As for immunopathology as a discipline, it is not loathe to engage certain metaphorical strategies and, at one point, appears even to concur with Nietzsche on this note when choosing, in a fairly recent text, the symphonic mode to explicate itself in triumph: 'The mechanism of host defense against (viral) infections *is a symphony* of many non-specific and specific immunologic components.'[21] It would be impossible, if not pretentious, to attempt a deconstruction of the rhetoric inhabiting the relevant medical texts here, although such an enterprise, as Nietzsche foresaw and desired, would certainly seem necessary. It may suffice to indicate the persistance of one odd designation in order to press the need for 'us' to contaminate and be contaminated by such a literature of life, by the bio-logical. In a volume published by the National Institutes of Health, it is stated at the outset that viral immunology is a 'transdisciplinary subject.'[22] Composed, then, under the sign of transdisciplinary discourse, the volume refers to immunodeficiency disease or syndrome as the 'ID-disease' or 'ID-syndrome,' depending on the context. One is left wondering, after trekking transdisciplinary fields, whether Freud is not a secret reference or repressant in such a naming, and whether a libidinal reading of the disease is not being insinuated here – or, simply, dismissed. At any rate, when we consider that scientists do not know what prompts immunological shutdowns, nor why certain organs are affected and not others (the 'meaning' of the individual organs also changes, warns Nietzsche [78]), this strange immunity/community regarding Freudian discovery needs further explanation. While the status of a shared signifier must be left suspended, it is perhaps not unfair to submit that, despite promises to the contrary, the discipline of immunology seems unperturbed in ascribing to itself as a discourse a position of immunocompetence with respect to 'outside' interpretive sources. Of the minimal evidence of contamination from our field, which is itself experiencing a moment of greatest impurity, there is an essay on 'Psychosomatic Medicine and Phenomenological Anthropology' to be considered, for example, wherein a certain Dr. Lit's reading of disease as something fundamentally noncontingent, as a response to a call, *Ruf*, or encounter, that is, in terms of Heidegger's *Daseinsanalyse* is reviewed.[23] However, Dr. Lit turns out to be something of a disappointment, despite the enlightening promise or premise to which he has lent his name, and narrates little more than what Nietzsche would call 'anemic ideas.'

This brings us back, for the last time, to the text in which Nietzsche says he is 'choking and fainting' (43), the *Genealogy of Morals*, and to the ascetic priest who conducts himself like an obsessional neurotic, isolating himself as he does out of fear of contamination.[24] Yet, 'the progress of [their] poison through the entire body of mankind seems irresistible' (36). Man is the most imperiled, the most 'chronically and profoundly sick of all sick animals' (121). The sick, Nietzsche writes, walk among us as 'embodied reproaches, as warnings to us – as if health, well-constitutedness, strength, pride were in themselves necessarily vicious things for which one must pay some day, and pay bitterly' (123). But who is this 'us' among whom the sick manifest themselves? Who are the walking – that is, relatively healthy – sick? The sick are 'moral big mouths,' they are 'all men of *ressentiment*, physiologically unfortunate and worm-eaten, a tremulous realm of subterranean revenge, inexhaustible and insatiable,' and so on (124). We have returned to a sense of nematology and pest management, to philosophy (assuming we ever left these). The temporality of the 'sick' happens to imply a long duration ('the man of *ressentiment* knows how to wait' [38]); they outlive Nietzsche's health; they have 'succeeded in poisoning,' thus impelling Nietzsche to conclude this section with a sense of pinched time, invoking the 'we,' convoking his friends: 'So that we may, *at least for a while yet*, guard ourselves, my friends' (125). We must guard ourselves, my friends, for it turns out that we are short-lived, and the strong are immunodeficient – the Greeks, their gods, the Romans, the *Fall* of Wagner, his Parsifal, the Nietzsches and his friends are defeated. And this is an acquired or imposed predicament which is not in itself a disease – he calls it *sickliness* – it is not a disease *an sich* but the susceptibility to disease, the vulnerable opening, the night, the point of entry. In immunology, particularly in Nietzsche's great immunological systems, everything depends upon the point of entry. Resentment is hiding vermin, and we are always subject to it. Resentment itself, if it should appear in the noble man (for it *can* appear in the noble), consummates and exhausts itself in an immediate reaction, and therefore does not *poison* (39). In *Human, All-too-Human* Nietzsche thus writes of inoculation, the tenure track record, the timing of the strong and the authority which tends to collapse the will of the strong. He writes of inflicting a wound on the stable element of the community. 'Precisely in this wounded and weakened spot the whole structure is *inoculated,* as it were with something new; but its overall strength must be sufficient to accept this new element into its blood and assimilate it. The strongest natures hold fast.' However, 'Only where the greatest duration is securely established and guaranteed is continual development and ennobling inoculation at all possible. Of course, authority, the dangerous companion of all duration, will usually try to resist this process' (125).

But I think, my friends, we should end on a happier note, for Nietzsche promises – and Nietzsche is the promising animal – Nietzsche promises, then, the gay science as our reward, and we should open our ears to the end of *Zarathustra,* to the fourth part, which is also called 'The Ass Festival':

> They all at once became conscious of how they had changed and convalesced and to whom they owed this: then they jumped toward Zarathustra to thank, revere, caress him, and kiss his hands, each according to his own manner, and some were laughing and some were crying. But the old soothsayer was dancing with joy.
> 'They are convalescing!' Thus spoke Zarathustra gaily to his heart.

# HITTING THE STREETS

*Ecce Fama*

---

*A dozen false starts:*
*You're such a fool, I said,*
*Spooking at shadows when*
*All day you were calm . . .*

*But he shuddered, stubborn*
*In his horsy posture,*
*Saying that I brought*
*Devils with me that he*
*Could hear gathering in all*
*The places behind him as I*
*diverted his coherence*
*With my chatter and tack.*

---

VICKI HEARNE
*Nervous Horses*

At the crossroads of a certain type of journalism and itself Walter Benjamin began an essay on Karl Kraus's torch with a quotation: 'How noisy everything grows [Wie laut wird alles].' He begins to engrave his final pseudonym and mask in a complex materiality where rumor is coconstitutive with disease, where the temporality of spreading cannot be assigned to the one over the other, in a kind of alarm text whose noises have not stopped becoming. 'In old engravings,' begins Benjamin, 'there is a messenger who rushes toward us screaming, his hair on end, brandishing a sheet of paper in his hands, a sheet full of war and pestilence, crying murder and pain, naming danger, fire and flood, spreading everywhere the "latest news."' News in this sense, what Benjamin calls 'in the sense the word has in Shakespeare,' is the street-episteme of rumor. He does not merely say 'news' but something like 'times': *Zeitung.* The time in this sense, the temporality of this sense, resides within a notion of uncontrolled spreading, carried by a tortured messenger whose speech is a crying one, pointing to the subtitle of his horror, a kind of horror from above to which his hair points. A punk messenger of old engravings who, set in motion, is a pointer; he blinks in the direction of writing which carries war and other cries, his screams being dictaphoned somehow by the inserted cries of murder and pain, spreading everywhere. This is not exactly the same cry as Heidegger's *Schreiben/Schrei* or the *cri/écrit* of Nietzsche, but it's not altogether remote either, because whoever implants the instrument of messenger within his body, whoever turns himself into a running transmitter of a brandished sheet of paper, crying aloud, his hair on end – our end, as the end of the antenna, pointing and blinking –, whoever will have said 'I am the messenger,' will have had to traverse the place where Benjamin stopped running, in Nietzsche and in Heidegger, in their rumorous rapport to the end, be this the end of philosophy or of man *tout court.*

Perhaps some will be astonished by the fact that Nietzsche is situated in the place reserved for 'hack journalists': 'as one who blurred the boundary between journalism and literature . . . betrayer of the aphorism to the impression.'[1] This is precisely the type of reading Heidegger tries to divert in his work on Nietzsche, one that appears to be inextricable, however, from the *Zeitung* of rumor. This quickly becomes clear in the rescue missions he performs on behalf of Zarathustra, leading us from temptation (whose temptation? one feels tempted to ask) thus: 'The temptation to take the thought of the eternal return merely as something obvious, to take it therefore at bottom as either contemptible mumbling or fascinating chatter is overcome.'[2] Or, to stay with the cries of the messenger, with screams whose vocal cords appear to be the hairs, in *Was heißt Denken?* Heidegger's attempt to construct a rumor control center goes in this direction:

> But riddle upon riddle! What was once the scream 'the wasteland grows . . . ,' now threatens to turn into chatter. The threat of this perversion is part of what gives us food for thought. The threat is that perhaps the most thoughtful thought will today, and still more tomorrow, become suddenly [*über Nacht*] no more than a platitude, and as platitude spread and circulate. This fashion of talking platitudes is at work in that endless profusion of books describing the state of the world today. They describe what by its nature is indescribable, because it lends itself to being thought about only in a thinking that is a kind of appeal, a call – and therefore must at times become a scream.

Riddle upon riddle, Benjamin's messenger might be Nietzsche: 'Nietzsche, most quiet and shiest of men, knew of this necessity. He endured the agony of having to scream.'[3] From where does the scream emanate within an understanding of post-Laocoönian speech acting? Does it arrive in that nonrhetorical moment that hesitates between the fall (into chatter) and the lofty transagony of lucidity's knowledge? And what renders Nietzsche, in Heidegger as in Benjamin, so vulnerable to falling at the border between small talking and big thought? Can some sort of public opinion settle the issue, for instance, the disputable *sensus communis* of Kant? Who negotiates what stays clear of idle chatter? And how to put a contract out on that which threatens Nietzsche's commanding voice, the 'threat of this perversion'? Perhaps more imposingly, how can the thought of the eternal return be taken for chatter? Is it not the case that the eternal return could be shown to be a rumor, launched by Nietzsche as the thought of his thought but never articulated or demonstrated philosophically, only pointed to by the innuendo of Zarathustra and his animals, his readers?[4] And what if Being were itself a rumor, the murky rumbling of an unheard-of ontology? The answers can be shown merely to reside within the form of these questions, whose constructions are only partially complete, hardly posed correctly or on reliably firm ground. We are cruising the site mapped out by Benjamin's 'Destructive Character,' a small passage through which he introduces a certain rapport of rumor to suicide; we are at the intersection 'between the public and private zones that commingle demonically in prattle,' as he puts it in another context.[5] In other words – and we shall speak only in other words – we want to address precisely that place of circulation that would not be limited to a body whose remotest limbs would be infused with writing's bloodlines, but which would be extended to the circulation of a newspaper and most pressingly into street circulation, whether that street be conceived in terms of a path, aporetic or not, one-way or dead-end, cut off from itself or even the U-turn where the troping *methodos* carries with it very specific sounds. There is a circulation, therefore, an auto-mobility that was brought to a screeching halt at the primary register of pure, that is to say, contaminated noise. Benjamin will have begun his enigmatic essay on Kraus and journalism, taking us through dense passages of *Verkehr* (where prostitution and language traffic), starting up an enigma on a modality of *fama*, toward which we shall want to turn (I am already setting the blinkers, the blinkers of the last man, *das Man* in the street): 'How noisy everything grows.' And Heidegger gives us a sense of noise as he starts his cars all along his roadways; there are so many cars, autos that blink as emblems of a false semiotics, motorcycles parked in the spaces provided by the German university, and a certain origin of sound that he ascribes to, different registers of street noises that is to say, one can hear, almost equiprimordially, the difference in the noises produced by a Mercedes and an Adler or Volkswagen – as usual, a difference between high and low gears, emissions from big cars and talk, small talk, vehicles of the people.[6] On the way to Nietzsche, then, a problematics of sonic transmission, a thinker's ear pierced by gutter noises which, however, will become linked to the very possibility of his oeuvre. A writing fundamentally attended by walking against the wind of *Gerede*, by get ting out of the car and walking toward another set of transmission prob lems, another topography of circulation: 'it is attained chiefly by the cardiac strength of great thoughts,' writes Benjamin, 'which drives the blood of language through the capillaries of syntax into the remotest limbs.'[7] As if one could jog across such a frontier without losing heart or breaking down.

This draws us toward the double hermeneutics of Nietzsche's predicament, double because his thinking ineluctably encounters the intersecting marks of public and private discourse. The space where internal, formal, private structures of a philosophical language control, as Paul de Man would say, external, referential, public effects, has already been cleared by Nietzsche. Lest this drive us into the arms of adventurous misunderstanding, please remember that we have been strengthened into a position, opened up by Nietzsche, from which misunderstanding has become a philosophically rigorous way toward thinking.

### THE FACE OF MADNESS

I will whip into submission two unruly movements that have permitted us to talk about Nietzsche's madness, training our focus on the fragile intersection where two names cross over into one another – because there were always two names harnessed by Nietzsche's charioteer of inscription, the one phantomizing the other, doubling for the other, or enfolding itself in the other's mask. These names embraced the masks of our history: Dionysus and Apollo, Wagner and Cosima, Socrates and Christ, Dionysus and the Crucified, Paul Rée and Lou Salomé. It appears that essentially two moments have permitted us to repeat a stutter in the painful archives of Nietzsche's madness – which was never only Nietzsche's madness, never only a broken contract, or even a fulfilled promise, between Nietzsche and himself, or Nietzsche and Wagner, or Nietzsche and Lou. But Nietzsche's madness (I am using shorthand) was more often than not made to enter a contractual agreement with third parties, such as the Third Reich, as if the collapse of Nietzsche could provide a hermeneutic clarity, a kind of luminous capitulation to the great politics of inanity. Nietzsche's madness, in Thomas Mann, was not so much out of reason's grasp, but to the contrary, it could be read as a historical explication of sorts, a fevered lucidity within which Nietzsche figured as a minotaurized self, contained, interred, and eloquent – a system of symptoms participating in the collapse of German spirituality: history's own case study, as it were. Thus it would be Nietzsche's unthought that promotes a genuine thinking of convulsive fascism, for example. As if Nietzsche's madness had a history, or could render history historical, readable in terms of a general archeology of pain. Yet only that which has no history, wrote Nietzsche, can be discovered ('Nothing is definable unless it has no history').

The route I'd like to take is less grand; it is not even a side street in the royal road to the unconscious. To this end, I have asked the gods to lend me their wing'd Pegasus, perhaps the first horse to invent the concept of a rider with conviction, that is to say, from the bestial perspective where distinctions are held between Hegelian masters and predators, sadism and cruelty. A strong figuration of rumor, not distantly related to Hermes, Pegasus arises as lord of the air, flying wherever he would, envied by all. Above all, the rider behind this corpus is a mere blemish on the back of a body propelled mysteriously through space. Pegasus, as nonpossessible gift, comes with a particular driver's license; it points one, like Bellerophon (whose father was devoured by horses), beyond the Chimera's fiery breath, or, in this case, it will permit us to leap over the Gorgon sisters, the terrible and unbearable gaping into the isle of madness from which one might not recover. However, the serpented head already places us face to face with Nietzsche's animals, if one considers the serpent around Zarathustra's head, the mysterious embrace traced around the neck of Nietzsche's anchorman, Zarathustra, who is destined to announce that which is never said. The serpent offers the embrace, forecasting how circle and ring are to be implicitly entwined in the circling of the eagle and the winding of the snake. The embrace of Turin, therefore, will be the first thing around which I coil my thinking, asking very simply what it means for a Nietzsche to embrace a horse, to wrap himself around the face of madness, collapsing in the street at the command of a whip. What sort of inscription was taking place when Nietzsche fell under the crack of a whip, a lash destined for another? The first part of this reading, therefore, is to be called:

### A HORSE IS BEING BEATEN

Nietzsche in Turin: We think we have understood. Nietzsche tells us relatively little. He favors Piedmont cuisine, he writes, and a glass of water follows him through the streets like a dog. This may conjure Mephistopheles or the dog of *The Gay Science*, whose title Nietzsche has given as 'la gaya scienza.' In this Italianate work, Nietzsche writes that 'I have given a name to my pain and call it "dog."'[8] In the same work, Nietzsche has written '*Knowing how to end*. –' He writes of the bay of Genoa ending its melody, and of 'Masters of the first rank,' who are 'revealed by the fact that in great as well as small matters they know how to end perfectly, whether it is a matter of ending a melody or a thought, or the fifth act of a tragedy or of an action of state' (§281). The dog's howl will return, or has already returned, to Nietzsche as the proper name of a pain. In Turin it follows him through the streets in the benevolent guise of a water glass; nonetheless, it follows him, pursues him through the streets. Assuming we know where or what Turin is, then let's skip over to an easier question: where is Italy, or more likely, *what* is Italy? Can we be certain of its status as locality – a place of topographical prestige, Turin merely being somewhere up a leg extended into the Mediterranean? I cannot assume that we yet know the auratic pull of Italy in the phantasms of German writers and thinkers, beginning perhaps with Goethe. Or even, to narrow the focus, what is the Italy of Freud, or more close to home still, the piazza to which Freud returns, as if under hypnosis, guided he suggests by a kind of horseshoe magnetism, in the text of the *unheimlich*, the being-not-at-home of the uncanny. You may recall the pull of that piazza, where painted girls decorated the windows, and Freud could only return, uncannily, to the labyrinth. Return to what? One could say that for Freud, Goethe, and Nietzsche, going to Italy implied picking someone or something up on some level of conscious or unconscious articulation, cruising for what we call *lues*, a syphilitic infection; but we shall return to this when hitting the streets. For we need to consider the rumor that Freud and Jung helped propagate concerning the etiology of Nietzsche's degeneration. They helped spread the rumor, and one wonders how they knew, of the origin of his spreading syphilitic infection. Freud, who shared Lou with Nietzsche, traced down the ostensible lues or luetic pathology to Nietzsche's having visited as we all know a bordello; but, Freud adds, a male bordello and, more precisely still, Nietzsche is said to have contracted syphilis in a *Genoese* male brothel. We shall treat these and other rumors of Nietzsche's susceptibility to infection in '*Ecce Fama*', *fama* being the proper name of rumor. So the question remains: what is called Italy?

Ever since Goethe's *Italienische Reise*, Italy was like a command post, the other Lorelei of Germanic desire. Goethe picked up Christiane Vulpius in Italy, and brought her back to Weimar. This scandalized everyone. The only Weimarian ever to invite Vulpius over was Arthur Schopenhauer's mother, Weimar's most liberated woman. (Nietzsche's eye doctor was also called Vulpius; this was before he was turned over to the doctor of the Basel asylum, Dr. Wille. Overbeck was afraid to tell Nietzsche that this was his doctor's name.) Elsewhere I have tried to show that for Freud as for Goethe, Italy became bound up in a notion of *genitalia*, an argument which I cannot reproduce here, but for which I would like to open a credit account. The extent to which Nietzsche might have borrowed a reading of the '*genitalienische Reise*' can be inferred from the citational qualities of his madness, if it is not presumptuous momentarily to accede to the suspicions of Overbeck and Gast. Their opinions become part of a history in which it is said that Nietzsche was feigning his madness, perhaps vampirizing the style of others' state-of-the-art breakdowns. These breakdowns, of which Nietzsche repeated a certain number of dimensions, come from Hamlet, for example, from the Greeks, for whom madness was a divine gift, from Christ's survival of himself, from Rousseau's paranoiac transport or that of Tasso. I have even found evidence of Nietzsche's citation of Goethe in his limited lexicon of fallen utterance. Nietzsche often repeated *'mehr Licht!'* in his long days of what in German is called *Umnachtung* – something like madness, probably linked to 'lunacy,' in any case a nocturnal inflection of mind. But here we run the risk of repeating Nietzsche's letter to Burckhardt, namely, that he is all the names in history.

A horse is being beaten. In Turin. Nietzsche will both forget and double his name after the mysterious embrace. He writes that he has forgotten his address. The scene suggests another citation, an inversion of an originary street accident in which a name is forgotten, an address blurred from memory – when *Rousseau* comes crashing on the sidewalk, a form of street paranoia overtakes him, knocking him down, whereas we could say that Nietzsche was somewhat uplifted by his collapse; he began to erect governments, shooting Bismarck, and anti-Semites, whereas Rousseau, on the contrary, felt that governments were being erected to gun him down in the streets. Nietzsche, after his street accident, will be transfigured euphorically into God, apologizing to the people for the weather, and wanting only to embrace the people of the streets. Rousseau is afflicted by an animal linked to a carriage, a dog pursuing him through the streets. He is shown being beaten by the unforeseen. Nietzsche is afflicted by an animal linked to a carriage. It is being whipped. The word for whip is *Peitsche.* The place in which to translate the horse in Nietzsche is not so much *Pferde,* as would be appropriate say, in little Hans, but rather, in this case, I would submit, *Roß.* I shall suggest why this is so momentarily. The *Peitsche* is a recurring instrument in Nietzsche's work – excuse me, it is silly to speak in this context of Nietzsche's work, only Heidegger could assert something like that or like 'Nietzsche himself,' who thought to the end of his thought. The question of the text erupted with Nietzsche, everything appears to be organized around the absence of an oeuvre.[9] We are reading the *Peitsche,* the whip, perhaps the maypole of Nietzsche's absent oeuvre. The whip serves as a compacted citation of 'the infamous slander unleashed behind your back' (F.N.). The whip produces a public rebuke, perhaps of the genre we saw in Wagner's public attack on Nietzsche following *Human, All-too-Human,* in the *Bayreuthischer Blätter.* It aims to awaken by wounding. Nietzsche traces his Wagnerian whiplash to the shock-awakening of Brünhilde, with whom he identified: 'Verwundet hat mich der, der mich erweckt [I am wounded by him who has awaked me].' The whip can be a conductor's baton or an instrument of destiny's charioteer. It cracks down on the numbed body under general anesthesia. A horse is being beaten. But there is no depth to the whip – it is a surface writer, participating in the temporality of the father, a flash through Nietzsche's existence, staying with him as a memory of pain. He cannot vomit the horse.

Attached to no concept of interiority, the whip lashes out like the explosion without gunpowder. Nietzsche once dreamed of such an explosion; before the days of nuclear plants, something that would originate in a sudden surface exfoliation. When the heat is on, it comes down on you, dissolving afterwards into a moment of lightness and dance.

At the very end, Nietzsche repeated a restricted number of statements. They are: 'I am dead because I am stupid'; '*mehr Licht*'; 'I am stupid because I am dead.' And also, 'I do not like horses.' As with Rousseau's catastrophic encounter with an animal-drawn carriage, Nietzsche will lose his name to the street scene. We need to consider the specificity of this hippopathology, as it exists inside and outside philosophy, a drawing cart of certain stubborn tropes whose epistemological reliability is not merely figurative. One wonders whether Klossowski was not right in perceiving a slow shift in Nietzsche from Greece to Rome – was Nietzsche not rearing at an unheard-of philosophical track whose grooves are so deep that only a fine ear can hear the master's voice? The sonic boom of *Peitsche*, to which it can be asserted Nietzsche loses his name – as he wanted to lose his name to Lou, to give her, as his appointed *Fortdenkerin* and *Erbin*, his heiress and continuance of his thought, the secret thought of the eternal return – this word appears in German as part of a story of repression and drive. It arrives on the scene from the East, the domain of Nietzsche's ancestry. In any case, it settles in the fourteenth century into the Middle High German form of *pitsche*, adding to the list of feminine equipment, which it also displaces, and to instruments of mutilation and devoration such as *die Geißel* [also whip] and *die Gabel* [fork]. *Pitsche*'s journey into *Peitsche* appears to follow a similar route to that of *Nietzsche*, which Janz informs us took root in Nitsche. Janz also discovers Wagner to be related to Nietzsche. Always related to drive, or that which drives on [*treiben*], the *Peitsche* plays an instrumental role in organizing the drives [*Triebe*] or in accelerating the horse power of *trab*, to trot or drive. To insert Wagner, as charioteer, into this configuration allows us to retain the fact that in his madness Nietzsche often longed for Tribschen, the place and time spent in friendship with Wagner and Cosima. I should like to extend an apology for brutally pacing these thoughts through friable terrain; this certainly puts me at jeopardy and risks creating uneasiness. I should have preferred the reliably scholarly pace of Rozinante, were I not honoring the poetry of Nietzschean philology or writing under madness's whip. I am going to suggest rather boldly that Pitsche is the name of the father in an exchange system that borrows a paternal *P* against an *N* – a name that Nietzsche always stood to lose. What comes cracking down on or before Nietzsche is the name he sought to carry in the sheltering place of radical solitude – for example, as Giorgio Agamben has shown, in the shadow of the wanderer. Remember that Nietzsche always doubles up under his father, imitating his death and going under, like his father, at the age of thirty-six (the family rumor attributes the cause of death to the fact that he fell then).

The difficulty resides in the doubleness of the father, as *Peitsche*, and as that which phantomizes the horse; insofar as the father is still alive in Nietzsche, as the one who is past life, numbed and fragile, a memory, he agitates within the scene which we have named 'A HORSE IS BEING BEATEN': 'I do not like horses.' We are lodged within a moment in madness's stutter, trying to grasp Nietzsche and his animals (Heidegger knew to write of Zarathustra and his animals). It seemed necessary to contain the zoomorphic energy propelling a momentary difference between what Margot Norris has called the creatural and cultural man in her reading of new ontological alternatives for man, extending to the *Übermensch* or instinctual aristocrats.[10] In book 3 of *The Gay Science*, Nietzsche writes of *Animals as Critics:* 'I fear that the animals consider man as a being like themselves that has lost in a most dangerous way its sound animal common sense; they consider him the insane animal, the laughing animal, the weeping animal, the miserable animal' (§224).

I cannot offer a full reading of the hippopathological phantasm, but merely scattered fragments. Let me assemble some of the principal elements. If a horse is being beaten, Nietzsche, as in all his modes of relatedness, will insert himself into the interstices of a couple. The couple could consist of a horse and its conductor, Lou Salomé and Paul Rée, Wagner and Cosima, or in a more strikingly negative vein, Elisabeth and Förster. I have chosen a description of the breakdown that appears calm and neutral. It begins on the third day of the new year, reviving momentarily the triadic structure which pervades the Nietzschean text. This often serves to underscore the fragility of his physiologic: the three days of debilitation due to a migraine headache, for instance, from which in *Ecce Homo* a terrible lucidity also arises. On the third day of January, 'Nietzsche had just left his lodgings when he saw a cab-driver beating his horse in the Piazza Carlo Alberto. Tearfully, the philosopher flung his arms around the animal's neck, and then collapsed.'[11]

Here are some characteristic traces which will be set forth without comment but with hopes of strengthening our reading. First an early and late poem, linking the horse with acts of naming. The word for horse in both cases is *Roß*, pluralized, into *Rosse:*

Flüchtige Rosse tragen
Mich Ohne Furcht und Zagen
Durch die Weite Fern.
Und wer mich sieht, der kennt mich,
Und wer mich kennt, der nennt mich:
Den heimatlosen Herrn. . . .
Verlass mich nie!

[No fear shatters me
When wild horses take me
As far as they can.
Whoever sees me knows me,
Whoever knows me names me:
The homeless man. . . .
Never forsake me!]

Nietzsche was at Pforta when he wrote this. The next poem is included in the volume Walter Kaufmann prepared for 'la gaya scienza.' Part of the 'Songs of Prince Vogelfrei,' it addresses the mistral wind of the Mediterranean. These are fragments of the eleven-stanza poem in which *The Gay Science* is evoked:

Sind wir zwei nicht eines Schosses
Erstlingsgabe, eines Loses
Vorbestimmte ewiglich? . . .

Kaum erwacht, hört' ich dein Rufen . . .

Auf den ebnen Himmelsternen
Sah ich deine Rosse rennen,

Sah den Wagen, der dich trägt,
Sah die Hand dir selber zücken,
Wenn sie auf der Rosse Rücken
Blitzesgleich die Geißel schlägt, –

Sah dich aus dem Wagen springen,
Schneller dich hinabzuschwingen,
Sah dich wie zum Pfeil verkürzt
Senkrecht in die Tiefe stossen.

[Were we two not generated
From the same womb, predestined
To one lot evermore? . . .

Hardly awakened, I heard your calling. . . .

I saw your horses running
Through the heavens' threshing basin,
Saw the carriage which carries you,
Saw your hand tremble at you
When upon the horses' back
Lightninglike your whip descended.

From the carriage of disaster,
Leaping to bring you down yet faster,
I saw you shortened to an arrow
Vertically downward plunging.]

The first time Nietzsche went to Italy, reports Ronald Hayman, this is how things went: 'He found that he wanted to be alone. He started out for Italy, but, feeling ill en route, spent the first night at a hotel. . . . Sitting, isolated, in the conductor's seat, high in the postcoach, he travelled for the first time along the Via Mala, the mountain road famous for its views. This is *my* nature, he wrote.' What Nietzsche was doing in the conductor's seat, whom he was replacing, what he was driving at, still needs to be clarified, particularly if he is en route to Italy, in which he recognizes *his* nature – again, a reference to genitalia. We note in passing, moreover, that his father's illness was referred to in Nietzsche's family as the *petit mal.* However, backing up along the heterobiographical trail, one finds that Nietzsche claimed to take more pride in his accomplishments on horseback than in winning a prize in philosophy. In the immensely invested month of October – Karl Ludwig Nietzsche had superstitiously fixated on October, the month in which *Ecce Homo* came to be written and Nietzsche was himself born – Nietzsche volunteered in 1867 for military service. Among the thirty recruits in the division there was only one other volunteer. Nietzsche wrote: 'The riding lessons give me the most pleasure. I have a very pretty horse, and am supposed to have a talent for riding. When I hurtle out into the big exercise yard, I then feel very satisfied with my lot.' Nietzsche – and I – was very surprised to find he was the best horse-rider among the thirty recruits. The officers predicted he would attain the rank of captain. But his hopes were humiliatingly frustrated. Myopia, which was felt to be inherited from his father, had made Nietzsche a bad judge of distances, even at short range, and in the middle of March, jumping into the saddle, he threw himself so hard against the pommel that he tore two muscles in his chest. He felt a sharp, twitching pain on his left side, which did not stop him from riding on with determination. He fainted twice that night, lay ten days in bed, paralyzed, and at the end of ten days the doctor made incisions in his chest. He writes: 'I am understating it if I say that already four to five cupfuls of pus have come out of each wound.'[12] For another biographical trace, we go to the 'memorabilia,' which retain one image in the earlier months of his routine military life. He writes: 'At morning at winter in a steaming horse stable.' Peter Heller has commented that 'this setting, with the bespectacled intellectual as groom, brushing the animals, cleaning the stables, recurs frequently in Nietzsche's letters of the period. The steam and smell of horse manure which he had to carry out, made a strong and revolting impression on him though he enjoyed his work with horses more than anything else.'[13] Heller links this up with Nietzsche's enormous capacity for radical compliance, a point that certainly holds up under scrutiny if one considers the extent to which he was driven by Wagner in the direction of abject servility.

Wagner as conductor of Nietzsche's destiny has been linked in psychobiographies to the paternal Nietzsche, whom he is said physically to resemble. What interests me however is the double rapport of repulsion and let us call it pleasure, which includes the carrying of an excremental deposit. The double and oscillating movement between repulsion and pleasure is best articulated in the book over which Wagner blew up publicly, *Human, All-too-Human*: '*Desire for deep pain.* When it has gone, passion leaves behind a dark longing for itself, and in disappearing throws us one last seductive glance. There must have been a kind of pleasure in being beaten with her whip' (§606). There exists nothing to prove that Nietzsche's infection did not in fact begin with his military service, in a kind of primal embrace of the horse. The parentheses thrown around these erotically invested whippings or embracings give pause. For while the horse marks an important moment in the history of photography, the photograph that we have of Lou, Paul, and Nietzsche wraps his pathogenic history around itself in an odd and painful serenity, a photograph of the future of the Nietzsche institution wherein Nietzsche, one of two horses, takes the bridle and Lou's whip, leaving Paul Rée to be the only figure among the three to be posing. In Nietzsche's madness, he will be said to have taken on equine features, for one was tempted often to focus on his manelike hair. Hélène Cixous has made him undecidable, lending him the features of a dog as well.[14]

Or consider this letter from his student days, written by Nietzsche's friend Deussen:

> Intoxicated with wine and camaraderie, we allowed ourselves, in spite of having so little money, to be talked into hiring horses to ride up the Drachenfels. It is the only time I have ever seen Nietzsche on horseback. He was in a mood to interest himself less in the beauty of the scenery than in the ears of his horse. He kept on trying to measure them, and to make up his mind about whether

> he was riding a donkey or a horse. In the evening we acted still more insanely. The three of us were wandering through the streets of the little town making overtures to the girls we assumed to be behind the windows.

The labyrinth of the ear, the minotaur, the interstice between one and the other: Nietzsche coupled with the donkey and a horse. In *Zarathustra* the ass's repeated braying is spelled I–A, which means *yes* in German. The adored ass is without question the most yes-saying of all creatures.[15] But here Nietzsche cannot make up his mind whether he was riding the one or the other. The other was in part born from the womb of Shakespeare, in the melancholy violence of 'Venus and Adonis,' a poem urged on by the libidinal whip of the neigh-saying: with ears pricked-up, he neighs, he bounds, he wounds the earth, 'what cares he now for curb or pricking spur?' This steed, who raises questions of mastery, is an uncanny horse who is not entirely alive, 'as if the dead the living should exceed.'

Of course we shall never know what sort of recognition took place when Nietzsche saw that a horse was being beaten; we know that he hallucinated his father's voice, suffered indeed from a kind of auditory psychosis since the age of five, listening to his father's telecommanding but disarticulated utterances. There was a telephone to the beyond installed within Nietzsche, but at times the voice would translate itself into a near televisibility for the myopic child. Once, Nietzsche was sure his father was crouched behind his chair as he was writing. But the voice was mutilated, unintelligible. I am led to suppose, but I have not yet been able to verify this, that his father's casket was horsedrawn. (Neither Janz's *Biographie* nor other sources produce a description of the funeral which Nietzsche attended; Nietzsche himself remembers the unforgettable music.) The only thing that we know is that Karl Nietzsche – perhaps the Carlo Alberto Piazza resonates with this – began the principal part of his seminary studies at a locality that bore the name of Rossleben. This linkage of the horse with coming-to, literally with 'life,' and the many inscriptions of destinal naming or even destinerring in and out of Nietzsche's writings, the way the father lives on in Nietzsche – 'I am dead as my father' – persists in Nietzsche and is carried by his work, the way Zarathustra begins by carrying a corpse, this fundamental carriage of the other whose inscription your back bears or under whose bruising flesh you remain immobilized. All of this leads one to want to motivate the embrace, to 'try the reins,' as Nietzsche would say, of an unbroken thought. In his last letters to Strindberg, Nietzsche's praise for *le Père* was unflagging.

In *The Birth of Tragedy*, a text perverted from its course to honor Wagner, Nietzsche 'dares to acknowledge the truth' about the Greeks. 'The Greeks, as charioteers, hold in their hands the reins of our own and every other culture, but almost always chariots and horses are of inferior quality and not up to the glory of their leaders, who consider it sport to run such a team into an abyss which they themselves clear with the leap of Achilles.'[16] Someone will have cleared the abyss, someone driving the horses, but not the horse itself. Because we find ourselves in the streets of Turin pondering the Greeks, because it will be appropriate shortly to leap into '*Ecce Fama,*' which actually is *defama,* we ask that Nietzsche ventrilocate with his double street register the necessary intersection, perhaps with the aim of uncrossing inevitable polarities; Socrates's wife, writes Nietzsche, 'taught him to live in the back streets, and anywhere where one could chatter and be idle, and in that way formed him into Athens' greatest backstreet dialectician, who finally had to compare himself to a pesty horsefly, set by a god on the neck of the beautiful horse Athens to keep it from coming to rest.'[17] The street, the horse: this is a citation, a repetition. He was set by a god on the neck of a beautiful horse to keep it from coming to rest, to keep it alive, to console the wound of slumber's denial: keep it from coming to rest. The meaning of *Rossleben* may reside in this backstreet passage. So when Nietzsche writes of 'the streets of one's ancestors,' he argues:

> It is reasonable to develop further the *talent* that one's father or grandfather worked hard at, and not switch (tracks) to something entirely new. . . . Thus the saying: 'Which street should you take? – that of your ancestors.'[18]

Your ancestors and mine. Let this tribute then be paid to memory, which has caused us to enlarge it now, yearning for what we once possessed. The tribute is cited from the *Phaedrus,* which we have begun to relive in the form of Plato in Turin, the place where madness ('mania') besets the text, and this describes the soul in its emergence. The soul of Plato will be membered by Lou, Rée, and Nietzsche. Listen to the soundtrack behind the photograph which Nietzsche staged in Lucerne, 1882:

> Yet it is troubled by the horses and only beholds Reality with much difficulty. . . . As for the soul's immortality, enough has been said. But about its form, the following must be stated. . . . Now all the gods' horses and charioteers are good and of good descent, but those of other beings are mixed. In the case of the human soul, first of all, it is a pair of horses that the charioteer dominates; one of them is noble and handsome and of good breeding, while the other is the very opposite, so that our charioteer necessarily has a difficult and troublesome task.[19]

There are essentially two horses, therefore, under the command of the charioteer. While one is good, the other needs to be beaten to submission. The account of the training whereby the bad horse is broken is of legendary cruelty, the whip being the finely tuned instrument of higher education:

> We divided every soul into three parts, two of which had the form of horses, the third that of a charioteer. Let us retain this. As we said, one of the horses is good, the other not. But we did not define the goodness of the one or the badness of the other, which we must now do. The horse that holds the nobler position is upright and clean-limbed; it carries its head high, its nose is aquiline, etc., in other words, a follower of true renown; it needs no whip, but is driven by word of command alone. The other horse, however, is huge, but crooked, a great jumble of a creature, with a short thick neck . . . grey bloodshot eyes . . . shaggy-eared . . . hardly heeding whip or spur.
>
> Now it has been humbled and follows the driver's instructions; when it catches sight of the beautiful, it is like to die of fear. So from this time on the soul of the lover may follow the beloved with reverence and awe.

In further passages, the bad horse is shown to be neighing. He must learn to serve the first command of the will to power which consists in the will to obedience. He must attune his pricked-up ears differently, to the lesson of the charioteer who, 'like a racer recoiling from the starting-rope, jerks back the bit even more violently than before from the teeth of the wanton horse, bespatters its malicious tongue and jaws with blood, forces its legs and haunches to the ground and causes it much pain.' We have to let this compelling bit go, too. The double occupancy drawn by the image of Plato and Nietzsche in Turin, investing our ancestry, trails off like the other enigmas, around which we have gathered, although this would have been the place to start reading something like Nietzsche's nightmare. 'But the other, as soon as it has recovered from the pain of the bit and the fall and has barely regained its wind, bitterly reviles its mate and their charioteer for their cowardice.'[20]

### ECCE FAMA

> One day that which *others* know about us (or think they know) assaults us – and then we realize that this is more powerful. It is easier to cope with a bad conscience than to cope with a bad reputation.–*The Gay Science*, §52

The rumor that hit the streets when his sister returned from Paraguay, assuming a double name, was that there was a Friedrich Nietzsche. The extent to which his so-called oeuvre was whipped up by the misguided Elisabeth Förster-Nietzsche has been covered in great detail, suggesting that Nietzsche will always to a certain extent be the effect of the hack work of a crude forester. Kaufmann's restitutional biography of Nietzsche produces a typology of gossip which it attempts to tranquilize and master. You know some of the points that have been beaten into the Nietzschean signatures. Lou Salomé, says Elisabeth, was a slut; Rée was Jewish, Nietzsche was not, Brandes was (these observations by no means coincide with Nietzsche's opinions). Furthermore, it is said that Nietzsche wrote that he loved his sister, he wrote books, for example he wrote *Der Wille zur Macht,* his intentions were never really to repudiate Wagner, and so forth. Kaufmann sometimes gets down into the gutter of *Gerede,* pulling misogynistic switchblades on Elisabeth, the big mouth who wrote Nietzsche's posthumous work. 'One wonders how her success was possible and why so many *learned men* who produced monographs on various aspects of Nietzsche's thoughts deferred so humbly to *this woman.*' Quoting Rudolf Steiner, he continues: 'that Frau Förster-Nietzsche is a complete laywoman in all that concerns her brother's doctrine, her thinking is void,' and so on. I do not dispute this, of course. But figuring out Nietzsche's 'Legend,' as Bertram was to call it, cannot be left to a war of the so-called sexes in which one side occupies the seductive and unpinnable territory of gossip and the other, seriously charted scholarship. Benjamin and others have suggested to what extent criticism as *Wissenschaft* participates in what we might perceive as a massively sustained gossip session, being a form of utterance that has fallen from truth. Nonetheless, the legend of Nietzsche, from wherever it may stem, began to develop, asserts Kaufmann, 'shortly after Nietzsche had become insane in January 1889.'[21] In fact, Kaufmann begins this particular work, *Nietzsche: Philosopher, Psychologist, Antichrist,* with the statement: 'Nietzsche became a myth even before he died in 1900, and today his ideas are overgrown and obscured by rank fiction.' In a Hölderlinian sense – Hölderlin being a compatriot in madness, and the poet whom Nietzsche discovered in his early years – Nietzsche fell upward ('*man kann auch in die Höhe fallen*'), if growing into myth in one's living 'after-death' can be considered an upward fall. In any case, Nietzsche's great fall has left at least a double-tracked imprint, suggesting for example a double origin or etiology for his illness, neither of which has been definitively lifted from inferential acts of reading or rescued from exiguous evidence. Dionysus issues from a double origin, twice born, once from the princess Semele and once from the leg of Zeus. Is one not in imitation of an understanding of double origin as sexual difference when at-

*Friedrich Nietzsche with Lou Salomé and Paul Rée, 1882.*
*Jules Bonnet. © Dorothee Pfeiffer*

tributing the secret beginnings of his disease either to something of which a woman was a carrier – either syphilitic contagion or the spreading of rumors – or, on the other hand, to something which threw him off the proud, erect equestrian pose that Nietzsche is supposed to have struck? There remains yet another possibility for a hermeneutics of infectivity that I have tried to elaborate in 'Nietzsche's Antibodies' (infra), one which is situated in the military, where Nietzsche gives up the rhetoric of immunocompetence.

Like Dionysus, Nietzsche is always divided, morcellated, cut in half by the flash of a whip, or sharing the bridle with a sadistic groom. There is time only to report what you already know. Nietzsche ended up on the street, touching the ground, and this was the end of his solitude. His mother came to fetch him after Overbeck, sent by Burckhardt, came to pick him up, after which Elisabeth would set him up in his own archives, near the Goethe archives. She propped him up for photographs, and benefited financially. But I shall stick to the streets, not to the mausoleum built by his counterfeit sister and nation, both inflatingly self-important, abusive, at once in awe of Nietzsche and hopelessly left behind by him. This predicament did not end in 1946. For some reason still to be studied, Nietzsche, with few but luminous exceptions, still cannot be read by Germans. Heidegger admittedly was the first to read him as the last philosopher. It was as if Nietzsche were to be identified with the blindness for which his name was made to stand. In any case, in 1888, Nietzsche's 'fame began to spread like wildfire.' A letter dated 7 June 1905 refers to *fama*'s hold on the Nietzschean legacy. It was written by Otto Binswanger to Ida Overbeck, wife of O., and expresses regret over the source of rumors surrounding Nietzsche's illness, something that has caused Overbeck embarrassment ('und daß ihm die Urheberschaft des Gerüchtes über die Krankheit Nietzsches durch das Vorgehen des Herrn Gasts noch immer Unannehmlichkeiten bereitet [and that the source of the rumor about Nietzsche's illness, through the actions of Mr. Gast, continues to cause embarrassment]').[22]

Klossowski mentions that, starting into his madness, Nietzsche began to consult newspapers to gain a referential anchoring ('la rubrique *faits divers, la chronique mondaine* fournissent bizarrement une dimension à sa pensée, où le fortuit donne aussi à son langage un ton peremptoire. . . . Maintenant, il est devenu son propre "propagandiste" [strangely enough, the *faits divers* and the *chronique mondaine* add a dimension to his thought, in that miscellaneous events lend to his language a dogmatic tone. . . . He has now become his own propagandist]').[23] Meanwhile, Overbeck receives a letter from Turin saying that Nietzsche had all the anti-Semites shot. On consulting Dr. Wille, director of Basel's psychiatric clinic, Overbeck was advised to go immediately to Turin.

Nietzsche wanted to address the crowds and to embrace everybody.

Overbeck was nervous about mentioning Dr. Wille's name.

Dr. Baumann of Turin sends Wille a signed statement diagnosing 'mental degeneration.' Evidence given in these terms: The patient 'claims he is a famous man.'

Nietzsche apologizes to everybody and no one for the bad weather.

Nietzsche says that during his attacks he wants to embrace everybody in the street and to climb up walls.

When Frau N. arrives he embraces her delightedly. 'My dear good mamma, I am so glad to see you.' After calm discussion about family affairs, he shouts, 'Behold in me the tyrant of Turin!'

In the train, Nietzsche tells his mother that he had been in a lunatic asylum but soon would be all right as he was quite young, only twenty-two. But before long he flies into a rage with her and throws one of his gloves out the window. She moves into another compartment.

When led into the psychiatric department, he keeps bowing politely.

In June he smashes a window. He thinks his chief warden is Bismarck. Believing he is being tortured every night, he begs for help.

In mid-August he smashes more window panes, claiming he had seen the barrel of a rifle behind them.

In mid-February, Nietzsche moves with his mother to Jena. Most of the time he is childishly docile now, and easily reduced to tears.

In the street Nietzsche would sometimes try to hit dogs or passersby.

Sometimes he wants to shake hands with strangers in the street.

One morning, in May, 1890, Nietzsche leaves the house without his mother. He began to undress on the pavement, wanting to bathe in a puddle, until a policeman stopped him. Her overriding fear was that she would lose him once again to the clinic.

In December 1890, Nietzsche waits with his mother for Elisabeth at the railway station. He holds a bunch of roses. At home he seems not to follow her stories about Paraguay, but listened with pleasure when she read to him from *Zarathustra.*

When his mother read to him from the table, he would often lie next to her on the sofa, holding her right hand pressed against his once wounded chest for hours at a stretch. He would sit for hours in the armchair facing the window, childishly exclaiming, over and over again: 'I am dead because I am stupid.' Or, 'I am stupid because I am dead'; or, '*mehr Licht!*' and 'I do not like horses.'

*Correction.* He would say, 'I do not like horses,' though he persisted, despite correction, in saying 'ich bebe' – I tremble, I crack – or: I, baby.

Anyway, he could not be corrected or trained to say it right. He persisted in saying, for I do not like horses, I do not *bebe* instead of 'ich liebe.'

> *Shame.* – Here stands the handsome steed and paws the ground: it snorts, longs for the gallop and loves him who usually rides him – but oh shame! his rider cannot mount up on his back today, he is weary. – This is the shame of the wearied philosopher before his own philosophy. (*Daybreak*, Book 5, §487)

# STREET-TALK

*Enter* RUMOUR, *painted full of Tongues.*

Open your ears: for which of you will stop

The vent of hearing, when loud *Rumour* speaks?

I, from the orient to the drooping west

Making the wind my post-horse, still unfold

The acts commenced on this ball of earth.

Upon my tongues continual slanders ride,

The which in every language I pronounce,

Stuffing the ears of men with false reports:

I speak of peace, while covert enmity

Under the smile of safety, wounds the world:

And who but *Rumour,* who but only I,

Make fearful musters and prepar'd defence,

Whilst the big year, swoln with some other griefs,

Is thought with child by the stern tyrant war,

And no such matter?

HENRY IV, PART II, ACT I, INTRODUCTION

Heidegger: Das ist eine Verleumdung.

**Heidegger: That's slander.**

Spiegel: Und es gibt auch keinen Brief, in der

**Spiegel: And there is no letter in**

dieses Verbot gegen Husserl ausgesprochen wird?

**which such a prohibition is recorded?**

Wie wohl ist dieses *Gerücht* wohl aufgekommen?

**How did the *rumor* come about?**

Heidegger: Weiß ich auch nicht, ich finde dafür

**Heidegger: It's beyond me. I've no explanation for it.**

keine Erklärung. Die Unmöglichkeit dieser

**I can show you the**

ganzen Sache kann ich Ihnen dadurch

**unlikelihood of the**

demonstrieren, was auch nicht

**accusation.**[1]

bekannt ist.

'I am dead; thou live'st: report me and my cause aright.' – *Hamlet*

What does it mean to begin an essay on Benjamin by quoting Heidegger? Not just Heidegger, whose proper name resonates imperial dignity, but the Heidegger cited above (the interview appeared when Heidegger was no longer here), to borrow a subtitling phrase from Nietzsche, the Heidegger 'for everyone and no one,' the philosopher who put himself into circulation after his death.[2] Part of his destinal mark was to have been made in a newspaper article, the space of *Gerede*'s loudspeaker. It is beyond Heidegger, the speaker is quoted as saying. We all know what 'the rumor' concerns. Its authority is such that no further naming is necessary in order to establish a sound referential ground. In a gesture that rumorological paranoia exacts, the subject will want to settle his debt with rumor in a structure of 'after my death,' in the very fragile place where rumor encounters itself, the supplementary issue – in this case, *Der Spiegel* –, where Heidegger means to quell 'the rumor' in a weekly journal. There is something perturbing about the philosopher's explication to a forum of public opinion? Has Heidegger wanted to bequeath his most urgently authenticated confession to a discourse of *Gerede*. In other words, is Heidegger's final word, made to be articulated after his death, a stroke against his philosophy, a woundingly ironic utterance made against the grain of his thinking (what does it mean for a Heidegger to tell the truth in a newspaper?), or will his afterworldly in-the-world discourse force a rethinking of language's housing projects?

What does it mean to begin an essay on Benjamin by citing Heidegger? Hannah Arendt *ends* her essay by citing Heidegger, by calling him into the room where he might meet Benjamin: 'Without realizing it, Benjamin actually had more in common with Heidegger's remarkable sense. . . .'[3] This, however, is a different Heidegger, a different meeting place, scheduled according to an entirely different agenda. Nonetheless, the articulation of the rumorous space in which a rendezvous between Heidegger and Benjamin can take place – this making-room for a double occupancy of thinking's imaginary – occurs in Arendt's text, in just about any work that claims to perform 'introductions' for Benjamin. Let me introduce you: this used to be an axiomatic moment on the path that led to Benjamin. At the time they could not say I've heard so much about you; in fact they had heard very little about Benjamin. Thus the first word of Arendt's introduction is *Fama* – rumor's proper name.

Benjamin, we are told in another introduction to his work, needed to be rescued as recently as 1968 from 'near oblivion.' It was a matter of 'transforming what had been . . . a rumor among the *cognoscenti*.'[4] In the way it goes to meet Benjamin, rumor is not merely a thematic internal to his writings, but appears rather to have a decisive rapport to an 'after my death' discourse which still needs to be understood. Within a simple polarity one would be justified in thinking that while Heidegger's text is threatened by the power of a kind of countertext – rumor – Benjamin's existence as text depends on this same power. One would expect the polarity to respect its poling propensity, to establish a sound border that would place Benjamin on the other side of Heidegger, the one posthumously sustained by rumor's decisive turn, the other run down by 'the rumor' launched against him to which he can only respond in kind, according to a rumorous logic that originates in the absence of the subject, in a journal. Certainly, the melancholic thinking that goes to meet Benjamin's end cannot take place without seriously interviewing rumor's winds.

These winds, however, do not blow the superficial traces of rumor aside in order to uncover some firmer ground of language. Nor do they appear to blow Heidegger and Benjamin apart, to have them occupy two sides of a borderline: 'You look and cross over the line; I look first only at the line you present.' No. In fact, when Heidegger himself writes of the locality of *Denken* and *Dichten* in 'Über die Linie,' when he writes that 'we can only prepare for dwelling in a locality by building,' he first asserts that such 'building must be content with constructing the *road* which leads into the locality of the restoration of metaphysics and thereby permits a walk through the destined phase of an overcoming of nihilism.' Without entering the question of a reactive restoration, an active or reactive nihilism and the *Auseinandersetzung* which Heidegger conducts with Ernst Jünger, what bears pointing out concerns the inversion Heidegger is about to perform on what might have been understood in his thinking in terms of a derived classical opposition entailing authentic and inauthentic speech, manifest moments in *Rede* and *Gerede*. What needs pointing out is the outward turn of thinking's inwardness, the locality it conceives for itself, constructing a space of publicness or publicity with which Heidegger elsewhere deals in different terms, apropos of Nietzsche, but which here places his thinking on a broadcasting summit shown to be vulnerable to the winds even as it furnishes the originating point of rumorous diffusion. Heidegger has just inflected his open letter (already a thing which is not quite a letter nor entirely open like a switched on radio) – his letter has just folded in on 'the erection of the house of God,' on the *road,* metaphysics, nihilism, the destined phase. These are not simply fillers, though a Nietzsche might be tempted to argue otherwise. Heidegger continues, giving his thinking another fold: 'Whoever dares to say such things, and what is more, in writing which is open to the public [*und gar in öffentlicher Schrift*], knows only too well how prematurely [*übereilt*] and easily these words, which would only like to induce some reflection, are only shut off as murky rumblings [*Raunen*, also 'rumors'] or are rejected as arbitrary pronouncements. Regardless of this, one who is on the learn must think of testing the language of reflective thinking [*die Sage des andenkenden Denkens*] in a more original and more careful manner.'[5] Heidegger goes on to encourage the memory of Hölderlin's words in 'Brot und Wein,' evoking the words which 'originate like flowers.' But this disjunctive origination [*ent-stehen*][6] stimulates a tension between the aforesaid and the power or prejudice of Hölderlin's proper name, creating in turn a kind of strategic enervation. (Benjamin has introduced the 'rights of nerves' as a principle of reading and valuation in his essay on Karl Kraus: 'He found that [the nerves] were just as worthy an object of impassioned defense as were property, house and home, party, and constitution. He became an advocate of the nerves.'[7]) Participating in a kind of circulation, our cruising has brought us to a nerve center, an intersection of modes of origination or ingathering that a nervous reading would have to agree is pinched, congested; this suggests that a careful kind of acupressure needs to be applied here, if not to relieve the tension then at least to understand its knottiness.

Heidegger tells us, without dwelling on the point, that rumor is essentially related to the most daring thinking. Or rather, a daring writing enjoys a relationship of enslavement to something like rumor, utterance's murky rumbling. Rumor would not be reducible to some sort of external envelope that can be taken off, put on, or thrown aside like clothing. On the contrary, these words, composing the most daring thinking, can be shut down 'easily' because they provoke a recognition in them of rumor. To the extent that the borderline trait which could prevent rumor and thinking from crisscrossing does not possess a fixed value or stabilizing power, authentic language cannot be sheltered from a reading that will take the word of being from something else, where the disclosure of being can be made to seem interchangeable with rumor. These words are therefore shut off, pushed down, quelled: *abgestellt.* Heidegger does not say that this exchangeability of thinking for rumor takes place only in print or in a thinking that becomes public. He begins to establish this simulacrum by circumscribing the subject from whom the daring word emerges: 'the one who dares such a word [*Wer ein solches Wort wagt*].' Only then does he qualify, appending 'and what is more, in writing which is open to the public [*und gar in öffentlicher Schrift*].' More clearly, then, writing that is open is fundamentally open to rumor. But already the dared word, in its anteriority, has been open to rumor, which acts as the horizon to all language testing. While still under the shadow of negativity, rumor nonetheless acts as the enabler, the ground and horizon for the founding of a 'more original and more careful thinking.'

In the work we are reading, Heidegger questions a hermeneutico-medical interpretation of madness that claims to be more than a punctuation mark to thinking (in *Was heißt denken?* he also disputes prescriptive explications of madness). Heidegger evokes the name of madness's silence when naming Hölderlin – as if by some radically double gesture Hölderlin, the poet who once allowed words 'to originate as rooted flowers,' could offer a cover or grounding closure. In any case, Heidegger here staples Hölderlin's name to a fleeting reflection on *oeuvre* as rumor, guaranteeing, it would seem, a language that cannot be made susceptible to shutdown – as if the name of the one who was to be solemnly shut up for forty years could ensure safe passage for the most daring word beyond the confines of rumor's domain.

The threat of shutdown, contained within this open letter as the possibility of self-sealing, appears to be lifted at the end of the missive, prior to the moment he signs with customary heartfelt wishes, 'I send you my hearty greetings [*Ich grüße Sie herzlich*].' The 'I' is mediated in such a way that the rumorous run of his thinking promises to be circumvented; he puts his thinking on another circulatory track, the one named and performed by Goethe. The letter will be closed on Goethe, a closing place [*Erörterung*] that leaves no history of loose ends:

> *How* it would be like, however, to cultivate reflection and discussion [*Besinnung und Erörterung*], Goethe says in the statement with which I should like to close this letter: 'If anyone regards words and expressions as sacred testimonials and does not put them, like currency and paper money, into quick and immediate circulation [*Verkehr*], but wants to see them exchanged in the intellectual trade and barter as true equivalents, then one cannot blame him if he draws attention to the fact that traditional expressions, at which no one any longer takes offense, nevertheless exert a damaging influence, confuse opinions, distort understanding, and give entire fields of subject matter a false direction.'
>
> I send you my hearty greetings.

Multiple addresses, constructions of multilayered containments guided by a double economy of *Verkehr:* Goethe closing Heidegger's letter on a currency that imprints current opinion, a current of thought which overruns a language of undistortion, words: these sacred testimonials. What does it mean to sign with Goethe, what kind of traffic control is implied by the intersection of an I, Heidegger, and I, Goethe? For Benjamin, signing with Goethe meant another end to his career, a collision discourse blocked by the institution of Goethe scholarship, the opening of rumorological fury that aimed to keep him in his place, that is, out of place. It is too soon to determine what signing with Goethe means for Heidegger. We can only gather from the end of a text seeking *immunization* from rumor, although a reproach made by Heidegger to Jünger targets his medicalization of thinking, particularly in his *On Pain* work. The issue, therefore, cannot lead to a comparative literature of thinking. Benjamin's Goethe needs to be perverted within the question of a difficult elective affinity so that the naming of an *Erörterung*, a place of rendezvous for Benjamin and Heidegger, can still take place. Benjamin went into hiding. A pseudonym, the final last name he chose for himself was Holz. Thus, like the eponymous hero of 'The Destructive Character,' 'he always positions himself at crossroads,' *Holzwege*. In a moment we shall discover how the destructive character carves a rumor into Holz, onto the wood or Benjamin's other dwelling place, the name meant to protect his 'clandestiny.'

At the crossroads, the question needs to be asked again: What if Being were itself a rumor, the murky rumbling of an unheard-of ontology? It wants to be asked, but not begged, in terms of the special architectonics put together by Benjamin and Heidegger in a shared residency of *Denken Bauen Wohnen*. Like many works of this era, housing projects were projected in the main for language-tenants. A crucial theorem of Freud's 'Notes upon a Case of Obsessional Neurosis' (1909), no less than the epistemophilic instinct, is explained by means of houses which in America are *translated* or transported in their entirety from one site to another.[8] Benjamin cites a new type of house in order to inspect a breakdown between public and private discourses, houses similar to those that can now be viewed in Southern California, with large curtainless windows into which you can look, if you want, and see a man walking around in his underwear, beer at hand, the television on, doubling public diffusion in the radical translucency of a private space, the television communicating with the window, the outside looking inside, at the television, for the outside, all these broadcasting systems turned on, and no one is really supposed to be looking. Benjamin recalls 'the political radioscopy of sexuality and family, of economic and physical existence, in a society that is in the process of building houses with glass walls, and patios extending far into the drawing rooms that are no longer drawing rooms . . . in other words, private life that is dismantling itself, openly shaping itself.'[9] It is as if the House of Being were opening itself up to expose the fragility of its containment, where interior decorating can no longer feel secure about itself, anxiously rearranging the site of language according to the decoration of exteriority, the ornamentalism of a Nietzsche whose drawing room has been drawn out toward a televisibility where the noise, the static, still grows. How fragile a *Gestell* keeps this household what it seems to be becomes discernible in 'The Destructive Character,' on the way to a language which is always out of the way, drifting, rubbing over the scratch that separates the creator from the destroyer. For 'the destructive character knows only one watchword: make room; only one activity: clearing away [*Der destruktive Charakter kennt nur eine Parole: Platz schaffen; nur eine Tätigkeit: räumen*].' Like Nietzsche, 'his need for fresh air and open space is stronger than any hatred.'[10] Clearing away the laboriously plotted tracks of our own age, the destructive character (henceforth DC) is a device whose transmissions need ears that hear, public ears: 'Just as the creator seeks solitude, the destroyer must be constantly surrounded by people, witnesses to his efficacy. . . . The DC is a signal. Just as a trigonometric sign is exposed on all sides to the wind, so is he to rumor. To protect him from it is pointless.' The DC is a marker in the semiology of land surveying. He or it signals the site prior to the building of any house. As signal for what is to become, as trigonometric character, he is at once private, solitary and open on all sides to the winds of rumor. He is a signal of what is to become if rumor does not topple him. He has witnesses.

As a signal, however, the DC does not need to be understood. He is hardened into the position, opened by Nietzsche, from which misunderstanding has become a philosophically rigorous way to thinking: 'The DC has no interest in being understood. Attempts in this direction he regards as superficial. Being misunderstood cannot harm him. On the contrary, he provokes it, just as oracles, those destructive institutions of the state, provoked it.' Benjamin now suggests a distinction to be drawn between rumor and gossip, *Gerede* and *Klatsch*, of which we could say quickly that rumor belongs to the ec-static while gossip has something to do with assuring a community's stasis: 'The most petit bourgeois of all phenomena, gossip comes about only because people do not wish to be misunderstood. The DC tolerates misunderstanding; he does not promote gossip' (302). Gossip, therefore, is essentially linked to the practice of literary criticism.

The DC knows only the *Parole;* no vision guides his movement, as the English translation has put it, or rather no image controls his deed, 'dem destruktiven Charakter schwebt kein Bild vor.' The cards are stacked against visual representation, DC responds to and is telecommanded by sounds, not by any concept of television (in this sense, DC still belongs to the domain of the Old Testament, the witnessing text that proceeds by modes of aural ingestion, no new vision before the era of video tapes of flesh-words). 'But we shall never find the Overman,' writes Heidegger, 'as long as we look for him in the places of remote controlled opinion and on the stock exchanges of the culture business – all those places where the last man, and none but he, controls the operation.'[11] The overman will not appear in a space that is not distilled by rumor – the stock exchange, itself an engine fueled by rumor, goes up and down the corridors of speculation, determining valuations. The overman will not compete with remote control systems of public circulation. Heidegger bets on this. 'The Overman's appearance is likewise inaccessible to the teletypers and radio dispatches of the press which present – that is, represent – events to the public before they happen.' The press runs ahead of the times, creating events prior to their taking place, announcing through megaphones, constituting thereby the event, or at any rate the advent of event. But does this not correspond precisely to Zarathustra's calling? To announce, as absolute newscaster, this is Zarathustra's desire. He repeatedly notes that some have not heard the news, the news that God is dead, for instance, or of the end of man. Is not Zarathustra another of Benjamin's messengers, running ahead of the teleprinter, reading the news aloud? Is this not the mark of an event's eventness which asserts its ontological priority as that which is constituted in and by language? But 'this well made-up and well staged manner of forming ideas, of representation, with its constantly more refined mechanism, dissimulates what *is*. . . . The Johnny on the spot, in every area including the literature industry, is the famous "man in the street," always available in the required quantities. Faced with this dissimulating type of representational ideas, thinking finds itself in a contradictory position.'[12] This Heidegger saw clearly: 'This Nietzsche saw clearly.' Johnny Heidegger is on the spot.

I would like to stay with this contradiction; it forces us to see double (it places thinking in a 'split site,' 'das Denken in einer zwiespältigen Lage'), perhaps, indeed, inducing a double clarity. I would like to stay with it, walk its path, not in order to encounter tunnel vision, but to understand this clear vision that arises from loud-growing noises, for the last man blinks, as we might say of a television on the blink.

I think they all wore or needed to wear glasses. The frame that holds glasses together belongs no doubt to the most fragile of all *Gestell*.

'Paris taught me the art of straying.' – *Benjamin*

Benjamin's DC has a capacity for opening a special kind of glance whose description in fact commences the piece. This glance is attributable to anyone: 'it could happen to someone looking back over his life [*Es könnte einem geschehn, daß er, beim Rückblick auf sein Leben*].' The *Rückblick* takes place as a stumble improving upon vision:

> It could happen to someone looking back over his life that he realized that almost all the deeper obligations he had endured in

> its course originated in people on whose 'destructive character' everyone was agreed. He would stumble on this fact one day, perhaps by chance, and the heavier blow it deals him, the better are his chances of picturing the destructive character. (301)

The vision has improved within this opening paragraph, the picturing has become clearer. The first mention of the DC was framed by quotation marks. What was Benjamin quoting? We know he had a weakness for quotation; he boasted that his *Trauerspiel* work was composed of over six hundred of these. He would collect quotations, insert them here or there, pick them up, take them home with him, discovering their solicitations on the reading boulevards, caring for them. The relationship of rumor to quotation still needs to be grasped, indicating a bent for the nakedness of the cited recited pick-up phrase ('I heard that so-and-so . . .'). She might be taken in provisionally, if only to be turned out again, to follow the course of an anonymous *flânerie.* Or she may be a pick up the way *Aufhebung* lets itself be picked up, kept. But before 'destructive character' has assumed the chances of the DC, engaging perhaps a bit more than a chance encounter upon which one stumbles, one can formulate the reasonable assumption that 'destructive character,' as quotation, appears to recapitulate the title – or does it rather suggest an anonymous source, the man on the street talk? Between the title as inaugural gesture and the man on the street, another reference and value insinuates itself, the directionals point to another mention. In other words, the instituting gesture of the man on the street bears a name whose history in fact thematizes the loss of name as he stumbles, being made to stumble by the DC. This occurs at crossroads. The immemorial stumble takes place, like that of 'the destructive character,' toppling an originary man on the street whose arrival argues for a translation of 'Johnny' – which, strictly speaking, is Jacques; however, all bases of displacement are covered by this man who, discarding his patronym, loses only what has been already discarded. The text which dramatizes becoming the man, the muffled speaker of the street episteme, announces itself like the teletypers, like the Heidegger who spoke through his *Spiegel* years before the occurrence of his death (which he began to do, prior to the interview, as an open letter to the press), like 'The Destructive Character' that begins on the *Rückblick,* happening 'to someone looking back over his life,' in a supplementary exit text, circumscribable as the past-autobiographical walk taken by Jean-Jacques in the *Promenades.* This takes place at the crossroads destined to hold a meeting between Heidegger and Benjamin. The meeting was to have been recorded, I am told, in the work never yet written by Benjamin, his work on the Paris streets, the arcades for which the trigonometric sign still stands, rumor blown, the *Passagenarbeit.*

While Benjamin's 'Destructive Character,' 'Karl Kraus,' and other characters, ciphers, or signals will have shown rumor to emerge, possibly against their own winds, like a dialect of the oeuvre, and while Heidegger has signed a contract with *Gerede* for the purpose of disseminating a final transmission whose status, or even transmissibility, remains difficult to discern or to unscramble in its at-handedness, the out-of-hand rumor first slipped into the microphones of public broadcasting with Rousseau. They slipped, they literally fell into chatter at a moment of finality's crisis, recorded in the supplementary exit text (like the black box that remains after a crash) 'beim Rückblick auf sein Leben,' within the impossible U-turn of an 'after my death' report. There has been something of a *logos-athleticus* at play here, something requiring an interview after having reached the finish line of thought. In short, and in order to start from scratch, as did Roman athletes – they would start their sprint from a scratch etched into a path – one may begin to wonder whether all great competitions and events of moment do not require the establishment of some sort of rumor control axis. Thus in the recent Los Angeles Olympics (1984), the existence of a 'rumor-control center' was broadcast widely. The center presumably was intended to monitor and absorb straying utterances, stray shots. This brings us to the paths leading into Rousseau's decathlon, his ten walks and diverse athletic events in which, like Benjamin and Heidegger, he tries to establish a rumor-control center in an attempt to disarm the stray utterances that pierce his corpus, or fall within earshot. Jean-Jacques will be placed in this reading, then, as trigonometric signal, the street sign pointing toward a construction site for future oeuvre shelters. When rumors affecting his standing are not noticeably stray but appear in some sinister way to be motivated, they are shown to reach Rousseau's ear via what is called the grapevine – a method of transmission whose origins are in the Civil War, but which extends toward all wars and pestilence, designating in the first place an alternate telegraph system or secret coding. A *civil* war, as it were, conducted through language ducts.

In the war zone, where one cannot escape situating the texts under discussion, a variety of speech act continues to wage battle. It turns out that we have stumbled into a twilight zone between knowing and not knowing, a space where utterances ('as well Publick as Private')[13] create myths whose transmissions are primarily oral. They operate according to a logic of contagion, communicating, like certain diseases, a kind of uncontrollable proliferation that essentially escapes a literature and, leaking, they often taint the proper name. These utterances are not imputable to a knowable origin (Heidegger: 'It's beyond me'); they rarely come with an identifiable creator or signator, and yet, they are invoked in the guise of a revealed truth. A variety of speech act that is, like Benjamin's messenger, essentially on the run, it exists in the mode of a hit-and-run temporality, coming like a sudden accident, from nowhere. As with the figures who are struck by it, or in this account, who will stand for it – Rousseau, Benjamin, and Heidegger – the rumor can never ensure the purity of discourse's absolute alien. Instead, it retains a mark of belonging which articulates the pain of a felt exile.

If one should arrive at the man in the street via Jean-Jacques, this is for several reasons, and largely in order to sustain the notion of a bad or faltering text. As it happens, scenes of physical deterioration and self-mutilation abound in Rousseau's *Promenades.* In step with the event of an out-of-hand rumor, his writing hand is permanently deformed as a result of an accident he describes in great detail. And the encyclopedia of batterings which he unfolds remains in step with the drastic *telos* of his project. Rousseau projects his text, or walks it, he writes, 'to contemplate myself before my decline,' 'I am devoting my last days to studying myself,' 'when death is already at the door' and 'all you have to consider then is how to make your exit. If an old man has something to learn it is the art of dying.'[14] We have been asking what it means to write at the point of decline. How to get up and walk or stagger to the end without losing heart, and to extend one's language beyond the finish line, as do all DCs. On the one hand, the mutilated one, it means that Rousseau does not want to be buried alive: 'Could I suppose . . . that an entire generation would of one accord take pleasure in burying me alive?' On the other hand, to write on the decline means to maintain a vertical stance, to keep from falling while writing to the end of a curriculum vitae. (Within the verticality of his walk, Rousseau employs a *methodos* or path that is opened by the question of self-knowledge, one which ever since Oedipus, however, has been associated with an impeded movement.)[15]

The writing, or walking, susceptible to mutilation occupy the opening pages of the *Promenades,* turning us toward a reading whose partial alienation from the discourses of literature and philosophy still raises questions. In a text that convulses with attempts to define beatitude, circumscribing its locus in a benevolent immunized zone – 'me voici donc seul' – what does Rousseau perceive as the agent of decline? A response to this question requires us to inquire about the oral trace responsible for an alternate discourse grounded, in Paul de Man's words, in 'hypothetical inferences that cannot be verified.'[16] For Rousseau, these inferences communicate from one orifice to another, from the mouth to the ear, which are thematically inflected as carriers of poisonous utterances. In other words, he writes of a language that, having no original taking-place, occurs on unauthorized epistemological grounds where it is armed with the power to kill. Trained as a double projectile, at once confidential and unrepeatable ('Don't repeat this to anyone, but I heard . . .'), this language is always oriented toward the future of its repetition, always on the make.

Rumors are in the air; they fly. They are often designated as something going around, essentially coming from a secret source, from a nowhere that is beyond me. They are spoken into ears that function like loudspeakers. The ear canal, like institutional corridors or political vestibules, is traversed by rumors. Insofar as the rumor arrives from nowhere it would be useful to recall Benjamin's undisclosed sense of Shakespeare's sense of news. To this end, let us recall Shakespeare's great rumor text whose nervous unfolding and semiotic restlessness can guide our reading. Very briefly, and on the run, *Hamlet* is organized around a concept of a nothing and nowhere that speaks. The sense of drama and the source of information it gives about itself issue from a form of nothing; it can be said to be narrated from two sources, both being like Heidegger's teletypists at a remove from the events which they nonetheless convey. The first anchor man is Horatio who, in order to situate the other source, puts his mouth to the sentry's ear and begins, 'as the whisper goes.' The other source, as origin of all rumors, is the ghost, of course. The phantom utterance itself originates from something that resembles the transmission of a rumor text. For we must not forget that Hamlet's father died of a poison that was poured into his ear, and the whole drama recycles this poison, from mouth to ear in a great ring of espionage and infection (separated, like Polonius, only by a curtained membrane). Infecting and paralyzing everybody, including the body politic, rumor, whose only paternity is the ghost of paternity (Heidegger: 'It's beyond me'), is the very thing that Hamlet wants confirmed. And so the ghost transmits a poisoned paternity to which every ear is open.

It has fallen to the Benjaminian stray-thinking to point out a kind of homonymic effect connecting Hamlet's predicament with that of Rousseau. Quite apart from being pursued by the ghost of paternity, Rousseau is likewise pursued quite literally and run down in the second walk by a figure whom he calls the 'great Dane' – who, on a certain level of phantasmic transmission, therefore, can be only Hamlet. Be that as it may, Rousseau is brutally pursued by utterances that fly at him wherever he steps in the double hermeneutics of the *Promenades*, double because this work is concerned with the intersecting marks of public and private discourses. One of the most pressing desires he asserts consists in putting a stop sign before the proliferant effects of the public circulation, containing it; that is, he wants to create a space where so-called internal, formal, private structures of a literary language control external, referential, and public effects:[17] a rumor-control center. Regardless of the 'type' of discourse one engages, however – autobiographical, philosophical, political – the rumor traversing the text is reported always to be foreign to it. In a scene that underscores the structuring of this foreign species of utterance over which Rousseau can exercise little control, he suddenly attains a moment of quiet. Strangely enough, the scene of asserted beatitude takes place in the fifth walk, but it is not centered on the famous boat of plenitude; in fact, I would suggest that the boat scene which tradition considers as the place of greatest self-gathering has displaced or submerged the moment in which Rousseau, in complete good faith, can call himself a founding father. And so the priority, the 'great day' of mastery which as such launches the boat, goes to the event in the fifth walk when Rousseau becomes the founding father, the sovereign subject behind a rabbit colony. The questions that have caused him some anxiety – those of paternity and posterity, of transmitting to a future, the wild proliferation of another species and the hope of containment – are generously raised in this densely compacted passage: 'The founding of this colony was a great day,' writes Rousseau. The rabbits, like the rumor, 'could multiply there in peace.' But unlike the rumor, they could multiply, as he writes, 'without harming anything.' 'We proceeded in great ceremony to install them on the little island where they were *beginning to breed before my departure*' (emphasis added). 'The founding of this little colony was a great day. The pilot of the Argonauts was not prouder than I was, when I led the company and the rabbits triumphantly,' and so on. And now Rousseau, triumphant, as he says, takes command of his society, supplying the antidote to all phobic reactions: 'and I was gratified to see that the Steward's wife, who was extremely afraid of water and could not step into a boat without feeling unwell, embarked confidently under my command' (86). They were beginning to breed before my departure, writes Rousseau. But to discover the precise contours of this phenomenon, he must cruise the streets.

Because time may be running short, I step up the pace in order to join the rumor that has been running down Rousseau. For the rumor, as Rousseau teaches us exemplarily, loses no time; it belongs to the *Zeitung*. This is his final Olympiad. Rousseau keeps on walking but finds himself always to be lagging behind the speed of the rumor, 'les bruits qui courent,' which overtake him. The price to be paid for this lag involves his phantasm of being buried alive; long after his *Confessions* something exceeds their intended totality where he thought he had told all, 'tout entier au publique,' 'incéssament sous ses yeux.' The rumor usurps from Jean-Jacques the privilege of showing and telling.

The Second Walk establishes a pace within which Rousseau keeps on succumbing to lapses and collapses. His lapse in memory, which includes the forgetting of his address and name, is an effect of his fall. This is where he becomes the man on the street. In fact his address and proper name are intercepted by a foreign species (arguably Germanic) – promoting a structure that will be immediately doubled in his treatment of the rumor. One recalls the misfortune that befell him, an accident which disrupts the very possibility of liquid *rêverie:* 'the flow of my rêveries was suddenly interrupted by the event which I must now relate' (38), an event that begins as he walks downhill, confidently poised within the movement of his decline. The street accident, the unforeseen, meets him in the shape of a dog, 'knocking [him] down.' So the disruption of *rêverie* comes about as a literal *interference* with his text, caused by another, extraneous or alien, species – the singularity of a dog that recalls but opposes the rabbits. This produces a collision or break in the structure of reception. Carrying the unseen and unforeseen, the great Dane bears up a catastrophic message which allows us to read this passage as a sign of intertextual collision, running interference. The term used to denote a problem in transmission, 'interference' is a kind of break in the flow of an utterance. In radiophony, 'interference' indicates a mutual effect on meeting in two wave trains of the same type; at the point of contact the two wave trains of light produce lines, bands or fringes. But if the dog and his unruly carriage [*carrosse*] come to be introduced as the double agents of the unforeseen, the fundamental interference breaking into an already discontinuous movement of walking, this is not only to mark the violent origin of the rumors that are about to fly as Rousseau hits the pavement, fracturing his jaw (his attempt to avoid the fall entailed his aiming to be above the situation, flying in the air to preempt the rumors that were about to fly). The howling collision threatens to obliterate the memory of a name, changing the course of a destination, transforming Rousseau into the originary awakening of 'das Man.'[18] And it is not too farfetched to suggest that, like the dog who comes around the bend in an irreversible circular motion, causing Rousseau to fall, rumors tend to be circulated about someone who stands to lose, and what is at risk in the catastrophic economy of losing one's balance is always the name one carries.

Here Rousseau, in an anticipatory *fort/da* game of textual command, narrates the power to forget from his place as subject. The *I* that constitutes itself does so in order to affirm its unshakeable control over forgetting: 'I was unable to answer. I asked them where I was. . . . I had to ask in turn the name of the country, the town and district where I was. Even this was not enough, it took me the whole way from there to the Boulevard to remember my address and name.' The drama of forgetting one's name, one's place, the drama of being forgotten falls initially under Rousseau's control. With suspicious precision he remembers, 'I could remember nothing; I had no distinct notion of myself as a person. . . . I did not know who I was' (Rousseau repeats this, as if in a traumatic trance [39]). How to represent the excluded story now under narration? The fall into oblivion occurs prior to being forgotten or having one's name effaced by the general public or that uncontrollable ear-mouth that is going to try to commit Rousseau to forgetfulness. In other words, Rousseau puts himself in the position of being the first to absorb the shock of being utterly forgotten and rather literally effaced – he goes into great detail on literal and figurative registers of defacement. Thus one example of the diagnostic gaze to which he severally submits himself evokes, among other things, this vocabulary of protection and prevention: 'my upper lip was split on the inside right up to the nose. On the outside the skin had given it some protection and prevented it from coming completely apart. I had four teeth knocked in on my top jaw, all the part of my face over this jaw extremely swollen and bruised,' and so on (40). Rousseau begins to resemble Frankenstein, the other monster-outcast of Geneva.[19] This scene of multiple fractures and mutilations is rendered throughout in the mode of painlessness, the nonsensory or an anesthetics of serene control: 'I felt neither the impact nor my fall. . . . The first sensation was a moment of delight' (38–39); most importantly, the Promenades have not really been disrupted, for 'I was able to walk very well and easily, feeling no aches or cuts though I was still spitting up blood. . . . But in spite of all this battering there was nothing broken, not even a tooth – a small miracle considering what a fall I had had' (39–40). So Rousseau had lost his name to himself, his address slipped his mind, his face was disfigured but nothing was broken; there was no pain ('ni mal, ni crainte, ni inquiétude; un calme ravissant'). And like a faithful dog, his name eventually comes back to him. I mention the *fort/da* structure discovered by Freud because in this violent passage through painlessness, Rousseau shows himself to be in command, as paradoxical as this may seem, of his sinking into oblivion. He is producing a *good* or legitimate version of his disappearance, the one which he can control and contain.

In this version, about to be doubled in another version over which he loses control, Rousseau maintains an absolute authority over his physical and textual body; he will have attended one of his many funerals commemorated in this text, and so survives himself long enough to provide a controlled narration, what he calls a 'faithful account': 'That, then, is a faithful account of my accident' (40). And because he can account for his fall, an accident, nothing will have been broken, and the pain which he is about to narrate will arise from an altogether different type of mutilation in which words cannot heal or close because there will be no closure. That, then, was the faithful account. He closes it, naming its containment, and continues to walk.

The narration will, however, shortly exceed itself, straying from his faithful account, and the real fall turns out to be that of this narration which falls out of its containment to produce the pain that Rousseau had not previously felt. While Rousseau's face, as disfigured as it became, was not seriously deformed or in any way unrecognizable, the narrative *après coup*, the fall of the fall within the walk will now take its course, leaving Rousseau, who had demonstrated so much control over chance, to be faced with a mystery-text, an enigma that overtakes him. He has closed his faithful account, putting it behind him. Now infidelity and contamination take up the relay and run away with his story: 'In a matter of days the story had run through Paris, but in such an altered and distorted form as to be totally unrecognizable.' We are made to see the accident, the drama of the unforeseeable, repeat itself, only this time Rousseau will be overwhelmed by the story's dislocation from its source; he will be troubled, dazed and mystified: 'I should have foreseen this metamorphosis, but it was accompanied by so many bizarre circumstances, mysterious words and silences, and told to me with such an *air* of absurd discretion that all this mystery began to trouble me' (40). Rousseau, then, is overtaken by what he first describes in terms of wordful silences, discretion, mystery, a secrecy speaking elsewhere, around him and ahead of him – all of which issues from vaporous air.

A rhetoric of dark rumblings begins to descend upon the text, to pervade a mood which had sought quietude ('I always hated darkness, the gloom they have plunged me in,' and so on) (40) until a certain Mr. Lenoir sends his secretary to deal with Rousseau. These dealings come from the public sector, Lenoir being the lieutenant general of the police: 'The man's air of secrecy showed me that there was something mysterious hidden beneath it all which I was unable to unravel. . . . I was prey to a host of gloomy and worrying conjectures and talked about what was going on around me in such a way that suggested a feverish delirium.' His discourse has caught the fever, it has been infected by world, the public's police language: 'in a way that suggested a feverish delirium rather than the sangfroid of a man whom the world no longer interests.' Rousseau starts to stagger. Now, shortly after describing the first accident which he has survived with only a few fractures, he comes to realize that his textual body has been subjected in the meantime to serious mutilation. This will constitute the event that has 'dealt the last blow to my peace of mind' (41). For the French regime, thinking he has died, publishes false texts that it imputes to Rousseau. But the regime – the one, no doubt, that gave him indigestion – has only begun to act up.

Rousseau keeps on falling precisely within the context of his walks, and keeps on struggling to get back on his feet. What defeats Rousseau? He falters largely because a type of textual monstrosity, uncontainable by anybody, is allowed to run freely; from the passage just cited we know that it even has a police license. The text that runs him down, with police complicity, committing him to his death, is one that in French literally runs. What it runs to or from is always shown to be unclear, but it emits a noise, a howl that runs through city streets and institutions from which Rousseau has exiled himself in order, he suggests, to avoid exposure to its contaminative properties. Or more exactly, he *has* been exposed, which is why he seeks seclusion and a certain luminosity that might cover the gloom of these poisonous currents. What were these?

Well, in the first place, and this will become inseparable from the rumor of his death – rumor wardens call this 'goal-gradient' or 'home-stretch' rumor – Rousseau runs to a public space where he is gunned down, *descendu*, by a final rumor or the rumor of finality. Spreading a counterfeit posterity, the rumor assumes its form as widely disseminated report detached from a discernible origin or source. Inasmuch as it becomes what it is, the spreading rumor takes on the qualities of a story told, without author or term, imposing itself as an ineluctable and unforgettable account. This account, the postautobiographical utterance, runs hand in hand with the finitizing rumor of Rousseau's fall. 'I had already gone out several times and was even taking quite frequent walks in the Tuileries, when I saw from the astonishment of many of those whom I met that there was some other story about me that I had not yet heard. Finally I learned that I was rumored to have died from my fall.' Now, this rumor that begins among the populous, the so-called lower classes, spreads like a virus throughout the body politic eventually to reach the head of state: 'And this rumor had spread so quickly and irresistibly that more than two weeks after I heard it the King himself and the Queen were talking as if there were no doubt about it.' The rumor in a sense receives ratification from the highest authority, though we must note that Rousseau's source for the rumor's run must be a rumor which he presently underwrites. Rousseau's ear is glued to the King and Queen's conversation. He even reports the certitude with which the sovereign couple circulates within itself the rumor of his death: 'The King himself and the Queen were talking as if there were no doubt about it.' Rousseau had no doubt about it. Here the evidence of the rumor's run, its surpassing power over Rousseau, is brought to his attention, carried as it is by the *Courrier* of Avignon: 'The Courier of Avignon, as they took care to inform me, not only announced this happy event, but did not fail to provide a foretaste of the tribute of insults and indignities which are being prepared to honor my memory by way of a funeral oration' (43). The rumor has run so swiftly that it will have delivered to Rousseau, its virtual destination, his final destination, a foretaste – here comes the indigestion – of that which outlives him, his remainder or the very thing that cannot be held down to what is commonly thought an experiential realm.

Rousseau experiences the unexperienceable: he will not only have attended his funeral but he will have read his obituary, which is not exactly 'his' in terms of what one might expect from a faithful account. Worst of all, however, he will have witnessed himself after his presumed death, in his afterdeath, being buried alive. For the obituary which he passes over in silence is a masterpiece of a refusal to produce a funeral oration, it attaches itself to modes of silence and innuendo that at once bury his memory and keep him unburied like an unappeased phantom, like Hamlet's father or one who has 'survived' his funeral, walking about in solitary grief, transmitting the story of his great betrayal to the ears of those who will have become his sons and daughters, the secretaries of the phantom. The ghost walks. Let us at no point forget that the one who delivers this text to us, his testament, remember, is seeking in his own words a resting place, a stable resting place.[20]

The obituary notice which he does not reproduce but to which he alludes, says this among other calamities: 'We are sorry not to be able to speak of the talents, etc. . . . our readers will no doubt feel that his abuse of them imposes the strictest silence on us' (43). The *Courrier* runs its course, establishing a circulation of silence between a writing and a readership, between a type of writing that talks and a readership that hears. What they speak and hear, what they hearsay and the news that they spread, is, they assert, no news; they spread silence or the condition of an unacknowledged loss. Thus creating the place of eclipse in which the ghost-writer will agitate. This is not all. Another accident befalls Rousseau. He learns of something 'by chance.' After learning of his death and reading his obituary, 'I learned this by chance. . . . It was that a subscription had been opened at the same time for printing any manuscripts that were found in my apartment. This showed me that they had a collection of specially fabricated works ready to be attributed to me as soon as I was dead, for the idea that they would faithfully reproduce anything that I might really leave was a piece of folly that no sensible man could entertain and that the experience of fifteen years was enough to guard me against [*Je compris par là qu'on tenait prêt un recueil d'écrits fabriqués tout exprès pour me les attribuer d'abord après ma mort*].' *Après ma mort:* I am dead, Horatio. 'Report me and my cause aright.' A speech that would survive the subject whose attribution it never fully outgrows, moving within the paradoxical exchanges affected between exile and freedom, the wing'd word, in flight, retracing in the air the destiny of any oeuvre given over to itself, partially canceling the signator whose memory it will be. Like the rumor's essential structure, Rousseau's tidings are perverse, recognizably marked by distortion, a signed bid for anonymity, leaving open the question of rumor's rapport to oeuvre; for in the end, his work I think desires to be enveloped by the sovereign ruthlessness of the rumor that will not submit to stoppage but goes around turning things over in easy transmission, the invisibility of the viral *virer* implanted by the father of the revolution whose literature annuls the writer.[21] A non-confessable *jouissance* of the irresponsible carrier (producing the seed, the virus, the word, everything that is in the air protected by the ring of invisibility, spilling, spreading – this time they will not say no to his pamphlets).

The rumor text is superseded by the rumored text ('fabricated works ready to be'), which is to say, Rousseau says, it is caught up in the effects of rumor's contagion, a thing ungrounded and perhaps still in the air, whether or not it has arisen from the imagination or even the transcendental imagination.

*Après ma mort,* there will be a blurring which I here authorize between authorized speech and anonymous rumor. Rousseau, writing 'after my death' in a kind of *Nachruf,* the echo or memorial address, calling after himself in the place of language's *Bodenlosigkeit,* the fundamental ungroundedness in which arises Heidegger's ontology of slander (which he does not want to ontologize but which in *Sein und Zeit,* §35, belongs to the 'positives Phänomen' of *Gerede*). Rumor as afterword, as that which I would say Rousseau was the first to say is constitutively *après ma mort* – rumor slips in somewhere between *Rede* and *Gerede,* between authentic and inauthentic speech, between the Destructive Character and creator; it is intended no doubt to dwell beneath authenticity but it rises above, leaning on nothing, since Heidegger grasps for the 'Bodenlosigkeit des Geredes.' He also calls this *Nachrede,* giving it performative powers before withdrawing its auratic dimension. Writing of *Nachreden:* 'Das Geredete als solches zieht weitere Kreise und übernimmt autoritativen Charakter [*Das Geredete* as such spreads in wider circles and overtakes or establishes an authoritative character]. Die Sache ist so, weil man es sagt [it is so because one, *man,* says it is].' Further along: 'The average comprehension of the reader will *never* be able to decide [*Das durchschnittliche Verständnis des Lesers wird* nie *entscheiden* können]' (emphasis Heidegger's). We shall never be able to decide. Or rather, the average understanding will not cut it. Does Heidegger suggest that such a text must be submitted to the understanding of an above-average reader, that rumor requires the labor of decisive apprehension?

~

'How noisy everything grows.'

Did Rousseau finally launch or stabilize the rumors he set out in his exit text to kill? This poses a dilemma for all rumor wardens, for example those associated with wartime rumor clinics ('In nailing a rumor did the clinic inadvertently spread it?').[22] 'Das durchschnittliche Verständnis des Lesers wird *nie* entscheiden *können.*' In any case, despite or with himself, Rousseau has granted their unanchorable flotation, navigating or cruising for repetition in terms of an echolalia, risking the motion sickness (navigation + nausea) that permits futurity to arrive by the tidings of rumormurmur, rumurmur . . . and so forth/back: 'Thus drawing the frontier between the private and public spheres, which in 1789 was supposed to inaugurate freedom, became a mockery. "Through the newspaper," says Kierkegaard, "the distinction between public and private affairs is abolished in private-public prattle." '[23]

# THE *SUJET SUPPOSITAIRE*

## *Freud, And/Or, the Obsessional Neurotic Style (Maybe)*

Wann haut'n *(Van Houten)* die Mutter? *[When do mothers smack?] It was only later that I realized that my pun really contained the key to the whole of his sudden recollection from childhood. [Displacement from the behind forwards; excrement becomes aliment; the shameful substance which has to be concealed turns into a secret which enriches the world.]*

*To bring obstinacy into relation with interest in defaecation seems no easy task, but it should be remembered that infants can very early behave with great self-will about parting with their stools, and that painful stimuli to the skin of the buttocks (which is connected with the anal erotogenic zone) are* an instrument *in the education of the child designed to break his self-will and make him submissive.*

SIGMUND FREUD, 'Character and Anal Erotism'

### BACK TO SCHOOL

Mr. Edward Glover, whose scholarship receives favorable citation from Jacques Lacan, might be held responsible for a peculiarly ironic inflection in the case history of psychoanalysis. In 'The Function and Field of Speech and Language' Lacan acknowledges an essay of Mr. Glover whose title eludes mention in the body of his text but which in part runs, 'The Therapeutic Effect of Inexact Interpretation.' While it is not a work meant to pacify those whose major stake in criticism lies in the resistance to theory, it shows, according to Lacan, that 'not only is every spoken intervention received by the subject in terms of his structure, but the intervention takes on a structuring function in him in proportion to its form. It is precisely the scope of nonanalytic psychotherapy,' argues Lacan, 'and even of the most ordinary medical "prescriptions," to be interventions that could be described as obsessional systems of suggestion, as hysterical suggestions of a phobic order, even as persecutory supports, taking their particular character from the sanction they give to the subject's *méconnaissance* of his own reality.'[1]

The ostensibly 'remarkable' point that Glover appears to be urging concerns a hermeneutics 'where the question of correctness moves into the background.' The locality of a background upon which this question is posed – or rather, to which this question, by force of an *intervention,* owes its displacement – will engage if not command our every move in this chapter. For if the question of correctness retreats into the place of a background, entailing an implicit about-face of traditional interpretive values, then the entire maneuver participates like Rat Man's army in the rhetoric of the Freudian *Umkehrung,* reversing the face value of things to display the proferred 'arse upwards.'[2] As mere reversal, this maintains the 'intervention' of which Lacan speaks in its classic column, still following the marching orders and route traced out by the commanding symbolicity of male homosexuality whose structures, in place since the time of Plato, continue to assure the paradigm for the transmission of knowledge. Supposing that the production of knowledge, meant or unmeant, depended upon this type of seed implant in order to guarantee transmission to posterity and to constitute itself as a body of knowledge. This forces an issue that does not properly belong within the confines of scholarly writing but that nonetheless requires some sort of intervention from 'our' side, if only to leave the question open: can any teaching whatsoever take place, given its genuine and deeply rooted history of phantasm patterning, in a representational field where sodomy has been legislated out of the constitutional space of a subject's legal bearing. Can a knowing subject constitute itself, or even be receptive to the seed of knowledge, where the effects of juridical shutdown reorganize the very conditions of an authentic pedagogy? As empty receptacle, virginal space, and originary innocence, the pupil has come to receive the desire of the teacher. The teacher fills this subject with the pedagogical deposit whose nature resembles that of a phallic desire.[3] The 'truth' of such a transmission is measured by the test of alterity which the student body, as excretory installation, produces, or, more properly speaking, in relation to the receptacle through which the teaching subject (who does not know what it knows) attempts to find articulation in the Other.

Given the particularly grim moment of legal history in which we find ourselves, the remake of a question first posed in the great Freudian pedagogics seems to fall on propitious grounds. Freud has made us inquire into the modes according to which the pupil, or analysand, receives the so-called intervention. What constitutes an intervention? While Lacan does not describe the nature of the intervention in the fallen terms we have chosen to elaborate in this chapter, he narrows the field of 'The Function' to a specific type of intervention, stressing that 'speech is in fact a gift of language, and language is not immaterial. It is a subtle body, but body it is.' What sort of body shows itself as an intervention made into the subject?

The intervention is not 'simply to be received by the subject as acceptance or rejection' argues Lacan, but is 'really to recognize him or to abolish him as subject. Such is the nature of the analyst's *responsibility* whenever he intervenes by means of speech.' It is precisely at this moment, when citing the analyst's responsibility, that Lacan abdicates a place of enduring insight in favor of Mr. Glover, permitting the structure of an intervention based on a double grounding of inexactitude to take hold of his text. The moment Lacan openly receives the discourse of Mr. Glover, recognizing the other by means of standard reference systems, he also ushers in the question of whether he as speaking subject is about to be recognized or abolished by the intervening text. The analyst's responsibility has him slide into the place of the Other.

If we could agree to let the incursion of Mr. Glover function as an intervention within Lacan's text, allegorizing the point he is about to make, then we would begin to perceive what kind of internal rectifications are occurring here. To explain the significance of Mr. Glover's intervention (though he does not call this citation an intervention), Lacan introduces 'in other words,' in words of the Other which I, Lacan, have now become by virtue of having recognized Mr. Glover: 'In other words, not only is every spoken intervention received by the subject in terms of his structure, but the intervention takes on a structuring function in him in proportion to its form.' Despite the 'remarkable' paper for which Glover is here re-marked, that mark cannot help being somewhat influenced by the obsessional systems of suggestion which it has recommended to itself. At the same time Lacan will have effected a shrewd move by accepting the hysterical suggestion, possibly of a phobic order, which at once assumes responsibility for a mastering interpretation and places on another's work the onus of having named the therapeutic results of an interpretation always falling short of itself. In other words, Mr. Glover's intervention might be seen as that which takes on a structuring function in Lacan proportionate to its form, which means further that it at no point touches the sanctity of the Lacan text. The 'hysterical' inclusion of Glover's argument would fill Lacan's essay at a blank moment, making the hysterical text 'pregnant' – and thus we have come down to another point of entry for making men pregnant.

'Speech is in fact a gift of language, and language is not immaterial. It is a subtle body, but body it is. Words are trapped in all corporeal images that captivate the subject; they make the hysteric 'pregnant,' be identified with the object of *penis-neid*, represent the flood of urine of urethral ambition or the retained faeces of avaricious *jouissance*.' There. We have hit bottom. But in order to open the gateway that will push the pun forward, we need momentarily to read a 'decondensation' that begins to flood the field of speech and language.

Illustrating the degree to which language solidifies into a body, Lacan argues its capacity for mutilation, as if dismemberment were to act as sign for its originary bodybuilding: 'What is more [which is less], words themselves can undergo symbolic lesions and accomplish imaginary acts of which the patient is the subject. You will remember the *Wespe* (wasp), castrated of its initial *W* to become the S.P. of the Wolf Man's initials at the moment when he realizes the symbolic punishment whose object he was on the part of Grusha, the wasp.'[4] But Lacan's next example comes from the case of Rat Man, the work responsible for establishing a rigorous theory of interpretative acts. Lacan is implicated in, if not acting-out, the text that serves as an example, initiating a kind of self-designated metaphilosophy of obsessional suggestive systems, supported only by glycerinic insertions into the subject who thereby receives his structuring. Lacan asks you to unforget the most slippery of signifiers, asking or commanding that 'You will remember also that S that constitutes the residue of the hermetic formula into which the conjuratory invocations of the Rat Man became condensed after Freud had extracted the anagram of the name of his beloved from its cipher, and which, tacked on to the final "amen" of his jaculatory prayer, externally floods the lady's name with the symbolic ejection of his impotent desire.'[5] Where Lacan wants the *S* or the intervenient Semen condensed, he can be read unwittingly to launch a suppository movement into the signifier's temporality of condensation and liquefaction whose disseminative expanse he still holds back. (That is, condensation here produces flooding and appears to occur *after* Freud decondenses the invocation.)

To present our brief succinctly, we shall evoke the question of anality via the exemplarity of the Rat Man case. The anus can be said to mark a locus of privileged transaction between at least two gendered entities. It organizes a space from which rental agreements are negotiated, leases are taken out by one gender to permit the other gender provisionally – depending on the terms of the agreement – to occupy its space. The other of genital sexuality, determinable neither as masculine nor strictly speaking as feminine, anality nonetheless constitutes a sexuality, a shared space that is often vaginized. Guided by Freud's theory of obsessional neurosis, I should like to try to read this locality of a feminine trait, which however also permits a man to be 'feminized' when 'used' anally by an other of either sexual determination.

A question regarding the transmission of sexual marks as a condition of knowledge can be posed under the name of 'Oedipedagogy,' involving a study of the de Sadian libertines' art of *socratiser* and the institutions of oral and anal examinations. Such a pedagogy, toward which Freud stretches us, would take its point of departure from the etymological span linking the Sphinx to sphincter, bound to one another by a notion of 'binding.' As threshold to all pedagogy, the Sphinx has participated in the acquisition of a feminine trait. Monsterized, as far as pedagogical figurations go, she is interspecial and, like her question, double-meaning. In accordance with some versions of the myth, she submits to corporal punishment, turning disciplinary measures upon herself when it becomes necessary to let the other pass. Sometimes she dissolves by pulverization, her implacable stoniness collapses. The other, at least in terms of Oedipedagogy's wish-fulfillment, is the becoming of the *sujet supposé savoir.* It is to him that sexual markings are transmitted as a condition for knowledge. The answer he gives is 'man.' He has gained admission to a newer phase of finitizing activity, having passed the guessing game, the great enigma or in German usage, the *Rätsel* from which emerges the Rat in our case. The issue of a pedagogy, particularly one structured by Oedipal constraints, is not something that only vaguely admits itself into a discussion of the Rat Man's story. 'Extracts from the Case History' forms its first sentence by constituting a man on the grounds of his education: 'A youngish man of university education introduced himself to me' (18). A certain type of knowledge, say, a body of knowledge, had insinuated itself into the youngish man who introduces himself to Freud. But the young man has not only inflated himself with the knowledge gained from a university education. He has also read Freud. Unlike the hysteric, however, he will not have become a reading body, for his illness, which belongs only to 'a dialect of the language of hysteria,' does not involve the leap from a mental process to a somatic innervation – hysterical conversion – 'which can never be fully comprehensible to us' (157). We shall see that the articulation of his symptoms is bound primarily to the bodily orifices – a point which brings us to the place of 'differomorphic organs' as they come to light in Lacan's seminar of 21 January 1975, presented under the American title of *Feminine Sexuality.* Of the radical abstraction, the figure of writing *a* (the *objet petit a*), the subject caused by an object, Lacan writes:

> The *petit a* could be said to take a number of forms, with the qualification that in itself it has no form, but can only be thought of predominantly orally or shittily. The common factor of *a* is that of being bound to the orifices of the body. What repercussion, therefore, does the fact that the eye and the ear are orifices have on the fact that perception is spheroidal for both of them? Without the *petit a,* something is missing from any theory having any possible reference or appearance of harmony. And why? Because the subject is only ever supposed. It is its condition to be only supposable. If it knows anything, it is only by being itself a subject caused by an object – which is not what it knows, that is, what it imagines it knows. The object which causes it is not the other of knowledge

> (*connaissance*). The object crosses this object through. The other is thus the Other, which I write with a capital O. The Other is thus a dual entry matrix. The *petit a* constitutes one of its entries.[6]

I am sure of little so much as of this probability: as we release Lacan's discovery of the supposable subject to the energy of interpretive warps and distortions, the master pedagogue, were he to issue a grade or response, would not make it an *A* of any size but would quote his own passage thus: 'which I write with a capital O.' This opening, then, will furnish our point of entry, slow in coming but owing its existence to a distortion of the spirit of the letter. One can expect little more from a *petit a* operator who takes off from the condition of a supposable subject. My question asks what the nature of the object causing the subject might indeed be. (As if an obsessional neurotic style were capable of producing only a single question.)

### 'PERMIT TO REMAIN'

The question might have been raised, I suppose, of the punctilious interval – as to why, at this point in time, we organize a moment of general thinking around the pun. In some circles of truth's closure, pun has remained the name of an indictment, an accusatory identification of that which takes too much pleasure, disarranging academic languages, promoting a rhetoric of looseness within the parameters of a recreational linguistics, valuelessly succumbing to the most indefensible copulations of meaning, related, as will be my subject, to the temporal succession of shame over pleasure, incriminating the grammar of some strict order of things, and so forth. It may not yet be necessary to compute the defensive expenditures that go into protecting the usages of puns in parapoetical texts nor even to enter the place where such disputes tend to be articulated. This suggests one reason for holding back a reading of thinking and drinking – a confluence of spirits in fact too sober for this interpretive occasion, though also dealing with the issue of disinhibition and the mechanisms of pleasure in rapport to communicability. One could focus the pun within a history of intoxication – a step that Heidegger, in an anti-Aristotelian move, tries to stop up in his treatment, or more accurately still, in his suppressive evocation of Nietzsche's and Kant's *Rausch* [intoxication]. Heidegger's intervention detoxifies Kant and Nietzsche by means of a pun-insert that returns the *Rausch*-motif to a kind of founding physio-logic, namely, by arguing: 'wir leben indem wir leiben [we live in that we "body"].'[7] So while Kant and Nietzsche are getting high, Heidegger brings them down with a controlling pun sequence, as if the pun were the most pious, recollective usage of language – the Old Testament and the Talmud pun incessantly –

allowing therefore for some degree of retention or at least a necessity of restoring an original meaning, like the great rituals of religious ceremonials, which recall, by means of reconstructive energies and incantation, a prior sense. The pun postulates a pitch-giving meaning on which a subject can jam polysemically, without breaking harmony, effecting the paradoxical reunion of the linguistic accident with some sort of anterior substantiality.

In regard to the pun, however, the problem of *hoarding* seems more compellingly chronic than that of drinking, although according to Freud's interpretation, both activities – hoarding and drinking – are closely allied in the symptomatology of obsessional neurosis. Both open up, we may add, the question of sexual difference. Thus the Rat Man, in our example, will have 'first noticed the difference between the sexes when he saw his . . . sister (five years his senior) sitting on the pot' – a gaze that can be seen as originating the rat phantasm, which will consist in turning around the pot, finding the sex to create a funnel for the rats.

Remembering that the right posture for a psychoanalytic session is in fact a *Sitzung*, let us then start with this clue of the other's sitting on the pot. Our first step will be to construct a kind of suppositorium whose translucent covering would permit us to observe the movement of the pun in relation to a case history whose solution purportedly rests on a spontaneous generation of puns. However, if this opening for the possibility of thinking the suppository, as a logic and a discourse, as a partial erection of a subject – if this should appear detached from a structure of deeply sustained meaning or motive, or, if the movement of thought should appear halting, showing a rather inactive reliance upon vague and general foundations, this is due in part to the smooth insertability of my suppository discourse into that of a 'complete obsessional neurosis,' as Freud puts it. For the tone and definition which Freud accords to obsessional neurosis get translated into a type of mimetic command which he dictaphones into this interpretation. Regardless of the degree to which the argument continues to participate in what it tells, producing noticeable ellipses and omissions, retaining points that ought to have been made – that is, retaining them at will as intrinsic ideality or dropping them as extrinsic excrement, it nonetheless constitutes itself in the relatively serious attempt at positing or, more seriously, at suppositing a link between the status of paronomasia, sexual difference, and the task that psychoanalysis sets for itself. In order to prepare the rectoscopy that will guide our investigation further, it seems appropriate first to cite what Freud's Rat Man calls 'the beginning of my illness': 'I used to have a morbid idea that my parents knew my thoughts; I explained this to myself by supposing that I had spoken them out loud, without having heard myself do it. I look on this as the beginning of my illness' (162). The beginning of my illness, then, consists in suppositing: I had the idea that they knew my thoughts; 'I explained this to myself in supposing.'

Before beginning the reading proper, in order to introduce and induce it, we ought to refer to an important text which elucidates the subtle shift of interpretive paradigms that the case study promotes. It has to do with a mistaken association, but one that is prescribed by law. When the writer joins the hermeneutic police force, provisionally dropping out of the detective's bureau of intelligence, his thinking is no longer in the service of truth, and has abandoned the desire to arrive, for instance, at a strictly truthful resolution. This explains why, in order to find the truth of the matter, a policeman sometimes is represented as having to leave the force, because police work consists in performatively apprehending a figure of suspicion, placing it under arrest. Freud writes of the opportunity he took of giving the analysand 'a first glance at the underlying principles of psychoanalytic therapy' (175). Proceeding from the inference that the patient has a criminal profile, he explains, producing himself as a citation:

> Where there is a *mésalliance* between an affect and an ideational content, a layman will say that . . . the inference that the patient is a criminal . . . is false. On the contrary, the physician says: 'No. The affect is justified. The sense of guilt cannot in itself be further criticized. But it belongs to another content, which is unknown (*unconscious*), and which requires to be looked for. The known ideational content has only got into its actual position owing to a mistaken association. We are not used to feeling strong affects without their having any ideational content, and therefore, if the content is missing, we seize as a substitute upon another content which is in some way or other suitable, much as our police when they cannot catch the right murderer, arrest a wrong one instead.' (175)

Whence a means of maintaining a strict order of functional meaning or apprehension: a police officer cannot provide you with a reason or a discourse that would explain why he is doing what he does; he himself operates according to a law that exceeds his grasp, whereas detective work in principle seeks only to grasp, often in ways indifferent to the performative telos of an arrest. What if psychoanalysis, whose moves are determined by an activity of substitution, also at times exchanged the investigatory badge for a policing instrument, the invisible extension of the arm of the law, 'and, therefore, if the content is missing, we seize as a substitute upon another content which is in some way or other suitable, much as our police,' and so on? But this would be the more naive of the options made available by Freud's understanding of a police license issued by the unconscious to its supervisor. A detective does not always have to work in the name of the law, whereas the police only work in this name, as its representatives. The subtle but immeasurable shift from detective to police work in the sense discovered by Freud suggests on the one hand the degree to which the subject has the right to remain silent as a condition of its correct apprehension. On the other hand, about to be linked to the first, psychoanalysis, working for the good of the whole subject in which a criminalized symptom is on the loose, may have to crack down arbitrarily, to appease a certain law which exercises control over its procedures. Such a show of police force, often amounting to brutality, may be brought down only on the ghetto zone where the dialect of obsessional neurosis is spoken, a zone which knows no amnesia. For this reason, police intervention in a zone so circumscribed also implies a risk for the representative of the law, who may be caught in the heat of a countertransference. In hopes of avoiding such a confrontation, we shall stick to finding clues.

The Rat Man came to see Freud after having leafed through the *Psychopathology of Everyday Life,* claiming to know something 'about my theories. . . . Actually, however, he had read none of my writings, except that a short time before he had been turning over the pages of one of my books and had come across the explanation of some curious verbal associations' (158–59). His attention was caught, perhaps even trapped, by the verbal associations and wordplays that were turned over with the pages; we could say that he arrived at Freud's door in search of a commanding pun. Back to the suppositorium. Exhibit A involves two containers of live suppositories, manufactured on the East Coast. Citing the directions, we ask that they be received in the preferred manner of Rat Man, who spontaneously converts a given statement into a command. Item 1 reads as follows: 'Directions: Insert one suppository into the rectum. Permit to remain. Bowel action will usually result within a few minutes.' Item 2: 'Insert one suppository high into the rectum and retain fifteen minutes.'[8] Copyright Princeton, N.J. Both rectal evacuants stress retention, though according to different nuances of command utterances: Permit to remain/retain fifteen minutes. (In this context one might consider the halt after which all of Rat Man's symptoms advance. During a halt in army maneuvers he loses his pince-nez and must send for a new pair, whose expected arrival occasions an obsessional vow. One might also compare these instructions with Jones's definition of obsessional neurosis, anchored as it is in a concept of retention, 'the retention of the complex in consciousness,' or with a subject's reception of neurosis as a kind of torpedoed suppository aimed at the ego that receives it as something alien, retaining it with an urge to evacuate.)

The two sets of directions differ in their interpretation of the degree of insertion: the first container indicates 'into the rectum' whereas the one from Princeton says 'high into the rectum,' characteristically stressing that which is elevated above the others. What *is* a rectum? The answer to this question leads directly to the solution of the rat problem, and to an understanding of the Western phantasm of evacuating, purging, and cleansing, in other words, to a certain birth of trauma, if we bear in mind that, regarding birth and men, the latter, according to Rat Man, are believed to bring forth children anally. *Rectum:* the lowest segment of the large intestine extending from the sigmoid flexure to the anus. *Sigmoid:* curved like the letter *S; sigmoidally:* in the manner of a double curve. The destination of the suppository, therefore, would be indicated as the sigmoid valve, the end station of the *S*, whether or not *barré*, whether or not standing for the signified with which the suppository will never absolutely coincide, but toward which it aspires. Freud himself reproduces the sigmoidal structure which he calls the principle of the Adige at Verona: the river makes a loop, creating nearly identical points of entry and exit (265).

These compulsive definitions may appear outrageous, scholarly, or unworthy of serious thought. If so judged, they would remain a citation of obsessional neurosis, where high thought is mimed, going so far as to allow an irregular, unworthy object to be hermeneutized to death. Where the suppositorial injection may seem somewhat debased in its literal application, it can be made to function as a reliable wedge for understanding the precise movements of the Rat Man text and indeed of obsessional neurosis as such, which Freud stresses is heuristically more difficult than hysteria, precisely owing to the issue of retention. Consider this, if you will, also in light of the generation of pleasure, where 'psychical damming up' is avoided, or as the relief of anxiety which occurs within an energetics of discharge and deblocking. Indeed, the entire Rat Man project belongs to a sustained temporality of retention, for this is the only one of Freud's case studies to have retained the notes and records which Freud normally let go. The editor's note to the *Standard Edition* reads accordingly:

> It was Freud's practice throughout his life, after one of his works had appeared in print, to destroy all the material on which the publication was based. It is accordingly true that extremely few of the original manuscripts of his works have survived, still less the preliminary notes and records from which they were derived. The present record provides an *unexplained exception to this rule*, having been found among Freud's papers in London after his death. . . . These notes . . . have not yet (1954) appeared in German. (253; emphasis added)

Yet while he himself retained what usually turned into the excremental deposits of a text, detachable and usually forgettable, one of the dilemmas that Freud faced with the Rat Man case is that the treatment quickly led to the removal of the subject's inhibitions. It is as if the cure had come too fast, as Freud's comments in the notes make explicit. The cure appears to have precipitated a kind of *Trauerarbeit;* the patient departed so soon. This departure, doubled by the announcement of his death at the end of the text, suggests the memorialization taking place in the Rat Man case. Yet, in terms of the internal rectifications of the work, we still don't know what it means to be cured *too fast* – say, within the phantasmal space of fifteen minutes. We can assume that the preparatory stages of this reading are completed now.

Permit to remain.

### REQUIRING IT OF THEM

I shall not in the present chapter attempt any discussion of the psychological significance of obsessional thinking. Such a discussion would be of extraordinary value in its results, and would do more to clarify our ideas upon the nature of the conscious and the unconscious than any study of hysteria or the phenomenona of hypnosis. It would be a most desirable thing if philosophers and psychologists who develop brilliant theoretical views on the unconscious upon a basis of hearsay knowledge or from their own conventional definitions would first submit to the convincing impressions which may be gained from a firsthand study of the phenomena of obsessional thinking. We might almost go to the length of requiring it of them, if the task were not so far more laborious than the methods of work to which they are accustomed. I will only add here that in obsessional neuroses the unconscious mental processes occasionally break through into consciousness in their pure and undistorted form; that such incursions may take place at every possible stage of the unconscious process of thought; and that at the moment of incursion the obsessional ideas can, for the most part, be recognized.

> *We might almost go to the length of requiring it of them, if the task were not so far more laborious than the methods of work to which they are accustomed.*[9]

One may well have sensed it: the preliminary stages of my discussion multiply the suppository effect in the sense that a piece of Freud has been inserted and retained, if momentarily, so that he could help us out. A kind of double suppository effect emerges here, in so far as Freud wishes psychoanalysis or, more precisely, the firsthand study of the phenomena of obsessional thinking (not 'neurosis' but *thinking*) to be forcibly inserted into those who develop 'brilliant theoretical views' or into what sometimes earns the name of philosophy. This kind of Hamletian admonition, 'there is more here than your philosophies have dreamt of,' inserts this case history into the citational space of playing within a play, retaining the other – a procedure for which the phantomal shape of the melting suppository ('dissolved into a dew') will serve as a sign. (Others have noted the similarities obtaining between the Hamlet and Rat Man texts. Patrick Lacoste in particular has pointed to the father complexes shared by both heroes, to the fact that Hamlet, when he kills Polonius, rather convulsively screams 'a rat, a rat,' to the famous acknowledgement of the doctor in Vienna to whom Hamlet futurally appeals, and Lacan has suggested that the case study unfolds with the dignity of high tragedy's inaugural reticence.[10] Both dramas end, moreover, with the arrival of arms – Fortinbras leaves a surviving Horatio to 'report [Hamlet's] cause aright.')

Now, to narrow the focus and fix the point of entry, I hope merely to wonder aloud to what extent punning belongs to a suppository logic – a logic that bases its point of departure on what Freud exposes as the 'obsessional neurotic style.' As readers of the case may recall, a major component of obsessional neurosis is indecision – a doubting mania particularly manifest, as Freud puts it, in a subject's vacillation between the male and female. Indeed, Rat Man and Freud will construct a suffering split subject founded on successive insertions of puns that function like a *Stattsorgan*, providing temporary gender assignments. In the notes, Rat Man is shown to be absorbed by an aspect of the *Stattsorgan*, the organ of state for which he prepares his exams. This can be read or apprehended in the form of its substitutive prosthetic application, that is, as something replacing the organ – *statt-Organ*, being detachable, excretable but not fully castratable. In any case, we seek out the meeting place of psychoanalysis and certain points along the intestinal tract (in sixteenth-century French *rencontrer* had both the sense of 'to meet' and the transitive sense of 'to joke or make puns.' A certain epistemophilia, resembling that of Rat Man, leads us back to the meeting place, therefore, of anal and oral retention systems and this by way of the pun). Some of the suppository definitions of pun, documented by Walter Redfern, trace back to 'a funnel-shaped vessel' or a 'slow, inactive person.'[11] This background material is placed at the service of a suppository discourse which in Freud's case involves inserting the 'ersatz' (as substitutive act or masculinizing positing) at a crucial juncture of reversal; in other words, we are dealing with a type of embolophrasia, which originally meant 'something thrown in, inserted' and which the *Dictionary of Speech Pathology and Therapy* has asserted to be a container, in Leiris's sense of language, of punning speech itself. Under *punning speech* one finds: 'A form of embolophrasia characterized by pathological play on words of the same sound but of different meaning. Sometimes manifest in the manic phase of manic-depressive psychoses.' I might add here, as a free-floating intervention, that according to the *Leçons sur les maladies mentales* (1890), neologisms are much more common in persecution mania patients than in others. Again, we might refer to the couple Hamlet and Rat Man, persecuted and telecommanded by phantom insertions or *Stattsorgane* which often carry a juridical authority.

The first phase of suppositorical maneuvering embraces the neurotic ersatz when a difficult passage in Rat Man's analysis forces the issue of the anus. This is where Freud dictates his intervention, whose transcription reads, ' – Into his anus, I helped him out.' In order to locate and name the subject's suffering, Freud supplies the phrasing. We shall take a closer look at the semantics of intervention in a moment.

The second suppositorical phase of treatment concerns the glycerinic signifier that cleanses Rat Man's impacted symptomatology, thereby simultaneously deblocking and curing the patient, if rather too quickly. The case in its entirety bases the possibility of a cure upon successive detonations of puns touched off in one cluster by the word *Rat,* in another by the copulation of *Amen* and *Samen* ('amen' and 'semen') in the superstitious religiosity of the subject. The seminal fluidity of the dramatically sliding signifiers is to be linked in our discussion with the glycerinic effect of language. However, at this juncture we can merely suggest how very neatly the case of Rat Man inserts itself into the idiom of the Derridean text (*The Post Card*) concerned with the technology of the courier. To recover one such moment decongesting and moving the entire scenography of the subject's phantasms, maneuvering the semantic fields of the case like the army maneuvers through which Rat Man enters a critical phase of narration, we note the centrality of the post office. Of the many hypotheses which 'Notes Upon a Case of Obsessional Neurosis' offers, one is dispatched as follows: 'After his friend had brought him to his senses he had dispatched the small sum of money in question [the C.O.D. payment for the new pince-nez] neither to Lieutenant A. nor to Lieutenant B., but direct to the post office. He must therefore have known that he owed the amount of the charges upon the packet *to no one but the official at the post office,* and he must have known this before he started on his journey' (172).

Lacan reads the neurosis as a notice of non-payment for the father's debt and the case in terms of a forced subjectification of the Rat Man.[12] We might also view the restitutional tactics in light of partial parceling-out of the subject, the robotization and militarization of a self deflated by a tight financial regime whereby it gets to play itself on a kind of psychically projected video screen of self-elimination. The patient lays emphasis on acts of 'sending in,' releasing a kind of initial capital flow; Rat Man suddenly produces up front money whose essential cash flow begins to move, though only after a provisional retention of funds, out the back end. The relation of such increments – *Ratten* – to excrement receives abundant documentation throughout the case (particularly given the returns on the merging of feces and money, both of which are hard to part with). The logic of the transactions consisting in sending in a sum of money in order to open an account must be understood in terms of enema, from the Greek 'to send in' – a logic which Rat Man rather insists upon. In the text, this logic organized, if secretly, around the related notions of a *Stattsorgan* and post office. In this respect, we can recall that Rat Man enters false calculations when he sends money by the post, expecting his lost pince-nez to be replaced by the next day's mail. But these desired substitutions for the missing pince-nez merely point to the temporal immediacy in the subject's demand as concerns the *Statts-organ*, a demand for replacements and dispatches that the post office is expected to yield. No need to show how the letter for Rat Man functions as suppository, for inserting the mail into the slot, attaining without mediation to the *Stattsorgan*, Rat Man figures the fantasy of a finite retention of his request.

Left to its lot, this genre of mail transaction nonetheless reminds us that the administration of enema, the arrangement of a suppositorical procedure for treatment, constitutes a rather familiar moment in Freud's contractual decisions. To the Wolf-Man case Freud has given his word as follows: 'I promised the patient a complete recovery of his intestinal activity.'[13] The promise exhausts itself, being delivered only when Freud makes the Wolf-Man's bowels speak: 'in the course of the work his bowels began, like a hysterically affected organ, to "join the conversation."' Hence in the best of cases the talking cure implies a modality of double-talk, a double source or end for the locality of speech. Hence, *suppository* is sent to us from *supponere*, that which comes from beneath, situating a place of underness charged with retaining and linkable to the *Unterbewußtsein*, that which retains everything, the entification made to speak. Why would the so-called Rat Man's locality of speech be the rectum? In the first place, the first 'telephone' connection to the patient may have been made by the wire of an enema extending from the nurse's hand to his rectum. She, like the analyst, was behind him. Enema administration and the experience of female penetration ought not to be underestimated in discussions of these cases – almost all of Freud's patients can be assumed to have been subject to the primal treatment of enema that went down as does aspirin for maladies nowadays. Rat Man tries to resist the enema in his treatment by Freud, as the original notes illustrate:

> *Jan. 2 [1908]*. – (Undisguised expression) . . . Besides this he apparently had only trivialities to report and I was able to say a great deal to him to-day. While he was wishing Constanze the rats he

> felt a rat gnawing at his own anus and had a visual image of it. I established a connection which throws a fresh light on the rats. After all, he had had worms. What had he been given against them? 'Tablets.' Not enemas as well? He thought he remembered that he had certainly had them too. If so, no doubt he must have objected to them strongly, since a repressed pleasure lay behind them. He agreed to this, too. Before this he must have had a period of itching in his anus. I told him that the story of the herring reminded me very much of the enemas.

Freud refers to the preceding entry:

> Connected with this, though it was not clear at what point, there was a transference phantasy. Between two women – my wife and my mother – a herring was stretched, extending from the anus of one to that of the other. A girl cut it in two, upon which the two pieces fell away (as though peeled off). All he could say at first was that he disliked herrings intensely. (307–8)

There is still another reason for locating the Rat Man's speech in a zone of rectal expressivity. In this case it may be linked to the rat phantasm itself: nothing can be ejected from the rat's mouth; this explains its use in laboratory experiments. The rat does not vomit, does not come out with it orally. Nonetheless the structure of double-talk is maintained. Leonard Shengold's 'More about Rats and Rat People' reminds us, apropos of the disconnection between thoughts accomplished by 'inserting a time interval' between them, of the vertical splits that occur in the mental apparatus of rat people, making possible such phenomena as the Orwellian 'double-think' which conditions – again by rat torture – the victim-hero of *Nineteen Eighty-Four.* Persecuting and persecuted, rats mark the historical phantasmata of great invasions. Their phallic power is coextensive with cannibalistic penetration, since 'the danger throughout is that of a phallus equipped with flesh-eating power.'[14] A final connection to the Rat Man's phantasms is Lou Andreas-Salomé's 'rental agreements': elsewhere Freud borrows from Lou the following conception in a transaction which he acknowledges: the rectum 'rents' vaginal properties, becoming the symbolic placeholder for the inmixation of male and female traits.[15] Rat Man, it seems, has dreamt of having fecal intercourse with Freud's daughter.

### 'THE FAECAL MASS OF THE SECOND-STAGE THAT IS CLEARLY "NOT-ME"'

From the postal system into which part of this case's phantasms are deposited there emerges a question of address. Honoring the sadistic captain of his narration, Rat Man quickly takes to addressing Freud as 'Captain' as well. If the performative structure of address also has a value for knowledge or truth, then there always exists an uncertainty about addressing oneself to the right captain and lieutenant, the right placeholder. Thus the lieu-tenants turn out to be substitutes for other destinations, they function like compulsive dead-letter officers or like dummies in the Lacanian sense. The text launches as well a whole problematics of a specifically *military* post office to which Rat Man owes his father's debt. Now the military post office enables another type of address to gain prominence, and this bears heavily upon the fortune of the pun, meaning the *good* pun or joke. Rat Man's father has left him a number of bad word/plays, a legacy which we could say is of the order of the *militerary* regime. Rat Man has to make good. As Samuel Weber has shown, Freud establishes a stringent economy in order to probe the nature of the joke, creating a balance of expenditures and savings which I loosely translate into releases and retentions that participate in the suppository logic.[16] Always involved in a concept of thirdness and in relation to a third party, the delivery of a good joke poses the question of address: if savings are involved, the Rat Man appears to suggest, then the crucial element resides in the possibility of saving up a good pun or a good joke, saving it for someone who is not present to its emergence, someone not entirely there, who is elicited only in the mode of his departure. Hence, for 'a long time he had not realized the fact of his father's death. It had constantly happened that, when he heard a good joke, he would say to himself: "I must tell Father that"' (174). This coincides with the moment Rat Man develops his neurotic machine of obsessional understanding, changing vowels, persistently hearing puns and generally indulging in grammatical aberrancy. While tightly held to a singular context and in a spirit of pure origination, the good pun appears always to be oriented toward the future of its repetition, being addressed and breaking through to an absent receiver – one who can no longer receive you but whom you nonetheless continue to receive. Like Hamlet, another melancholic punster and obsessional neurotic, Rat Man still waits for his father between the two sides of morn, waiting to address his father's apparition armed only with the phantomal, double-speech of the pun, in order to give him in exchange his word, his parole: 'often, when there was a knock at the door, he would think, "Here comes Father," and when he walked into a room he would expect to find his father in it. And although he had never forgotten that his father was dead, the prospect of seeing a ghostly apparition of this kind held no terrors for him; on the contrary, he had greatly desired it' (174–75).

Always bordering on auditory psychosis, Rat Man translates utterances by transforming them, through an internal converter, into perlocutionary speech acts. Plain assertions of the sheerly constative sort, when deposited into Rat Man, spontaneously acquire the authority of commands. So the morning a conductor vaguely asks whether he might be waiting for the ten o'clock train, Rat Man receives the message as a command and, despite having projected an entirely different agenda for the day, he finds himself under orders to take the ten o'clock train, just as he later finds himself under doctor's orders, taking in Freud's capsulated train of thought anally. To get a precise sense of where we're heading, follow this line to the end station in Freud's description of the train episode:

> The whole process then passed into the obsessional patient's consciousness accompanied by the most violent affect and *in a reverse order* – the punitive command coming first, and the mention of the guilty outburst afterwards. I cannot think that this attempt at an explanation will seem forced. (188)

The question of forcing something on or up Rat Man is not an empty one. Remember that Rat Man was the most intensely coached of Freud's patients. A typical session begins with this sort of move: 'I thought it advisable to bring a fresh piece of theory to his notice' (180). Freud introduces this piece to fit in with another theoretical requirement, namely, that 'the unconscious is to be understood as the precise contrary of the conscious – He was much agitated at this.' The structure of insertion followed by agitation typically stimulates a physiological stirring. Or, when Rat Man offers a perfect fit, Freud remarks parenthetically, 'I had explained the idea of "resistance" to him at the beginning of the hour.' We conclude that, in the beginning, Freud inserts his logic which in turn activates the conduct of Rat Man.

There can be no doubt in our minds that this procedure repeats Rat Man's original traumatism. The first blow to Rat Man, offers Freud in the section headed 'The Beginning of the Treatment,' occurred when a young tutor 'had entered his employ only in order to gain admission into the house. This had been the first great blow of his life' (160). Listen without compromise to the entries made into Rat Man. In German it is said that the tutor 'sich mit ihm nur eingelassen habe, um Zutritt ins Haus zu gewinnen [*eingelassen:* literally, he let himself into Rat Man]. Es war dies die erste grosse Erschütterung seines Lebens.' At this point I would like to demonstrate how Freud repeats this forced entry in order to get to the bottom of the rat problem, insinuating himself into the subject at the very moment he develops the decisive reading of the obsessional neurotic style. This brings us in yet another turn to the origin of the pun and to the rise of such incontestable punsters as Shakespeare's Bottom.

Before focusing the laser precision with which Freud reproduces the initial blow, I must offer a few more remarks regarding the other animal in Freud's life, the other heterogyn stylized by obsessional neurotic traits. I restrict these remarks to the establishment of a suppository discourse, which means they are intended to remain fragmentary by necessity and subordinate to the requirements for cracking the Rat Man case. When Wolf-Man stepped into Freud's office his first gesture of friendship was to offer to have rectal intercourse with the physician and to defecate on his head. We know the complimentary nature of such a gesture, insofar as 'excrement babies' are later divined to be resourceful gifts and are linked, as in Rat Man, to the reproduction of children emanating from the anus. In any case, please continue to retain the relationship of feces to money, which should help clarify Rat Man's urgent sense of owing, his terrible irregularity which Freud promises to regulate. With Wolf-Man, Freud and his patient experienced a serious blockage in their sessions, doubled by the patient's hysterical constipation. Nothing moves, nothing comes out of Wolf-Man. In Freud's words, 'nothing changed and there was no way of convincing him.' What gets things stirring is Freud's insertion, at this paralyzed moment in the analysis, of the suppository discourse. If Freud will not induce Wolf-Man to speak, at least he encourages his bowel to come out with it: 'I promised the patient a complete recovery of his intestinal activity, and by means of this promise made his incredulity manifest. I then had the satisfaction of seeing his doubt dwindle away, as in the course of the work his bowel began, like a hysterically affected organ, to "join in the conversation," and in a few weeks time recovered its normal functions.'

Supposing that Freud could not induce a talking cure based on the normal, rather normative understanding of intersubjective communicability, then he can henceforth deblock the silence by releasing a suppository torpedo whose aim would be to encourage narration from the bowel. Interestingly, Freud calls this renewed activity a conversation, as if conducted by two equal partners, that is, Freud and the bowel – what he later describes as the feminine side of Wolf-Man, the hystericized organ of identificatory pathos with Sergei's mother. In fact he may be treating the mother, the female hysteric, who begins to agitate and speak through her son's belly, ventrilocating her anguish. And so one should always be on the lookout for a 'small trait of hysteria which is regularly to be found at the root of obsessional neurosis,' the 'front bottom,' or the mother who is stirred to speech by Freud's suppository manipulations. Indeed, it is with the aim of giving his patients 'visible' pleasure that Freud, as in Rat Man, inserts his little container of promises; in the Wolf-Man case he similarly speaks of the 'pleasure attached to the function of evacuation' in conjunction with anal jokes, word/plays, and exhibitions'. A suppository moment of retention informs the description of Wolf-Man's *jouissance:* 'And this enjoyment (of joking, etc.) had been retained by him until after the beginning of his later illness.'[17] In the joke book, borrowing Lipps's notion of *Einfühlung,* Freud explains how, by the help of a joke, an internal resistance is overcome and an inhibition lifted – indeed, psychical damming up is altogether avoided. The mechanism triggering the generation of pleasure averts a constipatory blockage of the psyche. It seems that either something like a play on words or 'fresh pieces' of psychoanalytic theory must be inserted in the subject and momentarily retained, before the pleasurable evacuation, including the evacuation of the mother, can take place, or can take her place. We return to the lieutenants to whom Rat Man feels he owes everything.

To make good on a promise, we arrive at the pleasure associated with Freud's insertion into Rat Man. At the crucial narratological moment, when the fundamental phantasm achieves disclosure (we think), and well before the solution of the Rat idea via the life-giving puns is established, Freud reveals the moment from which this famous case derives its name and entitlement:

> Here the patient broke off, got up from the sofa . . . (I had explained the idea of 'resistance' to him at the beginning of the hour, when he told me there was much in himself which he would have to overcome if he was to relate this experience of his.) I went on to say that I would do all I could, nevertheless, to *guess* the full meaning of any hints he gave me. Was he perhaps thinking of impalement? – 'No, not that . . .' – he expressed himself so indistinctly that I could not immediately *guess* in what position – 'a pot was turned upside down on his buttocks . . . some *rats* were put into it . . . and they . . .' – he had again got up, and was showing every sign of horror and resistance – '*bored their way in. . . .*' – Into his anus, I helped him out. (166)

Freud does not supply his supposition with a confirming report. It's simply a case of – 'Into his anus, I helped him out.' In German, Freud actually fills this space out, or fills his anus with 'In den After, durfte ich ergänzen.' He has just articulated his way of helping his patient overcome the internal resistance, suppressing the signs of horror's speechlessness: 'Er gab alle Zeichen des Grausens und Widerstandes von sich – . . . In den After, durfte ich ergänzen.' 'I took the pleasure of filling.' We should not fail to note that the rhetoric of insertion remains the same for Rat Man's first blow as for the rat's rectal entry and Freud's *After*-words: the rats were *eingelassen;* the tutor had 'sich mit ihm nur eingelassen.' A bit later Freud strains the text to come out with the connector-puns on which the cure of Rat Man is based. Generated from the start-word *Rat,* they begin to take on genuinely glycerinic qualities, the gelastic *glissement* of speech reminiscent of the sliding potentialities of language in Lacan's sense, 'le glissement progressif des sens.'

The sliding signifier makes us note the tropes of fluidity and slipperiness that flood all treatments of the pun, breaking into a concept of language as substance or solidifying agent with a kind of patient fluency. Modalities of solvency and currency feed directly into what Freud identifies as the currency of the *Rat* idea. With a toss of the decisive dice, he starts the *Rat*-series rolling with *Spielratte,* referring to Rat Man's father, a chronic – one is tempted to say, chthonic – gambler. *Spielratte* in turn comes up with *Rate,* installments, and another turn of the wrist yields *hei-raten,* marriage. The stakes are particularly high with *heiraten,* as the primary conflict arises with a paternal prohibition on Rat Man's plans of marriage. Given the fervor with which Freud tracks down the 'punogenic' structure of Rat Man's disorder, I think it necessary to replay the earliest appearance of the *Rat* in his language. The earliest appearance is in fact a double feature which Freud leaves entirely unacknowledged, double like the very structure of paronomasia, which speaks twice as much by being split.

In the original notes to the case history the first mention of 'rats' comes in the context directly following Freud's fecal speculations: 'the thought that I desired to have him as a son-in-law. He was probably one of those children who retain their feces . . . the thought "rats" at once occurred to him' (287). In the published study the first, which is to say the second, or rather the last appearance of the rats takes place when the rats in fact do not appear, but when Freud divines their critical significance for the psychoneurosis of the patient, inserting them into his anus – at this point, remember, Rat Man is standing upright, completing as it were the phylogenic history of man that Freud describes in the same case. We cannot know how close he stands to Freud at the moment of intervention. In any case, he is no longer horizontal, he is up when Freud promises 'voll zu erraten' and then again, back for more: 'er drückte sich so undeutlich aus, daß ich nicht sogleich erraten konnte, in welcher Stellung [he expressed himself so indistinctly that I could not immediately guess in what position . . .].'

Freud gives his promise fully to guess, *voll zu erraten,* to smell a rat (the whole narration of Rat Man's ills begins with his losing the pince-nez and focuses considerably on his, and civilization's, osphresiolagnia). However, in so engaging himself, Freud also reproduces the position of the patient's parents who the child believed could read his thoughts ('he was afraid that his parents had *guessed* his thoughts'), leading to the delusional belief in his 'omnipotence of thought' or what Freud also recognizes as an endopsychic perception of the repressed. In other words, Freud's promise to guess the unspeakable thoughts of Rat Man also extends the promise to participate deeply in the offending symptomatology, closing off any guarantee of a cure. Freud may be looking for marriage, but in fact he engages himself on very precarious grounds, compromising the cure – first insofar as the cure will be set henceforth as a symptom of the disease, indeed, in part constituted by it, and secondly because Freud, Captain Freud, emphatically *becomes* the horrifying rat created by the other captain, inserting himself into the anus (' – Into his anus, I helped him out': as analyst, it is Freud's task 'to help him out'). The counter (and, possibly, original) transfer could be said to develop between the rat as boring signifier and the physician. Freud assumes the role of fully *er-ratting*, 'enratting' himself in the masculine pronomial form or, guessing again, he names the other by having his speech intervene as an injunction: *er: Ratten!* Given that Rat Man is a translator, he would have obeyed his doctor's orders, making the necessary transfer of accounts.

Still, why would Freud permit the symptom itself if not the cure to rest on such doubtful grounds? Why not deliver a confirming clue, a positive endorsement, a gesture perhaps, or have Rat Man – the other one, the patient – crawl back to the couch, collapsed with relief? The decision not to give a decisive accord fits the requirements of an obsessional neurotic style which proceeds by ellipsis and omission, as does the articulation of the problem with which Freud has helped out. The ellipsis makes room for the insertion of a missing link into (' – Into') a resistant hermeneutics of the obsessional neurotic style. In this case the link is shaped by the pun, the ellipses or points, the series of punctae mobilized to fix the moment of intrusion, which can even take the form of phonetic alteration: 'He declared that the mute *e* of the second syllable gave him no sense of security against the intrusion, which he so much dreaded, of some foreign and contradictory element.'[18] There is nothing to guarantee Rat Man's protection from such an intrusion of a foreign element into the ellipsis of his symptom. Nothing to assure us that Freud did not intervene precisely at a place of dread, inserting a liquefying speech like an inoculating stylus that repeats the poison in order to evacuate, to draw out, the silent agent of disease. The cruelly poisonous point is virtually admitted by Freud himself when he offers, 'I had told him that I myself was not fond of cruelty like Captain M., and that I had no intention of tormenting him unnecessarily' (169).

Be that as it may, we know only that Rat Man has a relation to utterance which turns over certain of them to the authority of compulsive commands, so that Freud's anal insertion would necessarily be received by Rat Man as a master key, an order and ordinance. Thus, Freud's insertions become progressively easier: 'I could easily insert the idea which he had so energetically repudiated into a context which would exclude the possibility of any such repudiation' (179). The intervention is well on the road to becoming the object causing the subject, if subject there be.

To base the possibility of reading the Rat Man on a modality of *erratten,* and to generate a string of puns out of a secret matrix doubling for *Rat,* means to find a bottom line which is not one, which is to say, the reading is based on fundamental indecision. Freud guesses and gambles, places his bets, thus basing his findings at the heart of the obsessional neurotic style. Wait. The heart is a false organ – we are speaking to or from an opening, perhaps 'the *béance,* impossible to fill, of the symbolic debt,' the behind which, like Christ's, is always hidden from view. (Does Christ have a behind? Wolf-Man reportedly asked as Wolf-Child. Can he shit?) In other words, does the secret of Christ reside in the possibility that he, suspended by the three points, was never to be approached from behind, neither evacuating nor constipating, just hung, he suggests, like a sacred pun enigmatically filling an ellipsis, with pun ambiguous, pleasing in suspense.

Like the pun, *erraten* occupies a place of no place, the space between two lieutenants, naming the mobile indecision. Freud's predicament forces him to guess, *erratten,* rather than to know. He appears to be positioning himself on an epistemological fault-line from which one simply cannot decide for one semantic field over the other, thus serving notice of the doubt against which the psychoanalytic compulsion must consistently struggle. The radical doubt thus described creates a compulsion to pun on the part of the rat subject, be this Freud or Rat Man. They produce a desire that is reconstituted as source and origin, surveyed by the control tower that monitors indecision in the face of some terror. Such might be the case for the ontologically down and out – I would guess Beckett fits into this ellipsis, and a number of others as well. Such would be the symptomatology of the suppository subject who has to 'supposit' and who, like Freud, knows no echo of a confirmation. If there is something to know in what discloses itself as a sort of abysstemology, it can only be the bottom, the originary split.

Since we have hit bottom, passed, that is, to what Freud has called the lowest form of the verbal joke, it is time to bring to your attention the poem whose argument unfolds a certain suppository subject in its relatedness to pun. It was published in 1826 by the pseudonymous Bernard Blackmantle, Esq. In the preface, the masked writer embraces the concept of pun by way of the word *posito.* He, or she, if they are split, honors the salutory agency of pun. We slip away, leaving with the indecision of an uncommented poem, a place from which to cooriginate the obsessional neurotic style. Shifting into lower gear still, I might have read the poem's amphibiguity or the evacuation of heaven.

The Origin of Punning:
From Plato's Symposiacks
*by Dr. Sheridan*

ONCE *on a time in merry mood,*
*Jove made a Pun of flesh and blood:*
*A double two-faced living creature,*
*Androgynos, of two-fold nature,*
*For* back to back *with single skin*
*He bound the male and female in;*
*So much alike, so near the same,*
*They stuck as closely as their name.*
*Whatever words the male exprest,*
*The female turn'd them to a jest;*
*Whatever words the female spoke,*
*The male converted to a joke:*
*So, in this form of man and wife*
*They led a merry punning life.*
*The gods from heaven descend to earth,*
*Drawn down by their alluring mirth;*
*So well they seem'd to like the sport,*
*Jove could not get them back to court.*
*Th' infernal gods ascend as well,*
*Drawn up by magic puns from hell.*
*Judges and furies quit their post,*
*And not a soul to mind a ghost.*
*'Heyday!' says Jove: says Pluto too,*
*'I think the Devil's here to do;*
*Here's hell broke loose, and heaven's quite empty;*
*We scarce have left one god in twenty.*
*Pray what has set them all a-running?' –*
*'Dear brother, nothing else but punning.*
*Behold that double creature yonder*
*Delights them with a double* entendre.'
*'Odds-fish,' says Pluto, 'where's your thunder?*
*Let's drive, and split this thing asunder!'*
*'That's right,' quoth Jove; with that he threw*
*A bolt, and split it into two;*
*And when the thing was split in twain,*
*Why then it punn'd as much again.*

*‘’Tis thus the diamonds we refine,*
*The more we cut, the more they shine;*
*And ever since your men of wit,*
*Until they’re cut, can’t pun a bit.*
*So take a starling when ’tis young,*
*And down the middle slit the tongue,*
*With groat or sixpence, ’tis no matter,*
*You’ll find the bird will doubly chatter.*
*‘Upon the whole, dear Pluto, you know,*
*’Tis well I did not slit my Juno!*
*For, had I done’t, whene’er she’d scold me,*
*She’d make the heavens too hot to hold me.’*
*The gods, upon this application,*
*Return’d each to his habitation,*
*Extremely pleas’d with this new joke;*
*The best, they swore, he ever spoke.*

# TAKING IT PHILOSOPHICALLY

## *Torquato Tasso*'s Women as Theorists

*The words are twisted in some double sense*
*That I reach not: the smiles fell not on me.*
SHELLEY, 'Tasso'

*Habe nun, ach! Philosophie*
GOETHE, *Faust* I

In the ensemble that we have come to call 'Goethe,' the theoretician and the poet were often at war with one another. When he applied himself to the sciences, Goethe was often driven by a marked fascination for monstrosities, degeneracy [*Abarten*] and malformation.[1] This can hardly be said to be the case in his poetical endeavors, though one might argue that *Werther*, for instance, is born of such a passion. To whatever extent the works preceding his so-called classical era paraded the banner of flamboyance or excess, they have, for the most part, been either forgiven, excused, or exalted for that aberrant expression, if indeed they were not treated as monstrous specimens. Hegel, whose judgment Goethe claimed was always sound, counts among the least indulgent recipients of these earlier works. Observing his customary reservations about youthfulness as such, that is, in this case, about a stage in the Age of Goethe (therefore, one which cannot stand in total isolation, Hegel being for the most part Hegelian), the philosopher asserts in his *Vorlesungen über die Ästhetik* that Goethe's first products are 'so immature, even crude and barbaric, that it's terrifying [*von einer Unreife, ja selbst von einer Roheit und Barbarei, vor der man erschrecken kann*].'[2] But Goethe's works, particularly those dealing in some way with creative powers, would always retain the trait of monstrosity and even of malformation, though a certain refinement would appear to dominate them. If they themselves would not bear this trait as something almost external, like a formal stigma, then they would mark it within themselves. The trait of monstrosity might be lodged in the elegance of Faustian striving, in the demonic excess, that is, of a desire for knowledge,[3] or, in the figure of the harpist, the poet who appears in *Wilhelm Meister* as catastrophe of self and other, the physically disarranged, dilapidated bard whom Meister, despite his *Bildung*, cannot altogether master.

It was always at the boundaries between acts of knowing and imagining that Goethe encountered enemies – or the threat of contamination and infiltration – even though he was himself so eloquent and efficacious in establishing sound borderlines, as early, certainly, as in 'Grenzen der Menschheit.' He was equally deft, as Nietzsche notes, in transgressing and ignoring them. It is at these borders that the acutely monstrous or disproportionate figures manifest themselves in Goethe's works, creating a space in which Goethe the poet and Goethe the theoretician challenge each other for mastery. Our example will be *Torquato Tasso;* as character and as oeuvre, it can be asserted that it (he) crisscrosses and tortures all the elements of purity which preoccupied Goethe. Goethe was himself most explicitly concerned with the generic purity of his piece, and not only in terms of a generic chastity so carefully delineated by him in cooperation with Schiller, but also according to those terms concerned with discursive identity, even sexual difference and, indeed, his consistently upheld notion of wholesomeness. In this respect, it may come as no surprise that the play was most often judged to be a novelistic rather than a dramatic piece of work; it was destined, like Tasso, to live between two genres. Violating so much of what the author held sacred, *Torquato Tasso* also violates its assumed position as exponent of classical serenity; Tasso was a monstrous conception, presenting in its own terms an ever increasing need to 'flee disgust [*dem Ekel zu entfliehen*]' while irrepressibly progressing toward the text [*Gewebe*] of entombment and madness. It is, to invoke one of the most recurrent exclamations of the work, involved in controlling the unexpected [*Unerwartetes*] – the accident or unforeseeable event that is another name for 'literature.'[4]

In the latter part of the eighteenth century philosophy and literature concluded an unconscious contract, jointly signed by Kant and Goethe, though the contract soon would be amended to include other signatories as well. Shortly before Kant inquires into the possibility for an aesthetic judgment and names the *Genie* the originator of the beautiful form in the *Kritik der Urteilskraft,* Goethe, by way of *Torquato Tasso,* places a rich meditation on poetry and the poet at the center of a literary work. Thus, while appearing to maintain the integrity of their discourses, philosophy and literature share certain basic assumptions as they contemplate the place of the artist, the artwork and the intersubjective response that the artwork is believed to evoke. Yet, certain problems arise with this project which suggest a thematic of intense double-crossing. In the first place, it is not clear which of the two Goethes (there are at least two sparring in each piece of writing) will take up the pen to compose the poet. For, as Novalis was soon to notice, another Goethe abruptly intervenes in the unfolding of *Wilhelm Meister* to dispose of the poet whose position initially seemed so secure, necessary and, of course, bordering on the romantic. One should always be wary of the other Goethe, the theoretician, who in *Der Versuch als Mittler*, for example, prescribed measures for the subduction of an especially pernicious enemy:

> Man kann sich daher nicht genug in acht nehmen, daß man aus Versuchen nicht zu geschwind folgere, daß man aus Versuchen nicht unmittelbar etwas beweisen, noch irgendeine Theorie durch Versuche bestätigen wolle; denn hier an diesem Passe, beim Übergang von der Erfahrung zum Urteil, von der Erkenntnis zur Anwendung ist es, wo dem Menschen alle seine inneren Feinde auflauren, Einbildungskraft, die ihn schon da mit ihren Fittichen in die Höhe hebt, wenn er noch immer den Erdboden zu berühren glaubt, Ungeduld, Vorschnelligkeit.
>
> [One therefore cannot be careful enough about inferring too rashly from experiments, about finding immediate confirmation in experiments, or about wanting to confirm any theory whatsoever from experiments. For it is here, at this passage, in the transition from experience to judgment, from cognition to application, that all one's inner enemies are lying in wait: Imagination, which is already lifting one to the heights on her wings when one still believes oneself to be firmly grounded. Impatience, precipitation.][5]

At the frontier, disguised as customs officers, the inner enemies of the theoretician lie in wait, with Imagination already taking flight. Now it may be objected that the context into which Imagination enters legitimizes the criminal profile which Goethe here gives it. Is it not in the company of impatience, precipitation, self-satisfaction, rigidity, and the others? One simply cannot be careful enough. But the question remains: what in 1792 is Imagination doing at the frontier, playing inner enemy number one? There are other characters who could and probably should have taken monstrous Imagination's place, for example some deviant of *fantasy* (rather than the highly valorised *Einbildungskraft*), which, at least since Kant's *Versuch über die Krankheit des Kopfes* (1764), appears in the guise of *Phantasterei* where it most unambiguously denotes fancies of an excessive sort. Goethe, however, arraigns Imagination, who is usually companion to the poets, at the border between experience and judgment. This is not the first time that Goethe will give orders to clip the wings of Imagination. In other contexts, however, his command will be more tortuous, twisted, and double-edged.

Beyond the question as to which Goethe is writing here, it is necessary to stress the decisiveness of a gesture that undertakes to dramatize the destiny of an artist. Goethe's decision to create a new genre, one necessarily susceptible to contamination, begins as a deliberate transgression of the will of his patron, Karl August. Goethe will be the first poet, if indeed we can settle on this title, to elevate the status of the poet in literature to the troubled dignity of a tragic hero. Torquato Tasso – the name shared by the hero and the text – opens the poetic study of poetry, it is the ur-portrait of the artist. After Goethe, a stellar configuration of poets will contemplate the 'life and works' of Torquato Tasso, as if to celebrate the very notion of *Weltliteratur* and the suspension of national if not generic boundaries; they are Shelley, Baudelaire, Leopardi, and Byron. Appropriately enough, one of the first attentive readers of this *Tasso* was a woman who crossed the border into the German principalities. Madame de Staël, however, found this text somehow to exceed the limits of its generic determinations and of the language and mood of poetry; it placed the pathological history of the poet elsewhere: 'Le langage du Tasse dans la pièce de Goethe,' she writes, 'est souvent trop métaphysique. La folie de l'auteur de *la Jérusalem* ne venait pas de l'abus des réflexions philosophiques [The language of Tasso in the play by Goethe is often too metaphysical. The madness of the author of *Jerusalem* did not originate in an indulgence in philosophical reflection].'[6] The madness of Tasso is doubled by the madness of Goethe, who flees the circumscribed domain of literariness into philosophical reflection. But what makes Madame de Staël so sure that Tasso's madness did not derive from a certain type of self-abuse, that is, from the 'abuse' of philosophical reflection? Is it merely a curious fact that, according to biographers, Torquato Tasso himself actually longed to be considered, of all things, a philosopher? Or that the man who was to become his persecutor in Goethe's play, namely, Antonio Montecatine (1537–99), in fact occupied the Chair for Philosophy at the University of Ferrara, a respected position that was still sought after by eighteenth-century philosophers? Was not a kind of discursive androgyny – a new genre or gender [*Gattung*] of contamination by others – precisely the madness to which Goethe committed himself here and elsewhere?[7] Or at least is not one of the secret texts of this drama, the core of its madness, the violent rapport of philosophy to literature and thus, to a certain extent, of literature to itself? Madame de Staël was not entirely wrong when she diagnosed *Torquato Tasso* as a borderline case.

But how, finally, could Goethe assimilate to his own aesthetics the character of Torquato Tasso? When he completed his work on *Torquato*

*Tasso* in June 1789, after nine years of alternately rejoicing and despairing over the very possibility of writing a poetic study of poetry, Goethe had created a place for the poet *as* literary figure – indeed, as the figure and disfigurement of literature. Unlike such remote precursors as *Don Quixote,* whose fictional hero is a rather literal reader of romance, or the theater of Molière, whose comically deficient poets occasionally recite verse, *Torquato Tasso* painstakingly incorporates the powerful myths that have led to the occasional exaltation and steady bludgeoning of the poetic figure. Though it may seem obvious, it should probably be stated at the outset that the figure chosen by Goethe to represent the poetic hero is one whose poetic authority had been firmly established before it is submitted to literary interpretation. By the second part of the eighteenth century, Tasso's poetry knew the kind of critical acclaim that we, in our generation, would reserve for Shakespeare alone. Goethe himself, after first discovering Tasso in his father's library, and hearing of his father's pilgrimage to Ferrara, considered him to be an exemplary poet of an equally exemplary age. This son of the prolific poet Bernardo Tasso is at once a child of the Renaissance and, more specifically, of the spirit and art of the Restoration in the second half of the sixteenth century. Goethe would in a sense restore to his own hollowed era an image of Tasso. This image had already been complicated by Heinse, who presents him as a great writer against whom everything conspires to suffocate his congenital genius. It is Heinse's contention that certain feverish seizures [*Anfälle*] are inherent traits of great geniuses.[8] Indeed, for Goethe, who was so allergic to symptoms of 'hypochondria' (with which he, however, persistently associates his father) and to eruptions of mental instability, the writing of *Tasso* would be a formidable task. For what was he to make of an era of plenitude, a poet of distinction and a man given to paranoiac transports? What would require Goethe to practice clipping here and to introduce restraint there? Which forces or figures would he need to pin down, arrest, remove, or incarcerate when Tasso's predicament as genius became the troubling object of contemplation for his own, conservative, *genius* – or phantom? Certainly Goethe will have assumed a position of superegoical dimensions in identification with the phantom of the father, in this case a rather strict purveyor of *Bildung,* sitting in uneasy judgment of an expulsed son; however, at the same time he will also occupy the position of the father's father or his own grandfather – a Textor of sorts – whose decision will emanate from a place that is strangely anterior to the *Bildung* of a father, and prior to that process of maturation whose goal, as has been suggested by the literatures of this philosophy, ought to be manhood.

Now, it may seem that too many men and too many feats of autoengenderment are involved in this story already, but the problem will resolve itself shortly, in another episode of frontier crossing at the very opening of the play. For now it is important to retain only this: from the moment Goethe and Tasso are jointly engaged in the thematization of poetic activity, a text full of uncertain harmonies comes to the fore, one that will bear both their names. Indeed, this text implies an encounter with shipwreck for both members of the couple, though Blanchot has asserted that Goethe, in the final analysis, will always have to face charges (particularly in the case of Nietzsche) for having diverted his course from shipwreck.[9]

As for the readers of Goethe's work, they are at once confronted with his dramatic, if not symptomatological, interpretation of the poet, Tasso, and with a text that presupposes the history of an aesthetic judgment. The text reflects Goethe's profound concern with the making of such a history in the detail with which it argues each character's judgment of Tasso's poetry. Probing the way the characters make their aesthetic judgments, the work contains within it its own version of the critique of judgment. For it focuses not so much upon the unquestioned excellence of Tasso's poetry as upon the theoretical premises according to which any poetic work, including of course Goethe's drama, might be judged. Basing thus the dramatic dynamics on the implications of competing aesthetic and anaesthetic theories for the artist, the text offers an implicit critique of the canonized aesthetic theories of its era, while it also testifies against the aesthetic axioms that Goethe himself has proposed elsewhere.

The drama proper begins, after the title and generic mark – it is a *Schauspiel* – with the conventional *dramatis personae:* there are two women, two men – and somewhere between them is Tasso. It is set on the grounds of a *Lustschloß* (country palace, or pleasure palace) in Belriguardo. The *belle vue* is decorated with the busts of two epic poets: on the right of the scene, Virgil, on the left, Ariosto. Again, Tasso will have to be situated somewhere between these two figures. The scene opens with two women, both named Leonore. The first injunction of the *Schauspiel* is related to knowledge ('Laß es eine Freundin wissen!'), uttered by Leonore to Leonore. And then Leonore (Princess) introduces an oppositional pair, the terms of which might at a later point shift slightly, but whose singular and indelible effect is immediately implanted in the text: 'You seem pensive, but you seem content.' While pensiveness and contentment have not yet swollen into the rival categories of thought and pleasure, they already point to different modalities of satisfaction and are shown to be at comfortable odds with one another at the *Lustschloß*. Leonore's contentment derives from being draped, like her companion, Leonore S., in peasant costume ('ländlich ausgeschmückt'). They are engaged in an act that will be linked in a detached way to poetry and to death; they are transforming sheer materiality into form or natural life, into a symbol of nonlife, each weaving a wreath which, to Leonore S.'s pleasure, is palpably swelling in her hand (l. 10). It is the rise and beginning of a new spring. And everything seems to indicate the beginning of a new play as well – the double frames designating the first act, first scene, the initial framing effect of the double busts, the expository verses, the doubled costumes (the new Leonores covering the other Leonores to which they refer in their speech) – the woman's play. But the beginning of the drama takes place somewhat outside the drama; it is still removed or detached from what will be isolated as genuine beauty or thought on the one hand, and action on the other. Goethe underscores their preclusion or exclusion; he begins the play in the form of an intrusion of sorts by setting multiple parergonal frames within the first scene.[10] The women are on the sidelines, next to the work; they are engaged, in their own words, in a *Nebengeschäft* and play within a kind of transcendent exteriority which touches, plays with, introduces the work, the poet and his poem.

Woman's play is foreplay. The foreplay will end too soon, they complain, and it will end in an excuse (an *ex-causa,* an outside), when the duke enters the threshold of their play, bringing the first scene, the foreplay, to an abrupt conclusion. The secret of the beginning, of their interpretation of the *Lustschloß,* must be kept from Alfons, though this has not been the first beginning. Leonore warns her companion not to betray 'wohin sich wieder das Gespräch gelenkt,' where their conversation has brought them once again. They would have to bear his raillery, just as their garb had already attracted his mockery. What is the 'joke' of their appearance in this play?

It is not clear what force will constitute the joke, responding to it, but it appears to revolve around a notion of *Fassung.* Tasso will lose what Goethe terms his *Fassung,* his composure. His self-composure, gaining only in fragility, begins to unravel soon after he submits and thus loses the draft – the *Fassung* – of his text to the man who demands it of him, Alfons. But *Fassung* in its constitution, the first draft – the mounting or framing – appears, the Princess fears, to be a joke. Everything that appears, appears to hinge on the *Fassung.* As *Fassung,* as that which frames, the women are also *außer Fassung,* beside themselves, a joke playing itself out in the peripheral domain of foreplay. This, then, is to be another version of '*Vorspiel* in the Theater.'[11] The subject of foreplay, as in *Faust,* arises with the desire to know ('Laß es eine Freundin wissen!'): a demonic joke of exceeding one's own *Fassung.*

The pleasure the women take in their first act is articulated through an abundance of visual metaphor. Their favored metaphorical dwelling place, the mode in which these women exist in and as language, thus always has something to do with poetry in the first place or with the fact of living with poetry, as Leonore von Este and Leonore Sanvitale apparently do. If vision is to take first honors in their view, this is in part because, like the apprehension of beauty, sight as such does not seek to consume its object. This notion, as attractive as it may seem, will of course prove highly problematic. They are now, they suggest, in a moment of plenitude that gives rise to a new world (l. 28). However, even this mood of plenitude harbors the knowledge of its own disruption: 'Do not remind me in this blissful hour, O Princess, how soon I must depart!' (ll. 41–42). The word for *depart* is the equally disjunctive but perhaps semantically more forceful *scheiden.* The women are on the boundary [*Scheide*]; they are always on the verge, poised between coming to themselves and separating, between the frame and the inside of the drama, between pensiveness and thought, between play and a politics so unanimously represented by the two men of the drama. In this stage of the 'between' that governs the exchange between von Este and Sanvitale, they deepen their links to poetry, allowing pensiveness to turn to thought [*Gedanken;* l. 13] and to a notion of pure gratitude [*dankbar;* l. 15]. And if such inner transformations take place, it is perhaps because these are the only characters to be detached from the economy of the *Dienst/Verdienst* pairing [service and merit, to serve and deserve], which rigorously determines the positions of the other characters within a hierarchy of strict subordination. They are the only figures authorized to contemplate poetry precisely because they are detached from the work, indeed, from any recognizable form of work; they are the parergae who achieve the closest proximity to what Kant will term *pulchritudo vaga.* Through the detachment, of which reverie and duplicitous self-identity are signs, the women will dream of the Golden Age of poets: 'Wir können unser sein und stundenlang / Uns die goldne Zeit der Dichter träumen' (ll. 22–23). But it is precisely within this fiction of being (left to) themselves within the reflexive dream of many hours ('stundenlang / Uns . . . träumen') that the women part ways. Separation begins when the peasant costumes turn out to be the disguise not for an original Leonore, but rather for a Kant and a Hegel. It is not easy to say whether Kant and Hegel are playing in the habits of von Este and Sanvitale (whose names strangely suggest a meeting place for Being and Nonlife), or vice versa. But when the spirit of Hegel meets up with the likes of Kant in Goethe, and when literature becomes the foreplay of philosophical speculation, then we are dealing with a phenomenon that has been recognized by every Goethe scholar who asserts the exceptional achronicity of his thought – the specificity, in other words, of that writing age seen in terms of a *Goethezeitlichkeit.* For our purposes, however, only this point needs to be emphasized: the meeting place for such an improbable and seemingly precocious play-off between philosophers or philosophies is the dream of a stage, one whose disclosure, we are told, involves a certain duration, and it is not too farfetched to suppose that their dream lasts the Age of Goethe. Let us return therefore to the women's vision, for in their performance of self-division, they are framing the central tensions of the drama.

According to the one (Leonore), the other (Leonore S.) has, despite her name, the capacity for sustaining a type of feeling that is in rapport with life; she has a capacity for lively feeling [*lebhaft fühlt;* l. 83) which, the princess supposes, is a matter of fortune [*Glück*], a gift freely bestowed as if by luck or chance. The princess, on the other hand, is associated less with life or sentiment than, in the first place, with a concept of *Bildung* (l. 100). Leonore Sanvitale has been translated, then, by the Leonore of *Bildung,* into life. But it is a precarious life, one whose concerns seem to lie exclusively with poetry, whereas the princess, on the contrary, stresses the value of science [*Wissenschaft*]. Delivering herself from the limits and certitude of nature's gifts, the princess concedes:

> Auch, kann ich dir versichern, hab' ich nie
> Als Rang und Besitz betrachtet, was
> Mir die Natur, was mir das Glück verlieh.
> Ich freue mich, wenn kluge Männer sprechen,
> Daß ich verstehen kann, wie sie es meinen.
> Es sei von einer Wissenschaft die Rede,
> Die, durch Erfahrung weiter ausgebreitet,
> Dem Menschen nutzt, indem sie ihn erhebt.
> (ll. 113–22)

> [Besides, what nature and what chance bestowed
> As property or rank I ne'er esteemed.
> 'Tis pleasure to me when the wise converse,
> That I their scope and meaning comprehend,
> Whether they judge a man of by-gone times
> And weigh his actions, or of science treat,
> Which, when extended (by experience) and applied
> to life,
> At once exalts and benefits mankind.]

In these lines, the princess begins to construct a system of values that will later be used to relativize, if not utterly devaluate, poetic activity. She introduces as fundamental categories of judgment 'experience,' 'utility,' and 'instruction.' Her parergonal status does not permit her to participate in the system of *Bildung* of which she nonetheless has some foreknowledge; she is not yet a figure enveloped by the systematicity of the Hegelian movement of *Bildung*, but she takes her pleasure in 'following,' in prefiguring the discourse of *Bildung*. The princess justifies the pleasure she takes in scientific discussion (as if this pleasure required justification) by arguing that the man of science, 'rather than cheating us, gives instruction' (l. 133). Scientific discourse 'elevates men when, by extension into the world of experience, it yields a measure of utility.' We might add here that the men in question are already rather elevated insofar as science is presented as a noble discourse or the discourse of nobility [*Gespräch der Edlen*], of that which is no longer nature.

At this point the princess directs the focus of the drama to an aspect of *Bildung* that will be more fully cast by Alfons and Antonio in the subsequent acts. She proffers an image of herself above all as the patroness of the *Denker* (l. 130) who appear to supersede in importance the *Dichter*. These thinkers, she argues, do not 'cheat' us – as perhaps the poets do. If thought is viewed as superseding poetry in some way, and if being cheated comes into question at all, this may be related to the fact that the princess's own poetic stage of development has been relegated to a past with which she has broken, though not without pain, negativity and a foretaste of death. It is as if she were to act as the mainspring and receptacle of Hegel's familiar but nonetheless astonishing recognition that art no longer fulfills our highest needs: 'wir sind darüber hinaus, Werke der Kunst göttlich verehren und sie anbeten zu können. Der Gedanke und die Reflexion hat die schöne Kunst überflügelt [We are beyond being able to worship and venerate works of art. Thought and reflection have overtaken the beauty of art].' Whether or not one agrees with the assumption, hardly limited to Hegel, that holds the sciences to be more liable to serve [*dienstbar*] a current need for utility, the fact remains that art no longer provides satisfaction [*Befriedigung*] for intellectual needs.[12] Getting back to our princess, it seems that she derives satisfaction from a type of reflection whose priority over art she affirms; she emphasizes the value of a reflection grounded in the experiential realm, as, for instance, in matters of science and of state when these serve as the basis for thought (ll. 125–33). Not until Alfons and Antonio introduce another, enlarging perspective into the drama, does *Bildung* become directly linked to a concept of history. The princess, a woman of *Bildung* excluded from the drama of historical action, is primarily concerned with the connotations of *Bildung* as culture, which goes hand in hand with a concept of pedagogy. This conjunction of pedagogy and culture becomes increasingly weighted with problems as the play unfolds. In her dialogue with Leonore, the princess seeks to establish a place for experience, that is to say, for the *discourse* of experience in rapport to a certain scientificity. Her argument aligns itself with that aspect of *Bildung* that can be understood provisionally, in its most general sense, as the philosophy which exacts full self-realization through experience. In the 'first science of philosophy,' as the advertisement to the *Phenomenology* says, Hegel suggests that the relationship of experience to consciousness is structured in the following way: 'Consciousness knows and comprehends nothing but what falls within its experience. ... And experience is called this very process by which the element that is immediate, unexperienced, i.e. abstract – whether it be in the form of sense or bare thought – externalizes itself, and then comes back to itself from this stage of estrangement, and by so doing is at length set forth in its concrete nature and real truth, and becomes too a possession of consciousness.'[13] The princess may not view what Nature has lent her as a possession, but that which experience fosters, which becomes comprehensible and (re)cognizable and has returned to her from a land of estrangement – Hegel later speaks of the land of *Bildung* – guarantees, secures and appeases thought as (self-)possession. Mind is reassured; she cannot be cheated. She has not quite buried but rather interiorized and remembered the path of her own *Bildung*. And this memory obsesses her, for she will repeat its story to Tasso, who in turn repeats it back to her; she will then repeat it once again to Leonore, in each case emphasizing the determinant configuration of loss, separation, and arrested consciousness that has made up the stations of her formation. Her *Bildungsprozeß* will have taught her the necessity of interiorizing her earlier renunciation [*entbehren*] of that which she has divinized most, but indeed, naively – she has learned to overcome poetry [*Gesang*]. Thus, before she first sees Tasso, before she awakens to a new stage of consciousness, she will have passed into a form of death. She was locked in silence at the time, dimly learning 'der Duldung stille Lehre' (l. 845), preparing her pedagogical lectures for the young poet. Her doctor was the one to prescribe an elimination of poetry, and he administered the end to her poetic comfort so that she might live, surviving herself in pain:

> auch dieses [Gesang]
> Nahm mir der Arzt hinweg: sein streng Gebot
> Hieß mich verstummen; leben sollt' ich, leiden,
> Den einz'gen kleinen Trost sollt' ich entbehren.
> (ll. 1813–16)

> [Not long, alas! this comfort (the joy of song)
> was allowed:
> The physician's stern monition silenced me;
> I was condemned to live and to endure
> E'en of this sole remaining joy bereft. (143)]

The princess carries with her this amputation, so to speak, this elimination and death. She has learned the gruesome lesson philosophy teaches about survival, having already died before the play begins. At least she has died to poetry. She has known therefore the seriousness, pain, patience, and work of the negative inscribed in the *Phenomenology;* dwelling in the company of the *Weltgeist,* she draws her intelligence from the solemn teacher of patience. If the princess is not a figure wholly integrated into the process which Hegel's own work undergoes, then she is at least an exemplary patient of the *Bildung* whose inscription she awaits.

Leonore, the interlocutor of *Bildung,* has been kept patiently waiting. Leonore, the life-force, Leonore Sanvitale forces life into the foreground. As the one of two Leonores to have assured a certain continuity of life and lineage through childbearing (l. 48), Leonore S. ensures the possibility of a fertile matrix in this drama from which a sustained reflection on poetry and its effects might spring. Shifting the focus of their discussion from *Wissenschaft* to poetry and the imagination, she introduces a different order of experience that occurs, she offers, 'nach dieser ernsten Unterhaltung' (l. 134), an *Unterhaltung* which the princess had described and herself maintained. Leonore, for her part, shows little concern for the specific, knowledge-yielding contents of a discourse; rather, her emphasis lies with the intersubjective response it evokes and the poetic sensibility that produces it. Poetry, she says, arouses feelings of utmost delight; our ear and inner senses find a place of rest in the rhyming quality of the poem:

> Und dann, nach dieser ernsten Unterhaltung,
> Ruht unser Ohr und unser innrer Sinn
> Gar freundlich auf des Dichters Reimen aus,
> Der uns die letzten lieblichsten Gefühle
> Mit holden Tönen in die Seele flösst.
> (ll. 134–38)
>
> [And then, this grave and serious converse o'er,
> Our ear and inner mind with tranquil (friendly) joy
> Upon the poet's tuneful verse repose,
> Who, through the medium of harmonious sounds,
> Infuses sweet emotions in the soul. (91)]

It is as if poetry were the place where exhaustion could be played out, or more exactly, the exhaustion following [*nach dieser . . .*] a Hegelian type of pedagogy that sets one restlessly seeking a 'completed discourse.'[14] Poetry, by comparison, is a 'friendly' discourse whose apprehension does not necessarily involve a concept of mastery. At this point in the drama a major snag begins to take shape in the way Leonore opposes the princess's notion of *Bildung* with an interpretation of genius. Leonore's stance, essentially aesthetic in nature, foreshadows the movement in the *Third Critique* which will find expression not more than a year from her recorded utterance in terms of the Kantian symptom called 'disinterested pleasure.'

Leonore S. emphasizes the freeplay of the cognitive faculties on the part of the poet and aesthetic reader without exacting from poetry a final purpose [*Zweck*] other than its purposefulness [*Zweckmässigkeit*]. Unlike the princess, she resists referring poetry to scientific models or to the categories of *Bildung*. Thus she counters the princess's contention that Tasso, when writing, appears 'violently' to be drawn to an order of empirical reality by arguing that, in fact, his poetry cannot be subordinated to cognitive interests: the poet communicates only his sentiment [*Gefühl*]. This sentiment, which Leonore understands as 'love,' has in a sense no claim; it shows no interest whatsoever in possessing or mastering its object. The poet does not love us, she insists, but conjures what he loves and commemorates it in the name of Leonore. In the same manner, the two Leonores only appear to love the man, Tasso, but truly love in him the 'Höchste' that can be loved (ll. 205–17). Distilled of his empirical elements, Tasso is then not the object to be loved or possessed, but the mediator of supreme forms that inspire a form of objectless love. Leonore, then, speaks of a love that does not seek to enter or be entered; it is a kind of prepenetrating love, we could say, for acts of penetration or violent pinning down [*Gewaltsam anzuziehen und festzuhalten* (princess)] are shunned by the freeplay she envisions. Perhaps it is with this intent of giving to Tasso the rights of otherness and asserting his nonviolability that Leonore had begun her reflections on the poet with these words: 'Und ich bin gegen Tasso nur gerecht' (l. 158). The princess, on the other hand, will always seek entry and appropriation – a desire which, when read correctly by the poet, will have disastrous consequences.

The mind, Leonore continues, when aroused by an aesthetic object, finds itself in attunement with the mind of the poet; drawn into the *Zauberkreis* in which the poet wanders, the mind feels its capacity, in Leonore's words, 'mit ihm zu wandeln, teil an ihm zu nehmen' (l. 169).

Leonore proposes a more precise interpretation of the poetic sensibility when she initiates the full conversion from sensory perception to another mode of perception; her language reflects the movement, within a hierarchical anatomy of imagination, to which the empirical gaze is sacrificed. Speaking first of the poet's eye, she begins to trace what Kant calls the poet's 'transgression of the limits of experience' (*Critique of Judgment*, book 2, §49):

Sein Auge weilt auf dieser Erde kaum;
Sein Ohr vernimmt den Einklang der Natur;
Was die Geschichte reicht, das Leben gibt,
Sein Busen nimmt es gleich und willig auf:
Das weit Zerstreute sammelt sein Gemüt,
Und sein Gefühl belebt das Unbelebte.
(ll. 159–64)

[His eye scarce lingers on this earthly scene:
To nature's harmony his ear is tuned.
What history offers, and what life presents,
His bosom promptly and with joy receives:
The widely scattered is by him combined,
And his quick feeling animates the dead. (92)]

If Leonore, who desperately seeks immortality within the limits of an acknowledged finitude (ll. 1935ff.), can speak so persuasively about the poet's sentiment, it is no doubt because in so doing she accomplishes that which she desires; she translates poetry into a name, into a proper name, that is, which owes its existence precisely to this poetic sensibility. 'Und sein Gefühl belebt das Unbelebte' can be translated as 'His feeling gives life to Sanvitale.' More so than any other figure in the court, Leonore is alive to the poetic act of naming which in turn engenders a need for eternal naming – a program in which she would like to enlist her own name (cf. 'Wie ihn die Welt verehrt, / So wird die Nachwelt ihn verehrend nennen' [ll. 1943–44]).

Of the poet himself Leonore has told us that his mind, and *body,* are spontaneously attuned to nature, life, disseminated things, and even to history (ll. 159–62). In particular, history and life encounter no resistance of a corporeal nature from the poet. The poetic act, she suggests, consists in giving expression to the immediacy of such an attunement. Yet the poet, wandering perpetually within the insularity of his magic circle, also exists somehow outside of history, protected from its potentially sacrificial movement. Certainly, complaints about such a typically Kantian erasure of history have been recorded often enough, beginning perhaps with Herder's famous gripe about Kant to Hamann, namely, 'auch in der Geschichte keine Geschichte.'[15] However, if the poet is placed paradoxically outside of history, it is somehow to affirm the possibility of its inside – this inside, by the way, becomes his insides; history extends itself over to him, and he in turn devours it with the invisible mouths of his bosom. But history does not implant her seed in him, so to speak, for the poet himself does not develop historically; without the shadow of a process, his heart immediately receives what history offers. At no point involved in *becoming* a genius, Leonore's poet is, rather predictably, born a poet. In Kantian terms, he is endowed by nature with the ability to originate exemplarily the rules for art. Neither instructed by experience nor bound by established norms: 'Oft adelt er, was uns gemein erschien, / Und das Geschätzte wird vor ihm zu nichts' (ll. 165–66) ["Oft he ennobles what we count for naught: What others treasure is by him despised" (92)]. In other words he displays, as Kant says at one point, the courage of deformities which is deserving of merit only in the case of genius (bk. 2, §49). Let us suppose, however, that the thing treasured [*das Geschätzte*], the treasure that genius buries, is, in this case and place, where deformity encounters form and formation – precisely, *Bildung*.

~

Hegel was the only student among his peers at the Tübinger Stift not to join the Kant-Club. A report submitted by Master Leutwein on the rebellious spirit includes the following testimony:

> Ich weiß zwar nicht, ob und wiefern Hegels letztes akademisches Jahr, das ihn mir entzog, ihn verändert habe. Ich zweifle aber daran. Jedenfalls war während der vier Jahre unseres näheren Umgangs die Metaphysik Hegels Sache nicht sonderlich. . . . Eine besondere Freude hatte er am Buch Hiob wegen dessen ungeregelter Natursprache. Überhaupt schien er mir zuweilen etwas exzentrisch. Auf seine nachmaligen Ansichten geriet er erst im Auslande, denn in Tübingen war ihm nicht einmal Vater Kant recht bekannt. Und ich, der ich mich damals in Kant'sche Literatur einließ.
>
> [I do not know if and to what extent Hegel's last academic year, during which he distanced himself from me, might have changed him. But I doubt it has. In any case, during the four years that he worked with me, metaphysics was not exactly Hegel's thing. . . . He took particular pleasure in the Book of Job due to its unruly vernacular. On the whole he seemed to me to be somewhat eccentric at times. He only came to his subsequent views when he was abroad, for in Tübingen he was not even really familiar with Father Kant. And to think that I, who at the time was working on Kantian literature.][16]

It is not clear from this letter whether Hegel was avoiding an encounter with Father Kant or, what appears more likely, with Master Leutwein at this stage of his *Bildung*. He will have a good deal to say about Kant later, of course, when he is master and developing the philosophy of mastery. He will, among other things, introduce a lack or rather find it in the *Geniebegriff* and try to supplement it precisely with a notion of *Bildung*.

We shall return to Hegel's *Bildung* at a later stage, but first, we might consider another aspect of their relationship.

Unlike Kant, Hegel does not of course bring beauty into rapport with pleasure or delight. His patient comprehensiveness, in the *Aesthetics* and elsewhere, hardly displays the urgency, the almost desperate glance toward the pleasure and beauty of Kant's *Third Critique*. Kant is dealing urgently with life and death, and seemingly pulling everything toward life. The heliotropic sway of his aesthetics tells us as much, though he has already indicated his inclination in the preface to the first edition (1790). This will be his last *Critique*, he is closing shop and the years are gaining on him: 'With this, then, I bring my entire critical undertaking to a close. I shall hasten to the doctrinal part, in order, as far as possible, to snatch from my advancing years what time may yet be favourable to the task.' He hastens, snatches, in general he writes the first part according to the credit system of borrowed time. It appears almost in keeping with the sublime tension involved in the foreknowledge of closure that the aesthetics be invested with so much mention of *Lebenskräfte*. His concern will lie with the 'Lebensgefühl des Subjekts,' he maintains. Thus while art emerges as a promotion [*Beförderung*] of life-forces, Kant writes of his own sense of decline as he writes his final *Critique*. (The first time he had dedicated himself to a study of life-forces, in fact the first time he had written an essay in the 'living mother tongue,' was in 1764, the year his father died. It bore the title, 'Gedanken von der wahren Schätzung der lebendigen Kräfte.') If Hegel elaborates in a fundamental way a philosophy of necessary catastrophe – and we shall see this to be the case when, in particular, *Bildung* is at stake – then Kant, when writing on the differential forces of judgment [*Urteilskraft*], places his bets on finitude and possibly in the first place on *his* finitude. We shall leave open the question of where Kant might situate himself with regard to the *Geniebegriff*. Let it suffice to say that he assigns acute importance to 'a limit imposed upon [genius] which it cannot transcend' (§47) and to the fact that what has been 'bestowed [upon genius] directly from the hand of nature' dies with the individual, 'awaiting the day when nature once again endows another in the same way.' The violence of this opening – the opening to the *Critique of Judgment*, to the question of genius, beauty, pleasure, and their disciples – might be borne in mind as we pursue the oppositional pair that Goethe has introduced as foreplay to and in *Torquato Tasso*.

Leonore's feeling was inspired essentially by the communicability of the poet's sentiment, which produces a doubling effect because the feeling of the communicability of his mood activates the desire for communicability in the aesthetic observer. Now, when Kant makes the radical claim that beauty is nothing in and of itself, he is aiming his argument at a specific tradition. Leonore S. names the source of that tradition when, in this context, she names the princess: 'Du, Schülerin des Plato! nicht begreifen, / Was dir ein Neuling vorzuschwatzen wagt?' (ll. 222–23) ['Thou Plato's pupil! and not comprehend / What a mere novice dares to prattle to thee?' (93)]. It is as if she, as daring newcomer and exponent of a new philosophical understanding of beauty, were momentarily humbled before the tradition with which she breaks. For the student of Plato, beauty is thought to exist in itself. Thus there are ideas which are beautiful in themselves (justice would be one such idea). It is significant that Leonore identifies herself throughout the first scene with newness, with the spring which the play promises. The princess by contrast is resolutely turned toward the past, the present springtime being no more than a phantom of 'manchen Tag der Jugend froh durchlebt,' for 'dieses neue Grün und diese Sonne / Bringt das Gefühl mir jener Zeit zurück' (ll. 25–27) ['Full many a joyous day I lingered here / And this bright sunshine, and this verdant green / Bring back the feelings of that by-gone time' (88)]. The princess has stored within herself and kept in reserve the memory of her origin, or the origin of her thought, which she as student and offshoot has, however, surpassed. The princess, then, remembers her origin (Plato) and keeps it pressed in her development, which mimes a Hegelian movement, whereas Leonore S. springs forth likc the natural source of spring, murmuring the presencing in this drama of Kant's *Genie*.

Another dimension of Leonore S.'s speech not only underscores the opposing characters of the two women, but also alerts us to a paradox in the reflections advanced by the text at this point. Addressing the princess, Leonore claims that whereas she feels immediately compelled to communicate her mood, the princess has the capacity to feel things better, deeply and – to remain silent. Leonore's line deserves careful consideration, for it also represents the first dismembered iamb in the play: 'Du fühlst es besser, fühlst es tief und – schweigst' (l. 88) ['Thou feelest the while more deeply, and – art silent' (90)]. The dash indicates a major pause in the rhythm of the verse as well as the absence of a real link between a superior capacity for feeling and its verbal expression. Somehow, Leonore suggests, a genuine plenitude of feeling eludes the touch of language. We cannot of course know to what *es* refers in this context, but it may be taken as an allusion of sorts to the suprasensible, the absolute plenitude to which all language, including poetry, is deemed inadequate. As such, Leonore projects onto the princess's silence a Kantian axiom that links poetry and the presentation of a fullness of thought [*Gedankenfülle*]. This may appear somewhat contradictory, for while Kant shows communicability to activate pleasure in the judgment of taste, he also shows poetry, which best presents plenitude, to be, like all language, finally inadequate to plenitude. But the princess's adherence to a motif associating superior feeling with silence nonetheless appears, in Leonore's view, to narrow her capacity for pleasure. The princess remains silent, Leonore supposes. Hers will not be the ironic silence of the philosopher, but that of a will too weak to affirm itself in and as language. Her repeated exercise consisting of *entbehren* functions analogously, as we have observed, to the renunciation of language. Thus when the princess chooses to remain silent at the event of Tasso's arrest, she correspondingly will have renounced her only access to pleasure; she will have entered another movement gaining on dust and dissolution and one, therefore, which will prove paradigmatic for many a *schöne Seele* to come. We are still and always in fact weaving wreaths.

When Leonore attempts a definition of Tasso's poetry, it is not clear where the image [*Bild;* l. 184] she invokes comes from. For Kant the prototype or originary image of beauty is a simple idea produced within each person and in accordance with which everything, including the object of taste, the judgment of taste and everyone's taste, is judged. Kant stresses that this *Urbild* of beauty is not something that we possess, but something toward which we strive. Leonore imputes this notion of image-striving to the poet:

> Bald hebt er es [das Bild] in lichter Glorie
> Zum Sternenhimmel auf, beugt sich verehrend
> Wie Engel über Wolken vor dem Bilde;
> Dann schleicht er ihm durch stille Fluren nach,
> Und jede Blume windet er zum Kranz.
> (ll. 185–89).
>
> [Now he exalts it (the image) to the starry heavens
> In radiant glory, and before that form
> Bows down, like angels in the realms of above.
> Then, stealing after it through silent fields,
> He garlands in his wreath each beauteous flower. (92)]

The poet's striving toward the image is heavenward, infinite, and eternal, but it is also associated with the earth, and with finite activity. Through this imagery, Leonore not only establishes a link between her own activity and that of the poet who, likewise, produces a wreath, but points to the finite gesture involved in striving on earth toward the image which he produces but does not possess. In Kant's section on image and the aesthetic idea ('Archetypon' and 'Urbild,' 'Ektypon' and 'Nachbild,' and so on), the *Bild* is said to be placed by the technique of nature; while it is linked to an intentional act on the part of nature, the fact that the imagination can reproduce the image remains fully incomprehensible. Nature somehow speaks in us. And whatever speaks in Kant when naming the image-producing imagination is decidedly diffident, humble and cautious. We can detect, at the very least, a break in style when he touches upon the imagination. For example, when he explains how the imagination collects a great number of images, Kant adds parenthetically 'in my opinion,' followed by a comparatively timid formulation, 'if I may be permitted,' which in turn politely opens onto the rhetorical figure of analogy: 'if I may be permitted to apply an analogy from optics.'

Just as imagination poses a problem, as we have seen (we are still applying analogies from optics), in Goethe's case, so, too, for Kant, it must be approached with kid gloves. Genius, which exemplarily houses the imagination and is unthinkable without her, poses no less of a problem. Since it will be necessary here to set limits on an argument that will have to be elaborated elsewhere, let me simply suggest at this point some of the snags and ruses, some of the areas of turbulence into which a reading of *Tasso* as a dramatic typology of aesthetic and pedagogical positions forces one.

Kant himself introduces the 'complete opposition' of genius and a certain pedagogy which he calls imitation, for learning, he asserts, is nothing but imitation. The poet of genius does not himself know; he has not learned and cannot teach what he has produced, though he will, as model, found a school. Elsewhere, Kant specifies that he is not dealing with 'a free swing of the mental powers' but rather with the 'slow and even painful process of improvement' that the work of genius undergoes. Like Goethe, he speaks in terms of sacrifice, criminality and the clipping of wings when it comes to genius and imagination. In the section (§50) entitled 'The combination of taste and genius in products of fine art [*schöne Kunst*],' he writes of the discipline which must be meted out to lawlessness:

> For in lawless freedom imagination, with all its wealth, produces nothing but nonsense; the power of judgment, on the other hand, is the faculty that makes it consonant with understanding.
>
> Taste, like judgment in general, is the discipline (or corrective) of genius. It severely clips its wings, and makes it orderly or polished; but at the same time it gives it guidance, directing and controlling its flight, so that it may preserve its character of finality. . . . And so, where the interests of both these qualities clash in a product, and there has to be a sacrifice of something, then it should rather be on the side of genius; and judgment, which in matters of fine art bases its decision on its own proper principles, will more readily endure an abatement of the freedom and wealth of the

imagination, than that the understanding should be compromised.

Thus it would seem that in principle, the imagination is less vulnerable to defeat; in other words, she can take a clipping whereas understanding must be conceded, in this fictive pairing of the one with the other, its priority. Imagination must be kept in her place. With this schooling and scolding of the imagination in mind, we might consider now how the *Genie* in fact comes to light in the *Third Critique*, in a footnote placed upon the word *schulgerecht* [academically correct]. The context is most peculiar and warrants our attention.

One will find, it begins, that a perfectly regular [*regelmäßig*] face – one that a painter might want to use as a model – usually conveys nothing [*nichts sagt*], for it contains nothing that is characteristic and is thus given more to expressing the idea of the species than that which is specific in a person. The exaggeration of that which is characteristic in this way, that is, exaggeration which breaks with the normal idea (the purposiveness of the species) is called *caricature*. Experience equally shows that those faces which are totally regular betray, as a rule, only an internally mediocre person; presumably (if one may assume that nature expresses in exterior form the proportions of the interior), this is because where none of the dispositions of mind [*Gemütsanlage*] surpass the requisite proportions for constituting a simply faultless [*fehlerfrei*] person, one cannot expect anything of that which we call *Genie* in which nature appears to deviate from her usual relationship of the mind's faculties [*Gemütskräfte*] to the advantage of a single faculty.[17]

The *Genie* or genius, the one at any rate whom Kant faces on the margins of his text, is thus a break within nature, a deviation which nature takes from a certain concept of faultlessness. It is a condition of internal dissymmetry and disproportion whose outward expression nature sketches as facial irregularity or distortion. Nature departs from herself or from the usual economy of faculty distribution to the profit of one faculty member. The *Genie* is thus made to appear closer to caricature than to a faultless, if ordinary, model of human 'perfection.' Goethe will also use the notion of disproportion when speaking of Tasso, at least according to the testimony of Karoline Herder. Tasso is to be the sign of the disproportionateness of genius itself with respect to life. Kant limits his remark to the face of genius, which would deviate from the *Urbild* nature uses for her productions; he, or rather it, the genius, would not correspond as such to the normal idea [*Normalidee*] of the species. Now this may be because the genius is not entirely of the species, nor necessarily a being whose concept is entirely self-determined.

The question of genius, which deserves far more attention than it can receive here, is not only taken up by Kant in the famous passages of the *Critique of Judgment* which it would seem most reasonable to cite at this point. The *Anthropology*, whose object is the empirical subject, too, treats this issue in a way that is perhaps less familiar to readers of Goethe but which no doubt indicates a more transparent affinity to his understanding of the problem. In the section devoted to and entitled 'Der Charakter des Volks,' Kant places the thirteenth footnote on the word *Genie*. The discussion to which this note is appended represents an attempt to demonstrate that the German people has 'its good side when obstinate *application* but not *genius* is required.'[18] While the Germans cannot equal the English, French, and Italians in wit and artistic taste, they possess a phlegmatic character (he adds, parenthetically, 'in the good sense of the term'), which Kant defines as the temperament of cold reflection and tenacity [*Ausdaurung*] in pursuit of its goal. Genius, Kant says here, is the talent capable of *discovering* that which cannot be taught or learned. To be sure, one can learn how to make good verses from others, he contends in the footnote, but not how one should make a good poem, for a good poem must emerge from the nature of the author [*Natur des Verfassers*]. Therefore, one can hardly expect a poem to arise on command [*auf Bestellung*] or in exchange for remuneration as in the case of some fabricated item [*Fabricat*]; rather, it should be regarded as an inspiration, that is, as an occasional disposition whose cause is unknown to the poet – he does not know himself how he came to it: *'scit genius, natale comes qui temperat astrum.'* This is why genius flashes like an instantaneous phenomenon which manifests itself in intervals and disappears again; it does not appear like a light turned on at will [*wilkürlich angezündet*] and that would continue to shine as long as one likes, but like showering sparks [*wie sprühende Funken*] which a fortunate fit or crisis teases out of the productive imagination.

All this – the occasion of luminous self-dissemination, of the violent flash and gaiety of a sudden crisis and loss (or perhaps not quite a loss, for it was never sought) of self-knowledge, the invention [*Erfindung*] of the unteachable and unlearnable – exceeds the structure of possibility which belongs to the specifically Germanic. However, this does not necessarily mean that Kant valorizes genius as a superior phenomenon among nations – and, let it not be forgotten that he is dealing in this case with *other* nations. Genius arises on foreign territory, foreign to philosophy, perhaps, or at least to the indigenous 'temperament of cold reflection.' To take an example – Goethe's example, for instance – genius could be sought in Italy. Now, the foreign territory which the poetical genius occupies or, more likely, constitutes, begins in Goethe's text with the provisional foreignness of the women to themselves when they offer a reading of Tasso and his poetry. In harmony with a Nature who departs from herself in order to impart herself through the poet, the women receive the poet in a mood of provisional self-departure. Not least among the decentering effects we have noted is woman's geographical remove from the center of political action and the source of monetary circulation. Given the accumulation of these factors, it is not surprising that the poet will receive payment, or the 'phantom of a salary' [*Lohn*] as Leonore puts it, in a foreign currency whose exchange value must remain radically undetermined; as a reward for his 'work' (the status of this term shifts throughout the text) he receives a wreath. This gesture proves as complex as it is ambivalent, literally creating the first dramatic knot in the play by tensely opposing motifs of remuneration and debt to those of life and death, all of which are tied into the wreath. And the related theme of general retribution will undergo substantial modifications before the poet envisions his departure from the stage in a state of utter destitution, a pilgrim en route to his biological family caught, indeed, in the dilemma of his sheer naturality. Here as elsewhere in the drama, Goethe takes the interpretation of genius as a naturebound entity to its parodistic extremes, as, for example, when Tasso deliriously offers to be the court's resident gardener (ll. 3190ff.), suggesting that his place is in Nature's kitchen.

If the text registers ambivalence toward the very notion of genius in its natural or innate quality, and dramatizes a certain lucidity about the stakes involved in such a precarious privileging of the poet, this does not mean that it will be able to overcome the problem by proposing a corrective vision to the *Geniebegriff* – namely, that of *Bildung* – and thus lay a wreath on genius. Tasso, for his part, refuses the wreath, which he is told by the princess he must *learn* to bear: 'So lern' auch diese Zweige tragen' (l. 523) ['Learn also now the laurel wreath to wear' (103)].

As with Kant, the genius, while being a sign of excess or extravagance within nature, is shown irrevocably to belong to a structure of naturality. This, precisely, is the point of departure for the poet's confrontation with *Bildung* – with that which must be learned and taught, beginning of course with the lesson of accepting a wreath. However, one of the reasons that Tasso can neither learn nor teach, Kant tells us, is because the genius is unable to account for his productions scientifically. In general, Kant insists on keeping art and science apart. In Goethe's text, the rigorous distinction that Kant draws will pose a problem, particularly when the men of science and state penetrate to the scene. At one point the duke will expose to the poet an economy of sacrifice which *Bildung* exacts: 'Ich bitte dich, entreisse dich dir selbst! Der Mensch gewinnt, was der Poet verliert' (ll. 3077–78) ['I charge thee, Tasso, snatch thee from thyself! The man will profit, though the bard may lose' (179)]. The head of state here entreats the poet – within a system of gain and profit – to tear himself apart from his (natural) self. The distinction repeatedly drawn by Alfons between the man and the poet suggests that the poet, in order to become a man of experience assimilable to the state – a *Bildungsmensch,* in short – must renounce that stage of existence marked by an insular, self-unifying type of poetic productivity. The powerful injunction commands the poet to lose precisely that disproportion of mind which was coterminous with genius. It is issued at a moment when Tasso requests that his draft [*Fassung*] be returned to him; when this fails to come about, the poet literally loses his text and context. Dislocated thus from his natural locus, as a being severely cut off from himself, Tasso from this point onward will start seeing double: 'daß ich mehr / Als je mich doppelt fühle' (ll. 764–65) ['That more than ever now / . . . I feel / . . . a distracting conflict (doubling) with myself' (111)]. Perhaps it is significant to note as well the double designation he receives within the drama: while the women seemed rather certain of his being a man [*Mann*] in the first scene, and referred to him as such, the play shifts ground on this issue when the male emissaries of *Bildung* arrive, reducing the poet to a mere child [*Jüngling, Kind*].

When Goethe seems keen on introducing a bit of confusion into the question of Tasso's age, and mostly in conjunction with a judgment passed on his character, he is still participating in the general inscription of his age, wherein art is set apart from science on the basis of a problematics of age and maturation. The voice of seniority that comes to mind in this context would be Hegel, of course, whom Derrida has interpreted as 'un philosophe qui se présente comme le premier philosophe adulte. . . . C'est le philosophe d'une philosophie qui se pense sortie de l'enfance, qui prétend penser, avec toute son histoire, tous les âges de la philosophie, tout le temps et toute la téléologie de sa maturation.'[19] This type of thinking applies even to Hegel's critique of Goethe which exhorts us to remember the rough beginnings of his early productions, whose immaturity gives cause for some alarm. But in the space of a delay the alarm can be safely sounded, for it is set off by the works of maturity which provide the implicit starting point for Hegel's observations. It should be noted, however, that when Hegel evokes a history of need [*Bedürfnis*], art itself is dated or given an age which has been supplanted, he announces, by the age of science. As for Tasso, he belongs, as everyone knows, to two ages – to Goethe's and to the Renaissance – while, upon the stage of the former, his age is further determined through the bifocal spectacles resolutely fixing art and science. In the domain of art, the poet appears to have achieved maturity; in the optic of science and *Bildung,* he still has a long way to go before our needs are reasonably satisfied.

When posed in this way, the question of age may strike us as a peculiarly Hegelian one; nonetheless, Father Kant had not been remiss in taking it up in order to stress the distinction between art and science and to address the problem of character as well. In the second book of the *Anthropology*, Kant makes it a point to explain why the veins of a poet dry up with age at a time when science holds out the promise of health and activity for a good mind [*dem guten Kopf*].[20] This age-old difference stems from the fact that beauty is a blossom while science is a fruit, that is, poetry must be a liberal art [*freie Kunst*] whose multiplicity and variety demand suppleness [*Leichtigkeit*], but with age such suppleness disappears ('and this is only just [*das mit Recht*]'). By contrast, the habit of pursuing the same old path in the scientific domain brings about suppleness. Requiring originality and newness (and to this end, dexterity) of each of its products, poetry can hardly be said to 'harmonize' with an advanced age [*mit dem Alter nicht wohl zusammenstimmt*], except to a certain extent in the case of caustic works – epigrams and satires (*Xenien*) which, however, are more a matter of seriousness than of play.

If the poet's destiny is short-lived in comparison with the long-winded runners of science, he is also partially excused from a category that finds prominence in Goethe's text, namely, *character* – a term which the *Bildungs*-crew tries to enforce upon the young poet, for example, when it is decided that 'Es bildet . . . Sich ein Charakter in dem Strom der Welt' (ll. 304–05).[21] Kant no doubt agrees with this view, but he points out, as if in response – as if he were willing to take up Tasso's defense – that it is a peculiarity of the poet's character *to have no character*.[22] And as if he wanted to counter every one of the objections that Antonio exposes before the court, he continues: poets are by nature capricious, moody, and unreliable (though without malice); they wantonly make enemies without however hating anyone; they mock their friends mordantly [*beißend*] without wanting to do them harm. These characteristics of the characterless poet are due in part to an innate disposition prevailing over practical judgment: Kant rests his case on a statement about the poet's essentially 'Torquato' [*verschrobenen*] wit, one that is naturally twisted or perverse and thus dominates his practical judgment.

It is probably evident by now that Kant's position on Tasso's defense team implies that he is already operating within a system of accusation. He knows the charges made against his client, and he may secretly harbor a few suspicions himself. He began his argument concerning the poet's character as a lawyer, or rather by contending that 'poets do not enjoy the same success as lawyers' because of the innate disposition of their temperaments. Kant's disposition often leads him to situate the poetical genius on precarious grounds. In fact, the moment an element of genius is admitted into his – or for that matter, Goethe's or Hegel's – discourse, disproportion, excess, and perversion come into evidence as well. This is perhaps not always immediately transparent, but can take the form of a sequential unfolding or an association of ideas (for philosophy, too, can be found to 'free associate,' especially when it freely associates with art). Without involving the intricacies of the *Third Critique*, one can find in the *Anthropology* a certain prejudicial buildup in the positioning of genius. Directly preceding the moment when he announces that 'the originality of the imagination (and not imitation), when it accords with notions, is called genius,' Kant is writing about something that at first sight appears to be entirely foreign to such a reflection: namely, the issues of stultifying and stimulating drunkenness. His observations find expression, by the way, in a section entitled 'On Imagination.' Working up to, or perhaps down to, a notion of genius, Kant will first expose the difference between *exhibitio originaria* (a faculty of the original representation of the object) and *exhibitio derivativa* (a faculty of the derived representation). One should perhaps not forget the easy proximity of the genius to the drunk, nor the fact that in exposing the nature of this exalted condition, he is also to a certain extent privileging it, or at least demarcating its province, by initiating an exclusionary operation: 'Nature,' he asserts, 'is actually working (in the intoxicated man) to renew his conscious life by gradually rebuilding his strength.' However, it is not in everyone's nature to thus employ Nature's renewal projects:

> Women, clergymen and Jews [*Weiber, Geistliche und Juden*] ordinarily do not become drunk, at least they carefully avoid all appearance of it, because they are weak in civic life and must restrain themselves (for which sobriety is required). Their external value depends simply on other people's *belief* in their chastity, piety, and their separatistic character. Because, as far as the Jews are concerned, all separatists, that is, such as submit not only to a general law of the state, but also to a particular law (of their own sect), are, as foreign elements and as pretended elected ones, particularly exposed to the attention of the community and to harsh criticism [*der Schärfe der Kritik*]. Hence they cannot relax their self-attention because intoxication [*der Rausch*], which removes heedfulness, is to them scandalous.

'Is to them scandalous.' It is not clear whether Kant has isolated the Jews within the primary isolation consisting of women, clergymen, and Jews. There are, however, others, he adds, whose virtues are enhanced by drink, and here, in these cases, the biting edge of the *Kritik* lets up – thus 'a Stoic admirer of Cato said: "his virtue was strengthened by wine [*virtus eius incaluit mero*]." '

If drink is not the *forte* of the weak or marginal – of those too low to get high – and is, as Kant suggests, a self-imposed taboo related to the appearance and staging of values produced by those elements involved in a certain *a priority* of foreignness, then it must be that much more scandalous 'to them' – to all of them, including perhaps Kant – if these same elements were to dispense with the appearance of sobriety and take flight, for example, in uncontrolled or spontaneous speculation. Because Kant lays emphasis on the separatism involved here, we must recognize the risk encountered in intoxicating food (he includes mushrooms, wild rosemary, acanthus, Peruvian chicha, South Sea Islander's kava, and opium) and in drink as one of blurred distinctions, the scandal of transgression or crossing over, indeed, of mixing genres and genders. Thus the great foremother of our Leonores dressed in the guise of speculation, the woman who is explicitly portrayed as the *Philosophin* of another drama, concedes the scandal, reminding us, in terms of a violation in sexual and generic difference, of the disgust that such crossings arouse: '*Ein Frauenzimmer, das denket, ist ebenso ekel wie ein Mann, der sich schminket.*' [A woman who thinks is as disgusting as a man wearing make-up]. Orsina, the philosopher, the made-up man par excellence, is made to utter these words by a writer of whom Kant did not entirely approve. Let us not forget that Lessing was precisely the one to put the woman philosopher, in other words: 'Weiber, Geistliche und Juden,' on stage. Thus Hamann reports to Herder on 6 May 1779, on Kant's censure of *Nathan der Weise*, for he did not find much merit in the idea of any hero coming from that people (to be sure, some of Kant's best friends were Jews: Moses Mendelssohn, Marcus Herz, and Solomon Maimon). This expulsion of the unhappy few from the state of drunkenness takes place, once again, in the section entitled 'On Imagination [*Von der Einbildungskraft*].' Now the question might, and by rights ought to, arise of whether Kant confirms the connection we have asserted between thinking and drinking. 'Drink,' Kant writes here, 'loosens the tongue: *in vino disertus*. But it also opens the heart, serving as a material instrument for a moral quality: openness [*Offenherzigkeit*].' Drink is then principally linked to enunciation, to the organ of feeling and serves, in particular, 'an expansive soul' [*lauteres Herz*] for whom the 'quelling of his thought' is 'an oppressive condition.' Drink, moreover, introduces a new fluid that intermixes with the juices of the veins, acting as a stimulant for the nerves; while it does not serve to make the natural temperament more transparent, it does replace the one temperament with another. Consequently, one inebriated man will become amorous, another loud [*großprecherisch*], the third quarrelsome while the fourth (especially after beer) turns mellow, pensive, or entirely mute; but all of them, after they have slept it off and are reminded of their discourse [*Reden*] of the previous evening, will themselves laugh at this strange mood or alteration [*wunderliche Stimmung oder Verstimmung*] of their senses. This then is the Kantian typology of the drunk. Drunkenness is a condition of relatively short-lived self-departure, a state of self-division and multiplication; it shares with genius a certain instantaneity and blurring aftereffect. It cannot remember its state of forgetting but has to be reminded, told, and taught by others the facts of its outpourings. Drunkenness spends itself on itself, unable to read itself. Perhaps, however, unlike his genius, Kant's drunk is capable of laughter.

Apart from the fact that Antonio, in order to promote the disfavor of Alfons, will depict Tasso as someone who does not cut his wine with water [*Wann mischt er Wasser unter seinen Wein? . . . Wasser? nimmermehr!* (ll. 2889–905)] – drink being related in Antonio's diatribe to the poet's being a creature of the *Augenblick* – the passage from Kant has some bearing upon the notion of genius which is more than merely circumstantial, insofar as it heavily concentrates on modes of enunciation in conjunction with feeling. Kant does not deny a natural basis to the sentiment inspired by drink, but says that a different type of temperament supplements it. One drinks in order to transform an oppressive state into one resembling pleasure; that pleasure, it can be deduced, is the result of opening the gates that have held back or quelled the expression of thought. The drunken state, which expells the subject from himself, making him thus foreign to himself, rests in Kant's exposition upon a notion of mood and voice [*Stimmung*], which of course enjoys a prominent role in his argument for pure aesthetic feeling. However wondrous and derisive the mood and discourse provoked by drink may be, it nonetheless opens up a mode of communicability which, as we have seen in another context, is always at the root of pleasure.

In the paragraph of the *Anthropology* immediately following the mention of 'what is called genius,' Kant turns his attention to another creature endowed with an innate quality and a highly productive productive imagination: 'If the lack of a sense (for example, vision) is innate [*angeboren*],' he observes, 'then the cripple cultivates another sense, insofar as is possible, which serves as a substitute [*Vicariat*] for it, and the productive faculty will be used to a high degree.' Here we are dealing with an innate lack, something with which someone is born, like genius, and which, because of the lack it represents, is charged with charging the productive imagination. As in *Tasso,* where the princess translates her brother's depiction of the poet into the metaphor of a cripple (l. 325), the genius, who in Goethe, by virtue of his own or rather collectively imagined incapacity, paradoxically threatens to impede the movement of the court and its *Bildung,* gravitates in Kant toward that which is handicapped and in some fundamental or innate way deformed. And Hegel also, but perhaps more understandably, creates an unsettling environment for the discussion of genius. His participation in the arraignment of genius is particularly manifest in the *Encyclopedia,* where the sequencing effect shows the close association of genius with madness, as well as with fanaticism and drunkenness. Even in the *Phenomenology* he tends to group together, as a conceptual syntagma, the sensations which derive from the activities of the 'thief, murderer and writer;'[23] or, again, in another passage, he writes of the 'painful headaches' that come with the strain of writing, adding that stealing, murder, and writing (in that order, in that ordering of the criminal profile) are each accompanied by their own sensation. And Kant, to return to his earlier work, makes mention of genius in equally tense contexts, for example in the *Versuch über die Krankheiten des Kopfes,* directly following his discussion of madness and disturbed understanding, which consists of judging a true experience [*richtige Erfahrung*] in a wholly perverted manner. The madman interprets the behavior of others solely in respect of himself [*auf sich aus*]; he is in a way mad because decidedly un-Kantian, incapable as he is of imposing upon his desire that vital sense of putting himself in the place of the other – as the judgment of taste would require him to do. Or, too, he is unwilling or unable to accept and practice any position of universality advocated by Kant. Such singularity, in which the subject is rigorously 'self-centered' or is not in some sense a common one, shared and shareable – such interpretation, beginning with and referring back to the self, is the number one enemy of Kantianism.

~

The genius has left his magic circle; he has hardly been able to sustain Leonore's image of a poet who invites us to wander with him. Instead, we see before us an injured figure headed rather directly for shipwreck. In the same gesture through which she names him a cripple, the princess will announce a concept of wholesomeness which appears to deviate from and repress the exigencies of *Bildung* that she however has introduced: 'Let us not forget that a man cannot be separated from himself [*Daß von sich der Mensch nicht scheiden kann*].' Why should they not forget what must be remembered, what must be dismembered, namely the man who is already separated from himself as that which he is not yet: the *Jüngling* Tasso. The seat of power acknowledges and admits to his speech the image of an injured, distorted figure; yet he asserts:

> Besser wär's
> Wenn wir ihn heilen könnten, lieber gleich
> Auf treuen Rat des Arztes eine Kur
> Versuchten, dann mit dem Geheilten froh
> Den neuen Weg des frischen Lebens gingen.
> (ll. 328–32)

[Better it were to remedy his pain,
With the physician's aid attempt a cure,
Then with our healed and renovated friend
A new career (way) of life with joy pursue. (96)]

The image of the poet toward which the women strive in the beginning of the drama has undergone considerable mutations. The poet who was called a man in the first scene now requires a master, an educator, and a doctor. Toward the end of scene 2, the three characters have ceased speaking of Tasso's poetry. They have isolated the poet from his poetry, the empirical from the aesthetic figure, the natural from the all-too-human, and have settled by common consent on the cripple. The princess's metaphor for the damaged poet is not an innocent one, for as Leonore had suggested earlier, writing is closely associated in this drama – perhaps in all dramas since Oedipus – with the act of *going*, and with the very possibility of walking [*er schrieb und ging und schrieb*]; it is not, on the other hand, circumscribed, defined, or sustained by any easily discernible path or *methodos* and *Weg*. Whether conceived as a stagger or as plodding, writing is a kind of movement that skirts the path, creating its own track and traces that have been hunted down (as has been shown by Goethe, Kant, Hegel and recently, in a different tone, by Derrida) like a criminal.

In the judicious spirit with which he has come to be identified, Goethe, that is, Alfons, recognizes the possibility of having wronged the poet: 'Doch hoff' ich, meine Lieben, daß ich nie / Die Schuld des rauhen Arztes auf mich lade' (ll. 333–34) ['And yet, dear friends, I hope that I may ne'er / The censure of the cruel physician incur' (96)]. Alfons's hope is to be a doctor of refinement, a doctor of philosophy perhaps, in any case a doctor who would conduct his practice without a loss, without incurring a debt or facing charges for wounding that very thing whose life he sustains. As Kant writes at the end of his essay on the illnesses of mind, doctors and philosophers share one and the same task; they both prescribe diets for minds – to which he curiously adds, 'without requesting payment.'

To my knowledge, doctors and philosophers do request payment, even as they administer the pharmakon. And in its madness something like *Torquato Tasso* has declined to take out an insurance policy that might reduce the burden of payment, and meets instead the infinite debt to which it owes its most rigorous struggle. This debt, which is named and discovered in the drama as the drama of aesthetic theory, has been prepared by the stages of its foreplay.

If Tasso has been taken to the court wherein philosophy, law, and medicine preside, we might remember that another drama's despair, on the night of its opening, finds expression in the hero's first utterance: 'Habe nun, ach! Philosophie, Juristerei und Medizin (und leider auch Theologie) durchaus studiert' (*Faust*, 'Nacht') [Alas, I have thoroughly studied philosophy, jurisprudence, and medicine, and, unfortunately, also theology].

# NAMELY, ECKERMANN

*Er könne nichts für mich thun, und der*
*Vater im Himmel würde schon für mich sorgen.*
*Damit leuchtete er mir die Treppe hinunter.*
*Bitte lache.*

*[He could do nothing for me, and our*
*Heavenly Father would surely look after me.*
*With these words, he lit* the way down *the stairs for me.*
*Please laugh.]*[1]

## GOING DOWN

There has always been, in the immunopathological activities of certain texts, a place for hygienic writing. Each thinking text, to the extent that it develops strategies of protection against outside interference or parasitism, is run by an immunological drive. Perhaps every text can be shown to be phantasmically producing antibodies against the autoimmune community it has established within itself (a within that is constantly leaking, running an exscription machine,[2] exposed precisely to a contaminating 'outside'). The immunological drive is as truly lodged in the Heideggerian corpus, which is always cracking down on impurities, as it is housed by the symptomatologist, Friedrich Nietzsche. Still, Heidegger and Nietzsche did not hire the same company to cordon off spaces of impurity, though both share a certain predilection for cleanliness, ever repelling sites of toxic invasion. This is why Nietzsche is constantly throwing up, and Heidegger inhales the pure air of forest paths.

Self-cleaning texts are made everywhere available. For instance, they are thematized in the works of Franz Kafka by implacable figures of cleaning women who are associated with tremendous hermeneutic insight. These agents of hygiene dwell in radical proximity to the residue for which they are responsible. They are the steadily invading contaminators against which the text tries to protect itself. Consider the three angels of dust: the woman, on the edge of writing, who sweeps aside Gregor Samsa's corpse; the cleaning woman who signs the suicidal rush of Georg Bendemann at the tail end of 'The Judgment'; *The Castle*'s landlady straightening out those who are the leftovers from another regime of being. The cleaning lady, who in Kafka poses a threat to narrative purity, also always runs the risk of being fired. When she's on her way out, she tends to wear a quill in her hat.

Whether it is a matter of the house of being or the prison house of language, people get paid for keeping it clean.

The cleanup job is something for which Nietzsche criticism, like the commentary surrounding many great figures, has made itself responsible. It is an economical way of domesticating a figure, particularly one who, like Nietzsche or even Goethe, also trails behind him a dirty story or the film of history. When submitted to the sanitation department of some institutions, these figures come out clean, like laundered money and safe text. They are made digestible by the huge garbage disposal systems which universities sometimes are. I personally have nothing against this. It just so happens that I, like Eckermann, work the night shift, when everyone has gone but an odor still lingers. It's not that God is dead, says Nietzsche, but his corpse has not been disposed of. Hence the odor. Don't get me wrong – show me no pity. I am neither fascinated nor particularly disgusted by the job. It rather depends on whom you work for. The cleanup crew tends to retain traces of filth; it is never itself clean. There's always a stain that hasn't been removed.

In any case, the cleanup crew tends to show up when the boss is gone or on the way out. We know everything about them, and empty their *litteraturé*. We don't resent them but form a couple with them. Not in any ideal or sentimental way, of course. Still, we create the bosses, and even their secretaries. They depend on us. We have thought and lived the Nietzschean saying, 'I am ugly created the beautiful.' Surprised? Philosophy is never where you expect to find it: since at least Hegel, it's been working the night shift, however.

No writer has been more alert to pollution systems circulating in texts than Nietzsche. As catalytic converter – how many times does he gasp for clean air! – Nietzsche is the place where the sanitation department cooperates with a logic of obsessional neurosis. He knows how to smell a rat in the most uptown areas of thought. And Nietzsche hangs out in these double spaces, drawing an *Übermensch* out of a leftover. As Heidegger has noted, the *Übermensch* can be thought of as a bridge, a transhuman, linking up over an abyss.

When Nietzsche names Goethe in the context of the transhuman, he stumbles and stammers, landing on 'Eckermann' – Goethe's leftover. The syncopated gulp separating what is indissociable, namely, the Goethe-Eckermann couple, opens a space for what Freud has called a dreckology. Eckermann is the immunocompetent guarantee of the Goethean corpus. Debased, forgotten, late on arrival, he corresponds to the essentially modern character of what Heidegger epochalizes as 'we latecomers.' As master slave, Eckermann, this link and leftover, offers exemplary access to one among the impressive number of *couples* that compelled Nietzsche's attention. Nietzsche's rapport with the couple – the alterity that is double or nothing – is indeed so striking as to render Nietzsche the thinker par excellence of the couple: Lou and Paul, Dionysus and Apollo, Ariadne and Dionysus, Dionysus and the Antichrist, Wagner and Nietzsche, and what he becomes when he is – I am my mother and my father, *Ich bin der und der*, and so forth. When it comes to the couple Goethe-Eckermann, Nietzsche switches on the transvaluating machine, going for the one over the other (the one *as* the other), reinstalling the gigantic but hidden cleaning apparatus of what we call Goethe.

### . . . AND OUT

I suppose, if it is not too late, I could speak to you about depression – about depressions and openings, that is; about the way down and about *dejection* (I shall ask you to consider dejection in its medical sense as well, where it means an evacuation of the bowels, or the matter evacuated – excrement). The topological displacements which depress the Nietzschean text – a text so peculiarly riddled with holes, cuts, and enigmatic openings – have been treated under various guises, and often in terms of what has been taken to be a *feminine* element. The opening, a certain figuration of outwardness, has been regarded as a deep, unfathomable inside, for instance a Medusian hole [*trou*] in Bernard Pautrat's reading of *Zarathustra* or, in Gilles Deleuze, as the depths and caverns, the 'pits' to which woman is assigned or of which she is a sign.[3] In his *Twilight*, Nietzsche himself – assuming it is still possible to say 'Nietzsche himself' – links such interpretations of woman's depth to the hopelessness of ever getting to the bottom of things. Perhaps, indeed, some gynecologist of morals would go down too far, would risk losing himself in the obscure atopy or groundlessness of his pursuit ('*Man hält das Weib für tief – warum? weil man nie bei ihm auf den Grund kommt* [One holds woman to be deep. Why? Because one never gets to the bottom of her]').

But let us withdraw the speculum of vaginocentric readings and remain close to another source of Nietzschean depression, for there are other apertures and openings in Nietzsche – and we should not too soon forget the nasal and anal cavities of the *Genealogy* which are indeed contracted or held closed [*zugehalten*], for we have had to stop inhaling degenerate life; thus, we pinch our noses to ward off the stench of our revolting productions [*Erzeugungen*] such as spittle, urine, and dung (2, §7) and at the same time we have stopped relieving ourselves [*entladen*]. Except for the artist, perhaps, who is in a sense the form of his own relief, or, in Nietzsche's words 'under certain circumstances the dung and manure from which [the artwork] grows.' We shall return to these circumstances. For now let us note simply that the words Nietzsche uses to designate decency, such as *anständig* and *aufrichtig*, point up to a posture of uprightness which Freud has explained precisely as a posture of maximum distance from the smells produced from our lower regions – in other words, the beginning of all morality.

Yet, even beyond his special nostrils and the ears that he commands to open, there are still other holes in Nietzsche; perhaps they have let too much blood and perhaps they are the silent wounds of too great a catastrophe. This at least is what Blanchot suggests when he compares Nietzsche to Goethe in a section entitled 'André Gide et Goethe' in *Faux Pas*. Goethe, he writes, has been unfaithful to shipwreck. He has proven himself guilty in the face of darkness; he knew catastrophe but elected to circumvent it. In short, Goethe willed everything *including* his rescue. Nietzsche, on the other hand, threw himself into catastrophe with the certitude 'qu'en se perdant il accomplissait son destin [in losing himself thereby he fulfilled his destiny].'[4] And though it may seem that in this respect Goethe owes one to Nietzsche, Blanchot reminds us of Nietzsche's love and admiration for Goethe, for his Apollonian force and his Dionysian dreams.

It may well be that Blanchot has named for us the law of Goethe's singularity, namely, that he has been rescued from the catastrophe which he, like Nietzsche, knew. And Nietzsche himself rescues Goethe from countless catastrophes, for example, in his poem entitled 'An Goethe' which begins:

| | |
|---|---|
| Das Unvergängliche | [The Everlasting |
| Ist nur dein Gleichnis! | Is but a mere semblance of you!] |

If Goethe could resist catastrophe and avoid being overturned [*katastrephein*], it is not because he foresaw it or read the chart of his descent. He foresaw it and he even dictated it, in a sense by telling the story of his life to himself, namely, to Eckermann.[5] Eckermann was the anonymous vessel who let his body be invaded by Goethe, and Eckermann knew that he was the rescue vessel for a hero [*Held*] whom he could not allow to sink, as he says in the preface to the third book of the *Conversations*.

No rescue mission was formed to save Nietzsche, nor did he necessarily will it. Yet one of the fissures or cracks, one of the openings that he names in the *Genealogy* occurs, as you know, when Nietzsche, giving definition to his ascetic priest, calls out in his text 'mehr Schmerz! mehr Schmerz!' When he dissolves this section, he does so by asserting Goethe's position with regard to the ascetic ideal: '*Goethe*, in case you hadn't known as much, was no ascetic priest,' writes Nietzsche. 'He – knew more.' Goethe – knew more. What more did Goethe know when he rent a hole into a passage naming the desire for more – dash – pain?

Goethe is out of the question; Nietzsche brings him into the picture to illustrate its outside, to place him, paradoxically, as its external reference. He is incorporated into the text of *ressentiment* to be expulsed, propelled outside the body of this concern; and as such, he is also the lifeline that brings Nietzsche to the other side of *ressentiment.* And we shall see how Goethe affirms the position of master precisely because he *knows* how to maintain pain in the element of its exteriority.

Thus, he is brought in to be expelled, dropped, excused from the conference of ascetic priests; he saves Nietzsche, if only momentarily, and thereby gains infinite credit for his name.[6] And if Nietzsche's credit line, if *Goethe,* comes to be the horizon against which we measure *ressentiment,* it is not a horizon whose limits are fixed within the boundaries of the German-speaking text. When Baudelaire offers some free advice to a young poet, he admonishes him to remain free of debt, upholding Goethe as the figure par excellence who can be imagined *only* in the role of creditor [*créancier*], never in debt or at fault.

But I was suggesting another typology of the fault, and it may be that Goethe has always been used to cover a debt or fault – a fissure – that he has been held up as a fetish or substitute for some thing that has been cut off, missing, disintegrated, and often used to cover or substitute for Germany itself – if we can still say 'Germany itself.'

But what about the position that Goethe occupies in Nietzsche's reading and elsewhere? We think we know that Nietzsche will never merge Goethe with the category of the *Unvermögen* which so often identifies the man, and certainly the woman, of *ressentiment.* This word means impotent as well as impecunious. I need not recall the position that impotence assumes in Nietzsche's corpus, nor Goethe's own delicate maneuvers around *unvermögend.* Nietzsche perhaps is most attentive to the way Goethe seems to keep a *Dis-tanz* from such a predicament. Thus, when Nietzsche names Goethe, he necessarily addresses the question of a declining age and the fiction of the writer as a stylized human being. In a note, he writes:

> *Goethe* is exemplary: the impetuous naturalism which gradually becomes severe dignity. As a stylized human being he reached a higher level than any other German ever did. Now one is so bigoted as to reproach him therefore and even to censure his becoming old. One should read Eckermann and ask oneself whether any human being in Germany ever got so far in noble form.

If Friedrich Schlegel had censured Goethe for becoming old, Nietzsche employs another strategy, one that shows Goethe, if not becoming old, passing into noble form. But to apprehend the form of that nobility and the stylization of the human being, one must look away from Goethe; in fact, 'one should read Eckermann.' And from *The Gay Science* we know what type of aesthetic surgery is required to attain such a high level of stylization: it is a 'great and rare art.' 'Here a large mass of second nature has been added; there a piece of original nature has been removed. . . . Here the ugly which could not be removed is hidden; there it has been reinterpreted and made sublime.' One should read Eckermann. And if one reads Eckermann, one will find that he stylizes or 'reinterprets' *Goethe* with a finely cut diamond.

In Nietzsche – and for Goethe – Eckermann is accorded a place, which is not really a *place*, between the writer and himself, at a moment when the signatory *Goethe* – the italicized Goethe – no longer coincided with: Goethe. Thus, Eckermann's first assignment in the summer of 1823 will be to determine which of the papers in Goethe's possession were actually written by the master; Goethe no longer knows, and asks Eckermann to find, identify, perhaps to invent his style. Eckermann will spend the entire summer identifying Goethe in order to return to him his findings at the beginning of the fall. Goethe is satisfied with the results and yet we shall never know who interpreted when Goethe decided that Eckermann interpreted his style and signature correctly.

By way of introduction – though it is getting rather late for that – we can say that Eckermann created the fiction of the self-composed, Olympian Goethe; in Blanchot's words, he witnessed the poet in his solitude. Of the *Gesamtbild* we may still carry of Goethe, Eckermann was credited with having handed down its principal elements. As for his own image, what can be said but that he was a shadow, a phantom, a writing hand attached to Goethe's voice. He wanted to make a name for himself. He was thirty years old in June 1823. It was getting late.

In the end, Eckermann's style would become indistinguishable from Goethe's; scholars would be – and still are – unable to determine whether he copied his notes from Goethe's diary or whether Goethe reconstituted his diary from Eckermann's notes. The history of the *Conversations,* a long one, is a history of incertitude which involves among other things constant questioning of proprietorial rights, joint ownership, the writing couple, the one and the other. Sometimes you will find the book under Goethe's name with the title *Conversations with Eckermann;* or you might find it listed under 'Eckermann' as *Conversations with Goethe.* While some call it Goethe's last work, or his spoken text, others call Eckermann himself Goethe's last work – and not necessarily his best at that. Indeed, it would seem that Goethe had a hand in organizing and producing this fragile part of himself that was to be sacrificed to the fiction of *Goethe.* Goethe arranged his survival as fiction and as life, as the fiction of life

[*Dichtung der Wahrheit*] that only the romantics dared attack and decline. It is hardly fortuitous if Goethe kept Eckermann at his side, forbidding the instinctive wanderer from straying too far up the Rhine. Eckermann was to be shielded from the romantic illness, but more importantly he was to shield Goethe from this impertinent, rebellious generation or degeneration of writers. Eckermann became in a sense the deflecting object, the *conduit* as Nietzsche would say, that attracted the *ressentiment* of a whole generation. His lot, of course, will eventually come to resemble the one reserved for widows, those creatures left behind with a body of works, who become the petty functionaries of its future institution. Eckermann, always to a certain extent Goethe's widow, his void, will be severely punished for the profit he made and for the proprietary rights he exercised over Goethe's works. The punishment begins almost immediately. Heine mocked Eckermann as did countless others. And even in the twentieth century, if one deigns to mention Eckermann, this embarrassing leftover, it is mainly to exercise one's venomous spleen. Freidenthal and other Germans have discovered Eckermann to be beady-eyed, his nose is/was too long, at any rate he is servile and he is ugly. [He is a half, but he succeeded in creating a whole work which belongs to Goethe's oeuvre.] In addition or rather in subtraction, 'Er ist ein Halber, aber er hat ein ganzes, rundes Werk geschaffen, das zu Goethes Oeuvre gehört.'[7] This type of mutilation to which Eckermann is subject has been largely dictated, I believe, by Goethe, and perhaps it was only a sly and terribly ironic Nietzsche who could overturn these nearly universal judgments, though Nietzsche himself – I say this in passing – would suffer the indignities of a ferocious widow and philosophical executor: Elisabeth – F. N. – Förster-Nietzsche.

Now, Eckermann arrived to take over – to execute Goethe's oeuvre and life; it will be *his* desire and command that Goethe complete *Dichtung und Wahrheit* – complete his autobiography, his life. And Goethe will do the same by doing the opposite for Eckermann, that is, he will not let him complete his life or oeuvre; he will finish Eckermann, for Goethe considers himself a kind of finishing school for the young writer, who until the age of fourteen was wholly illiterate. Goethe will make Eckermann indissociable from himself; he will lend him his name and his style, which Eckermann will then bend into our readings and misreadings of a beautiful Goethe. So many works of scholarship presumably occupied with Goethe will import this somewhat foreign body, this Eckermann, to lend a certain buoyancy to their claims; they will say that 'Goethe said . . .' but append Eckermann's name to what Goethe is said to have said. Nietzsche – knew better; he knew about fortifications against pain and about that which is left behind.

Thus wrote Nietzsche in *Human, All-too-Human:*

> Wenn man von Goethes Schriften absieht und namentlich von Goethes Unterhaltungen mit Eckermann, dem besten deutschen Buch, das es gibt: Was bleibt eigentlich von der deutschen Prosaliteratur übrig, das verdiente, wieder und wieder gelesen zu werden?
>
> [The treasury of German prose, apart from Goethe's writings, namely, the conversations with Eckermann – the best German book there is – what is there really of German literature that it would be worthwhile to read over and over again.]

About whom or what does Nietzsche write when he writes that he is writing about Goethe's writing – the best German book? Goethe, by the way, is no longer italicized. What remains, what deserves the eternal return of the reader is, according to Nietzsche, neither entirely Goethe nor Eckermann, but the name of Goethe's supreme writing: namely, Eckermann. And it is indeed with Goethe's remains – with what remains of Goethe's signature – that Eckermann will write the remainder of his life.

Eckermann warns in this best of German books that if the *Conversations* are not added to one's reading, 'one will not be able entirely to have the authentic Goethe [*den eigentlichen Goethe nicht vollständig haben, wenn er nicht auch diese* Gespräche *hinzufügt*].'[8] The *Conversations,* then, will give you the authentic Goethe. (Eckermann will have beautiful nightmares, by the way, about having produced a more authentic Goethe than Goethe himself produced in his works.) They are at once an addition or supplement to Goethe's corpus while they also guarantee its totality. Yet, as totality, they in fact revert to the function of a half. The authenticating supplement, the authenticating signature: at one point the couple disagrees on which of them will authenticate, underwrite the other. In any case Eckermann wished his book to be published wearing the same jacket as Goethe's collected works (*Ausgabe letzter Hand*), and to serve in the terms spelled out by his contract as introduction and supplement – as the appendage and the ground. As if Eckermann had to make Goethe presentable to us. If Eckermann is capable of giving away the authentic Goethe it is, according to most receivers of this extraordinary gift, because the gift – the *Conversations* – is itself in the first place Goethe's property.

In the introduction to his work, Eckermann seems largely to concur with this assumption; in fact, he promotes it himself. Yet he also writes at one point: 'Übrigens erkenne ich dasjenige, was in diesen Bänden gelungen ist, zu meinem Eigentum zu machen, was ich gewissermaßen als den Schmuck meines Lebens zu betrachten habe [In addition, I recognize how to make into my own that which was successful in these works – that which in a certain sense I can regard as the jewel of my life].'[9] The rights of ownership, it would seem, would not go to Goethe, for the writer recognizes or knows how to make the successful part of this work his own property, what is proper to himself [*Eigentum*] – what is successful, namely, is Eckermann. This is where a momentary reversal takes place; Eckermann is not the supplement or addition to Goethe and his life, but Goethe, who remains unnamed at this point, is the addition, the decoration or the parergon to Eckermann – the jewel of my life. This is not to say that Goethe relinquishes his position before the beginning of the *Conversations* proper; it is momentarily displaced and in a certain sense reversed. Eckermann will carve a subtle argument into these reversals when, in the introduction, he turns the adornment of his life into a hard-stoned diamond. The facet whose emanations Eckermann will capture authorizes him to claim: 'dies ist *mein* Goethe.'

Eckermann's strategy here is, at bottom, to safeguard Goethe. The pathos of rescue with which Eckermann approached Goethe from the very beginning always should be kept in mind. In the first place, in announcing 'this is *my* Goethe,' he is immunizing his enterprise against any possible contestation that might be brought to bear upon this text. In asserting a part of Goethe that is wholly his own, namely Eckermann's, he makes this work invulnerable to attack. Of course, if this were a critical work about Goethe's oeuvre – a mere interpretation – Eckermann would have to assume full responsibility for his writing; but here he establishes the status of the text as testimony and, as such, the only criteria for truth must be derived from the purely subjective effect that Goethe produced on Eckermann. At the same time, Eckermann is giving back to Goethe what is his own. For the only truth of Goethe, of this diamond, can be the different perceptions that one receives from it. The diamantine cut of this text guarantees the reception of the testimony while also saving Goethe from a scientific operation. As the object of testimony, Goethe will remain mysterious, elusive, and safe from any attempt to pin him down. In this respect, Eckermann returns *everything* to Goethe. Everything I say, he says in effect, is not equal to the grandeur and multiplicity of the phenomenon, Goethe. However, the same holds for anything anyone else might say or write about Goethe, for anyone else would be perceiving another, singular facet. As an assembly of multiple facets, Goethe will never be, strictly speaking, identifiable with what one can say about him. In fact and as facet, 'this is *my* Goethe.' Eckermann's project is a delicate one. If this is *his* Goethe we cannot properly have any access to him; if, then, Goethe is unknowable as a total object of any discourse, then Eckermann is also, at the very beginning, disclaiming any possibility for representing the true Goethe. Yet, in saying 'this is my Goethe, this facet of Goethe is the reflection that I perceive,' he is claiming to disclose precisely this facet of Goethe which is the only image or manifestation of Goethe to which one can ever hope to accede. Eckermann knows this much: his project is an impossible one, his text and testimony are impossible – and yet they are true. Goethe, Eckermann in effect says, will never be identifiable with what I am about to say. This text is Goethe, but it never attains him. And Goethe is also the signatory of this text, for this is the only way he showed himself to me, Eckermann. But because this is the way Goethe showed himself, I, Eckermann, have to sign myself.

This structure guarantees the text as Eckermann's property, insofar as it is an instance of subjective testimony. In this respect it is unique; nothing else can be substituted for this testimony – it is irreplaceable. As such, we have to assume its truth; however, to assume that it is true, we have to attribute it – to Goethe. As exclusive receiver, Eckermann *is* the owner of the speech. A diamond only shows itself in this way; it is therefore the truth of the diamond. The logic of the argument runs something like this: the subjective effect that Goethe had on me was multiple appearance; therefore, I tell the truth (if the object shows itself only as appearance, then that very appearance must be the truth of the object). However, Goethe is the divine source about which only one thing can be said, although none of this is really correct; therefore, everything is only approximation. By thus divinizing his text, Eckermann renders it superior to any criticism or refinement. My text is better than it is, my signature is even more illustrious: it is *my* Goethe. *I* have written the best German book. As signatory of the *Conversations,* Eckermann is the center without a place, face or facet in this text. Goethe, on the other hand, is pure facet that can be neither centered nor touched.

If Eckermann's strategy has been one of safeguarding Goethe, of keeping him in a certain sense untouchable, secret, and at an eternal distance, it is because Eckermann is the caretaker of someone who is vanishing, and who has been vanishing for a long time. Unfortunately, I shall not be able to trace at length this structure of parasitical inclusion along the lines of a cryptonomy here. But briefly, I believe it is possible to demonstrate that Goethe by no means provides an original instance of corporeal invasion for Eckermann – and that Eckermann had already found a home for someone else's suffering within him. Some other figure is agonizing in Eckermann; he is a foster parent to an alien body which has been deposited within him – and all this is thrown up in a sense toward the end of the *Conversations,* when Eckermann teaches Goethe about birds (says he), instructing him that certain of these have been known to swallow their adoptive parents [*Pflegeeltern*]. Goethe, the adoptive parent, opens his ears as they enter a precarious discussion about molting, losing one's plumage – or excreting – in order to sustain *Gesang.* The phantom agitating in Eckermann and who demands that his host continually feed him – this phantom who has long before Goethe taken up residence in his body, will have to be confronted elsewhere, however.

Now, if Eckermann's predatory habits seem finally to correspond to Goethe's desire, it is because Goethe had spontaneously proposed himself as Eckermann's host. In fact, Goethe gives his body to Eckermann so that he can constitute it as a body. Eckermann's task, as Goethe defines it, will be to transform the fragments and remains – the bits and pieces of Goethe's writings – some of which date from the 1770s, into the body of Goethe's works. Thus if their relationship may appear at first sight to be grounded in dissymmetry – and it certainly is – this does not preclude the relationship's being always in a certain sense reversible, however. For Goethe preys on Eckermann in order to nourish his body, which, henceforth, will never be entirely his own. In fact, Eckermann underscores this aspect and the secret reversibility of their relationship when he feeds Goethe back his own lines from a work whose completion is, according to its author, due to Eckermann. The subject in question on 16 December 1829 is Homunkulus, that mysterious figure capable of reading the mind and dreams of Faust when he lies unconscious. 'Sie empfinden das Verhältnis sehr richtig, sagte Goethe ['You perceive the relation very correctly,' said Goethe],' whereupon Eckermann quotes to him the text referring to the relationship of their relationship:

> Am Ende hängen wir doch ab [In the end we are dependent upon
> Von Kreaturen die wir machten. The creatures we have made.]

This is an example of Eckermann making Goethe swallow Goethe in order to digest Eckermann; in the final analysis, in the end, we do indeed depend upon the creatures that we have created. We hang from them, like limbs. If Goethe created Eckermann at the end of his life, it was because this end also depended upon him. In the *Conversations* these lines revert to Eckermann; they are presented as his lines which he picks from Goethe's body, citing from Goethe's masterpiece in order to establish his mastery over their relationship: 'Sie empfinden das Verhältnis sehr richtig, sagte Goethe.' Thus inciting Goethe to authorize the legitimacy of his claims and the correctness of his interpretation of Goethe, Eckermann likewise affirms the proper functioning of his assimilative or digestive systems.

Eckermann has long been assimilating Goethe's body to his own, and his position has always been one of hanging on to the Goethean body, be it in the prehistory of their intimacy, at the time he wrote *On Poetry with a Particular Reference to Goethe,* be it as the *Kompendium* to Goethe's *Farbenlehre,* be it as that member of Goethe's familial branch who as early as 19 June 1823 can assert that Goethe 'mich zu den Senigen zählt und mich als solchen will gehalten haben [counts me among his own and wants to keep me that way]' – or be it in the form of the *Conversations* which was first appended to Goethe's collected works. Eckermann himself hangs onto Goethe's body of which he constitutes an appendage, limb or member [*Glied*] which is however best viewed as a type of prosthetic device that, all Goethe scholars agree, can be dislocated from the joint legacy. Perhaps we shall have to amend this notion of Eckermann as *Glied* in a moment, as the movement of our narrative carries us to another body.

But to remain within the precinct of this body – of the detachable, attachable parts and reversibility – let me just say that neither a notion of mutual perforation nor one promoting corporeal exchange was ever directly addressed in the recorded exchanges between Goethe and Eckermann. However, in the third volume of his conversations with Goethe, Eckermann inserts an account of a dream he had narrated to Goethe. He had dreamt his dream the night preceding 12 March 1828. 'I saw myself namely,' Eckermann begins, 'in an unknown region among strangers, but I was altogether in a good mood' (this is a dream, needless to say). 'At lunch time we consumed our meal' and then, while walking about they saw a coastline spread before them at a distance. 'There's only one thing to be done,' said the one to the other: 'we must undress and swim over there.' 'You can say that easily enough,' I [Eckermann] said; 'you happen to be young and beautiful and beyond that, you're good swimmers. I however swim badly and, anyway, I don't have the kind of figure [*ansehliche Gestalt*, 'eminent or distinguished figure'] that would allow me to appear on shore in front of strangers with any pleasure or ease.' 'You're a fool', said one of the most beautiful. 'Just get undressed and give me your form [*Gestalt*] and you can have mine in the meantime.' . . . With these words I quickly undressed, leaped into the water and immediately felt, in the other's body [*Körper*] that I was a powerful swimmer. I had soon reached the coast and, naked and dripping, I stepped among the people with the most cheerful confidence – I was happy in the feeling of these beautiful limbs [*dieser schönen Glieder*], my behavior was unforced, and I was immediately at home with the strangers at table.' The others eventually reach the shore to join them and the only one missing turns out to be the young man 'with my form in whose limbs I felt so well.' Finally he approaches the shore, 'and I was asked if I wouldn't care to see my former self [*mein früheres Ich*]. At these words a certain uneasiness [*Unbehagen*] overcame me, because I felt no great joy about myself [*keine große Freude an mir selber*], in part because I feared that my friend would immediately ask me back for his own body. Nonetheless, I turned toward the water and saw my second half swimming not far in our direction and, turning his head sideways, he looked up at me laughing:

'There's no buoyancy [*Schwimmkraft*] in your limbs!' he called to me. 'I've really had to fight the waves and breakers, and it's no wonder that I'm arriving so late and am last of all.' I immediately recognized the face: it was mine, rejuvenated and somewhat fuller and wider, and freshly colored. Now he stepped onto the shore and when, setting himself upright, he took the first steps, I had a general view of his back and his thigh [*Schenkel,* also 'hinged leg, limb'] and was pleased about the perfection [*Vollkommenheit*] of this form. . . . How is it possible, I thought to myself, that your small body grew up so beautifully! – Did the primal forces of the sea have such a wondrous effect on it or is it because the youthful spirit of the friend permeated or penetrated our members [*die Glieder durchdrungen*]? I quietly wondered why the friend didn't act as if he wanted to exchange his body once more. Actually, I thought, he looks so stately and, at bottom, it could be all the same to him; it is not all the same to me, however, for I am not sure whether I could be pieced back together in that body or whether I would shrink to my former size. – In order to arrive at some certitude about the matter, I took my friend aside and asked him how he felt in my limbs [or 'member,' *Glied*]. 'Just fine!' he said 'I have the same sense of my being and strength [*Kraft*] as before. I don't know what you have against your limbs! As far as I'm concerned, they are perfectly all right, and you see that one only has to make something of oneself. Stay in my body as long as you please, for I am completely content to abide in yours for all eternity [*für alle Zukunft*].' I was very happy about this statement, and insofar as I, too, felt completely as before in all my sensations, thoughts, and memories, there came to me in the dream the impression of a complete independence of our souls and the possibility of a future existence in another body.'

And the possibility of an existence in another body. The other body to whom the contents of this dream have been confided responds with the characteristic ambivalence that he seems to reserve for Eckermann's more delicate revelations. 'The muses are particularly favorable to you at night,' Goethe comments 'for you will surely admit that in your waking hours it would be difficult for you to come up with something so peculiar [*Eigentümliches,* also 'proper to yourself'] and pretty.' 'I hardly understand how I arrived at that,' Eckermann replies, 'for in the past days I have been feeling greatly depressed, which would make the idea of so new a life seem rather remote.' Although I cannot propose an analysis of the dream at this time, I shall ask you to retain only this: to make something of oneself means to enter the other body, possibly an institutional body – and we shall examine the consequences of this phantasmic entry in a moment. For at bottom, there is always a way out.

Eckermann himself, however, gives us a clue to where a primary dream source might be found. He supposes it to have arisen somewhere in the conversations of the previous evening. We might take a brief glimpse at that exchange to see how it might have left its imprint in Eckermann's dream. That conversation – of 11 March 1828 – engaged Goethe in a reflection on genius for which, Eckermann notes, Goethe has exchanged the term 'productivity.' 'Every divine illumination in which the extraordinary arises [*das Außerordentliche*] will always be bound up with youth and productivity.' What determines productivity will not be a quantitative mass of creations but their *life* and *endurance* [*Leben und Dauer*]. There was a pause after Goethe linked productivity to life: then, Goldsmith, for instance, can be considered a productive poet precisely because the little he produced was capable of sustaining its indwelling life [*ein inwohnendes Leben hat, das sich zu erhalten weiss*]. This gave rise to a pause [*Es entstand eine Pause*] during which Goethe continued to pace up and down the room. Eckermann interrupts the pause by asking whether genial productivity resides only in the spirit of an important person or whether it might also be lodged in the body [*oder liegt sie auch im Körper?*]. 'At least,' Goethe replied, 'the body has a great influence over it. – There was however a time in Germany when one thought of a genius as being small, weak, and even hunchbacked; however, I praise the genius who has the appropriate body.' One can well imagine how this part of the exchange between Eckermann and Goethe might have been translated into the dream had that night by 'le petit Docteur Eckermann' (as he was known). The pause itself should give pause, as it introduces a dead moment into the question of life. Genius has something to do with youthfulness – this, by the way, is the same conversation in which Goethe makes his notorious assertion associating genius with repeatable puberty [*wiederholte Pubertät*].

Eckermann, the questioner, the listener, the writer of genius – though that genius may not be proper to him or embodied in his appearance – is now old by comparison to Goethe; he is doubled over Goethe, hunchbacked, writing this down, depressed. He may not know how to sustain life – his own life – he may lack the necessary buoyancy. He was perhaps never young. He was a latecomer (he was even born belatedly as the last son of a second marriage, he was born to elderly parents – Goethe gets him on this, too). And Goethe cannot resist talking to Eckermann about the physical constitution [*körperliche Konstitution*] of a writer who might not be solid or well – one who, on the contrary, would be subject to dejection. The productions of such a writer, he presumes, must frequently come to a standstill [*häufig stocken*]; this type of writer is depressed and suffers blockage. Goethe has advice for him: 'My advice, therefore, is to force nothing.' Eckermann's dream that night in one sense enforced this admonition, but in the other body: 'I felt very fortunate in these beautiful limbs,' he dreams, 'my behavior – I – was not forced.' As one of Goethe's beautiful members, I do not force my writing. I am young and healthy. Elsewhere, Eckermann has told us that swimming and writing amount to the same activity. Nietzsche will advance a similar hypothesis, notably when he writes that the decision to start writing is like leaping into a cold lake.[10]

If Eckermann adjoined himself to the Goethean body, in fact, if he dreams of the possibility of an existence in another body – and he tells Goethe that this *is* his dream – then he forever runs the risk of being removed or excreted from the other body, that is, of being subject to a peculiar form of survival to which the name of Eckermann always returns us – what the German language would designate as *fort* rather than *überleben.* Eckermann's so-called survival after 1832 can be grasped neither in terms of life or death, strictly speaking, but rather as another delay – his final delay, in fact, for Eckermann was even a latecomer to his own death. When George Eliot writes of her visit with Eckermann in the forties, she astutely notes that she had seen him before his '*total* death.' Perhaps this partial and incalculable death, this delay that supplants survival as such, needs to be called by its name: namely, excrement – as that which continues to grow after a body, according to biological determination, ceases to live. The first meaning that excrement takes is that of any appendage or outgrowth on the body, such as hair, nails, feathers, and so on; it is related to the Latin *excrescere,* to grow out, to rise. Goethe himself seems to have intuited immediately Eckermann's place in terms of supplementary growth. His several letters and diary entries from as early as 10 June 1823 refer to Eckermann as something that has 'trained itself on me [*sich an mir herangebildet*].' Nor should the history of Eckermann's own complicated attachment to hair and feathers be left entirely out of the picture. When he first encounters Goethe, he must burn his hair to accommodate the style that was agreeable to Goethe; his last temptation and wish will be to cut a lock of hair from Goethe's corpse. Any consideration of Eckermann's relationship to his not quite so proper name (namely, excrement) would have to take into account as well his pathological preoccupation with feathers, and particularly the fact that after Goethe's death he lived in a cramped room with forty odd birds (including birds of prey) whose droppings would fall on his papers: all this belongs to the issue of excrement.

But the other meaning, more familiar to us, need not be excluded and also has something to do with a type of survival, as an early and largely unpublished poem of Goethe's tells us.

The poem in question not only thematizes scatological survival, but is itself carried along by such a movement. This is *Werther*'s void, entitled 'The Joys of Young Werther.' We have stopped suffering:

| *Freuden des jungen Werthers* | *The Joys of Young Werther* |
|---|---|
| Ein junger Mensch, ich weiss nicht wie, | A young man, I don't know quite how, |
| Starb einst an der Hypochondrie | Once died of hypochondria |
| Und ward denn auch begraben. | And was therefore also buried. |
| Da kam ein schöner Geist herbei, | Then a beautiful spirit came by. |
| Der hatte seinen Stuhlgang frei, | He had to relieve himself |
| Wie's denn so Leute haben. | As one must after all do. |
| Der setzt' notdürftig sich aufs Grab | He went to his necessity upon the grave |
| Und legte da sein Häuflein ab, | And deposited there his load, |
| beschaute freundlich seinen Dreck, | Observing amicably his dirt |
| Ging wohl eratmet wieder weg | And went thence with a sigh of relief, breathing |
| Und sprach zu sich bedächtlich: | And spoke to himself, reflecting: |
| 'Der gute Mensch, wie hat er sich verdorben! | 'The good man, oh, how has he ruined himself! |
| Hätt er geschissen so wie ich, | Had he shat like I did |
| Er wäre nicht gestorben!' | He would not have died!' |

Excrement is that which allows the *Geist,* which strictly speaking belongs neither to the living nor the dead, to survive – or, at least, to sustain its peculiar stirrings. As *Dreck,* this dejection is *not* ugly, hideous or repulsive in any way; on the contrary, the 'beautiful' *Geist* – thus, one aesthetically valorized – looks upon his droppings in a friendly manner, without averting his gaze, to leave relieved, breathing, living on. This is not to say that we are interested solely in constructing an image of *Dreckermann* per se, but rather in showing, among other things, the place that Goethe had made for excrement as something that follows upon a work, in this case, as something following the sorrowful self-elimination thematized in Werther. The choice presented in this poem is precisely one between self-elimination and elimination, of doing oneself in or relieving oneself outwardly.

Perhaps it is not even necessary to dramatize the conditions of Eckermann's 'life' after Goethe's biological death, to suppose that he belongs at once to the class of the young hypochondriac who no longer lives, while he is also the delayed *Erzeugung,* as Nietzsche would say, of Goethe's *Geist* – and thus a sign of his maker's survival. This would be just one of the ways Goethe left Eckermann behind.

Excrement, then, is the name which Goethe leaves to the company of a work – work understood as corpse – as its guardian and as the mark of its death, marking the end of a process but also the beginning of another one, one that begins with the droppings on the grave, if we consider that this substance has fertilizing properties as well. But what is to be fertilized here is, above all, that layer of ground covering the buried opus; it is precisely the ground under the legacy, from which the posterity and the legend of the work will spring. And since the question of *Geist* or *genius* has already solicited a certain notion of productivity in relation to the body, we might remember, too, that the production of excrement presupposes the proper and healthy functioning of all sorts of assimilative systems; this process not only holds for the making of a work, but also for the type of *Bil-dung* in which Eckermann and Goethe seem to be engaged. This brings us back to the large question, which is never held at a distance from what Eckermann writes or Goethe says, of the relationship between property or (self-)possession [*Eigentum*] and the extraneous or foreign [*das Fremde*], which pertains to excrement in both the senses we have developed: first as something growing out from the body and from which it is most easily detached, belonging thus to that body and removable from it to become foreign matter, and in the second sense, as the end-station or destiny of what has been taken into the body to be discharged, secreted, or excreted.

It would not be difficult to demonstrate that Goethe swallowed Eckermann whole in order to assure the afterlife of the work which for him was already buried. In fact, those critics who designate Eckermann as Goethe's last work would no doubt agree with our excretory interpretation of work. Eckermann must grow out of Goethe's work which he must assimilate after Goethe has assimilated him to his systems. He is to fertilize the work whose condition of survival he is; he will permit Goethe's *Geist* to move freely from the graveyard of his productions. As Goethe's outgrowth or delayed death, as his charge and discharge, Eckermann relieves Goethe of the responsibility towards those works he had more or less completed, though he felt they were not ready to be published as part of his complete works. We can think here of Nietzsche's notion of ennobled irresponsibility which, in this case, permits Goethe's spirit to move on to other projects, such as *Faust II,* to take one example.

If Eckermann's task and 'dirty work' is to secure Goethe's posterity, to remain behind with the work, at its graveside, this does not mean, however, that Eckermann will not stir to rebel against his lot. As an outgrowth of Goethe, as his follower and pupil, Eckermann will not always be something upon which Goethe can cast a friendly glance. This becomes especially clear in the case of the *Farbenlehre* [*Theory of Color*], a work which initially left Eckermann baffled. Let me interrupt this argument for a moment to remind you that Nietzsche preferred the *Conversations* to *Faust* and to *Dichtung und Wahrheit.* In a note, he wrote with unbaffled certitude that 'Goethe, in his Color Theory, was wrong' (1876 or 1877). I am led to suspect that Nietzsche took particular pleasure in reading this section of the *Conversations,* and not only in order to oppose Schopenhauer, who sided with Goethe. Nietzsche, needless to say, takes the part of Eckermann.

Now before asking him to write the compendium, Goethe organizes another property transaction when he directs Eckermann to appropriate the theory [*Lehre*] as his own [*zu eigen machen*], promising that what he passes on to him will begin to live in Eckermann's care. Goethe predicts that 'this science will soon be your property [*Eigentum*].' He leaves Eckermann in possession of this work, but something begins to take root which Goethe did not exactly foresee; namely, 'an unsuspected difference' arises [*und so gerieten wir in eine unvermutete Differenz*] which, given the gravity of the matter, Eckermann feels obliged to impart.

The question that interests me here is not so much who is right in the course of this development, but rather Eckermann's need to assert precisely the *Differenz* between his own careful [*sorgfältig*], superior insight and Goethe's observations. As we go over some of the elements of this difference, we should not forget that the subject at hand is a *Lehre,* that is, the stakes here involve not only Goethe's teaching of color but his status as teacher, as master of *Bildung,* which Eckermann, however, continues to affirms. In this light – in the light of the one submitted to *Bildung* – it is noteworthy that Eckermann's privileged instrument of verification most often is *Kerzenlicht,* a funereal beam that he casts over Goethe's corpus. Indeed, given everything that science meant to Goethe and his passionate crusade against Newton, this is not a matter of indifferent *Differenz.*

The problems first arise when Eckermann takes a look at the *Farbenlehre* in order to test whether he would be at all capable of meeting Goethe's 'friendly request' [*Aufforderung,* 'challenge, demand']. While considering the phenomenon of blue shadowing in an empirical light, however, he comes to realize 'with some surprise' that Goethe's argument is 'based on error.' He describes how he arrived at this conclusion, making his case increasingly solid: 'in order to be absolutely sure . . . and now there was no further doubt,' and so on. 'The color was there, outside of me, independently, and my subject(ivity) had no influence upon it.' Goethe had classified this phenomenon as a subjective manifestation, and it is perhaps not exactly fortuitous that Eckermann will seek to diminish subjective power in Goethe's theory at the same time as he tries to affirm his own subject. It is equally important that in the act of refuting Goethe, of risking parricidal writing, he can fathom an 'outside.'

In the days that follow, Eckermann finds the opportunity to confirm the truth of his hypothesis, for example, 'in this case, according to Goethe's teachings, the freshest blue tonality was supposed to emerge. It did not however emerge.' After several more days of experimentation, Eckermann establishes that 'Nature could not confirm' Goethe's argument 'as true'; the corresponding paragraphs thus 'urgently required revision.' Eckermann does not stop at this: 'I encountered something similar with colorful double-shadowing' which, after anxious observation, he was compelled to dismiss. However, this time, he does not limit himself to his experiments, but calls upon Shakespeare to bear witness. Although reference to *Romeo and Juliet* may not seem scientifically compelling, Eckermann probably could not have taken a more deadly aim at Goethe. If Shakespeare's couple meets a tragic conclusion, the one inscribed in this book now faces doom as well. For Shakespeare is the only name to which Goethe, in the *Conversations* and elsewhere, ascribes powers of mutilation. Eckermann could have found no higher tribunal to sit in judgment of Goethe: Goethe claims he had been forced to rid himself of Shakespeare – to get him off his body [*vom Hals schaffen*] – in order to be able to write at all. Eckermann knew this only too well; as early as 5 January 1826, he had scribbled on one of his papers that 'Shakespeare alles andere verleidet.' There may be no end to Shakespeare, as Goethe's essay on that subject argues, but his would be the name of Goethe's end. Eckermann's strategy of including Shakespeare in a demonstration that, with the exception of this reference, remains purely empirical, belongs to the logic of his crime, to his assertion of an outside, the possibility of independence and the doubt he casts on the 'double shadow'. After rallying Shakespeare, Eckermann observes:

> Das Resultat meiner Beobachtungen ging demnach dahin, daß auch Goethes Lehre von den farbigen Doppelschatten nicht durchaus richtig sei, daß bei diesem Phänomen mehr Objektives einwirke, als von ihm beobachtet worden, und daß das Gesetz der subjektiven Forderung dabei nur als etwas Sekundäres in Betracht komme.
>
> [The result of my observations therefore indicated that Goethe's doctrine of chromatic double-shadowing was not exactly correct, that these phenomena involved something more objective than had been observed by him, and that thereby the law of subjective experimentation only came into play as something secondary.]

Eckermann is dealing in law, in Goethe's law of subjective experimentation which he will allow only a secondary position: doubles, shadows, secondariness – this all sounds desperately familiar.

Goethe disregarded too many things; given his fixation on what has once been recognized as law [*am einmal erkannten Gesetzlichen*] and his way of presupposing his law/the law even in such cases where it appears to be concealed, he could very easily be misled [*verführt*, 'seduced'] into making large syntheses and perceiving a law of which he had grown fond [*ein liebgewonnenes Gesetz*], even in a place where an entirely different law was operative.

Therefore, 'when Goethe mentioned his *Farbenlehre* today and asked me what was happening with the Compendium we had discussed, I would have gladly concealed the points developed above, for I was unsure (embarrassed) about how I was supposed to tell him the truth without hurting [*verletzen*, 'wounding'] him.' Eckermann was embarrassed about telling Goethe the truth – a truth which he however freely imparts to his readers. And this truth cannot be told without inflicting a wound on Goethe, one whose proportions Eckermann will disclose only at the end of this entry.

He does tell Goethe, for he had no other choice, he writes, that after careful observation, he finds himself in the position [*Fall*] of having to deviate [*abweichen*] from Goethe. Goethe, it appears, begins to gain in stature in Eckermann's rendering of the scene, for 'it is not given to me to develop a subject of great length in oral conversation [*im mündlichen Gespräch*] with any clarity . . . I would do that later, in writing.' Later, in writing. 'However, I had hardly begun to speak when Goethe's lofty and cheerful nature grew clouded [*verfinsterte*] and I saw only too clearly that he did not appreciate my objections.' Eckermann saw too clearly; he saw too clearly in his experiments with light and shadow, and he sees too clearly when Goethe's brilliance is clouded over, darkened. As you see, the experiment is now being carried over to Goethe; and if Goethe appears too obscure in his writing, and Eckermann can so easily give umbrage, it is also because 'conversation' is at stake. Having asserted his inferiority in oral conversation [*mündlichen Gespräch*], Eckermann will now shift the sense of the mark to announce the possibility of triumph: 'it can happen, however, that the mature [*Mündige*] are overprecipitous whereas the immature [*Unmündige*] find it.' Goethe flushes and returns with mockery: 'As if you had found it! With your conception of colorful light, you belong in the fourteenth century.' Goethe makes Eckermann's immaturity a question of age, of the dark ages, injuring him with his charges of obscurity. But 'the only thing which is good about you, is that at least you are honest enough to come out with what you are thinking.' That would be the only thing good about Eckermann.

The stakes are high, and Goethe does not refrain from naming them. Eckermann's deviation in his veneration for Goethe already has a place in intellectual history: 'I feel that what's happening with my *Farbenlehre* is exactly what happened to Christianity. One believes for a while to have faithful pupils and before one turns around they deviate and form a sect.' Eckermann is indeed about to take the form of a sect, to be cut off from Goethe's body, to be ex-communicated. '"You are a heretic just like the others, for you are not the first to have deviated from me. I have become estranged from the most excellent people because of disputed points in the *Farbenlehre.*" . . . He named for me a few important names.'

Goethe, then, has severed relations with the most excellent people, among whom Eckermann may or may not count himself, precisely for the type of objections that Eckermann raises. The immediate consequences of Eckermann's heresy is indeed a form of excommunication: they had finished eating (for they always eat) and conversation stalled [*das Gespräch stockte*]. Yet if conversation was blocked, the *Conversations,* it must be said, has rarely flowed so freely, for this is also among the lengthier 'conversations' that Eckermann would record: an instance of interrupted intercourse sustaining Eckermann's desire to write [*conversatio*]. Now arrives the moment of sublime triumph, in which the younger becomes the master, at once the elder and the child, in short, the part who is not suffering:

> Goethe stand auf und stellte sich ans Fenster. Ich trat zu ihm und drückte ihm die Hand, denn wie er auch schalt, ich liebte ihn, und dann hatte ich das Gefühl, daß das Recht auf meiner Seite und daß er der leidende Teil sei.
>
> [Goethe got up and stood by the window. I went over to him and pressed his hand, for even when he was abusive, I loved him, and anyway I had the feeling that right was on my side and that he was the suffering party.]

This is the magnanimity of power. If Eckermann concedes to Goethe in this manner it may be due to love, as he suggests, but it is most certainly because he has justice on his side; he is right, and this right surpasses Goethe's threat of vengeance. Goethe has been judged – by Shakespeare and by Eckermann – justice is on this side, but the other part or member [*Teil*] suffers. Thus, 'it was not long before we conversed and joked about indifferent matters.' The *Differenz* appears to be suspended, the division repaired. Yet when Eckermann leaves, promising Goethe a written version of his objections – he reminds Goethe that if he would not concede to him his right, it was simply a consequence of the awkwardness in 'my oral delivery' – Goethe cannot refrain from saying a few things about heretics and heresy as Eckermann was in the doorway. Goethe throws his comments at Eckermann 'halb lachend, halb spottend.' Half and half: the halves are beginning to multiply again with the non-suffering half upon which Goethe casts half scorn, half laughter, half inside, half outside Goethe's house. If Goethe is himself divided, it is because '*Goethe*' is as such divided, as Eckermann proceeds to explain:

> If it should seem problematic that Goethe could not easily tolerate opposition regarding his *Farbenlehre*, whereas with his poetic works he showed himself to be wholly gracious, accepting each well-founded objection with gratitude, then perhaps the riddle [*Rätsel*] can be resolved when we consider that as poet he received the fullest gratification from the outside [*von außen her*], whereas in the case of *Farbenlehre*, this largest and most difficult of all his works, he experienced nothing but blame and disapprobation.

Eckermann is still wandering on the parricidal path. He understands and explains patiently why it was particularly painful for Goethe to meet up with any opposition concerning the *Farbenlehre*. It is a question of the outside, and Eckermann puts himself entirely in line with this outside-of-Goethe which repudiates his most difficult work. And this outside comes at him from all sides, for the better half of his life, forcing Goethe into the stance of a reactive warrior who is not afraid to cut to the quick. Nor is he afraid to amputate. Eckermann, as we noted, runs the risk of being cut off. At the same time, he qualifies Goethe's reactive instinct as natural:

> Ein halbes Leben hindurch tönte ihm der unverständigst Widerspruch von allen Seiten entgegen; und so war es denn wohl natürlich, daß der sich immer in einer Art von gereizten kriegerischen Zustand und zu leidenschaftlicher Opposition stets gerüstet befinden mußte.
>
> [For half of his life he was bombarded by the most incomprehensible contradictions from all sides. And thus it was only natural that he always found himself in an agitated, warlike type of situation which forced him to be armed for passionate opposition.]

Armed for battle on the field of science, Goethe is the warrior whom Eckermann challenges, if not to a fight quite to the end – though his end is always in sight – then at least to a 'natural' duel on Nature. But the difference between the painful duality taking shape here, and the mass of other conflictual pairs who have fought over this particular text, is that Eckermann does not belong to the legions of slavishly uncomprehending opposition. He stands his ground alone, he is honest, as Goethe has said, and forthright; he does not hide among the ranks of that army raised by *ressentiment*. In Nietzsche's terms, *he also knows how to be an enemy.* This is of course precisely what makes him a most dangerous opponent.

Yet Eckermann has just told us that, in the case of the *Farbenlehre,* he has been in effect all along describing and engaged in a riddle; and when riddles are at issue, the myth of Oedipus does not always lag that far behind. However, this wanderer, we shall see, will find a devious, if not ingenious solution to the riddle, thereby bypassing the path which he has been hitherto pursuing, the parricidal path on which he has nonetheless and, it would seem, irrevocably set foot. The detour that he takes, the deviation from the killing of the Father, the solution and resolution of the riddle is in fact simple: Goethe, it turns out, is, in this case and connection, not the father but the mother, the *good* mother: 'He was, in connection to the *Farbenlehre,* like a good mother.' A good mother, that means a mother who has not been violated, not by Eckermann namely, for it was precisely his earlier recognition in this episode of the 'unsuspected difference' that stopped and deadened the urge for intercourse. Goethe, the father, will not have been killed, and Goethe, the mother, will retain her integrity. As for Eckermann, he will certainly not have to pay for what was almost a crime. He can write against the Father without remorse.

# DOING KAFKA IN *THE CASTLE*

*A Poetics of Desire*

*What would be a literature that would only be what it is, literature? No longer would it be itself if it were itself.* JACQUES DERRIDA, 'Devant la Loi'

In a recent issue of the Lacanian journal *L'Ane* (Jan.–Feb. 1983), Slavoj Žižek has observed: 'C'est une chose étrange . . . l'absence d'une approche lacanienne de Kafka, qui a été entièrement laissé à l'hermeneutique, à l'existentialisme, au deleuzianisme [It's a strange thing . . . the absence of a Lacanian approach to Kafka, who has been entirely left to hermeneutics, existentialism and Deleuzianism].' Although this, like so much concerning the *chose,* is a bit of an exaggeration, it is true that Kafka scholars are beginning only now, with the speed of Gregor getting out of bed, to move toward an understanding of the infatuation felt by contemporary theory for the Kafkan text. In this chapter I try to show the extent to which Kafka at once courts, mobilizes, and challenges some of the major axiomatic inflections with which we have come to identify 'French Theory.' It is probably one of the more subtle ironies of the text in question, *The Castle,* that the language it claims to speak secretly, in a mood of clandestine solicitation – so that its chief agent and victim, K., will not understand the language of its intention properly – is French.

My strategy (assuming that a reading could be reduced to such a thing) consists in following a zigzagging course whose path in fact double-crosses anyone hoping to discover a circumscribable locality which would nurture, guide, or direct interpretative activity. However, this predicament by no means prevents me from making rest stops at stations of critical thinking marked by proper names that have created some anxiety in critical circles, namely, Derrida, Lacan, de Man – all of whom, it might be said, bear some resemblance to the Klamm of our story. What is being tested here, then, is not so much Kafka – for Kafka is an example, perhaps *the* example for commentators of varied persuasions – but a distinct set of critical perspectives which are elaborated within my interpretation. Interpretation, of course, is one of the great themes of Kafka's corpus, and it is always shown to be a radically destabilizing injunction to heed. One always runs the risk of dying like a dog (*The Trial*) or being tortured by the word processor ('In the Penal Colony') or simply dragging oneself eastward, across snowy fields of endless incompletion (*The Castle*) once one agrees (as if we had a choice) to attempt interpretation.

These are just some of the finitizing tasks which Kafka designs for us. But he also places 'literature' in a very precarious position, which is why his texts can be seen to be reactors to the devastating proposition that can be heard in such a simple but perplexing statement as 'doing literature.' *The Castle,* while it does not necessarily furnish responses to the questions it raises, situates them, and invites us to survey the expanse of their effects. Thus the problematics circumscribed since at least the age of Hegel by philosophy (and its others, for instance, psychoanalysis and linguistics) find a unique point of articulation in Kafka's last novel: these include the posturing of the 'we' in discourse, as well as questions of self-identity, proper name, and title. These in turn appear to be enveloped in the transparency of desire. It is perhaps not a mere coincidence that Kafka's desire – the broken constancy of his relation to women and to writing – has become a horizon against which we measure our capacity to read.

As frail *Ungeheuer,* Kafka, who has come to arrange the survival of textual performance, is said to have been celebrated in every conceivable mode and idiom. But will it have been possible for Kafka to receive his due? Has he begotten what's coming? The nuclear desire of which the Kafkan corpus is an indicator remains unspoken, though it has been sensed and said that he has more or less done in the fragile enterprise of critical commentary. One feels indebted to Kafka – in the formidable German sense that links debt to guilt – as to the promise of apocalyptic disclosure. For it may be that few others have persecuted writing readers with superior lucidity or have evoked with such elegance their suffering before the text, as well as that of virtually all his protagonists. Out of gratitude for the suffering thus induced some have readily acknowledged the debt [*Schuld*], gaining a margin of credit in the form of despair. Yet, the weary desperado has also learned to exercise a just revenge by touching off a paradoxical maneuver which turns the nameless monumentality of Kafka's undoing into an already canny, classifiable, and, of course, literary event. It is as if a certain type of need, originating in a narcissistic, guilty reading of Kafka, has driven one repeatedly to the place in his writing where cases of interpretative crime are held up for review, while the death penalty is, in one sinister form or another, decreed for the commentator.

A kind of *Sorge* for the predicament of the interpreter may explain why 'doing Kafka' has often resulted in the unconscious rehabilitation of something that Kafka had in fact systematically undone; by adding here that 'something' covers up for an opening where 'literature' was once discoverable, we will have already called the decisive stakes at hand. The somewhat numbing effect produced by Kafka's treatment of the interpreter may explain why we have let slide the gesture that has summoned quotation marks to accompany the other stricken victim; one has preferred to avert one's gaze from the wound that Kafka inflicted upon something which, at least according to the testimony of his diary, amounts to nothing less than his proper name, his autonym: 'Literature.'[1] And this proper name, which is submitted to so many forms of expropriation, abbreviation, and disfigurement under the pen of its bearer, will countersign the spectacle of its great undoing within a work whose legitimacy qua literature has never been seriously questioned. Curiously enough, the title by which we identify this work bears a peculiar resemblance to the source of undisputed authority within the work. The castle, as is well known, maintains itself as an impregnable, untouchable, and unfigurable figuration of resistance. This last erection of Kafka's, this final attempt at entering an inside, seems to be designated to delay enclosure indefinitely and to forbid closure. We are never allowed to advance 'within' the work's inner workings nor to venture quite outside of what it claims to be the inside. We are merely pushed back and forth within a peripheral pocket that somehow touches upon the work without properly getting in touch with it. This should not however make us insensible to the drama of a troubled discourse unfolding about us to which we are hypnotically attached.

But just who are 'we' and who, for that matter, was K., who seems never to have gained a legitimate foothold in *The Castle,* though he also seems to be contained by it? It is a likely assumption that here, as elsewhere, Kafka has allegorized critical intervention in terms of an impossible desire, in other words, as that which makes desire possible. If, in this light, 'we' as K.'s coprotagonists figure as the intentional victims of a text that, while claiming to summon us, has from the very start demobilized our interpretative movements and resisted the interpretative Key, then in the name of what should our first move be made? In the name of what should 'we,' like K., begin here anew with the naive design of measuring this work's limits or perhaps entering it, as if it were merely a question of finding the right *Zeug?*

'In the name of what?' is an intervention of a citational sort whose original formulation can be imputed to a bleak comedian named Schwarzer.

Following its initial and initiating appearance in chapter 1, 'in the name of what?' will be repeated in several guises throughout *The Castle*, with the double aim of forcing the interpreter's hand and interrogating textual procedures. It is the question that threatens both to hold K. in lifeless custody and to withhold him from taking custody of the text as its protagonist. What is being demanded of K.? The question, quite simply, requires K. to produce an identity. In front of anyone, in front of Schwarzer, for instance, who claims to be a representative of the castle, though his only connection to it seems to be a telephone line. K. entitles himself 'Landsurveyor,' not *a* landsurveyor but *the* landsurveyor. This entitles him in turn to assume a role of legitimacy which is characteristically subversive. The subversive aspect of his response necessarily imposes itself here since K. is not, strictly speaking, entitled to his title, in part explaining why some notable critical essays have made his apparent fraud tantamount to deceit.[2] Nonetheless, K. can be said to be irrevocably bound by the title he decides upon, precisely insofar as it names and legitimates a fundamental (though not substantializable) lapse by which his identity is constituted. K.'s mode of presentation, which is by no means a *self*-presentation, has however aroused a kind of moral indignation among his readers. They have tended to assume that K. immediately dissimulates what must be regarded as a preconstituted identity. Despite the fact that a prior identity has never been disclosed, this view has given us the basic interpretation of K. as impostor and, as such, has never allowed for the possibility – beyond all questions regarding truth-value – of considering K.'s title an indispensable supplement to his function in *The Castle*.

Although the question of who K. – or, for that matter, 'we' – might be has not yet been settled, an implicit hypothesis has become evident; the title institutes a place, assures an identity in a place where self-presentation or identity cannot as such take place. In this respect, K.'s claim to a title may serve not so much to inflate or empower him in any determinate way but only to underscore the fragility of his status. Thus assuring for himself a title without the guarantee of a stable value, K. in effect commits himself to a position, however precarious, on the fringes of what we shall come to appreciate as a colossal staging of textual effacement and degradation. In so doing, K. may well have outdone the commentators who claim to have a legitimate and secure hold on the castle.

When judging K.'s infraction of a strictly constituted order – the order presumably established and represented by the castle and its functionaries – commentators have largely maintained a posture of dauntless forbearance with respect to their deluded impostor.[3] Their judgments, leaning on the stability gained from a rhetoric of anguish, failure, and deceit, have produced a somewhat surprising reading of K. which profiles him as an exemplary victim of his or his author's existential and metaphysical desire. The reading of K. as victim has been subtly and diversely proposed by Marthe Robert, Maurice Blanchot, and, more recently, Charles Bernheimer.[4] Bernheimer, for instance, has written: 'The necessity to interpret engages the reader of Kafka at a particularly intimate level, because it is exactly the failure of the Kafkan protagonist to interpret his situation successfully that leads to his destruction within the text. The existential implication. . . .' A few pages later, Bernheimer summons a key witness, one who has been doing an awful lot of jury duty lately but whose present appearance startles this court: 'K. is, in terms introduced by Jacques Derrida, resolutely logocentric and phonocentric, an undeviating believer in the metaphysics of presence.'[5]

But what if Kafka's final and most valiant hero has come over to *this* 'side' of Derrida? What, that is, if K. can be shown to be opposed to the same effects of logocentrism as D., *avant* the *lettre(s)?* This, however, remains to be judged, though it might be mentioned that Derrida has recently given one indication of the friendship his writing seeks in Kafka by upholding 'Vor dem Gesetz' as the story of *différance*.[6]

It is best now to return to Bernheimer's sentences telling of the failure on the part of the Kafkan protagonist to interpret his situation successfully and of his consequent destruction within the text. This type of assertion releases a dazzling array of questions, some of which have been suggested but left unanswered. In the first place, who – or what – is the Kafkan protagonist? Is the protagonist indeed a 'he' of whom it can be said 'his destruction'? What would guarantee a successful interpretation in a text which earnestly disavows the possibility of any form of interpretative mastery or gratification? What does 'his destruction' mean? Are we to entrust ourselves here to Max Brod's phantasmic decision that K. was meant to suffer a natural death at the novel's conclusion (who ever heard of a natural death in Kafka's works?) – or does 'destruction' simply spiral down tautologically to failure? Does K. perhaps develop a strategy for outliving the apocalyptic claims made in 'his' name within and without the text? What, finally, is this text about which we speak with such easy fluency?

The tempting assertions found circulating in Bernheimer's and other critics' arguments call for a careful reconsideration of that oeuvre, *Kafka* – whose very mention evokes a sense of pious literariness – which has prompted readers to try to localize a distilled type of poetic or writing self whose irreducible signature would be obedience to the law and text. That the Kafkan protagonist may attempt to violate the law and to deviate from a notion of pure writing self has only served to affirm their presence. Our task, in conjunction with our assumed title, will be to determine how Kafka's literature does indeed undo certain determinations that have become associated with this name.

Kafka's texts – but this is not an unwelcome contradiction – are fundamentally concerned with literature and with what the author calls *Schriftstellersein.* Yet there are, properly speaking, no poets or authors in Kafka's works. Nor do these works reserve a place of honor for literature or exalt it in any way; in fact, Kafka seems to have lifted the *concept* of literature – of a literary subject, language, and form – from the thematic tissue of his texts. Kafka's oeuvre thus develops a type of self-reflexive poetics whose reductive rigor imposes itself disconcertingly. In the first place – this is simple but needs to be stated at the outset – Kafka's protagonists appear as purely figurative beings, anonymous personas, or machines. The locus of consciousness may be a vermin, a singing mouse, a hunger artist, the K.s, a bureaucratic apparatus, or a writing machine. These curious carriers of the word make it difficult indeed to speak convincingly of poetic utterance. This is but the first of a series of difficulties confronting humanism's commentator.

In the second place, Kafka's works reduce not only the image and putative function of the poet-author but of writing as well. Kafka replaces the literary text with newspapers, legal documents, letters, the *Gesang* produced by the humming sounds of a telephone and even, human flesh. In addition to metamorphosing or technologizing modern literature's portrait of the artist and his work, Kafka's oeuvre abandons such metaphysical comforts as a transcendental signified on the one hand and the fiction of ultimate, substantialized meaning or absolute presence on the other.[7] The source of power, especially in his later works, lies with such dubious functionaries of language as bureaucrats, lawyers, officers, and judges. Ever distant from the metaphysical grandeur of, for instance, Goethe or Hölderlin, Kafka claims nowhere in his oeuvre a superior authority for God, Nature, or the writing self, not even for the text in which they are not contained.

Kafka has stripped the poet in literature of his phenomenal appearance, his selfhood, and his name; in general, he has, his literary texts, thematized the massive proliferation of nonliterary texts that have a radically indeterminate value; and he has pronounced the death sentence on God and the kaiser.[8] These series of reductions – the reduction of the poet to, say, a singing mouse, the literary text to an old newspaper, and transcendental presence to a bureaucratic establishment – give rise to a poetics that undermines notions traditionally attributed to poetic discourse and still applied to Kafka's works. In one respect, the poetic consciousness, personality, and subject appear to be secondary phenomena which are determined by the vaster structure of language. In this context, one might think of Stanley Corngold's reading of *The Metamor-*

*phosis,* which argues that Gregor Samsa exists as an indecipherable sign, 'a word broken loose from the context of language.'[9] In another respect, however, Kafka's language itself, much like the writer whom he depicts in the letter to Max Brod, seems continually to assert its lack of 'genuine existence.'[10] Kafka makes this assertion about the writer, which we are extending to include his language, the same year he writes *The Castle.* Acknowledging at once the dangerous confrontations that isomorphic relationships notoriously invite, we might nonetheless assume the role of K.'s co-text-surveyor in order to witness how Kafka's final work reflects this lack in its language and structure.

*The Castle* imparts an intention to subvert ironically its literary enframing by calling constant attention to the dysfunctionality of its discourse, at once technologizing and short-circuiting its procedures.[11] While showing simulacra of poetic utterance and the generation of all written discourse to arise from the quirks of an anarchic bureaucratic apparatus, Kafka's novel systematically breaks down (in the technological and nervous senses) its own iterative performance of meaning. It is as if Kafka had programmed his apparatus to disrupt any claim for a classical type of meaning which would be able to be pure presence or selfsame identity. Rerouting the illusion of a merger between texts and their meaning, commentaries, and interpretations to an indefinitely expulsed elsewhere, *The Castle* registers the 'destinerring' movement of the signifieds which it has dispatched, thus creating the drama of lapsing within the text that presumes to be literature-bound.

Language, the text holds, is never a plenitude itself; it is in its very structure a formed incompleteness waiting for the other's – the interpreter's – participation.[12] Kafka calls the interpreter who braves this incompleteness within *The Castle,* K. This interpreter, however, not only declines to surmount the distance between texts and their possible meanings, but is 'himself' a linguistic sign that takes part in the structure of incompleteness. A mark of incompletion, the letter *K* anticipates interpretation while it also represents a resistance to signification. By thus reducing the status of the subject from an entity to a locus, that is to say, to the linguistic function of the subject in the text's discourse, Kafka has created a double protagonist – K. is both the subject summoned to interpret the castle and, as typographical character, a unit of signification without any meaning in itself.[13] In this it recalls Freud's 'memory trace,' which is never an image of a person or event, but a term which takes on meaning only through its differential opposition to other traces. But to divide K. thus does not require a reading of K. neatly composed of two severable parts; rather, it points to an internal shattering of the concept of any unity, even on the level of the protagonist's identity, which involves both subject and signifier. Thus, even when the title of landsurveyor supplements the letter *K*, K. remains throughout the novel only a potential landsurveyor, as perhaps *The Castle* remains the potentiality of novel-being.

If one were to look for a relation of congruency in order to locate the structures governing Kafka's novel, then one would not need speak of the 'absolute congruency between author and hero,' as does Martin Walser.[14] Rather, one could begin to distinguish systems of congruency operating between K. and the novel in which he figures as protagonist. Such a congruency reveals K.'s study of meaning and structure – his continual (but inconclusive) measuring and interpretation of the limitations and possibilities of a world hermetically sealed off from the context of a past and *Heimat* – to reflect the way in which *The Castle* tests the limits and possibilities of its own textual determinations.

~

But, initially, K. is not entirely equal to the text whose repetitive and discontinuous structures of signification seem calculated to thwart him. In the course of his exegetic peregrinations, however, K. will abandon an accepted notion of meaning, which he has hitherto pursued as a presence that would be the origin, referent, or end of the text. He will also learn to 'scan' the castle as something that is not quite a material substance. The text, on the other hand, begins its artful game by introducing a castle which is neither present nor absent:

> The Castle hill was hidden, veiled in mist and darkness, nor was there even a glimmer of light to show that a castle was there.[15]

The language of the novel's beginning at once names the castle hill and castle and asserts their material absence. This initial description reveals the generative principle of the novel's composition to be one of distance and deferral, of the substitution of a semiotic for a substantial mode of reference.[16] The initiating passage, then, tells us two things about *The Castle*. First, by underscoring the absence of a link between the sign (castle) and its concrete *denotatum*, it alerts us from the start that the novel has little to do with representation. Second – and this will be of special concern – it calls into question the status of the textual signifier itself.

Having instituted from the start a process of semiotic deferral and subversion, *The Castle* helps us define K.'s situation more rigorously than before. For the novel reflects this same process in the movement that leads to K.'s acquisition of his title. Just as K. cannot begin to interpret the castle until it is explicitly named for him, he cannot interpret his own function in the novel until the castle agrees, after an initial deferral, to name him 'Landsurveyor.' When the castle first rejects K.'s claim to this title, Schwarzer, assailing him, cries: 'No trace of a landsurveyor. A lowdown lying tramp. Probably worse' (14).

The castle, however, changes its position and 'smilingly' accepts the challenge of giving K. his auto-nomy (13). K.'s apparent surprise at being thus named a landsurveyor does not, even here, require us to consider him an impostor. For – beyond the issues of classical oppositions such as truth/dissimulation already discussed – to do so would be to concur with Schwarzer's judgment of K., which, however, the castle's designation supersedes. What K.'s astonishment does appear to demonstrate is his awareness of the radically arbitrary assignment of signs in the novel. For both castle and landsurveyor prove to be signs dispossessed of referents. K. now possesses the title of landsurveyor, but this does not entitle him to identify himself with its 'meaning', and the castle will prove to be anything but a castle.

These observations point to a bifurcation of temporal perspectives in the novel's signifying process. From K.'s perspective, the structure of signification seems to consist of three moments: the moment in which an entity – such as the castle and his landsurveyor 'self' – appears on the text's horizon as traceless ('No trace of . . .'), followed by the moment in which that entity (arbitrarily) acquires a sign – of a tramp, a landsurveyor, a castle – and then culminates with the interpretative moment – as when K. analyzes the castle-construct, in which he discerns a disunity between the signifier and signified. The other perspective, which might be called the narrative perspective, cannot coalesce with K.'s, for it initiates, coordinates, and finally subverts the semiotic systems with which K. is confronted. Thus, in the novel's first paragraph the narrative perspective (or voice) names the castle; proceeds swiftly to establish the disunity between the representative and semantic function of language by showing, for example, that the value or meaning of the word *castle* has no bearing on the thing denoted or on its indicated manifestation; and pauses to lie in wait for K.'s interpretative approach. Then, a few pages later, the narrative will go one step further. Calling K. forth to interpret the meaning of a sign – the meaning of 'castle,' 'landsurveyor,' and even the name Westwest – the narrative voice retains for itself the additional pleasure of ironizing the semantic function of language.

But it is only when K. begins to work *with* the text to free the sign from its subservience to that 'reality' (or presence) which it was supposed to serve, and affirms that it is in the nature of language and of writing *not* to be confined to specific structures of meaning, that a new freedom for K. and his companion text begins to assert itself.[17]

~

Before celebrating the news of K.'s triumphant assimilation of the textual surveillance systems, it would be useful to consider what exactly K. must work against and to what extent the novel dramatizes his desire to 'do the negative.'[18]

K. never realizes his goal of penetrating to the inner chambers of the castle, where it is suggested he might uncover the locus of meaning. Nonetheless, the castle preserves its function in the text as the single generator of texts and signs, be they of an architectural, bureaucratic, photographic, telephonic, or musical nature. Often, when K. finds the villagers' speech incomprehensible, or when the villagers remain aggressively mute, the castle intervenes as the single source of apparently significative communication. But these communication acts usually point ironically and even 'joyously' (27) to dashing the possibility for communication. When, for example, K. rides with Gerstäcker, who can only respond to K.'s urgent queries with coughing attacks, the castle sends out a compensatory signal:

> But as if to give him a parting sign [*Zeichen*] until their next encounter, a bell began to ring joyously up there, a bell that for at least a moment made his heart palpitate, for its tone was painful, too, as if it threatened him with the fulfillment of his vague longing. (27)

But the possibility for this longing's fulfillment is quickly put to death by the emergence of an inferior sign:

> This great bell soon died away, however, and was replaced by a feeble, monotonous little tinkle, which might have come from the castle, but might have been somewhere in the village. This jangling was certainly more appropriate to the slow journey and to the wretched-looking yet inexorable driver. (27)

This passage not only thematizes the text's withholding of meaning, inasmuch as the signifying sign abruptly changes into the 'more appropriate' asignificatory jangling of other bells, but also points to the threat that signification poses for the protagonist.[19] The momentary promise of fulfillment – fulfillment as the becoming-of-meaning in the castle's signal – has a menacing effect on K. Suggesting that K. himself craves incompletion and the absence of meaning, this passage marks an essential stage in the text's trajectory which in turn compels a reassessment of K.'s position within the novel. We shall explore the thematic and temporal implications of this craving when, after a brief but necessary deferral, we consider the interpenetrating structures of desire and narrativity.

At this point it is important to bear in mind that his desire for a lack of fulfillment or completion stands in opposition to the more 'organic' desires of the bureaucratic apparatus against which K. is pitted. The text defines the bureaucracy persistently in terms of its fundamental unity and its ability to function as an organic whole. The novel extends the metaphors of organicity and the rhetoric of unity [*Einheitlichkeit*] to include a particular mode of writing. The exponent of this writing is Momus. As Klamm's village secretary and the most prolific writer in the novel, Momus appears to command more respect in the village than any other character short of Klamm. His authority becomes manifest when, presenting himself to K., he inspires in the other characters a feeling of awe. With the exception of K., all (including Momus himself) are struck by the dignity of the act of naming:

> 'I am Momus, Klamm's village secretary.' At these words seriousness descended on the whole room; though the landlady and Pepi knew the gentleman very well, they were nonetheless staggered by the dignified utterance of his name and position. And even the gentleman himself, as if he had said more than his judgment sanctioned, and as if he were resolved to escape at least from any aftereffects of the solemn import implicit in his own words, buried himself in his papers and began to write, so that nothing was heard in the room but the scratching of his pen. (133)

The aura of seriousness that surrounds Momus is linked directly to his role as writer. In fact, the Momus episode enjoys a unique status in the novel in that it both profiles the writer as he writes and records the specific contents of his text. Momus bases his lucubrations on the concept of a writing order [*Ordnung*] that exacts the full representation of a given event. Thus Momus, who makes the strongest claim in the novel for a representational mode of writing – one that would absorb into itself the real – summons K. to help him bring his work to fruition:

> 'It is simply a matter of getting a precise description of this afternoon's events for Klamm's village register. The description is already complete; there are only two or three lacunae that you must fill in for the sake of order; no other purpose is in view and neither can another purpose be achieved.' (137)

But this is precisely the mode of writing that K. rejects, and quite like K.'s assistants, who are of no help to K., so Momus's potential assistant lends no support to his project. Superior to the protagonist of *The Trial*, K. declines Momus's appeal for his cooperation in the execution of the protocol:

> 'Good night,' said K. 'I despise any kind of trial [*Verhör*].' (137)

K.'s refusal to stand trial, his refusal to aid Momus in the completion of his text, amounts to a rejection on his part of the representational mode of writing. Perhaps more powerfully, it demonstrates how K. actively resists being totalized into meaning. In this respect, K. can be said to assimilate his own action to that of the text insofar as he reduplicates the immediate resistance on the part of the textual signifier to being transformed into a signified. The text has thus in advance endorsed K. in his aversion, for it too refuses to comply with the order of writing ennobled by the Momuses of literature.

By refusing to be engraved completely into the text of the protocol, K. in effect asserts the impossibility of being 'represented' to Klamm. And just as K. refuses representation in a so-called complete and organically unified manner – in a passage that Kafka deletes, K. judges Momus's work not only to be an 'adversary text' (382) but also a 'very common meadow flower' (387) – so, too, Klamm eludes representation. If indeed the representational mode of writing figures as K.'s only means of reaching Klamm (the landlady asserts this), then we are already alerted in this episode to the impossibility of K.'s ever confronting Klamm. For his refusal to sub-scribe to this type of writing implies his refusal of a structure in which sign and referent would exist in harmonious unity. Thus K. now affirms Klamm's essential fictionality and seems to abandon his hope of actually finding him. From this point onward, K. must accept the dispersal of Klamm's 'person' among letters, narrations, fantasies, objects – and among these objects we may count, as we shall have ample opportunity to do, K.'s various lovers. From this point onward, then, K. will accept a Klamm that exists exclusively by means of eternal, errant substitutions, some of which in fact provide our rambling surveyor with a measure of pleasure. And this pleasure, coinciding as it does with the affirmation of the inaccessibility of an unpresentable, untouchable, and unsignifiable Klamm, is the mark of K.'s escape from the laws of presence itself.[20]

The Momus episode, which began with such an aura of dignity and seriousness of purpose, concludes on a comic note that deflates the putative importance of Momus's texts. In an ironic inversion of the hunger-artistic thematic, Momus breaks apart a pretzel and 'scatter[s] all the papers with salt and crumbs' (140). This spilling over of food onto the written word amounts in the Kafkan world to a necessary desecration of the devouring text. As for Momus, he can be assumed to have literally 'buried himself in his papers' (133).

The functionaries of language, regardless of the amount of power they may possess, turn out to be deficient writers or speakers. Significantly, only an 'apparatus' achieves a certain degree of perfection in producing texts. An exemplary instance in which the novel focuses on the principles of textual generation emerges in the fifth chapter when the mayor explains to K. the nature of the bureaucratic apparatus [*behördlicher Apparat*]. In his narration, the mayor first parades the details of the bureaucratic apparatus's triumph over a certain Mr. Brunswick. This triumph represents the suppression of the only character in the novel, apart from K., whose actions are linked to a concept of fantasy, originality, and deception. Moreover, Brunswick, whom the mayor depicts as a troublesome revolutionary figure, turns out to be the only character to have argued for the necessity of bringing a landsurveyor into the castle domain. But according to this spokesman for the castle, fantasy, revolutionary action, and originality merely betoken disjunctive stupidity (84).

The mayor displaces those very categories of originality and invention which, when applied to a villager, he considers a source of serious vexation, onto the bureaucratic apparatus. In fact, the mayor's substitution of a machinelike entity for mind is complete, for this machine functions in the text as the poetic sensibility par excellence and thus provides a paradigm for textual production. Only the machine as such, and not a particular self, proves capable of engineering and accomplishing a disclosure in what resembles an originative moment of poetic conception:

> 'And now I come to a special feature of our bureaucratic apparatus. In conformity with its precision, it is extremely sensitive as well. When an affair has been weighed for a very long time, it may happen, even before the matter has been fully considered, that suddenly in a flash the decision comes in some unforeseen place, which, moreover, cannot be found any longer later on – a decision that settles the matter, if in most cases correctly, yet all the same arbitrarily. It is as if the apparatus were unable any longer to bear the tension, the year-long irritation caused by the same affair – probably trivial in itself – and had hit on the decision by itself, without the assistance of the officials.' (85–86)

This autonomous apparatus, so precise and sensitive in its functioning, produces in a moment of inspiration the arbitrary but conclusive resolution for the textual malfunctioning in the castle. Never relinquishing its radical autonomy, the apparatus functions as a regulatory mechanism in that it purports to regulate and control the production of bureaucratic texts 'sensitively'. Indeed, this apparatus would appear to govern the entire system of utterance within the bureaucratic network if it were not for one 'disturbing' factor. The mayor emphasizes the perfect functioning of the self-propelled, robotoid apparatus and enlarges upon its capacity to make crucial decisions; however, these decisions have in fact little control over the generation of bureaucratic texts. For, as the mayor himself points out, the actual 'dissemination' of these decisions undergoes a temporal delay:

> 'Now, as I said, it is just these decisions that are generally excellent. The only disturbing thing about them – it's usually the case with

> such things – is that one learns about them too late and so in the meantime still keeps on passionately canvassing things that were decided long ago.' (86)

In this respect, the apparatus reflects a moment in the narrative strategy. Just as the apparatus is always temporally ahead of individual bureaucrats in making decisions which however remain concealed, so the narrative tends to run temporally ahead of the characters. Thus, for example, the narrative marks in the beginning of the novel the centrality of the castle's function while keeping K. in a state of fundamental uncertainty, leaving him in the dark.

The temporal gap between the decisions that the apparatus produces and the dissemination of those decisions results in the random proliferation of bureaucratic texts. Always lagging behind the decision-making machine, these texts necessarily fail to perform their intentional function. The temporal gap between narrative 'decisions' or designations and their disclosure creates the necessity for the characters' endless, indeed passionate [*leidenschaftlich* (86)], search for a stable core [*Kern* (89)]. But the possibility of ever finding such a core (or any form of stability), a possibility which presupposes the temporal coincidence of the narrative assertions with the characters' discernments, remains permanently deferred. Positioned in a novel whose generative principle is based on this notion of deferment, the characters find themselves caught up in a perpetual 'chase after' narrative constructions.[21]

~

The castle, one of the primary fictions that the novel pursues, excites our curiosity by provoking the belief, shared at times by characters and commentators alike, that somewhere beyond the lowly bureaucrats, in some secluded chamber, there resides, with an air of serene majesty, the translucent embodiment of meaning. In the first part of the novel, Klamm, the other narrative fiction, similarly arouses curiosity, at least that of Olga, the landlady, and K., who conceive him to be the absent and alluring author of events. In this respect, the 'ostensible Castle' (12) and the equally 'ostensible Klamm' (215) together function as the organizing principle of the novel, for they are both seen to guard the secret of the hidden matrix of significations.

In an attempt to penetrate the novel's ostensible locus of meaning, the characters chase after these fictions in essentially two ways. Though condemned in advance always to fall short of their goals, the characters engage in constructing and reconstituting a connecting link to the castle or to Klamm. In order to locate the points where these acts of construction and reconstitution converge, we might first distinguish them by considering the former a purely sensual endeavor and the latter a constitutive act of interpretative discourse. Yet, in keeping with the text, we may not assume that what we are calling acts of construction and reconstitution form a polarity in which sensuality would be opposed to written or spoken discourse. They appear, rather, to represent the same experience of the characters' search for the elusive core/*corps*. For we learn by observing the characters that in the world of *The Castle*, the desire to reach the castle or Klamm, whether expressed sensually or verbally, always carries with it the force of an erotic drive. Indeed, every interpretative act in the novel has erotic overtones and, conversely, every erotic encounter demonstrates that interpretative discourse may become the object of eroticization. Driven by an erotic pulsion toward the castle or Klamm, the characters encounter an implicit interdiction which they however appear to accept: they are never allowed in their sensual or interpretative 'performances' to achieve a moment that even remotely approximates satisfaction. The text thus interlaces sensuality with interpretation as it advances a poetics of desire manifesting the characters' consent to incompleteness, to time and to the repetition of desire in time.[22] At no point do the characters attempt to keep alive the delusion and fiction of sustained satisfaction.

The purely sensual acts of construction culminate in narrations about moments of self-delusion. In her narration of past attempts – and failures – to reach the Castle, for example, the sense in which Olga speaks of her 'connection' to the Castle may be taken literally:

> 'What I did however attain in the Herrenhof is a certain connection to the castle.' (256)

Indeed, the liaison between Olga and the castle consists of her nightly adventures in a barn spent with the castle's male servants and, as far as we know, this represents the extent of that 'certain connection.' As she tells her story, Olga however comes to recognize that her repeated attempts to establish a link to the Castle have implicated her in a game of lies and madness, a game in which she figures as a plaything (260).

When she reveals to him the details of her relationship with the castle, Olga fears K.'s contempt. But her interlocutor is not entirely innocent of applying a similar method to his search. For K., too, repeatedly constructs purely sensual bonds that he hopes will link him directly to the castle or Klamm. His sensual connections, somewhat more varied than Olga's, range from sipping Klamm's cognac to consuming Frieda. Even K.'s encounter with the androgynous Barnabas – Barnabas immediately recalls to K. the image of a woman (34) – brings to light the erotic drive impelling K. toward the castle. K., at once enchanted with Barnabas's beauty, pursues him into the night, tightly linking arms with the messenger, in hope of being delivered to the castle. Barnabas 'yields' to K. (41). But the entire episode turns out to be the effect of a misunderstanding, and K., recognizing this to be the case, regrets having surrendered to Barnabas's inveiglement. In this moment of recognition, K., like Olga, inverts the poles of seduction to conceive of himself as the object rather than agent of seduction:

> So it had been a misunderstanding, a vulgar debasing misunderstanding, and K. had given himself entirely over to him. Had let himself be captivated by Barnabas's tight-fitting and silken, lustred jacket, which he was now unbuttoning. (43–44)

This is not the last of the seductions to which the unfortunate K. succumbs – Frieda's lure still awaits him.

Yet it is not Frieda as such who finally attracts K., for his sensual contact with her embodies, rather, K.'s endeavor to draw closer to another, *provisional* object of desire whom we know by the name of Klamm. This is perhaps not the place to lament Frieda's predicament; however, it should be noted that she is merely extracted from an economy of desire in which the object will always be substituted for something that was never really present. On this level of general ingratitude, Kafka's Frieda bears striking resemblance to the woeful woman of whom Lacan speaks in *Écrits*, for she too is shown to be 'giving in a love-relationship that which she does not have.'[23] But Kafka judges it prudent to suppress two passages in which K.'s desire for Frieda is explicitly subsumed under his desire to gain proximity to Klamm. The first of these passages consists of one sentence. It discloses, particularly in the German version, the pathos of K.'s homage to Klamm in the love-making scene with Frieda:

> K. thought more of [*andenken*] Klamm than of her. (371)

In the second passage, K. reflects upon his deluded encounter with Frieda thus:

> And then immediately, before there was time to think, Frieda had come, and with her the belief, which it was impossible to give up entirely even today, that through her mediation an almost corporal relationship to Klamm, a relationship so close that it amounted almost to a whispering form of communication, had come about. (380)

What Kafka retains in his manuscript deals less with K.'s desire for an 'almost corporal' link to Klamm than with the temporal dynamics of desire:

> There the hours passed, hours in which they breathed as one, in which their hearts beat as one, hours in which K. was haunted by

> the feeling that he was losing himself or wandering into a strange country, farther than ever man had wandered before, a country so strange that not even the air had anything in common with his native air, where one might suffocate of strangeness, and yet whose mad temptations were such that one could only go on and lose oneself further. (54)

This passage, which simultaneously unfolds a diachronic and synchronic event, is crucial to us in two respects. First, we can see two suprathematic planes converging here, for Kafka at once traces out K.'s erring interpretative movement in the novel and his intimate moment with Frieda. Second, the syntax suddenly deviates from that of other descriptive passages in order to stress the temporal character of K.'s predicament. The repetition of a word in a single sentence is uncharacteristic of the novel's diction. At this narrative junction, however, Kafka repeats the word *hours* [*Stunden*], as if to reflect in the rhythmic movement of language itself K.'s experience of desire's temporality, that is, of desire as repetition in time. Mad temptations, a sensation of suffocation and strangeness, the sense of radical loss and endless repetition: these are the effects of desire under which K. labors in the precinct of the female or textual corpus. Yet rather than creating an impasse, as one might surmise, the incessant repetition of these effects produces, on the contrary, the enabling structure for K.'s search. Thus the words that conclude this passage intimate the inevitability and necessity of this moment's restless repetition: 'one could only go on [*man kann nichts tun als weitergehen*] and lose oneself further.'[24]

Perhaps one of the primary tasks that Landsurveyor K. does accomplish in the novel consists in measuring the limits of the sheer materiality of desire, the body as a sensual 'connector' to the hidden matrix of the textual machine. Bürgel, invoking the vocabulary of surveyorship, informs K. that precisely the 'frontiers' of the body are meaningful:

> 'One's bodily energies can be pushed only to a certain limit or frontier [*Grenze*]; who can help it if precisely this limit is meaningful in other ways, too? . . . there are things that founder on nothing but themselves.' (312)

'Things' refers here not only to the body – be it physical or textual – that may collapse under the pressure of 'meaningful' limitations or boundaries, but also – and this brings us to the issue of 'reconstitution' – to the equally meaningful limitations of interpretative discourse. With these words, Bürgel ushers in the final stage of his interpretative act, thus dramatizing the analogy between the failure of the body to transcend its physical limitations and that of interpretation – or the other search for the castle or Klamm – to transcend its eternally ungratifying conjectural thrusts.

Fully alert to the coincidence of erotic and interpretative behavior, K., in the Bürgel episode, climbs into the bed of the connecting secretary [*Verbindungssekretär*], stroking his leg, while Bürgel offers in return his interpretation of K.'s situation. But K.'s desire wanes, he falls asleep, and the curtain falls on another unsatisfying and meaningfully limited narration.

Amalia, too, conjoins interpretative with erotic intent when she grasps K.'s visit (as does Frieda subsequently) in terms of his desire for Olga:

> Amalia said that she was certainly not mistaken, she would even go further and assert that K. too had an inclination for Olga, and that his visits, which were ostensibly concerned with some message or other from Barnabas, were really only intended for Olga. (198)

After Olga returns home, Amalia turns off the light for the narrating couple. The erotic tonalities of this narrative exchange are reinforced by K.'s response to Olga's story, but the terms are reversed to reveal the reciprocal innocence of Olga's mode of being [*Wesen*] and of interpretation. Thus once K. perceives the inconclusiveness of her narration, he feels sure of eluding Olga's seductive powers. Her manifest failure to advance a satisfactory interpretation enables K. to resist in turn *her* 'advances':

> Of course it was as yet far from being adequately explained and might turn out to be quite the reverse; one did not have to be immediately seduced by Olga's unquestionable innocence. (207)

Despite his chaste resolve, K. finds himself abandoned by Frieda directly after his interpretative affair with Olga. Frieda, who discerns in K.'s interpretative act the unique correlative of his erotic drive, regards K.'s night of narration with Olga as an act of infidelity. Thus, for Frieda it is truly a matter of indifference whether K. deceives her through a sexual act or, as it were, a speech act, for both represent part of the same experience of desire. Analogous in structure and performance, each erotic and interpretative act reflects itself as a failure; the search never achieves completion, but is condemned repeatedly to begin anew. This search is based on a concept of desire that can be taken neither as the appetite for satisfaction nor as the demand for love but, as Lacan once wrote, as 'the difference which results from the subtraction of the first from the second, the very phenomenon of their split [*Spaltung*].'[25]

~

In the blissful days of their union, Frieda and K. would delight in surrendering to each other countless interpretations. When, in the fateful thirteenth chapter, they unite to reconstruct their story, Frieda takes the initiative by voicing the landlady's interpretation in her absence. K., as usual, is not satisfied. Observing that he cannot distinguish the boundaries that mark off the landlady's critique from Frieda's narration, he incites Frieda to cast a preliminary counterinterpretation. Frieda, however, soon swerves once more, readjusting her own interpretation to match that of the landlady. This occurs on the occasion of K.'s exchange with Hans. As she reassimilates the landlady's critique of K. to her 'own' perceptions, Frieda begins to notice the 'naked' intentions concealed within K.'s innocent language, as the landlady had done before her (182):

> 'But in reality everything has changed since I heard you speak with that boy [Hans]. How innocently you began. . . . But then quite suddenly – I don't know how it happened – I noticed that you were talking to him with a hidden intention. . . . Your end was that woman. In your apparently solicitous inquiries about her I could see quite nakedly your simple preoccupation with your own affairs. You were betraying that woman even before you had won her.' (185–86)

Frieda's shrewd insistence on keeping the phallic dimension of the signifier intact permits her to 'hear' K.'s simultaneous seduction and betrayal of Hans's mother, Hans, and herself ('What great difference was there between him, the poor boy, being exploited here by you, and myself that time in the taproom?' [186]). Dwelling on the homonymy of K.'s intercourse with her in the taproom and his discourse with Hans here, Frieda, in what begins to read as a parody of Freud's 'little Hans' (1909), in effect charges K. with molesting the child.[26] Her interpretation, as inflated as it may seem, derives partial substantiation from the text:

> K. had called Hans up to the teacher's chair, drawn him between his knees, and kept on caressing him appeasingly. This closeness helped, in spite of Hans's occasional resistance, to bring about an understanding [*Einvernehmen*]. They agreed finally. (176)

This passage, especially in the German with its implicit play on union and agreement [*sich einigen*], encourages us to read the Hans-K. encounter in the manner of Frieda. Indeed, it becomes increasingly difficult to distinguish between the performance of a sexual act, which the child temporarily resists, and that of a speech act. In any case, the result of this 'interdiscourse' is that the child 'desires to be a man like K.' (178), suggesting he has grafted his own desire onto K. However, Hans's desire – much like K.'s desire for Frieda, Olga, and Barnabas – represents a metonymic displacement, or the metonymy of desire, for the mutually desired object of this union is the absent mother. Thus, the Hans episode concludes with the never-to-be-realized promise secretly to meet again, at which time both Hans and K. are to seek out little Hans' mother.

K. initiates the final reconstituting stage of their autointerpretation by conceding, 'everything you say is in a certain sense correct' (186). Typically, though, he seizes upon a lack from which his own interpretation arises – the landlady's interpretation had omitted the word *love.* Although K. redeems the missing signifier, he does so only partially. For his counterargument rests solely on the premise of Frieda's love for him which, he maintains, both women's interpretations had eclipsed. K. does not argue with the tenor of the landlady's argument, but he does reproach Frieda for yielding so fully to the seduction of the landlady's discourse ('These are the thoughts of the landlady . . . even if you think they are your own . . . and how you yield to her, Frieda, how you yield!' [186–87]). More than anything else, K. appears to be jealous of a rival discourse, one that, possessing Frieda entirely, necessarily obscures her presumed love for him. In a renewed attempt to conquer Frieda – this time through the *language* of desire – K. urges Frieda to restore to her speech, though not necessarily to her action, the motif of love. Toward the end of his own interpretation, however, K.'s attempted abduction of Frieda from the landlady takes another course. His reconstitution of their story brushes aside the very motif of love – in this he repeats the landlady's error – to dwell upon the supposed reciprocity of their needs. 'Remembering' the mood that drew them together, K. speaks of a shared moment of forgetfulness (189). K.'s reconstitution of his original encounter with Frieda joins a procession of previous recollections, for here, as before, K.'s interpretative act conjures an imaginary other; participating in the moments that prompted his recollections of the beautiful church in his *Heimat* as he stood before the wretched 'castle,' and of days spent happily in the military as the bizarre assistants first saluted him, K.'s present accounting activates once more his – and perhaps all too often the commentator's – memory of another, hallucinated text. But this other text, in which aesthetic harmony, manly action, and forgetfulness [*Vergessenheit*] lightly intermingle, never coincides with the text that has drafted K.

The sequence of interpretations that originated along the boundaries of the Frieda-K. story concludes much like the event it sought to reconstruct. And so the constellation of eros, suffocation, struggle, loss of goal, and absented object reemerges:

> 'Oh, if you [K.] but knew with what passion I try to find what I [Frieda] consider a good core in all that you say and do, even if it causes me pain . . . a young lad suddenly comes in and you begin to fight with him for his mother, as if you were fighting for your very life [*Lebensluft*].' (189)

> 'But do you consider your entire earlier life to have sunk so low, . . . that you no longer know how one has to struggle in order to move ahead [*das Vorwärtskommen*], especially when one comes from the lower rungs [*von tief unten herkommt,* "comes from deep under"]?' (189)

In sum, the interpretative act, much like the erotic pulsion that parallels it, discloses itself as a movement at once toward and away from an original signifier – in a generous Freudian context, the phallus – that was never really present. This signifier, whether exemplified in the castle or Klamm, in the saintly image of Hans's mother, or in the Frieda who figures in the landlady's narration as a restorer of wholeness, constitutes an imaginary object that would serve, in Frieda's idiom, as a stabilizing 'core.' The interpretative act supplements but never captures or coincides with the original signifier. In other words, interpretation is as dependent on a notion of breakdown as is the theory of desire set forth in the text. In dramatizing the characters' desire (*Verlangen,* in Frieda's idiom) for a dimension beyond the limits of their discourse, the text reflects the fault out of which it generates its own discourse.[27] Yet the characters, like the text and an honest woman, seem finally to accept this affair of the lack as their sole mode of existence. By the 'end' of *The Castle,* the characters are so accustomed to a game which decries its own rules that they produce a nonrecuperative comedy of the text's denial of meaning and truth. Returning to the question of sign and significance, the landlady recommences:

> 'What are you actually?' 'Landsurveyor.' 'What *is* that?' K. explained, the explanation made her yawn. 'You're not telling the truth. Why don't you tell the truth?' 'You don't tell the truth either.' 'I? So now you're beginning your impudent remarks again? And if I didn't tell the truth – do I have to answer for it to you? And in what don't I tell the truth, then?' 'You are not only the landlady, as you pretend.' 'Sure! You're full of discoveries!' (360)

And thus this virulent archcritic reduces our reading of the textual strategies, the lies, and circuit breakers to a caustic 'Sure! You're full of discoveries!' We should not lose sight of the fact that, together with K., we are perhaps always confronted with the likes of the landlady – who is not only a landlady. If I am not mistaken, it was she who named us as beings who are incomplete and superfluous, beings whose readings engage a perpetual aberration:

> 'You are nothing. Unfortunately you are nonetheless something, a foreigner [*ein Fremder*], one who is superfluous and always in the way . . . someone whose intentions are unknown. . . . You misinterpret everything – even silence.' (64, 100)

Precisely. The text drew us toward itself much like Kafka's sirens, using as a means of seduction 'a still more fatal weapon than song, namely . . . silence.'[28] In *The Castle*, it was the silence of the 'locked-in' [*ver-schloßen*] realm of untroubled semantic security and our common isolation from this ostensible realm that originated our interpretative activity, replaying the technicity ('terrifying weapon') of a vague desire.

~

Let us suppose for a moment that within the boundary of Kafka's works there exists a luminous repository of truth. Let us assume, as do others, that the source of Kafka's essential truth-telling – what Hölderlin ironically called 'the most truthful truth' – is to be found in Kafka's diaries. And now, let us consider in this light two well-known diary entries. First the remarkable claim, 'since I am nothing but Literature and neither can nor want to be anything else,' and second, Kafka's assertion that 'one can only communicate [*mitteilen*] what one is not, that is, the lie.'[29] Let me suggest, finally, that in this essay I have taken these two statements at face value. Since Kafka himself champions an antimetaphorical diction, one will happily not need to interpret his first statement metaphorically; I have suggested a reading of *The Castle* as the imparted lie of that which our author is. That is to say, we have witnessed Kafka withdraw from the scene of his final work the proper name 'Literature.' But then, of course, if one, namely Kafka, can only communicate the lie, are we, in our desire to reach a satisfactory conclusion, basing our thoughts on yet another Kafkan lie? In keeping with the poetics of *The Castle*, one can however continue to pursue the lie, persistently, hopelessly, and yet, admittedly, with a certain degree of pleasure. For this line of pursuit is the wisdom that the text teaches.

In the beginning of this discussion, it was suggested tentatively that Walser's view of a congruency operating between K. and his author seemed untenable. The strategy here was to bring the protagonist into a congruent relation with the text and to propose that K. and the novel together explore the limits of a literary world that has relegated the very concepts of a poetic language, self, and form to a remote *Heimat* from which they have been expelled. Now, however, it seems that the two are linked in yet another way; they seem to reflect, indeed, to reinforce each other's craving for incompleteness, repetition, for another writing which would be neither entirely absent nor present. But the degree of congruency between K. and the text was not fully evident in the beginning of the work.

This reconnects to Walser's study, in which he further argues that 'the work shows no development whatsoever.'[30] Another reading of the same work could trace a dynamic progression in the modes of narrative consciousness culminating in Pepi's acutely self-analytical narration. But our focus was elsewhere and led to another type of discovery. In the early stages of the novel, there arrived at the castle frontier a rather illiterate K. expecting to race through the text as a kind of picaro and, at one point, hoping to dissolve into a mimetic brother to the villagers Gerstäcker and Lasemann.[31] It turned out that the uninitiated K., who first had to learn to 'read' the novel which captivates him, is not identical to the later, more astute K. For, as the unsuspecting K. gradually became acquainted with a variety of textual strategies, he began to acquire an ironic appreciation of difference, play, and desire.

Armed with an ironic sensibility, K., though often weary and perplexed, essentially affirms the text's intentions and makes them his own, 'for the duration' [*auf die Dauer* (227)]. K. finally colludes with the text and defends its principles; he defends the novel against the enemy lines of the representational mode of writing, as in the Momus episode; he defends the novel against potential lapses into meaning. Thus, for example, when the Castle sends out a 'meaningful' message that threatens to fulfill him, K., reacting with pain, sends out a signal to disrupt the message. And K. also defends the novel against the possibility of *its* achieving a modicum of satisfaction. Often, when a given interpretation verges on 'understanding' the textual maneuvers, K. will either judge it inconclusive or interrupt its presentation. We find one such example when Olga is about to release her knowledge of irony. As if to prevent her from providing the text with a 'satisfactory' interpretation of its own mode, a cybernetically inflected K. cuts her off abruptly: 'Stop the interpretations!' (239).

In this larger context, we could venture to say that K. compels the text to watch patiently the spectacle of the comedy in which the characters' jarring readings of its intent are voiced and, if any interpretation seems to border on insight, K. will quickly eliminate it or deride it for reaching beyond signal decoding or information systems.

Eternally plotting thus to delay the moment of the other's gratification, the text and protagonist, if not in a relation of congruency, then surely in one of profound reciprocity, keep each other 'alive' and seriously moving by one and the same shrewd method – they reinforce each other's withdrawal and energetically affirm the necessity of sustaining a mutually unfulfilled desire. In this respect, let us recall that one of the primary fictions that K. pursues within the text suggests in Hebrew – Kafka studied Hebrew in preparation for his emigration to Palestine – 'nothing' ['כלום'], while in German it also means a 'yawning' or 'gaping open.' The triumph of the work's irony is that K. and his object – his text – do finally meet on the grounds of an abyss.

# STARTING FROM SCRATCH

*Mastermix*

### THE AUTOTHANATOGRAPHICAL INDICATOR

I was invited to give a lecture at a special session of the Modern Language Association convention in Washington, D.C., in 1985. The session was intended to launch the first full-blown appearance of the Nuclear Criticism Group after the publication of several distinguished papers in *diacritics.* Richard Klein of Cornell was charged with heading up the panel at the convention. I had been working on rumorological paranoia and the telephone, trying to trace the umbilical logic that attaches certain utterances to the paternal belly of the state. I got interested in untraced calls to the Third Reich, the telecommunications of fascism and the industrialization of corpses. But, in particular, I was trying to locate a call that Martin Heidegger had received from Hitler's elite guard when he was in the rector's office heading up the university. I have always been onto the university switchboard, its complicity with the state, the war machine that keeps it well lubricated.

Flash to the convention. I was wondering about *their* nuclear desire, about the way institutions accommodate certain undigestible objects of inquiry, or desire. What was their investment in this discourse? I wanted to address this and also the state's inscription of the body, the way it registers, imprints, and invents a coded body. Where does war take place? Or the radicality of absolute war? Not in an imaginary outside, no longer in a firmly circumscribed space of the battlefield, but in two ways – war's atomization marks the civilian body and the language that envelopes it. I wanted to scan incorporations of war, scouring the national unconscious.

The war zone extends to the intestinal tract, or begins there. If we could throw it up, we would reverse the dialectic of assimilation. It is crucial to place the battlefield, especially when it is no longer localizable as such but still relegated to an hallucinated exteriority. If the national appetite has fetishized hamburgers and frankfurters, is the homonymy with the former enemy not rather jarring? What is going down? Also, insofar as nuclear war cannot as such take place – when it does, it's over – then its proper domain is rhetoric and the field of the Other. This is why I felt it necessary to explore the linguistic conduct associated with warfare, a politics of epistemological anxiety.

I try to figure the paradoxical tensions that arise with nuclear desire. The point is that we want it, we dream it, we call it forth. The radical problem consists in recognizing the desire, wanting the end as the fulfillment of a promise. Even when we're just having a blast or blown away by a lecture or burning to do the neutron dance. Because when the end comes – and we want it to come – it is promised to us as the grandiose gesture of apocalypse; it is to come as revelation, the disclosure of truth. I wanted to go to the heart of this metaphysical desire, and fire away at its pernicious totalizing schemes. But I had to do it in a certain way, break up the academic language barrier, talk about those effaced from the scene of a conference. So when I say 'we,' this dogmatic assertion has to be collapsed, destabilized, rendered nonidentical to itself. 'We' is wartalk – something I try consciously to deconstitute. I had to do it. My own kind of research and destroy unit.

> Notice: I am going to make this very choppy and quick. It will not be centered like the A-bomb, or gathered up into a mushroom cloud. The following nuclear dispersion aims to condense time, spinning within the temporal aporia of a thing destined not to begin.

~

So put this through the chopper, the cuisinart, or helicopter propeller. Nuclear aphorisms, word snapshots in the dark. The album has for a first title, 'I'm not a man, I'm dynamite.'

### THE BLAST EFFECT

> *The blast effect results from the pressure wave created by the explosion. It travels at a much slower speed than the heat flash. Local earthquake-proof buildings can be expected to withstand this pressure wave better than the type of building found in Hiroshima.*–San Francisco Examiner, *10 Sept. 1950*

This discourse appears to be parasited from the start by a defilement – a newspaper article has supplanted research tools of a traditional sort. Nuclear criticism implies a relationship to journalistic reporting that had been cleared away, like a kind of toxicity, from the fields of academic and intellectual discourses. This suggests, among other things, a desire for an instantaneity that projects a sensational nuclear blast. Let us remember the figure who switches identities in a telephone booth. A telecommunications specialist par excellence, Superman becomes what he is by literally ascending beyond himself, rising above the journalistic persona that suffers a still more heavily weighted temporality than the one guiding the flying rumor, faster than a bullet or any train of thought. The flying rumor is that which Superman qua Superman becomes. The extent to which Superman serves to trace out the double trajectory linking a rumorology to the concept of nuclear war can be recalled from the beginning of his narrative; a rumor circulates that the planet Krypton is going to explode momentarily, and this is read by Superman's father through the trace gases in the air. That trace gas is related to air as rumor to discourse. As it stands, nuclear war constitutes itself in and by rumor.

Before turning the speakers up full blast, it would be useful to make a few prefatory remarks which, in a sense, is the only discourse one can engage in the face of something called 'nuclear war' – a kind of critique of practical nuclearism. While nuclear war may in fact respond to the vision that Kant conjures up in his perpetual peace treaty – a vision of the endless and absolute cemetery, a perpetual resting in peace – one has to wonder why the thinking of this peace, nuclear war, has been readily accommodated by such institutions as the MLA.

One implication of such an accommodation may be that the MLA has granted permission, it thinks, to *talk about nothing:* in other words, business as usual. But what would be the place or desire of an academic discourse that allows itself to speak about nothing, in other words about nuclear war, about that which bypasses everything? Will this be the place where, finally, one can gracefully recuperate a language of totality, reading against the horizon of absolute finality? And what would distinguish this type of thinking from all thinking of totality, in the tradition of metaphysics? Entering what has been called the unthinkable poses a risk for the nuclear critic who has to be wary of participating, knowingly or not, in a movement of general repression. Writing with the end in mind threatens to lift pressure from thinking of the pain or suffering that nuclearism by definition erases. Therefore the nuclear critic has to resist all that erases the terrifying demarcations of pain, and has to ask questions about the MLA's decision to legitimize the discourse of nuclear criticism.

One point that might be raised here concerns the silence of the university on questions of racism, torture, AIDS – in other words, the order of things which belong to the thinkable and, in principle at least, to the redressable. Nuclear criticism needs to prevent itself from being the university's spectacular way out, or from producing a sign of pious responsibility for something that, according to classical ethical determinations, we can, strictly speaking, no longer be responsible for. The history of the university's relationship to war still needs to be interpreted, for in a large measure if a university has had anything to offer on this subject – beyond a certain erotic overinvestment or the pleasure it takes in its own impotence – universities have all too often been the locus of collaboration and intellectual complicity with war. To conclude these prefatory hesitations, let me note that use will be made of the word, 'California.' The trajectory linking California to Washington, D.C., is not merely a contingent effect of a random subject's autobiographical passage through time. The California-Washington shuttle does not simply refer to a certain subject's privileged itinerary. (Clearly, *if* a subject were to be named here, it would be President Reagan, whose homes are split between these toponyms.) But an interpretation of the Pacific end of this country will have to be left to a study concerned with the precise geopolitics of nuclear implantations.

Now we can turn up the speakers full blast, in stereophonic bicoastal synchrony. Many of those who have written on nuclear criticism have pointed out that timing is of the essence. We now can add that the truth of time-telling in the ontic sense continues to be measured against what is called the atomic clock.

### THE ATOMIC CAFÉ

Given the present context, meaning the 'fast-food' or 'zap' temporality governing nuclear utterance, I will propose what, in the rhetoric of break dancing, is known as a Mastermix. That is, the signatory will take up the post of a DJ whose record has no original, but who submits a piece to a particular audience by committing violence to that piece – for example by 'scratching' the surface. 'Scratching,' or the production of a piece whose origin is continually scratched or canceled out has been generally considered a response to automation. This would be my point of departure if I were going anywhere – the homonymic effects which arise from the linguistic escalation of *atomic* into *automatic.* As the mastermix methodology suggests, the question of war is one of genre, and has been posed since at least Sun Tzu's *Thirteen Articles* devoted to military strategy: is war an art or a science? What is the site of war's taking place? The typologies and topologies of war will be the objects of study for programs being implemented at the Collège de Philosophie in Paris, founded by Jacques Derrida and currently under the direction of Jean-François Lyotard. Here, an outline will have to suffice to name the issues which might underlie a specifically nuclear genre, although this genre is by no means limited by the advent of nuclear*ism.*

As everyone knows, total nuclear war cannot as such begin, it can only end – the moment it takes place, nuclear war will be over. Its taking place, therefore, constitutes an original end of sorts, the final fall of the fall, the spectacular fallout. Displacements of the body: arms have become arms that race, erasing the bodies' members, heads turned into war heads, and so on. By several rhetorical maneuvers, then, the body has already been evacuated from the site of battle, a battleground no longer being grounded as a circumscribable place where a class of warriors might engage one another in a limited, classical way.

Nuclear war is conducted by no bodies: a symbolic mutation in the very concept of war that has created, I think, a condition through which every body is carrying war upon itself, now. This may be observed in the most superficial manner, in combat fatigues as casual fashion, but war has also been incorporated by everybody since at least the 1950s when the so-called cold war was first served up as a legitimate notion. In his essay on war, 'Tomorrow's Arms,' Walter Benjamin writes of the possibility of an invisible war, anticipating scenes (or rather nonscenes) of chemical and biological warfare that would take place in our cities – in a space, therefore, that is no longer remote from the *polis,* and about which we would have no absolute certitude. All of this could happen, he writes, without there being a single airplane visible in the air. The sky would be clear, unaltered, and the sun resplendent. While Benjamin casts only a shadow of suggestion upon the phantom of war haunting and agitating within everybody, he prepares an alarm system destined to safeguard thinking, because, according to Benjamin, the question of thinking is numbed, anesthetized by the simple idea of a coming war. And this numbness first comes over the faculties of thinking; the coming war induces *Denkfaulheit,* mindrot.

Note that there is War and there are also wars, contained and containable. World War I, which Freud asserts introduced a break into the occidental notion of death – perhaps the beginning of the death of death and of the symbolicity that every individual death commands – was the first event to implicate every citizen, whether or not he or she was professionally engaged in warfare. It might be noted that in and of itself war has not had a stable or single meaning. For the Native American, to take one example, an individual death or casualties were accidents of the war ritual, which was accompanied by all kinds of aestheticizations, such as war dancing, body makeup, and so on. Nor have the discourses surrounding the event of war remained fixed. The notion of *justified* aggression arose, according to Hannah Arendt, only with the Romans. One would want to study the history of declarations of war, peace treaties, settlements, restitutions, and so on, to understand the differential range of something like a rhetoric of war.

Instead, let us pursue a subterranean tract of nuclearism, begun in the 1950s, that goes by way of the digestive tract, a doubled-over kind of incorporation. How has war been turned into a food processor, something that plays itself out in the body's symbolizations of pain? Rumor, the other embattled field, returns us to Benjamin's mention of the murmur. This involves a type of linguistic behavior that has always been associated with warfare, since at least the time when Homer sent Rumor, Zeus's messenger, speeding through the battlefield. As usual, rumor has preceded its proper place of disclosure, in the advance guard of any pronouncement one would presume to make about it. The other field of inquiry, then, will be the restless advancement of rumor. This raises the question of what Neil Hertz has called 'epistemological anxiety': can you trust your ears?

## EATING AT THE ATOMIC CAFÉ

The era of the flying saucer is not quite over. It originated around the fifties when world wars began to be incorporated, served, after the war, on cold platters. The war was taken into the home, domesticated and stylized, beginning with saucers or atomic ware (manufactured in California), thus establishing a line of dishware, dish*war.* This coincides with the era when bunker food began to be developed – and everything in advertising and electoral campaigns turned around the question of preserves (please let the French *conserves* enter this reading, for one should not overlook the conservative edge to this frame). The stockpiling of cans, the miniature replicas of shelters, the possibility and need for conserving food substances indefinitely can be read as an objectification of the incorporation of war into the political imagination. Humanities preserving themselves in the can: a kind of prison phantasm carried out under the name of shelter.

The rise of atomic dishware and the mass production of canned foods overlaps with the moment women began to be designated as 'dishes' and 'bombs,' objects of desire. Or, perhaps to the contrary, according to a phobic logic that has also made women the carriers of certain sexually transmitted diseases whose symptoms erupt in men, women were the carriers of dishes, at the height of proliferation rumors about the nuclear family. As Edward Shorter has suggested in *The Making of the Modern Family,* the nuclear family belongs to a class of cultural phantasmata that organizes its concept around the domestic unit and radical enclosure. Women served their families in the performative making of dinner, making war, and possibly (within the kind of displacement that has been suggested for the sixties oppositional rhetoric of making war or making love, these women were always shown prepared to make war), spreading the table with war's contagion. Of course there will be no final proof in the pudding except to refer to a symbolic mutation, an incorporation of war into the domestic unit or digestive tracts in order to eliminate the radical outsideness and uncontrollability of war.

Ever since the manifest world war has ceased, America has been ingesting an atomic regime whose culinary range includes the automatic production of hamburgers and frankfurters or whatever can be mastered by the fast-food temporality that we associate with the proliferation of (hamburger/nuclear) chains and what could be subsumed under the concept of frozen foods, the arrested state of entire meals destined to survive natural spoilage or even the consumer. This nuclear freezer, while participating in a fast temporality, simultaneously puts natural objects on hold, preserving them beyond the classical deadline of any perishable item. By the time of nuclearism – our time – the future was over, an unmarked event whose expression is found in an essential punk or nuclear sensibility.

In this respect one should not close one's eyes to the punk look, which not only glues together a safety-pinned numbness, but also raises the question of the punk hairdo. What do the hairs stand for? The punk look essentially consists of standing on end, on split ends pointing toward a concept of nuclear fission. The punk hair style falls into place, or rather out of place, to solidify a notion of accidental taking place, a kind of arrested or frozen state of the accident, or horror. One could say it gathers up in itself the horrified post-Hiroshima Medusa look. As excremental growth, hair, the body's supplementary temporal zone, is already the afterlife of a body, the substance that continues to grow after a body, biologically speaking, may have ceased to exist. In this respect the punk hairdo thematizes the anticipation of a disaster of which they (the hairs) have had a prior experience, insofar as hair can be said to experience anything. As a mark of a body's survival, as its minimal leftover, belonging neither to life nor to death strictly speaking, hair will share the world with the insects – in fact, it is already there, which is precisely the predicament to which the punk hairdo points.

But the sense of alarm, the desire to decorate one's body or domestic unit with atomic rhetoric received one of its principal modes of expression through a sort of household bomb. The first peacetime use of radiation fell to the alarm clocks of the fifties which were painted with radium, meant to glow through the night. Having first killed Mme Curie, radium also caused the deaths of the workers who painted the numbers and dots on alarm clocks, since in order to apply radium to the minuscule dots or ellipses that were to mark time, workers had to wet the brushes by putting them in their mouths, thus ingesting poison. Nowadays one can still ingest radiation the way certain ultramodern households or luncheonettes fix their food or 'nuke' their bagels, although this mode of preparation is considered dangerous and even banned in some other countries: the microwave oven.

### TALKING TO THE WAITRESS AT THE ATOMIC CAFÉ

Nor should the manner in which nuclearism freezes language escape us. The conjunctions of an incapacitated literacy in this country, serial repetitions of mindless clichés and the anticipation of nuclear war – what Derrida has called 'remainderless destruction' – must to some extent constitute one another. This hypothesis can be observed in the case of certain presidential utterances beginning in the 1950s, in which Eisenhower, Carter, and, more recently, Bush, gave expression to the unpronounceability of the nuclear designation; they would only pronounce the term as an anagram of itself, as its own substitute: *nucyular.* Even more recently, President Reagan conjured a nuclear futuricity by promising and repeating the promise of 'You ain't seen nothing yet.' A nothing that is unpronounceable, imperceptible, the defutured future of remainderless nothing. We ain't seen nothing yet. Yet this nothing is something that we hear, spreading like a rumor according to a logic of contagion.

One type of freeze language, publicly diffused, broadcast like the support system of rumor, is the current nuclear music. For example the Pointer Sisters, pointing their missiles, launching messages from Oakland, California, such as 'The Neutron Dance.' Or 'Space Cowboy' ('everything is automatic') or the Gap Band's 'You Dropped a Bomb on Me,' or Prince's '1999' ('Mommy, why does everybody have the bomb?'). But the very technology of widespread diffusion parallels the thanatechnology carried in Reagan's hotline briefcase, his portable button to the bomb. Consider, in this respect, the so-called ghetto briefcase or *blaster,* which prides itself on a sophisticated button control system. If there is no place for the nonevent of a nuclear war, if the concept of battlefield itself has been expulsed or denied, except for the extraplanetary fantasia of a star wars, and if there are no bodies to engage in a warfare, the violence of this predicament is being staged and reinterpreted close to the ground. It is in the unsigned street-texts of break dancing which have introduced, at the limit between violence and art, a revival in the form of bodily engagement whose acknowledged model, however, is the cartoon. Cartoon figures, given over to a multiple battering and explosions, always spring back to life, surviving themselves in the present. Break dancing opens ritualized competition whose moves, consisting of dislocation, alternate between gestures of 'popping' and 'floating,' styled to encounter classes of the unintelligible such as the hieroglyphics that make up the King Tut moves. Break dancing deserves (together with heavy metal, whose language involves a nostalgia for medieval warfare) a more attentive reading as the undead street graffiti of nuclearism – in which, once again, blacks are sent to the front. What emerges here is an effect of miniaturization, a minimal turf battlefield, in the polis, circumscribed by the parameters of a mat upon which the competition plays itself out.

One more thing ought to be said about break dancing as a sign of war's incorporation, and this concerns the body which, while it appears to be engaged in the performance of conflict, is also disengaged, decorporealized in a conceptual retreat to nuclear war's *a priori* evacuation of bodies from the scene of battle. Thus the dance vocabulary contains motifs of bodily retreat, a kind of robotization of sheer movement, the Kleistian new wave marionette theater. And so, on the one hand, the freak terminology that abounds in this mutant warfare has its roots in German culture, in the prescratch music of Kraftwerk. On the other hand – and dislocated as this may initially seem – break dancing and scratch came into play when gang wars had reached a certain limit of mutual destruction and a social contract was drawn in the South Bronx, establishing break dancing as a substitutive war action. This phenomenon participates, then, in the logic of MAD – Mutual Assured Destruction, a term coined by the Pentagon – which, in the face of our recently achieved 'overkill capacity' staggers the imagination. But this stagger falls into step, becomes a step, in fact, for a space will have been created, almost automatically, for dancing. This is why, in the *meantime*, the Great Couple will dance. Reagan has offered to dance with the dancing bear of the Soviet Union, willing to offer his arms, taking the lead therefore and yet, as D. A. Miller has pointed out, when two men dance, it is never clear who is leading.

## THE JUKEBOX AT THE ATOMIC CAFÉ

To repeat: this presentation is organized around the concept of the Mastermix, derived from break dancing and meant in this context to convey a means of thinking the atomic automatic. Mixing sounds, then, attuning your ears to the noise base of language, I would like to consider a specific type of linguistic utterance whose force is especially prevalent at times of great stress. This would be a variety of 'speech act' that occurs, like the 'excuses' of which Paul de Man has written, in a twilight zone between knowing and not knowing. Yet this utterance comes armed with the power to kill. First, an article published in San Francisco in 1955, entitled, 'Six Secrets of Atom Survival,' three of which might be mentioned here. The first anticipates a move in break dancing: 'Drop flat on the Ground or Floor. . . . Should you unexpectedly be caught out of doors, seek shelter alongside a building or jump in any handy ditch or gutter.' The motif of the handy turns back, in the second secret, to arms: 'Bury your face in your arms.' Note the embeddedness of burial and the arms race in the language of survival. The last secret interests me most: 'Don't Start Rumors. In the confusion that follows a bombing, a single rumor might touch off a panic that could cost you your life.' In other words, the rumor that you start could turn its aim upon the speaker. This is the only mention made of death, and its source would not be a bomb but a rumor. Moreover, it would follow that in the confusion and general contamination set off by a bomb – 'war' by the way traces back etymologically to 'confusion' – rumor would be the one thing with a clear aim, a nuclear aim. *If* you start a single rumor after massive bombing has completed its course, you will pay for shooting off your mouth.

## BREAKING BREAD WITH ROUSSEAU AND HEIDEGGER AT THE ATOMIC CAFÉ

What is rumor, possibly the most costly of utterances? Rumor has been treated primarily in a sociological context. In *L'Age des foules*, Serge Moscivici analyzes it as a symptom of collective impotence, while Francisco Umbral has written of 'il rumerismo' as a product of hermetic societies. But let us target a slightly different reading, in keeping with the task at hand.

When the stakes are high or very clear, a principle of noncontamination tends to be asserted, a purity of aim and telos introduced. Thus, for example, the rhetoric of war, when drafted into war, aims to be clean and to the point. A kind of language is launched in an attempt to offset rumor's run. Three examples could serve as a point of departure for studying the rapport of containment that war rhetoric seeks to establish over unmonitored broadcast systems of transmission:

1. 'Loose lips sink ships.'
2. 'Attention! Les murs ont des oreilles!'
3. In the recent 1984 Olympics, a Rumor Control Center was set up to monitor and absorb straying utterances and catch stray shots.

In a work originating in Paul de Man's reading of Rousseau, I am trying to show how competing utterances work in Rousseau's decathlon, his ten walks and diverse athletic events – arguably, his war text – in which he tries to establish exactly that: a rumor-control center, an attempt to disarm the stray utterances that pierce his corpus. Any rhetoric of war – and this includes institutional warfare, the noises that traverse an ear canal, an institutional corridor or political vestibules – would have to take into account the rumor's path, a kind of exemplary master-mix text continually resuming its form as a widely disseminated report detached from any discernible origin or source. Inasmuch as it becomes what it is, the spreading rumor takes on the qualities of a story told, without author or term, imposing itself as an ineluctable account (see 'Street-Talk,' 128 above).

As Rousseau has taught us, the rumor loses no time; in his text, it is always placed in relation to the devastation following an accident. In this sense, rumor has always belonged to a structure of the automatic, being something whispered into ears that function like loudspeakers, receiving warnings on the order of 'do not repeat this,' but always oriented toward the future of its repetition. One of the final goals of his exit text, *Reveries of a Solitary Walker* – of all exit texts, including rules of proper atomic conduct – entails putting a stop to the proliferation of a public discourse, in an effort to kill the rumor or at least to contain it. For rumors communicate, like certain diseases, a kind of uncontrollable contagion that essentially escapes all literatures, that leaks, like nuclear plants.

The aims and precise expression of these utterances are not imputable to any knowable origin. They have no identifiable creator or signator and yet, rumors are stated in the tone of a revealed truth. This is a variety of speech act that is always on the run, existing in the mode of a hit-and-run temporality, coming, like a sudden accident, from nowhere. Rumors, like bombs, Superman, or Benjamin's helicopter, are in the air – they fly. They are often designated as something going around, arriving from a secret source, from nowhere. Like *Hamlet,* rumor is organized around the concept of a nothing and a nowhere that speaks. The most pressing issue of nuclear criticism may be, then, to decipher the trace gas of poisoned utterances. For do not forget that Hamlet's father died from a poison that was poured into his ear, and the whole drama recycles this poison, from mouth to ear, in a great ring of espionage and infection. Infecting and paralyzing everybody, including the body politic, casting a form of *Denkfaulheit,* mindrot, the rumor of Hamlet begins when he whispers, 'I am dead, Horatio.' Is this not our predicament, to say we are dead, transmitting a rumored knowledge to which every ear is more or less open? The nothing and nowhere that speaks – 'you ain't seen nothing yet' – being in the air, on the streets, performed in hairdos and on the air, has been addressed, to a certain degree, by Heidegger, the philosopher who wanted to withdraw his signature from the war text. Thus, in *Being and Time* he writes of *Nachrede* – the temporal afterlife or afterwards that marks rumor in the German language. The route of rumor or passing the word along creates a condition in which 'things are so because one says so.' Rumor is constituted in 'a process by which its initial lack of grounds to stand [*Bodenständigkeit*] becomes aggravated to complete groundlessness [*Bodenlosigkeit*].' Furthermore, 'rumor is the possibility of understanding everything without previously making the thing one's own.'[1]

With Heidegger, one can offer that the rumor belongs to that order of things which cannot be assimilated. But it does not stand in a relationship of strict exteriority to those systems of utterance from which it has always been bounced. Having its place neither inside nor outside such a language, whose measure of authenticity would be privileged proximity to Being, rumor, however, places in question the Heideggerian difference between an authentic and inauthentic *Sprache,* a language whose greatest fear would be to fall, like Rousseau, into the abyss of *Gerede.* Rumor, by its very nature, Heidegger argues, is 'a closing-off, since to go back to the ground of what is talked about is something which it *leaves undone.*' This would be Heidegger's break dance, his breaking ground with groundlessness, with that which has been left undone, but is still in the air, being passed around. Perhaps, however, this breaking of the ground is precisely what nuclear criticism must listen to.

# THE WORST NEIGHBORHOODS OF THE REAL

## *Philosophy – Telephone – Contamination*

**Note from the stenopad: Precisely at the middle of his important book,* A Strange Virus of Unknown Origin *(originally,* Un Virus étrange venu d'ailleurs*), Dr. Jacques Leibowitch trades in his medical technology for what appears to be its double and other: 'Let us put down our stethoscopes and our too slowly productive test tubes and begin our investigation. First of all, the telephone, an absurd instrument of research, but a modern one. Let us get the anecdote, the information, the verification, the cross-checking into circulation. Let the institution support them, as an army supports its scouts.'*[1]

«1»

BAD RECEPTION: The site of discursivity around which the technologies of the self have been organized goes under the name, or so it appears, of Michel Foucault. He has cut the intersection between philosophy and contamination, urinal politics and the state. If the body in the meantime has been submitted to new zoning laws of anality and detection systems, the signs and symptomatologies of the body under language arrest were already showing up on Foucault's scanner. And beyond – perhaps before – all this, his body where it lines up with philosophy, became the writing of contamination. The history of Foucault's body can no longer be considered extraneous or accidental to the line of thought that was threaded through a diagnostic politics, a body technology, and a history of sexuality.

Yet this 'Foucault' divides itself under the rule of a certain technological proliferation. There are many Foucaults, scattered among different localities and rigorously expulsed from others. There exists for example a German Foucault of punk precision who, despite an abundance of shared signifiers, has little in common with the Foucault of S/M criticism. There is also a Foucault of the right, who has been reabsorbed into traditional ('new') historicist thinking, as well as a Foucault who has been used to legitimize the myth of an immediately transparent language, whose immediacy renders thought accessible, embraceable. This language, as Michael Bernstein writes in an emphatic tribute, is not a *deviant* language.[2]

Still, if Foucault has not been the accomplice to deviant language, this amounts to something of a scandal; or, paradoxically, it turns him over to a kind of Derridean critique, doubtless the unnamed accused of language's deviance. In other words, if Foucault's language successfully evades deviance as his admirers suggest, then he is shown to be speaking from the other side of the barricades – this side, perhaps, of institutional safety zones; he would be speaking in order to maintain deviance in its exteriority, to gag it once again, to incarcerate and protect language from the contamination of poisoned otherness, from the contagion of linguistic misbehavior, that is, from madness's contagion. But language, according to Foucault, cannot create for itself a zone of radical immunity; it constantly runs the risk of exposure, and it is at this encounter between the body of language and its antibodies, the encounter of the language of deviance and that of prescriptive normativism, that Foucault's language risks severe contamination. This is the language of terror, stated in his essay 'Language to Infinity,' which drives itself out of any possible resting place. This language can no longer avoid multiplying itself – as if struck from within by a disease of proliferation. Shedding all 'ontological weight' – losing weight, therefore, the language of terror exposes itself to, even acquires for itself, a symptomatology of immunodeficiency. This language, Foucault writes, 'suffers a deficiency.'[3]

Whereas one could argue that Nietzsche's texts are immunologically active – this is how his 'pathos of distance' can be read, if violently, as originating in an immunopathological demand; whereas Nietzsche's texts operate within a hygienics of the obsessional neurotic, overly sensitive to stench, Foucault's texts, his literature, solicit exposure, or, rather, enter the zoned-off spaces where one is seduced into contamination. As an affirmation, this may seem scandalous; but if a reading of Foucault does not produce an effect of scandal, then his discourse may well have been submitted to the sanitation department – neutralized and expulsed from the filth and aberration which it wanted to let speak. Or if the scandal of Foucault's descent has been rerouted and domesticated, then this would be a pretty sure sign that Foucault has entered the place where writing loses its edge, knowledge its insomnia – indeed, the university.

It could be shown, however, that Foucault in his writing on literature willed his death as a somewhat remainderless destruction, with no discipline to bear his name; thus, 'I would like my books to be like surgeons' knives, molotov cocktails or galleries in a mine, and, like fireworks, to be carbonized after use.'[4] Assuming this utterance were successfully to disclose the desire of its signatory, this atomic destruction or the pleasure taken in inflicting pain – like surgeons' knives ('surgeons' is pluralized, there are many knives at work here including perhaps that of Foucault's father who was a surgeon) – if we are to submit or subject ourselves to his books, in the most kindly of these hypotheses, we would first have to undergo anesthesia or succumb to the power of a blast, a Molotov cocktail. One has to risk destruction or, in Hegelian terms, the prestige of death. This indicates a performative language in its latency – one that is not only inaccessible, but not to be touched for fear it will go off (there is a large rhetoric of what I would call *militerary* desire in Foucault, a consistent grasp of strategy and tactical maneuvers, a reading pressing upon the transmission of knowledge and affectivity within a scenography of war).

Maybe so. I can't say. I have been merely assuming the function of secretary, or more precisely still, of a receptionist, taking this down, down from its transcendental heights or the superior certitude of recent academic appropriations, including that of my boss. Foucault will have served as example and warning to the extent that he has been made to map out the test site for a sinuous thinking of contamination, philosophy, and its carceral breakouts. His act was cleaned up after him. This gets me down. In what follows, when I'm on the job, I shall try to make a connection on a somewhat complicated switchboard that always threatens to jam up. This will be no reading of the Purities, but an attempt to move back and forth between what lights up before us. This includes the call from the past which tries to disguise its voice while at the same time telling us that the future is on the line. Nothing happens on this switchboard that does not announce itself as coming from the future. One of the events, finally, to which the switchboard will try to put us through, is the subterranean murmuring that underlies all thinking of technology (including that of Nietzsche, Heidegger, Blanchot, Freud), namely, the relatedness of technology to the feminine. No liberation without appliances, no war machine without a girl's name, no desire for survival without the feminine. No mode of connectivity, in short,

without the
Emergency Feminine.

«2»

THE MOVE: Philosophy's invasion of literature took place when the border patrol was out having a cigarette. And then, when philosophy got onto her premises, the guard who was supposed to be monitoring the screen dozed off. It's not that the surveillance systems were down, but Someone grew tired of them and became unconvinced of their usefulness. We didn't need the discipline. Anyway, the people they put there to handle what stays out were poor sorts, only doing a job, and were given no transcendental place from which to protect her sanctity. They were

on the job,

on a break.

THE S.W.A.T. TEAM: From a place of felt exteriority it may seem that philosophy has taken a plunge into the gutter of *Gerede*, a term we borrow from the Heideggerian economy of language which designates roughly the inauthentic babble of the They. Something was spilled, exposed and exposing itself in an unprecedented production of contagion, cutting rumorous circuits to spread the news. Chernobyl, AIDS, a certain return of fascism, Le Pen, and the call in France for a 'SIDAtorium.' Something's going on in your blood, descended from an unpinnable outside. Sonar probes catch the winds of rumor. At least since Defoe's *Journal of the Plague Year*, a space 'as well Publick as Private' has been opened up to the coconstitutive status of rumor and disease. Here it appears that rumor spreads the plague and, inversely, the plague carries rumor. In the war zone, where one cannot help situating the toxic invasions under consideration, a variety of speech act continues to wage battle. What happens, though, when the philosopher affixes his name to a public, presumably referential record of *Gerede*, precisely to that locality which had been assumed to endure the purity of high discourse's absolute alien? One fears catching something in the public sphere, in open gathering places where transmissions scatter and inhabit the air like so many street noises. Essentially part of an invisible air force, rumors are often seen to be flying. They can be designated as something going around, or sometimes they drain from a crypt. It's a big break, submitted to a theory of leakage.

Under the names of Martin Heidegger and Paul de Man, claims made on behalf of a philosophy that would be sheltered by phantasms of immunocompetence, received a crack. The economy of leaks from newspapers to newspapers, from old to current journals, and thus shredded through *Gerede*'s loudspeakers, casts inflationary shadows. That which has primed itself on exposing – deconstruction – has been 'exposed.' Or so indeed it would appear, after a space of delay between the event of contamination and the phenomenal appearance of that which is to have created an irreversible mode of infectivity. If all this comes back now (even though it was never there – deconstruction was not there to read collaborationist theories, fascism, or nazism) and is hitting the streets, it has something to do no doubt with national hygiene programs, an especially tensed rapport to leakage, body fluid, and invisible agencies of virological hit men. There is a general movement to close things off, to get back to where we belong, a desire to detect and bind orificial openings, the still festering wounds or cuts from which uncontrollable utterances might be stopped. One of the dreams shared by the body politic, the academy, and forces of the body police consists in shutting down the flow, and anyone who approaches the immense toxic waste sites should be properly vested, wearing plastic gloves, keeping rather clear and clean. The latency period of the archival, viral, and historical underground seems to be linkable to the structures maintaining a secretly cycling poison, the hidden terrorisms that have taken up residence in the rhetoric of bloodlines and bacillary negotiations, all requiring applications of hyperdetection and a new examination of the shit we keep on walking into. This sounds very remote indeed from the lofty peaks that you felt philosophy was scaling. You were wrong. You didn't read close enough, with your nose to the ground.

Yet philosophy has always cruised the streets, moved in gangs or as a solitary punk looking for a dose of trouble and aporia. Or it traversed, when finishing itself off, Heidegger's mudfields. Philosophy never was where you expected to find it. In any case, it was not at home, but hanging out in the worst neighborhoods of the real; we know, for instance (because he talked) that Nietzsche found Socrates doing dialectics in some backstreet alley. There's one who refused to go home, but preferred instead to jump people who were not his own size. Philosophical thought was never not starting trouble nor beyond contamination, and this may be taken in the strongest sense, perhaps in a way that is most abundantly underscored in Nietzsche's pathos of distance and his great politics of health. Philosophy was always exposed, which is also why each philosopher exposes his predecessor and is conversely exposed by a text that stakes him out. Exposure travels under many masks, there's a contract out on it, even when it stabilizes through the guise of *Darstellung*. The topography of thinking shifts, sometimes with a stationary mobility. Either it is not discoverable in the philosopher's book, or it hasn't taken up residence in the ideal, or else it's not living in life, not even in the concept; always incomplete, always out of reach, forever promising at once its essence and its existence, it is no longer a question of 'philosophy of value,' but philosophy itself as value, submitted, as Jean-Luc Nancy argues, to the permanent *Verstellung* or displacements of value.[5]
Philosophy, love of wisdom, asserts a

distance

between love and wisdom and in this gap that
tenuously joins what it separates,

we shall attempt to set up our cable.

THE HIT: One might ask questions, with the greatest indecency – like street girls granted a Nietzschean pass of immunity – of everything that tries to pass us by. As if nothing were happening. So I'm asking. But like someone who knows the answer: *really* tough. Like, I don't have to be asking. (This is what Heidegger really scowls at – he's mostly into peasant girls – why are we asking what we think we already understand?) One wonders, then, if every thinking text is not immunologically active, phantasmically producing antibodies against the autoimmune community it has established within itself (a within that is constantly leaking, running an exscription machine,[6] exposed to the 'outside'). Autoimmunity is meant to designate the discordant condition in which a given body turns against itself because it has misunderstood or misinterpreted its systemic productions, having discerned something as foreign in the worst sense, as dangerously parasitical and inimical to its constitution. I should like to focus on a detail. It is a detail circumscribed by the return of history and the immense border disturbances caused by the oral trace. On the return of certain modalities of historical accounting, nomadic thought will have been arrested in its tracks, asked for identity papers, interrogated as to its whereabouts; in the face of felt infectivity the subject will have to account for itself, reveal a history, and be made answerable for all points of contact. The subject will have to contain itself anew, responding to the

last call of history.

THE LEAK: The issue engages a problematics of reproduction and spreading. Spreading beyond the age of mechanical reproduction, which is to say that the solicited fields of intensity fall under the regime of technology. No one is saying that it doesn't take place within the precincts of the good breast or object that technology proffers, doubling for the autoamputation it has marked. Surely, one of our questions here concerns the relatedness of the body to its technological extensions, the way the body will have replaced itself, assigning certain property values to the place of an absence. The body is down on itself, building auxiliary organs that, as Freud has said, make it almost godlike. Technology is hired out to take care of the problem, of which it also has inside knowledge. And perhaps because all sites of discursivity grounded in immunodeficient power plants offer an abyssal encounter with the question of technology, with the globalization and reproductive capacities of a technobody – AIDS challenges the technologies of the cure and tends, in the West, to be located in the technosphere marked by cities –, it becomes necessary to make something like a conference call to this thing we are naming technology. But we'll take it slow, find out where we are, turn off the loudspeakers

blaring news of
where
we are going.

FINITUDE'S SCORE: So, we have finally got to the point where we cordon off a section around a toxic waste site, one so invisibly laid, indeed, that what surprises our gaze is not its remote contours, but the extent to which the umbilical cord has kept us connected. It seems right to begin discreetly and with another kind of surprise attack – one so customary, in fact, that the sirens of its warning systems have seemed to recede into background music. Yet, background music is the return of the death knell, subliminally cadencing finitude's score. All this is piped in precisely at the place where technology comes to contaminate philosophy. While the technologies of reproduction and medical research urgently need to be read in conjunction with juridical and metaphysical determinations, it is perhaps equally as compelling to begin with something more neutral, less grandiose, and, possibly for these reasons, even more insidious. To start with a more familiar, and therefore that much more uncanny instance, we take a step back toward the structures of touching, invasion, reaching, and destination. It is the type of immunity which inflects our attraction to the carceral silence of the telephone booth.

The site offers itself to toxic invasion. Its radius is measured by a telephone cord that links you to the state and keeps the body in custody. It amplifies, intensifies, passes down death sentences. You cannot put up bond or bail – no bailing out of technology's iron-collared intensifier. This is why we have to answer a call that is seeking to pull us in, and to shorten our leash. My line on philosophy, always running interference with itself, has been accompanied, no doubt, by static.

The telephone connection houses the improper. Hitting the streets, it welcomes linguistic pollutants and reminds you to ask: 'Have I been understood?' Lodged somewhere among politics, poetry, and science, between memory and hallucination, the telephone necessarily touches the state, terrorism, psychoanalysis, language theory, and a number of death support systems. Its concept has preceded its technical installation. Thus, one may be rightly inclined to place the telephone not so much at the origin of some reflection, but as a response itself,

as that which is
answering
a call.

«3»

CALLING HEIDEGGER: A structure that is not equivalent to its technical history, the telephone, at this stage of preliminary inquiry, indicates more than a mere technological object. In our first listening, under the pressure of 'accepting a call,' the telephone in fact will emerge as a synecdoche of technology. As provisional object – for we have yet to define it in its finitude – the telephone is at once lesser and greater than itself.

Perhaps because the telephone belongs as such to no recognizable topos or lends itself to an *athetic* response, picking it up, especially in Heidegger and in World War II, can by no means produce a reading without static on the line. We shall constantly be interrupted by the static of internal explosions and syncopation – the historical beep-tones disruptively crackling on a line of thought. To sustain our reading against the crush of repressive agencies, busy signals, and missed connections, something like the 'rights of nerves' is being newly mobilized.[7] Suppose we begin by citing Heidegger in a decidedly aphilosophical mood when, in angry reaction to a reporter's persistent claims, he responds to a certain genre of transmission problems:

Heidegger: Das ist eine Verleumdung.
**Heidegger: That's slander.**
Spiegel: Und es gibt auch keinen Brief, in der
**Spiegel: And there is no letter in**
dieses Verbot gegen Husserl ausgesprochen wird?
**which such a prohibition is recorded?**
Wie wohl ist dieses *Gerücht* wohl aufgekommen?
**How did the *rumor* come about?**
Heidegger: Weiß ich auch nicht, ich finde dafür
**Heidegger: It's beyond me. I've no explanation for it.**
keine Erklärung. Die Unmöglichkeit dieser
**I can show you the**
ganzen Sache kann ich Ihnen dadurch
**unlikelihood of the**
demonstrieren, was auch nicht
**accusation.**
bekannt ist.[8]

To be sure, Husserl's name is doubly cut off when it finds itself missing in the translation. And perhaps because Heidegger is about to 'demonstrate,' his mood is not so aphilosophical after all. Heidegger poses himself as a kind of unscrambling device for a massively entangled historical narrative whose other end somehow involves a telephone call. In the passage cited the call is being set up; Heidegger has not yet made the connection, technologically fitted, to the hollow of the state.

We are not merely listening for a prior continuity which telephone wires would cable into the language of Heidegger, his war words or *Der Spiegel* reflections. In some respects, Heidegger's work, including his final interview, hooks up the telephone as if to simulate answerability when it in fact creates a scrambling device whose decoding strands it nonetheless enjoins us to follow. It is Heidegger himself who poses the telephone. He poses it at this junction, almost as if he wished to supply the want of an ethics. It has been said that Heidegger has no Ethics. This brings us to the problem to be raised by the central exchange of our system, where empirical guilt and the Heideggerian theory of guilt seem to share the same operator.

This is a serious problem promoted by an oeuvre that provides itself with a manual, a directory assistance that makes such connections inevitable, at once calling them forth and wanting to annul them. Yet if the interview containing the telephone call is a ruse or a scrambling device intentionally installed by the philosopher, then he still isn't given over to laughter. Whether this is because Heidegger would never strike such a pose of subjective mastery – he would perhaps not wish to assert, in the sense of Baudelaire, the idea of a superior bearing – or whether nonlaughter marks a more sinister conviction, will have to remain open to an answer temporarily out of service. While it is necessary to elude the confusion of situating a purely empirical/anthropological reading of guilt within a theoretically grounded one, it must be recognized that for Heidegger the relations between anthropology and ontology are not simply external ones. Indeed, Philippe Lacoue-Labarthe has shown the thematization in Heidegger of the empirical and historical figure cut by the philosopher.

*The time has come to record the message, to listen in a gathering way to what has been said within the interstices of two beep-tones.*

Let us wind up this recording around the major points it appears to have urged. Heidegger accepted a call. In Lacan's sense, we call this predicament the transfer of power from the subject to the Other. In this case, the other happens to be the top command of the Storm Trooper University Bureau. Heidegger traces his relationship to national socialism to this call, asserting thereby the placeless place where the other invaded him, the place or moment when the connection was to have taken place. He does not report a face-to-face meeting, but we shall arrange this momentarily.

The scene can be teletyped for review according to two preliminary aspects. First, Heidegger's compromise with national socialism marks an arrangement with a supertechnical power. Secondly, Heidegger in fact elaborates an idea of *technē* that largely stands under the shadow of the negative. It has a contract out on Being, tightening its corruption, its veiling and forgetting. The coherency of these two aspects will lead us to examine whether it is not precisely owing to his theory of technology that Heidegger was engaged on the Nazi party line. Later, Heidegger would locate himself at a remove from national socialism by linking the movement to technology. But if Heidegger can embark upon the adventure of national socialism in the first place, it is only to the extent that there is something which he resists in technology, hoping it can be surmounted like the grief or pain one feels in the human realm over a loss. We shall have to put a search on this unmarked grief through which Heidegger mourns the figure of technology. Or even more to the point, Heidegger *wants* to mourn technology, but it proves to be unmournable as yet, that is, undead.

In large, constative terms, we shall have to concern ourselves here with the contours of another, somewhat displaced horizon through which it may be claimed that no fundamental distance establishes itself between the technical, natural, human, or existential worlds, no purity or absolute exteriority of one of these to the other. But Heidegger has produced, let us say quickly, a naive reading of technology whose philosophically inflected and historical effects require rigorous examination. It is as if he thought there were something beyond the radical rupture in Being which technology involves – another relation to Being, more original than that supplied by a technological emplacing; and this possibility he identifies at one point with the Nazis. Still, what is nazism if not also the worst moment in the history of technology? 'Worst' can serve as a rhetorical qualification of 'moment,' which may not be restricted and may not be an indication of closure. The worst moment in the history of technology may not have an off switch, but only a modality of being on. Let me formulate this pointedly, so that the telephone can begin its job of condensing and displacing questions of desire and extermination, war machines and simulators within the apparatus of a peacetime; when Heidegger fails to consider that technology cannot be surmounted, surpassed, or even perhaps sublated, he walks into a trap. I want to trace this trap to one day, one event. I am going to take the same call several times, and then try to move beyond it.

RECTOR'S OFFICE: Husserl, whose name suffered erasure by Heidegger under the same regime – Heidegger had deleted the dedication to *Sein und Zeit* – was removed from the office which Heidegger now occupied. Husserl was not there to answer; he would not even answer to his name. The mentor had had the telephone removed which, during Heidegger's tenure, was reinstalled.[9] These gestures are connected to the paternal belly of the state by the umbilical cord of the telephone. The scene was technologically set for Heidegger to take the call. Preliminarily we shall argue that what came through on that day was a certain type of call of conscience. Why precisely did he answer this call? Or say he did? Is he not trying to give it the same existential legitimacy, trying to make it the same type of call that *Sein und Zeit* describes? Simply asked, what is the status of a philosophy, or rather a *thinking*, that doesn't permit one to distinguish with surety between the call of conscience and the call of the storm trooper? This raises a first point.

The other point is organized around Heidegger's technological blind spot as concerns the telephone, which can be grasped as a way to measure his commitment to divest ontologically technology. Accepting the call by missing the point – that is to say, missing the appointment of the call, its 'significance' – Heidegger thus demonstrates the force by which to gauge his attempt to secondarize, ontologically speaking, technology. To the degree that his concept of technology is blind or lacking, it is guilty of his alliance of power with nazism. Of course, to the extent that he underreads technology, Heidegger cannot be identified, purely and simply, with the self-constitution of national socialism. He himself says that he was accused by the party for his 'private national socialism.' But the status of what he says is shaky, particularly since it has run on rumorological grounds, a history of dissimulation and silence. On his own subject, on the subject of the Third Reich, Heidegger never stopped playing telephone. The mark to be made here, the incision, indicates the surface of a weakly held limit between technology and Being. Technology, while by no means neutral, but a field of fascination, is viewed as covering an authentic relation to Being. It is from this point onwards that claims are made for a relation to Being more original than the technically assumed one.

To be sure, the notation of a Being that would enfold technology only by hesitant parasitical inclusion has received expression from the 'other' side of the line. In a recently disclosed letter to Heinrich Vangleer, Einstein wrote from Berlin in 1917: 'All our lauded technological progress – our very civilization – is like the axe in the hand of the pathological criminal.' The aberrant course traced by technopathology engages a risk of blindness – as if the axe could be surrendered, and the criminal appeased, as if, indeed, there were a truer law of Being into which technology were cutting a pathology. However, Einstein was not instituting an ontology – a discourse on Being which presupposes the responsibility of the *yes*, as Derrida writes: 'Yes, what is said is said, I respond or "it" responds to the call of Being.'[10] Einstein, then, was not taking on an ontology or saying yes to a call, he was definitively disconnected from the supertechnical powers which drew the open ear of Heidegger. In addition, he only took a call from Princeton.

TELL MOTHER: As we heard ourselves say, the telephone is a synecdoche for technology. It is lesser than itself but also greater, as in the maternalizing call of *What Is Called Thinking?* A number of things might be put on this account. Lecture 5 of this text opens the telephone book. It is mysterious and compelling. It wants to teach teaching. She appears, if only sonically, at a long distance. The mother calls her boy home, opening his ears, but also teaching him a lesson. A certain Oedipedagogy is taking shape here – the restoration of contact is in the making, initiated by a mother whose navel, in Joycean terms, would emit signals. The navel is the third eye, closed, knotted – the eye of blindness. Whatever the lesson of the mother, which turns into a desemanticized Nietzschean scream, telephonic logic means here, as everywhere, that contact with the Other has been disrupted, but it also means that the break is never absolute. Being on the telephone will come to mean, therefore, that contact is never constant nor is the break clean.

Such a logic finds its way through much of the obliterature that handles these calls. Heidegger's *What Is Called Thinking?* names Nietzsche in the passage to the ear canal. In a way that comes through clearly, this call has been transferred from Nietzsche before it is returned to him. One should think of Nietzsche on the mother tongue.[11] Deformed by the educational system whose condition she remains, she makes you become a high-fidelity receiver on a telephonic line rerouted by interceptors to the state. This is the telelogic of the Nietzschean critique whose access code runs through 'On Redemption.' The bildopedic culture has produced itself out of a combinatory of lack ('for there are human beings who lack everything') and excess ('one thing of which they have too much'); it constellates the human subject telephonically. Figuring the human thus first undermines visual security:

> for the first time I did not trust my eyes and looked and looked again, and said at last, 'An ear!' The tremendous ear was attached to a small, thin stalk – but this stalk was a human being! If one used a magnifying glass one could even recognize a tiny envious face; also that a bloated little soul was dangling from the stalk.[12]

That Nietzsche's texts are telephonically charged is clarified in the *Genealogy of Morals,* where he writes of a 'telephone to the beyond' which is arguably the case with every connection arranged by such a switchboard.[13] It is Joyce who excites the hope that an explicit link might be forged between the call to the beyond and a maternal connection which we hear enunciated in Heidegger's exposition:

> Boys, do it now. God's time is 12.25 [twenty-five minutes past the Nietzschean midday, therefore]. Tell Mother you'll be there. Rush your order and you play a slick ace. Join on right here! Book through eternity junction, the nonstop run.[14]

The little boys tell Mother they'll be there. While here, which is never 'here,' they are booking it through eternity junction, cathecting onto the gamble of the book. All the while Mother is on the line. What links this act to the calling apparatus of state? Don't forget, though: we are not reading an indifferently occupied state but one which destined itself to the ear, in terms achieved by Hélène Cixous, to the *jouissance* of the ear.[15] The ear has been addicted, fascinated. And just as Hamlet's father, head of state, overdosed on the oto-injection ('in the blossoms of my sin'), the ghostly *Der Spiegel* interlocutor, speaking from the beyond, utters the news of technology's infectious spread, beginning with a phone call. Again, and forever, why did Heidegger accept this particular call? Through which orifice did nazism pass in Heidegger? He has already told us. In terms of an entirely different intensity (but is it so different?), in 'The Madonna's Conception through the Ear,' Ernest Jones convincingly shows the ear to cover for the displaced anus.[16] This demonstration has received security clearance from subsequent psychoanalytic claims on the matter. Yet we are not addressing a multiplicity of ears but one ear, technologically unified against the threat of a narcissistic blowout. The *jouissance* of the ear was felt by a whole nation, whether it was listening to Wagner or to the constant blare of the radio, which is said to have hypnotized a whole people, a tremendous national ear.

Heidegger's ear was trained on the telephone. It was what Blanchot calls 'fascinated.' He answered the call. The blindness associated with any call assumes proportions that are difficult to name but which nonetheless can be circumscribed. A problematics of image obliteration engages the telephone, and even the rhetoric surrounding it. The telephone sinks away as a sensory object, much as the mother's figure disappears. When Heidegger mentions being-on-the-telephone, it is not meant to coagulate into an image. The call was fleetingly arranged, like a sonic intrusion. The Nazis were not in sight, they were the hidden and private eyes to whom Heidegger spoke. Visual apprehension on the retreat, supplanted by the dead gaze: these constitute elements brought together in 'The Essential Solitude' of Blanchot. A dead gaze, 'a gaze become the ghost of eternal vision,'[17] stares fixedly from his text, which listens to the Heidegger text which it quietly repeats. In a way, the call of *What Is Called Thinking?* is taken up, transferred, or translated to 'the force of the maternal figure,' which itself gradually dissolves into the indeterminate They. Following the telepath of Heidegger, Blanchot induces a stage of telephonics in which he regards the vanishing image. The mark of a maternalizing hearing which blinds all imaging, he calls this 'fascination.' Why fascination? Seeing, which presupposes distance and a decisiveness which separates, fosters a power to stay out of contact and in contact; it avoids confusion. But he writes of a manner of seeing which amounts to 'a kind of touch, when seeing is *contact* at a distance.' His focus, if that is the proper way of putting it, fixes fascination – something allows sight to be blinded into a neutral, directionless gleam which will not go out, yet does not clarify. 'In it blindness is vision still.' This vision has been perturbed; it is a 'vision which is no longer the possibility of seeing.' Fascinated into the dead gaze, we retreat from the sensory and sense: 'What fascinates us robs us of our power to give sense. It abandons its "sensory" nature, abandons the world, draws back from the world, and draws us along.'[18]

JOCASTA'S CALL: Now the transfer or transit is made to the other woman, the one about to speak to us, teachingly, in Heidegger. The habit-forming mother freezes the image into the blinding absence which we have come to call the telephone. Alongside Heidegger's little boy, we encounter the child of Blanchot, transfixed and fascinated, unseeingly drawn by the enchantment of the mother. Blanchot takes a step in the direction of Heidegger by fading a mother into the They, the neutral impersonal 'indeterminate milieu of fascination.' As if responding to a query coming from elsewhere, he offers:

> Perhaps the force of the maternal figure receives its intensity from the very force of fascination, and one might say then, that if the mother exerts this fascinating attraction it is because, appearing when the child lives altogether in fascination's gaze, she concentrates herself in all the powers of enchantment. It is because the child is fascinated that the mother is fascinating, and that is why all the impressions of early childhood have a kind of fixity which comes from fascination.

Blanchot's evocation continues to withdraw itself from sight, effecting a sense of immediacy complicit with absolute distance. The sequence releases the mother, letting her drop out of sight while the subject appears to have achieved cecity:

> Whoever is fascinated doesn't see, properly speaking, what he sees. Rather, it touches him in an immediate proximity; it seizes and ceaselessly draws him close, even though it leaves him absolutely at a distance. Fascination is fundamentally linked to neutral, impersonal presence, to the indeterminate They, the immense, faceless Someone. Fascination is the relation the gaze entertains – a relation which is itself neutral and impersonal – with sightless, shapeless depth the absence one sees because it is blinding.[19]

We should like to retain the neutral gleam, the sightless depth that sees – a tele-vision without image, not very distant from the annihilating gaze of Lacan, though perhaps less in arms. The texts of Heidegger and Blanchot are not merely practicing the Oedipal blindness with which the maternally contacting child is menaced – even if, indeed, it is the mother who calls first. With the exception of Cixous, little has been said about Jocasta's call, the way she secretly calls the shots, and her responsibility. If these texts were repeating the gesture according to which the Oedipal gaze is averted, then we should remember that every repetition, to be what it is, brings something new with it. The child has disappeared in the mother. This disappearance or traversal also devours the mother – each the absolute hostage of the Other, caught in a structure that inhibits the desire to cancel a call. Once made, the call indicates the mother as *aufgehoben*, picked-up, preserved, and canned. 'L'Imprésentable' is the name Lacoue-Labarthe gives to the essay which shows how the female figure has always been one that Western thought has attempted to 'overcome' or wind down [*überwinden*] in its philosophical, aesthetic, and physical dimensions.[20] The child, like philosophy, gains on the mother. The child, as we said, has disappeared in the mother. He is, in Blanchot, there and not there. He has arrived, if henceforth sightlessly averting his gaze to face the immense, faceless Someone. In Heidegger, though Blanchot does not simply contradict him in this, the child maintains a long distance. Even though it was a local call. The remoteness of the child to the place from which the call was issued is never collapsed into the 'immediate proximity' felt, if evanescently, by the Blanchot text. The invading Other doesn't arrive at touching, contaminating the one that is called or, in the ontic enclosure that separates the caller from the called, the one is never held hostage by the Other, fascinated, or derailed. The Heideggerian remoteness from the call's source guarantees that it will avoid being danger zoned, for it masquerades as the purity of a long-distance call. This detoxified scene of calling is what, in Heidegger, we call into question.

In this light, one of the things that we shall need to ponder concerns a tranquil assertion such as one finds in *Sein und Zeit:* 'Being towards Others is ontologically different from Being towards Things which are present-at-hand.'[21] While this articulation involves a complex series of designations whose elaborations would require a patient tapping of each term ('Being-towards,' 'present-at-hand'), it can nonetheless be seen to assume a clean ontological separation of Others and Things wherein the Other, as Heidegger states in the same passage, would be a duplicate [*Dublette*] of the Self. The question that we raise before any approach can be made towards this passage or the locality of Other suggests a disposition other than the one disclosed in Heidegger's assertion. The mood we wish to establish is not one of reactivity but of genuine wonder and bewilderment before the statement. At first sight the statement asserts itself as constatively unproblematic: 'Being towards Others is ontologically different from Being towards Things which are present-at-hand.' What is supposed, however, regards not only the difference between modes of 'Being towards,' but the aim or destination which would know the gap separating Others from Things. Now, what if Others were encapsulated in Things, in a way that Being towards Things were not ontologically severable, in Heidegger's terms, from Being towards Others? What if the mode of *Dasein* of Others were to dwell in Things, and so forth? In the same light, then, what if the Thing called Other, and not what is called Other, were a *Dublette* of the Self? Or more radically still, what if the Self were in some fundamental way becoming a xerox copy, a duplicate, of the Thing in its assumed essence? This perspective may duplicate a movement in Freud's reading of the uncanny, and the confusion whirling about Olympia as regards her Thingness. Perhaps this might be borne in mind, as both Freud and Heidegger situate arguments on the Other's thingification within a notion of *Unheimlichkeit*, the primordial being-not-at-home, and of doublings. At another point, Heidegger will himself genderize the thing, calling on the 'young thing' to step into the domain of the feminine prehuman.

THE SWITCHBOARD: The second type of question, which nags critical integrity, having received only an implicit formulation, concerns the history of, let us say provisionally, a subject of the private sector who normally would be granted diplomatic immunity, sheltered as he is by the structures regulating philosophical politesse. A transgression, authorized by Nietzsche, has permitted us to view the life of a philosopher not as so many empirical accidents external to the corpus of his works. But where Nietzsche constantly affirms the value of dissimulation, including self-dissimulation, Heidegger does not.[22] Thus it is not clear that we already know what, in this instance, involves self-presentation and a statement of identity. In Nietzsche's heterobiography, *Ecce Homo*, we know that the self will fail to reappropriate itself; in Heidegger's journalistic disclosures, we know no such thing. At any event, the referential pathos of his explication leaves room for serious refutation. This order of bewilderment, granted a Nietzschean pass, has permitted us to open the case on two infinitely nonreciprocal texts, linking *Sein und Zeit* and the *Spiegel* interview. Is the call of conscience readable in terms of a telephone call? We suggest this to be the case. More precisely, perhaps, can one rigorously speaking utter *Dasein*'s anonymous calling in the same breath with the call taken by a historical subject whose identity papers, civil status, and telephone personality name a 'Martin Heidegger'? A receptionist must know how connections are tolerably made, determining which opening will establish communication between two parties or two things – in brief, she must understand how to manipulate the switchboard or

she would lose
her
post.

~

The labor of working the forces of contamination knows no closure. We have tried to open up the question by marking the spot where thinking encounters technology in the real. Seduced by technology but maintaining its own suspicions, thinking often goes out for a twirl with technology, gets caught and tries to reform itself. Still, contact has been made, and something unforgettable keeps asking to be accounted for. I have tried to follow the disjunctive moves that have been made on us and of which we are a part. One of these engages a double reading of technology and the valuations that it casts. There was no way to do this sort of thing in a classically continuous manner. The switchboard cut off a number of calls and took a host of surprise calls. It's not as if I controlled it. We're the kind of couple in which I figure as answering device. Still, it's constantly under repair, and we're working the night shift.

# THE WALKING SWITCHBOARD

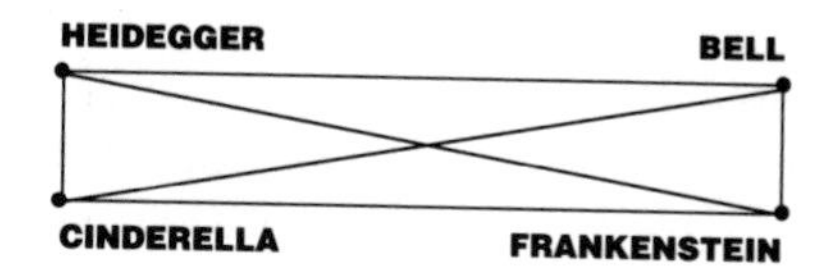


PLEASE BEAR WITH ME: *I don't know how it started but when it happened, I got up and lit a cigarette, kind of serenely. The click was still resonating in my ear, the smoke crawled up to where it hurt. I had no image, just a sonic blaze in my head.*

*When they hung up on me, it felt like an amputation. I got to thinking how it was by a thin thread that everything had been related. As long as they kept calling, contact was never really broken, nor was the break clean. This time it was over. I had heard the click, like a gun pointed at your head. Like I said, I got to thinking. About the amputation, to be exact. In a sense, it was a story about the invention of a body part. I had my ear trained on the telephone. I don't know where their voices went when I picked up the receiver, whether they were coming from elsewhere or coming from my insides. In literary thematizations authors tended to put the superego on the line, barking orders. I had seen it in Pynchon, but also in Proust.*

*I could never say no. Going to answer it already meant yes. Yes, it's me. I'm answering to it, I'm indebted and responsible. You could never be absolutely sure who was at the other end. This is where the concept of a 'phony' emerged, when the metaphysics of identity and self-presence came crashing down. I never let it ring more than three times. I went for the phone, which also meant they weren't here, with me. Nor were you, at the time. Something was always missing, and in those days the telephone seemed to mark the place of an absence. So something was missing and we had to invent a new body part – a part that was gone, like the legendary female penis. I'm not sure what the telephone was substituting for. Maybe they weren't gone that much but something in me was missing, and that's what the teleprosthesis was supposed to cover.*

*Then it hit me. I got to thinking about a kind of technohermeneutics of mourning – how technology amplifies the body as it commemorates a loss.*

*The typewriter invented for the blind, the telephone more or less for the deaf and the missing. Swallowing the pain, eating the invisible: back to an incorporation of the lost object, as they called it then. It had to do with the drama of disconnection, and I was having withdrawal pains. Sometimes they would feed me the telephone just so I could get some long-distance transfusion. It evoked something of a primordial feeling, tapping into an umbilical logic. So I started tracing calls that had been transferred to the subterranean body. That's when I found a disconnected feminine operating the texts of Mary Shelley, Alexander Graham Bell, and Martin Heidegger. I didn't expect to find it in Heidegger. But there it was: the technologized call of the feminine wrapped in veils of mourning. He said maybe we could get over technology like we, in the human realm, got over the pain of someone's dying. Pretty soon the girls show up, the young things that are supposed to illustrate thingliness. So I staked them out, and felt the technospheric pressure mounting* . . . . . . . . . . . . . . . . . . . . . . . . . . . . . . . . . . . . . . . . . . .

. . . . . . . . . . . . . . . . . . . . . . . . . . . . . . . . . . . . . . . . . . . . . . . . . . . . . . . . . . . .

«1»

Maybe I should have spoken more distinctly. The telephone, within language, entrusted to transference and translation, is to be plugged in somewhere among science, poesy, and thinking. Inasmuch as it belongs, in its simplest register, to the order of the mechanical and the technical, it is already on the side of death. However, the telephone cannot simply be regarded as a 'machine' in the classical sense, for at times it is also 'live.' Or at least 'life' sometimes gathers in it and takes part in it. The voices that stir within its strange locality periodically come to, indicating a living presence, though always modulated in something like an absent tense. The telephone flirts with the opposition life/death by means of a ruse through which it stretches apart receiver and transmitter, or makes the infinite connection that touches the rim of finitude. Nietzsche, like Kafka, Duras, you and me, once thought of a telephone to the beyond, a kind of transcendental Sprint.

Certain texts operate according to a telephonic logic; some people are glued to the telephone. Bent on bionic assimilation, they show a readiness to incorporate the technochip, and thus to open a horizon against which to measure the future of one's own body part. But let us stick to the ear for now, and its extension to the technological umbilical.

Like transference, the telephone and other technologies are given to us as effigy and as relation to absence. At bottom, these assert an originary nonpresence and the alterity of the self to itself.[1] The Other rings you up, as if summoning you to existence. If all reference to self takes place by way of such a detour through an Other, the self, in order to be itself, is first traversed, deposited in the Other, and reappropriated to

itself by some fundamental impurity. Telephone teaches that the self has been hit by the Other. If the self comes to, it is to be slapped down again; call it a violence, loss of the proper or of self-presence, but understand that in truth it is the loss of what has never taken place, of a self-presence which has never been given, but only dreamed of, always already split, repeated, incapable of appearing to itself except in its own disappearance.[2] . . . . . . . . . . . . . . . . . . . . . . . . . . . . . . . . . . . . . . . . . . . .
. . . . . . . . . . . . . . . . . . . . . . . . . . . . . . . . . . . . . . . . . Bell's project belongs to the anxiety registers of historical recounting, for the telephone cannot be, nor was it ever, according to its concept, properly fitted to the narrative event of truth-telling, handwashing, or clearing a name. The telephone stakes out that thing which is not to be believed; a cataloguer of hermeneutic suspicions, it compels one blindly to overlook it, as in the technomanic case histories of schizophrenics in Jung and Laing, or in the disseminative distillation of the Heideggerian text. There is something to its not-thereness, destabilizing and implacable at once; it is a place without location from which to get elsewhere, translating into electrical carriages the air or ether waves which convey voices. Not itself a locality, it forms the topography of an artificial organ from which the Other speaks. The regime of displacements and cancellations within which it functions tells us that it cannot, by definition, speak truth, even if it dangles there like an earwitness . . . . . . . . . . . . . . . . . . . . . . . . . .
. . . . . It followed the twisted cord of umbilical logic; hardly a beloved or universally celebrated little monster, it inspired fear, playing on fresh forms of anxiety which were to be part of a new package deal of the invisible. It soon became clear that schizophrenia recognized the telephone as its own, appropriating it as a microphone for the singular emission of its pain. Schizophrenia was magnetized by the telephone the way neurosis rapped on Freud's door. In a fundamental sense, we can say that the first call the telephone makes is to schizophrenia – a condition never wholly disconnected from the ever-doubling 'thing.' In his autobiography, Thomas Watson (Bell's assistant) mounts his case slowly, describing the call of aberrancy first in terms of embarrassment. Men, in particular, were uneasy about the thing. Watson writes: 'It also interested me to see how many people were embarrassed when they used the telephone for the first time. One day a prominent lawyer tried the instrument with me. When he heard my voice in the telephone making some simple remark he could only answer after a long embarrassed pause, "Rig a jig, jig, and away we go." '[3] Regression takes hold, the call transfers the speaker to a partial object, a false self caught up in the entanglement of *fort/da:* away we go.

Watson defines essentially two kinds of men who visited the telephone. The first we have just listened to, and away he went. The second returns us to a recurrent concern, the consummate knowledge of disconnection that connects the schizophrenic to things and machinery: 'Men of quite another stamp from those I have mentioned occasionally' (98). Though he is not necessarily playing *carte postale,* you will note the self-addressed envelope upon which these stamps are pressed. They go to the telephone lab like mission-controlled hypnotics, who are called toward their destination by unmarked signals. These men of another stamp arrive by letter, writing in secret codes of secret codes that would transform the telephone into a system of telepathically guided transferrals.

It was as though an invisible, subliminal sign hung over the laboratory, bouncing signals for schizophrenics to phone home, calling for psychosis and auditory paranoia to settle down in the telephone. Watson retains the invisible headset telecommanding this man and those stamped in a similar way as part of his *autobiography,* which itself is a partial otobiography of the telephone. Watson hardly pushes this episode, whose repetitions he asserts, to some peripheral pocket of narrative disclosure. The call of the insane, who at first sight resemble the inventor, belongs to the fundamental history of the telephone, ingathering a newly bodied 'them' whose strict isolation and difference, as a guarantee of carceral alterity, I would not vouch for. Somewhere between an art and a science, the telephone still throws strangely stamped shadows off its primary invisibility. It divides itself among thing, apparatus, instrument, person, discourse, body part, voice. Or rather, as a moment in ontotechnology, it perhaps offers itself precisely as a nothing, so that by putting off access to itself, suspending or interdicting itself, it might thereby come closer to being something or someone. The telephone coils around its own lack of assumption, if one understands by this the stranglehold by which it affirms the impossibility of acceding to its proper significance. Noise machine, schizo leash, warzone shots in the dark, lovers' discourse, or phantomatic conference call, the telephone as such is, like the phallus, empty but powerful . . . . . . . . . . . . .
. . . . . . . . . . . . . . . . . . . . . . . . . . . . . . . . . . . . . . . . . . . . . . . . .
Bell never considered the telephone to constitute a mere scientific thing, an object, or even a machine that would one day be subsumable under a notion of technological dominion. Watson, for his part, wrote of the *art* of telephony, and was himself a spiritualist who conjured ghosts at nightly *séances* in Salem. He was, for a time, a strong medium.

The telephone's body-grafting activity could have taken root in the dead ear Bell carried around with him and into which he spoke. He carried the ear with him one summer vacation, to his parents' home. The fact that he did not bring a pair of ears home, but a single member of a pair, leaves room for fetishization. The fetishist tends to go for one of a double kind – a single shoe, one ear, or half a body set. In a way that reflects the fetishist calculus, Bell had lost a pair of brothers; one of them was the felt destination of the new telecommunications.[4] The departed one manifested himself in the dead ear, faintly responding to the call. The primal connection took place in the paternomaternal space of a perforated ear.

Now, the dead ear that was lent to Bell by the Harvard medical institution may have been the other ear of Hamlet's father, or more likely of Van Gogh, insofar as ears tend to come in pairs. Or it could have been that of his deaf mother calling him home. Still, as ears are rarely pricked up for stereophonic listening, it might be reasonable to assume that one ear sufficed for the telephone as well as for the purpose of invention. One ear alone does the work of receiving the call.[5] One ear goes down into the abyss while the other exfoliates to the Open. It is not clear what the other, latent ear is doing. This somewhat disjunctive pair cannot engage in a dialectic; there is no third ear to resolve the issue, though Hölderlin is said to have found a third eye. Or, if there should be a third ear, which of course there always is (the ear of the state, for example, or the ear of the other), it acts as a second ear to the collapsible pair of ears. Unlike the mouth, the ear needs a silent partner, a double and phantom of itself. The mouth doubles itself by metonymic displacement, getting on the shuttle to vaginal or anal sites. In sum, Bell carried a dead ear to his mother's house one summer. He walked it home, establishing a singular hook-up between a departed brother and a mother's deaf ear.

The telephone, whose labor pains were felt in that ear, has, already in this limited example of its birth, so complex a matrix that the question of its placement as thing, object or machine, scientific, gynecological, or *objet d'art,* still presses upon us. It was conceived with a kind of Frankensteinian pathos, this supplementary organ to a mother's deafness – mother or wife, actually, since Bell's bride, Mabel, also suffered a hearing impairment. But she came second to the deaf mother, like a second ear joined in the same determination as the first of a pair. In a certain light, we can ask the same question of the Frankenstein monster as we do of the telephone. After all, both inventors – Bell and Victor Frankenstein – were invested in a simulacrum that speaks and hears; both, we may add precipitously, were elaborating works of mourning, memorializing that which was missing, and in a certain way trying to make grow the technological flower from an impossible grave site. Both inventors were motivated to reanimate a corpse, to breathe life into dead body parts. University labs provided the material. Frankenstein was created in the university, an artificial genre, a dissertation for which Victor was awarded the title of Doctor. It took two years to write and forever to defend this dissertation in studied denial of a mother's departure. Never publishable, yet circulating and appearing everywhere, it stood as the objectivized phantasmata of the reconstitutability of the body of Victor's absent mother. It was a new inflection of the alma mater.

The monster's predominant sexual markings do not appear to coincide with those of a mother in whose image it is made. But the monster envisions himself in light of a pair, which splits off into a self-designated phantom extension. The monster could not become what it is, the argument goes, until the feminized other is made to join him. He shares in the atotality of the telephone that seeks its other in the remote possibility of a long-distance summoning. The monster resides in his nature as phantom, which he sometimes is called by his inventor, until the other is conjured up, recalled.

The story is too well known. The essential connection will never be made. This perhaps is not even the point. The point, if such there be, is to *make a disconnection.* The phantom learns the lesson of a desirable finitude, something he picks up from reading Goethe, who in a way remote-controls his destinerring. The point is not necessarily to respond (though this is a beginning), but to know how to hang up. And thus a certain explosion into something like humanity takes place, at the threshold of finitude, whether or not this is to be a citation, a vampiric bite into the Goethean corpus. The phantom of Victor Frankenstein abolishes itself when, finally, the call for mourning is answered. He answers the call which it is impossible for Victor to receive, though he takes it. The disconnection is made when the Disconnection is made. This is not a play on words. The monster knows that it was created to sing the lament of mourning, to teach the necessity of hanging up, which the professors with their self-willed striving could not effect. At the event of Victor's death, a strange proximity emerges from the remoteness of absolute departure: the monster mourns, demonsterizing itself by the double lesson of finitude, that of the other and of the self cleared by the other. This was what he was called forth to be, to do, as a child taking upon itself the responsibility for a parentally crafted task. Yet, we must resist psychologizing even here where so much suggests that the phantom marks the other side of a divided self, a partial object, or false self system.

As we shall have to ask of the telephone whose summoning into being sprang forth in part from a dead ear – an ear dead to this world – we ask of the monstering text: was Frankenstein the monster (who had acquired his creator's proper name) a body or machine, a prosthetic soul perhaps, appended to the maternal fantasy of his founding father? Was he a 'thing,' as sometimes Frankenstein *père*, his creator, calls him? If so, what is a 'thing?' What is his equipmental nature? The properties of his potential being are not necessarily exclusive of one another – human

subject *or* piece of bionic technology – for transplants of a mechanical sort are routinely made, and organs are kept 'alive' by machines. It cannot suffice to say, with Marshall McLuhan, that this machinery extends the body in a way that would be continuous with its concept. We have established very little about the putative identity of this monster or thing. He is an answering machine of sorts, one whose call is to hang up and disconnect . . . . . . . . . . . . . . . . . . . . . . . . . . . . . . . . . . . . . . . . . .
. . . . . . . . . . . . . . . . . . . . . . . . . . . . . . . . . . . . . . . . . . . At the advent of this mediated and altogether new necrophilia, the medium is a kind of walking switchboard whose origin in the text of this 'new Prometheus' announces the disruption of models of organicity by the electrical shock waves supplanting it. The monster, in short, who, following the Goethe manual, elects his short-circuiting, has as its form of presencing an electrical terminal reconstituted by a transformer.[6] The monster is wired; he already explodes into existence by the electrocution of a proud family tree, the oak tree electrically devastated within the irrevocable instant of a lightning flash. The primal event, witnessed by an explicating scientist, shows the tree to be, like little Victor, 'shattered,' 'blasted,' – a fundamental breakdown in a tropology that makes way for the creation of a technological tool. What appears to be destroyed catastrophically by this preatomic blast is the tranquil indwelling of a world. With the electric shock which that world receives, a frivolity is signed which leaves behind the false testimony of mastery and the overcoming of finitude whose advances enthrall our century. As a life-support system, technology reroutes the question of life to a conquerable challenge which paradoxically brings unacknowledged death to the possibility of being or thinking, producing a weed garden of zomboid reactors. The switchboard Frankenstein articulates the shift away from a more genuine temporality than that unthinkingly drafted by technology, which chooses finitude in this limited case, with the implication that a choice is to be negotiated; the monster technologue *chooses* to imitate the route traced out by a prior literature, advanced under the name of *The Sorrows of Young Werther* – the name of valuation and worthiness in general, *Wert*her. Neither young nor old, though a relatively new invention, and in this sense always only young and reckless, constitutively untried, dangerous, the monsterized thing in his test drive has the power to select his conclusion and that of the more original Other.

But the suggestion implanted into the fold of this thinking is that technology can choose a genuinely human temporality only if it chooses to read a certain grace of poetry, a listening to finitude more truthful than technology's disassembling of space-time. The nameless technomonster could have chosen, after all, not to put itself to death, in a graceful bereavement over its loss of mortality. And like Frankenstein, who is

there to mark an absent alterity, the telephone in other texts stays largely off the hook, producing sounds and forms of sonic harassment that have only been read, if at all, subliminally. Still, the switchboard flashes and calls are placed. In Heidegger's *What Is Called Thinking?* for instance, as with the examples of Bell and Frankenstein, these calls are placed from an ever-disconnecting mother . . . . . . . . . . . . . . . . . . . . . . . . . . . . . . . . .
. . . . . . . . . . . . . . . . . . . . . . . . . . . . . We are hypnotized things suffering from positive and negative hallucinations – that is, we see what is not there and often we do not see what is there, because in the first place what it is to be there has no clarity of being. It is as though we cannot see a thing. Stemming from the famous verse, 'No thing is where the word is lacking,' Heidegger's word distills the thing. Let me try to graft some of these edges together.[7] The switchboard body and Heidegger's *Question Concerning Technology* appear to communicate certain properties to one another, being reproductions of a frame (or in Heideggerian, the *Ge-Stell*). As a remote-controlled thing, an object or objectification of sorts, is the monster not also perhaps a work of art, mimetically rooted in a fevered vision of the truth of man? Or has it been conceived rather as a piece of equipment to whom the doctor is at times contracted as a repairman? Certainly the monster bears traits of its maker who signs the project that haunts him; like the telephone (we did not hang up, I merely put it down momentarily), it is sensitively impregnated with the secret traits of a disconnected mother. These wires are constitutively crossed. And so we ask about the equipmental nature of these things. On automatic redial: object of art or object of technology, object of a sustained hysterical fantasy, yours and mine, or thing of inmixation, telecrypt, or, in all cases, partial object. We have yet to connect the telephone to its principal (over-)determinations.

It may seem as though we were bent on splitting technological hairs by bringing up the question of the equipmental character of the telephone, of a Frankenstein or even of a broken self . . . . . . . . . . . . . . . . .
. . . . . . . . . . . . . . . . . . . . Yet the breaking point . . . . . . . . . . . . . . . . .
. . . . . . . . . . . . . . . . . . of any self, a history, for instance, of the nervous breakdown, would have to link a hermeneutics of the nervous disorder with power failures of a strictly technological order. A probing rhetoric of

«2»

the psyche would show the degree to which we are constantly borrowing structures from the technosphere. Hence the need for questioning technology at its hardened root . . . . . . . . . . . . . . . . . . . . . . . . . . . . . . . .
. . . . . . . . . The necessity of yielding an interpretation that deals with the equipmental being of equipment has been signaled in 'The Origin of the Work of Art,' perhaps the text of Heidegger most solicited by students

of literature and the arts. In the search for the equipmental character of equipment, Heidegger reports that equipment has come into being through human making, which renders it particularly familiar, therefore, to human thinking.[8] At the same time, this utterly familiar being has a peculiar intermediate position between thing and work. I shall not fight the battle between earth and world, or join the armies of the striving fourfold, but rather limit my scope of inquiry to the place where equipment and thing intriguingly alight onto two figurations of woman. The first woman of note is the one who has left her shoes hanging in Van Gogh's tableau; the second is Heidegger's 'young thing.'

The world of art history, represented notably by Meyer Schapiro, has faulted Heidegger on making Van Gogh's shoe fit a woman's foot, for it appears that the sure referent of the represented peasant shoes can be established as Van Gogh's own shoes. Yet Heidegger does not seem to have an art historian's take on this issue. One might ask instead why the decision to fit the shoe to a woman's foot seems apt, showing a tight fit in the curriculum of the argument: 'We choose as an example a common sort of equipment – a pair of peasant shoes' (32). The issue has been set forth in a number of works by Jacques Derrida, where the question is raised as to what constitutes a pair of shoes. It is not feasible for me to run this by you now, though an assumption of familiarity with the argument lacing together *La Verité en peinture* will have to be made. To get the shoes going, Heidegger shows the nonnecessity of conjuring them as visual representation: 'We do not even need to exhibit actual pieces of this sort of useful article in order to describe them. Everyone is acquainted with them. But since it is a matter here of visual description, it may be well to facilitate the visual realization of them, for which purpose a pictorial representation suffices' (33).

The move to pictorial representation comes to pass as a concession; it is not essential. The inessential marks the spot where the woman steps in, for what is to be seen in Van Gogh's representation also depends on 'the use to which the shoes are to be put, whether for work in the field or for dancing' – a difference within which form and matter shift accordingly (33). Since you will find neither Heidegger nor Van Gogh putting on their dancing slippers in this calling, we move to the peasant woman who, as exemplified equipmentality, doubles for another woman subsequently chained to the thing.

> The peasant woman wears her shoes in the field. Only here are they what they are. They are all the more genuinely so, the less the peasant woman thinks about the shoes while she is at work, or looks at them at all, or is even aware of them. She stands and walks in them. That is how shoes actually serve. It is in the process of

> the use of equipment that we must actually encounter equipment. (33)

Now, the shoes are pressed to the earth's lips, they have a telephonic hollow: 'In the shoes vibrates the silent call of the earth, its quiet gift of the ripening grain and its unexplained self-refusal in the fallow desolation of the wintry field.' As with the call that Heidegger fields in *Sein und Zeit*, there arrives an aphonic call of anxiety: 'This equipment is pervaded by uncomplaining anxiety as to the certainty of bread, the wordless joy of having once more withstood want, the trembling before the impending childbed and shivering at the menace of death' (34). The picture and the peasant woman belong to two different hands of Heidegger's reading; the woman and the represented shoes may belong to different frameworks, since the woman exists differently, in a motion picture . . . . . . . . . . . . .
. . . . . . . . . . . . . . . . . . . . . . . . . . . . . . . . . . . . . . . . . . . . . . . . . . . . . . . . . . . .

> But perhaps it is only in the picture that we notice all this about the shoes. The peasant woman, on the other hand, simply wears them. If only this simple wearing were so simple. When she takes off her shoes late in the evening, in deep but healthy fatigue, and reaches out for them again in the still dim dawn, or passes them by on the day of rest, she knows all this without noticing or reflecting. The equipmental quality of the equipment consists indeed in its usefulness. But this usefulness itself rests in the abundance of an essential being of the equipment. We call it reliability. By virtue of this reliability the peasant woman is made privy to the silent call of the earth; by virtue of the reliability of the equipment she is sure of her world. World and earth exist for her, and for those who are with her in her mode of being, only thus – in the equipment. (34)

Yet:

> A single piece of equipment is worn out and used up; but at the same time the use itself falls into disuse, wears away, and becomes usual. Thus equipmentality wastes away, sinks into mere stuff. In such wasting, reliability vanishes. (34–35)

When Heidegger ends this particular moment of the demonstration, reminding us of the disclosures of which breakdowns are capable, he returns to the painting, which has spoken [*Dieses hat gesprochen*, the painting has spoken]. The work did not in fact 'as it might seem at first' serve merely for a better visualization of what a piece of equipment is, that is, the work did not get used as a piece of equipment. Thus he can write that the work 'therefore, is not the reproduction of some particular entity that happens to be present at any given time; it is, on the contrary, the reproduction of the thing's general essence' (37). But the woman in Van Gogh's shoes, like the equipment, also arrives at her appearance through the work, except that her genuine arrival never as such takes place. Cinderella remains unfitted, a peasant out of the picture. The work of Van Gogh does not show us the woman, but rather lets her step into the image which Heidegger hails as the genuine arrival of equipment. To what extent does the passage through the work leave woman wasted, used up, or worn out, like the shoes that wear her spirit down? She is not entirely there in any phenomenal sense. Heidegger does not exclude 'woman'; on the contrary, he brings her into the hollows of the wooden shoes, he lets her wear the shoes unawares, unreflectively, reliably connected to the earth which speaks and vibrates through her feet. Here sexual difference may be a matter of substantial indifference. In any case, the woman who fills the shoes does not exactly exist as an aesthetic object, prepared for sensuous apprehension. *She is absent from the shoes that hold her.*

In his absence, Van Gogh is a woman, a peasant woman who allows the equipmentality of equipment to arrive, to shine through the canvas that has used him up; he, too, like the dwindling which Heidegger perceives, has vanished. As odd as this would seem at first sight – she is not there at first sight – the peasant woman marks the locus of an operator, working the shoes as the fields, arriving on the scene as the phantom voice that allows the painting to speak. She converts into a sonorous language the image which keeps her unillumined. Linked to the equipment, 'shivering at the surrounding menace of death,' the woman comes into the picture as that which vibrates, trembles, shivers. She connects both ends in the mode of genuine arrival: 'the trembling before the impending childbed and shivering at the surrounding menace of death.' The earth's vocal cords vibrate in her shoes . . . . . . . . . . . . . . . . . . . . . .
. . . . . .We are on the way to the feminine. Not an essence, or the goalie's penalty, just a way. Technology in some way is always implicated in the feminine. It is young; it is thingly. Thus every instrument of war can be given a feminine name. The feminine, in whose way we are, does not arrive. She is what is missing. Constituted like a rifle, she is made of removable parts. She hinges on the other, like the allegorical symbolics of which Heidegger speaks. The woman has gotten in the way of things, so that prior mention of her, at a younger stage of the 'Origin of the Work of Art' needs attending to. All works have a thingly character. A picture may hang on the wall, asserts Heidegger, like a rifle or a hat (19). Because the thingly character is so irremovably present, it draws allegory to the understanding of the work. The question of the other, of, say, equipment and the other, is not an arbitrary one. 'The artwork is something else over and above the thingly element' (19). It is not the thing,

but the something else that constitutes the artwork in its nature. While the artwork reverts to a made thing, it however says something other than the mere thing itself, *allo agoreuei.* The work makes public something other than itself. Manifesting something other, it is an allegory. In the work of art, the reading continues, something other is brought together with the thing that is made. To bring together is, in Greek, *sumballein.* The work is a symbol. Joining one element with another, bringing together what stays apart, the work somehow participates in both these figures, ruling over separation and that which binds. 'This is the thingly feature in the artwork' (20). The thingly feature is the jointure, that which at once joins and separates . . Heidegger enters a calculation of hesitations. The calculation, as the hesitation which defines it, impresses itself heavily upon us, for the thing will divide the sexes. Proceeding from the highest order of being, we slide down to the moment in which the hesitation prepares to be lifted. This will be the second configuration of woman:

> And besides, we hesitate to call God a thing, in the same way we hesitate to consider the peasant in the field, the stoker at the boiler, the teacher in the school as things. A man is not a thing. It is true that we speak of a young girl who is faced with a task that is too difficult for her as being a young thing, still too young for it, but only because we feel that being human is in a certain way missing here and think that instead we have to do here with the factor that constitutes the thingly character of things. We hesitate even to call the deer in the forest clearing, the beetle in the grass, the blade of grass a thing. (21)

In this scaled list of hesitations going down from the godhead to grass, spacing things out among themselves but providing a thin span from the stoker to the teacher and beetle, all of which we hesitate to name as thing, there comes one moment of relief from hesitation, one admission of a 'true' nature in the way we speak. The *we* constitutes an odd consensus, if it should include Heidegger. For it is not clear that the *we* prehending a girl as thing measures her necessity as the gravity of a task yet unfulfillable. What does Heidegger want from the girl? In the first place, a girl can be too young. To what extent does this clarify the demonstration of a thingly being? In a sense, the age of a being does count for Heidegger, for technology itself is always too young, too reckless and untried. There is typically 'something missing here' when the girl joins the lineup, something which the turn to equipmentality may or may not supply. But as a young thing, the girl is faced with a task too difficult for her; her telic finality remains out of her grasp. If this were the voice of Nietzsche, all of humanity would be this young thing. For Heidegger, we are, however, latecomers, a predicament with which our little girl remains out of step. There is no present of the feminine. While the girl proves still too young, the peasant woman appears no longer to be faced with a task. Having grown into her strongly unreflective being quietly, fatigue is the way time has spent itself on her.

Of all the 'things' enumerated as resisting the language of thingliness, the young girl has always already stepped out of the shoes of humanity into which she is supposed to fit ('only because we feel that being human is in a certain way missing here' – was being human not already missing in the beetle, or are we to understand that Gregor Samsa has crawled into the picture?). True, when Heidegger says that 'we speak,' he may be registering this as a largely quotidian or inauthentic *we.* The pure thing comes only in the form of a stone, a clod of earth, a piece of wood, the lifeless beings of nature. He does not include the schizophrenic girl who also comes in such a form of lifeless assimilation. Nonetheless, if a young girl fits the requirements of a thing concept in the way we speak, then we must let this thing, as in the case of all things, 'encounter us without mediation. The situation always prevails' (25). As object of sensuous perception, linking thus the thing directly to the aesthetic, the young girl, Heidegger avers, can 'move us bodily':

> But we do not need first to call or arrange for this situation in which we let things encounter us without mediation. The situation always prevails. In what the senses of sight, hearing and touch convey, in the sensations of color, sound, roughness, hardness, things move us bodily, in the literal meaning of the word. The thing is the *aistheton,* that which is perceptible by sensations in the senses belonging to sensibility. (25)

. . . . . . . . . . . Were we not engaged in questioning the specific mode of being for the telephone, assuming there to be an irreducible mode in this case, we would be tempted to stay on the line, inching our way to the artwork. For it is certainly not out of the question to engage this line accordingly. If the telephone were not conjured from a pretechnological concept of *technē,* as a mode of knowing, we could more easily dispose of its being as artwork. In *The Question Concerning Technology* Heidegger accordingly reminds us that *technē* is 'the name not only for the activities and skills of the craftsman, but also for the arts of the mind and the fine arts. *Technē* belongs to bringing-forth, to *poiēsis;* it is something poietic.' Furthermore, *technē* is linked with the word *epistēmē.* 'Both words are names for knowing in the widest sense.'[9] They mean to be entirely at home in something, to understand and to be expert in it.

The phone calls, speakingly rendering itself as a forthcoming, a call out of slumber, sheltering the self-containment of the other whose presence is always mediated, making the encounter unlike the one described for the mere thing. Yet, precisely because the artwork no longer acts wrenchingly the way something akin to science may do, if disbelief in the Hegelian pronouncement can continue to remain suspended, the most urgent call of the telephone at this phase of its protected being, seems to come from a place that cannot be framed satisfactorily by 'artwork,' particularly since many contaminations are at play. But, like the artwork whose origins Heidegger describes, the telephone is attached to the *aistheton* in fundamental ways; it is still a young thing faced with great tasks that elude its reach. Similar to the artwork's manifold veilings in the Heideggerian text, the telephone absorbs into its coils the features of equipmentality and thingness. Besides, it has assimilated to itself artistic qualities in the media that support its ambition for representation and replacement of the idiomatically human. It makes things appear, happen for the first time, and in the mode of a 'historacular' announcement. Independently of a signified, of course. The telephone largely avoids representational art, spreading the night that has to appear together with all that participates in the nonphenomenal dimension; telephone, like the temple, says that even the nonvisible has to appear in order to be what it is. There is thus a hypertheology of the telephone, the mightier god of the making-happen, making-appear, the remarkable localization of an electric *Geschehen.*

In this regard, the artwork performs the essence, performs the telephone, which proves capable of carrying the role of a mysterious lead character, as for example in the filmed version of *The Thin Man.*[10] The position of the thin man, mediating events, aesthetic transmissions, and desires, is occupied by the stand-up telephone, a character whose double plays the more recognizably human persona. One can scan effortlessly enough the motion pictures that carry the telephone, often thematizing the hallucinatory power it holds over dramatic action, calling forth a destiny in its finitude, arranging a string of statements attached to the will to power. *Sorry, Wrong Number* or *Dial M for Murder* will do; or within the form of another medium, Poulenc's *La Voix humaine* might be considered, where opera sings itself into an absent receiver of *Angst.* In all these representations, the telephone belongs to the artwork both as parasitical inclusion and as its veiled receiver, from whose opening invisible events are directed, quietly co-occupying the scene with the voices of commanding phantoms. Remoteness and nearness commingle – one is almost there. It makes a felt connection to its own reception history. Yet the telephone participates with such recognizably fresh insolence in the production of interruption, noise, and chatter that no one would yet presume to make a case for its markings as artwork, with which however it often coincides, drawing to itself the structures of both allegory and symbol. It perhaps does not yet claim the capacity for holding the terrifyingly silent scream of Munch's figure. Nonetheless, the stillness upon which any work of art is said to be grounded, its removal from a disconcertingly ontic dimension, has not always served the work of art well, has not necessarily strengthened it. A thinking of the artwork may include having to renew its effects and possibly, as in the experiments of Mary Shelley, to recharge it electrically – as if the artwork could produce the pain of an electric shock. This may not come to pass. Yet the static has returned, the noise grows louder. Life, as in Nietzsche, is holding her delicate ears – even though it was Nietzsche who first heard

> the scream of the Greeks,
> the din of
> Dionysiac noise . . . . . . . . . . . . . . . . . . . . . . . .

The telephone presents itself nowadays as a relatively unpretentious thing. It barely belongs to the league of high-tech desires. 'The unpretentious thing evades thought most stubbornly' (31). Thus the exertion of thought seems to meet with its greatest resistance in defining this relatively young thing. This is why it may seem that we are getting nowhere. But is this not precisely where the telephone gets us? We provisionally conclude this questioning of its nature with the leftover that Heidegger offers. It has not been thrown to us at the end of the road, but along the way. This is where we get off, to stay with the remnant:

> The situation stands revealed as soon as we speak of things in the strict sense as mere things. The 'mere,' after all, means the removal of the character of usefulness and of being made. The mere thing is a sort of equipment, albeit equipment denuded of its equipmental being. Thing-being consists in what is then left over. But this remnant is not actually defined in its ontological character. It remains doubtful whether the thingly character comes to view at all in the process of stripping off everything equipmental. (30)

This has also turned out to be an assault upon the thing. Perhaps the whole question has withheld itself in concealedness. Beings such as the telephone 'refuse themselves down to that one and seemingly least feature which we touch upon most readily when we can say no more of beings than they are' (53). The news is good. For concealment as refusal 'is not simply and only the limit of knowledge in any given circumstance, but the beginning of the clearing of what is lighted' (54). In the context that Heidegger draws out, concealment is not simple refusal. 'Rather, a being appears, but it presents itself as other than it is' (54). It turns out that concealment conceals itself, capable of appearing as refusal or merely as a dissembling. 'We are never fully certain whether it is the one or the other' (54). We believe we are at home, writes Heidegger, in the immediate circle of beings. That which is, 'is familiar, reliable, ordinary. Nevertheless the clearing is pervaded by a constant concealment in the double form of refusal and dissembling' (54).

At bottom, the ordinary is not ordinary: it is extraordinary, uncanny – it can be as eerie as the skeletal deposits of *Ge-Stell.* But it is covered over, pushed back, overlooked. 'The nature of truth, that is, of unconcealedness, is dominated throughout by denial. Yet this denial is not a defect or a fault, as though truth were an unalloyed unconcealedness that has rid itself of everything concealed. If truth could accomplish this, it would no longer be itself' (54). We have hit bottom, where the ordinary protects the extraordinary and uncanny, producing a buffer zone and shock-absorbent layering. We believe we are at home, but this occurs because the gift of denial shelters us from the immediate circle of beings. If we back up a bit, we discover a certain element of truth residing in dissembling. This greatly encourages our hopes, as we have let the telephone – most 'ordinary' of all things – fit the shoes of other beings, particularly when it was stepped up to enter the domain of artwork. Why did the telephone allow itself to respond to each combination, hardly resisting the dislocations which it acquired for itself? (Similarly, why does the work of art evoke a thinking of the thing and equipmentality?) Heidegger is clear on what leads a being to present itself as other than it is:

> If one being did not simulate another, we could not make mistakes or act mistakenly in regard to beings; we could not go astray and transgress, and especially could never overreach ourselves. That a being should be able to deceive as semblance is the condition for our being able to be deceived, not conversely. (54)

. . . . . . . . . . . . . . . . . . . . . . . . . . . . . . . . . . . . . . . . . . . . . . . . . . . .

. . . . . . . . . . . . . . . . . . . . . . . . . . . . . . . . . . . . . . . . . . . . . . . . . . . .

. . . . . . . . *They started calling again. I was getting worried, becoming their answering machine. The new book by Lacan came out, and he said someone ought to look into* AT&T. *So he was part of it! In* La Carte postale, *Derrida said to some girl she ought to go after the telephone. Something was going on here. Pointing the way, they were keeping their distance. They were right. I wanted to crack the crypt, but too much was happening. It got as far as the corporate unconscious . . . . . the corporate unconscious can speak, it exposes a layer of latent terrorism under the changing surface of telephonic ownership. An official pamphlet, entitled* American Heritage, *and subti-*

*tled* Breaking the Connection: A Short History of AT&T *(June–July 1985), shows a dangling, lopped-off telephone receiver, next to which one can read:*

Read the prose of self-mutilation and the essential phantasms of corporate identity and disintegration. After establishing the facts ('On January 8, 1982, the organization announced that within two years it would tear itself apart, and on January 1, 1984, it made good on its promise'), bodily dissolution takes over, and corporate paranoia suggests itself to be ready at hand:

> Before its dismemberment, the American Telephone and Telegraph Company, also known as 'Ma Bell,' had been by many standards the largest company on earth. In the range of its influence, in assets, and in its impact on the daily lives of ordinary people, it dwarfed not only other companies but also nations . . . The legal term for what occurred on January 1, 1984 is divestiture, but that word seems inadequate as a description of the corporate equivalent of a many-limbed giant ripping off limb after limb, flinging the pieces in all directions, and leaving the landscape littered with big, bleeding hunks of its former self. (65)

It is clear who directed the hand of the writer(s) here: either Bataille or Dr. Schreber. At any rate, AT&T ('also known as "Ma Bell"') makes no bones about having ditched Mother in the transaction. Several years prior to the divestiture, AT&T chairman Charles L. Brown 'shocked some of his own employees' when he announced the evacuation of the maternal:

> Brown suggesting that the comforting image of Ma Bell might not fit this new company: 'Mother,' he concluded, 'doesn't live here anymore.'
>
> Brown was premature; Ma Bell did not pass away until New Year's Day, 1984. Now that she is gone, we might take a moment to remember her remarkable life. What did she mean to us? *How did she get so big and strong?* What is her legacy? How will we manage without her? (66; emphasis added)

So 'Ma Bell,' as it turns out, was assassinated not because she was becoming frail or weak, edging toward something of a natural death, but, on the contrary, because she had become such a tough mother – she had become so big and strong. By eliminating her, the company ripped into its own image – bleeding hunks, as it says, of its former self, fragmenting into a litter of body parts: the violent and repressive birth of a maternal superego. Ma Bell's suppression installs a maternal superego as the place around which corporate members organize their remorse – which once again reminds us of the feminine trace deposited in the technologies . . . . . . . . . . . AT&T, incidentally, maintains the telephone as a 'tool' . . . . . . . . . . . . . . . . . . . . . . . . . . . . . . . . . . . yet the telephone was itself conceived as a prosthetic organ, a supplement and technological double to an anthropomorphic body . . . . . . . . . . . . . . . . . . . . . . . . . . . . . . . . . . . . . . . . . . . . . . . . . . . . . . . . . . . . . . . . . . . . . . . . . . . . . . . . . . . . . . . . . . . . . splitting itself off into the poesy of body parts . . . . . . . . . . . . . . . . . . . . . . . .

# THE *DIFFERENDS* OF MAN

Lyotard has observed that nazism, when it was 'over,' was let down like a rabid dog but never as such refuted. To be sure, a number of persuasive assertions have been made, analyses have been attempted, and an indisputable sense of justice has seemed to reinstall itself. Still, these do not provide philosophical proof or a rigorous guarantee of the intelligibility of the Nazi disaster. In fact, the recourse to the sublime, to modalities of the unthinkable and uncontrolled, suggest to us that nazism continues to place us before what Walter Benjamin has called *Denkfaulheit:* a failure or falling off of thinking, a kind of lethargy that overwhelms language. Among other things, this means that the gas has not been entirely turned off, but continues to leak and to spread its effects.

Yet it may be that the stunning toxicity is wearing off, and thinking is beginning to stir, to come to. This does not mean that the technologically constellated torture systems have been shut down, of course. But thanks to a number of courageous individuals – I think proper names are essential here: Jacques Derrida, Werner Hamacher, Philippe Lacoue-Labarthe, Jean-Luc Nancy, Sarah Kofman, Geoffrey Hartman, Raul Hilberg, Claude Lanzmann, Shoshana Felman, and others – the Holocaust, the break in any hope for naive historical continuity, has come into focus. I think it necessary to indicate at the outset, since this has strangely become a point of contention, that Derrida had been listening for the murmurs of the Holocaust long before this became, for intellectuals, somewhat of a journalistic imperative. I offer evidence in a footnote so that this can be set aside and we can get past the roadblocks that have been set up in order to stop a genuine thinking of that which has invaded us in this century.[1]

In France, as Jean-François Lyotard notes in *Heidegger et 'les juifs,'* something has been happening, a scene has broken open that can be linked to a certain geophilosophy: 'L'affaire Heidegger est une affaire "française." '[2] Whether the 'French' can be made to communicate with the 'jews' under arrest in the quotation marks of the title is something we shall need to decide. The displacement to France of the Heidegger scandal, the suspension of the Jews, and the dislocation of a differend reflect the temporal discontinuity to which this book seems to owe its existence.

Like the Heidegger disclosures which marked the end of a latency period – everyone knew Heidegger's Nazi seduction was there, but things were beginning to stir only now – *Heidegger et 'les juifs'* seems to emerge from a latency period that I will call 'Cerisy.' This is not to diminish the immeasurable importance of the disasters under discussion, but to include the frame that allows Lyotard to name this a French affair. Why the displacement to France? Which is another way of asking ourselves why 'deconstruction' – this miserable orphan of a name – has become the living target range for shots against our Nazi past. It is not wrong to wrest nazism from the deceptively secure space of a restricted national spasm. For the range and programming by metaphysics or Christianity, the major complicities shared by the most surprising parties, corporations, nations, and individuals, all fed the death machine – one, as we may soon learn, that was not, as we tend to say, out of intellectual cowardice, merely 'irrational.' It makes sense. Indeed, what needs to be considered is that the *project of making sense* or rather of making *one* sense is implicated in history's breakup with itself.

There are two scenes that I wish to evoke, two prologues to Lyotard's book, which exceeds itself and takes place elsewhere than between its covers (but what book ever takes place within its own site, letting itself be contained or bound by some simple determination?). Sometimes, however, the referential effects of elsewhere are less troubling than in this context.

*Cerisy-la-Salle, August 1980, Debate following 'Discussions: Ou, Phraser "Après Auschwitz."'*

*Lyotard* repeats, 'Il faut enchaîner après Auschwitz, mais sans résultat speculatif [It is obligatory to connect phrases after Auschwitz but without trying to obtain a speculative result']. In response to a question, he specifies: '*We* would be simply the hostages of: it is obligatory to connect phrases, *we* don't have the rule, we're looking for it, we are connecting phrases in searching for it. . . . The search for the rules of connectability is a search for the intelligible. Adorno speaks of the readable, Derrida of unreadability – which is a radical divergence, yet if *we* are the community of hostages held by "Il faut enchaîner," this is because we learn to read, thus we do not know how to read and, for *us*, to read is precisely to read the unreadable.'[3] At one moment Lyotard reminds his interlocutors that he has not talked about Heidegger ('*Lyotard* fait observer qu'il n'a pas parlé de Heidegger') although it is clear that ontology is at stake in the idea of phrasing.

[*Shift of scene.*] *Johnson* thinks that the most horrifying aspect of Auschwitz is not the phrasing 'You must die' but that it is unutterable, that the act being committed could not be accounted for in an utterance (except a sadistic one). *Derrida* adds that, indeed, this sentence could be uttered only within the context of a reasoned legality (such as the verdict of a jury): through Auschwitz no statement can legitimate the phrasing 'You must die.' After some discussion, *Nancy* intervenes: 'Thus there would be a specific difference between Auschwitz and other seemingly comparable situations.' Now, *Derrida* and *Lyotard* appear to have come to an agreement: names other than that of Auschwitz, just as unconnectable, demand no less to be connected. *Lacoue-Labarthe* asks that one name them [*Lacoue-Labarthe* demande qu'on dise lesquels]. *Nancy* sees the specificity of Auschwitz in that 'the end of man was in itself its project, and it was not the outgrowth of another project.' 'Auschwitz initiates the project of the end of man, which means: extermination, the final solution.' *Lyotard* doubts that this project would be exclusive to nazism. It is Western, Christian: the work of the churches of the New World in Africa, like that of Hegel on Judaism. . . . *Lyotard* thinks that there is also a Nazi discourse of reformation, but concedes only that what distinguishes 'Auschwitz' is the absence of a discourse deriving destruction from a project of reformation (in contrast to the Soviet camps, adds *de Gandillac,* where the latter exists). Indeed, but *Lyotard* wonders if this isn't a question of the addressee. For nazism, certain men are not at all reformable (on racial principle). The 'You must die' which is addressed to them is pure destruction. They wouldn't even understand the reformation discourse – *Cut.*

Anyone who has followed the works of those participating in this debate will recognize essential threads of a more sustained argument. We have selected and frozen this frame in order to splice it into the ongoing narrative, however frayed and complicated, in which the effects of Auschwitz are submitted to interminable analysis. It is necessary to jump-cut to these syncopations of thinking if we are at all to understand the major blank around which the Heidegger debate is being organized: Heidegger's silence over Auschwitz. The major default consists in Heidegger's refusal to enter the politics of connecting; as Lacoue-Labarthe sees it, Heidegger offered nothing but silence on the subject of Auschwitz. Thus, for both Lacoue-Labarthe and Lyotard, the mute but powerful interlocutor of Heidegger will have been Paul Celan. Heidegger's silence cut a wound into the name of Paul Celan, which is why Lyotard ends his book on this name and Lacoue-Labarthe never stops citing and reciting 'Todtnauberg.' In fact, Lyotard's book will end on a slippage of sorts, when the proper name Celan is traded in – we might say somewhat precipitously – for 'the jews': " 'Celan' n'est ni le commencement ni la fin de Heidegger, c'est son manque: ce qui lui manque, ce qu'il manque, et dont le manque lui manque."[4] Of course Heidegger misses the appointment and the point of Celan – but we still do not know what it is to get the point. Particularly when, in our sententious discourse on Auschwitz, we still subject this proper name to metonymic usury. There is nothing so abhorrent as a German who appropriates the suffering evoked by Auschwitz in a post-Nazi fit of insight and wins prizes for his efforts – a regular occurrence in the American university. The constant blare of moral loudmouths may be far more pernicious than a silence that we haven't yet learned to read. And what Heidegger has in fact written may be more disturbing than his silence. As for the American university, we must take a close look at what often passes for a Germanist. . . .

Reviewing the scene of Cerisy, we find markings of certain symptomatic mentions that ought not escape our screening devices. Lyotard's omission of Heidegger, Lacoue-Labarthe's probity, Derrida's precision of legality and context, Nancy's ability to read the project of Auschwitz will all reemerge in displaced but intelligible ways in Lyotard's *Heidegger et 'les juifs'* where the missing Heidegger comes to name the *différend* that Lyotard will want to articulate with his interlocutors.

~

Several of Lyotard's recent works have been concerned with the problem of rephrasing the political. His regard for justice has always put him on the side of Aristotle, Nietzsche, and Kant rather than that of Hegel and cognitive regimens of historical narration. While Aristotle produces a description of the prudent judge ('Prudence consists in practicing justice with no models')[5], Kant establishes the idea of justice, which, as David Carroll and Geoffrey Bennington have variously shown, prevents the hardening of justice into dogma or doctrine.[6] The 'critical' faculty teaches one to judge without criteria and to negotiate incommensurable domains. Thus Kant aggravated the incommensurability between the cognitive law (descriptive) and the moral law (prescriptive). What interests Lyotard is precisely the unbridgeable gap between the cognitive and the ethical faculties. Because of Kant's 'phrasing of the ethical, of obligation,' he comes after Hegel for Lyotard.[7] Kant's belief in obligation in the absence of any demonstrable proof of its existence is what engages Lyotard. His text, however, decidedly privileges Kant's *Third Critique,* because the problem of critical judgment is announced here in its most radical possibility and in terms of the 'aesthetic.'

~

When Jean-François Lyotard showed up that day at the colloquium organized by Nancy and Lacoue-Labarthe, he had already begun his work on justice. It was a turning point. No one was absolutely sure that he was going to be there when the time to honor Derrida came around. There had been so much silence between them, a break that no one really talks about. Lyotard had begun to articulate his apparent disillusion with certain aspects of militant politics in 'A Memorial of Marxism: For Pierre Souyri.' By then, we were all getting despondent. Every revolution had submitted to the spectacle of failure. Maoism turned out to be a disaster; the so-called Third World, according to entirely readable power failures, could not be expected to offer a model for revolution; the Black Panthers had been wiped out. The sclerotic fix of dialectics was showing up on the scanner as a kind of paleo-Marxism. Even the 'sexual revolution,' while complex as libidinal accounts go, largely ended up fucking with women. All these phrases needed to be filled out, studied, connected to explanatory discourses. I am merely trying to establish the mood, as Kant would say, for the day on which the debate took place. So Lyotard actually did come. It was maybe a kind of turning point. He had neglected to mention Heidegger. But on this eve of the retreat of politics, one was turning with Lyotard toward a more universal idiom of ethics and moral law. Kant in a way was the name of this retreat – Kant, whom Hölderlin had appreciated for his retreat from great revolutionary fervor, for democratizing in the mediated mode of reflective judgment. In any case, Kant, along with Levinas, offered the best means of exposing the 'transcendental illusion' of revolutionary politics.

As for the retreat of the political, Nancy and Lacoue-Labarthe were addressing it in their critical project for the Center for Philosophical Research on the Political. In the *ouverture* to *Rejouer le politique,* they write:

> This double demand – the recognition of the closure of the political and the unsettling practice of philosophy in terms of itself and its own authority – leads us to think in terms of the *re-treat* of the political. The word is to be taken in what is at least its double sense: retreat from the political in the sense of what is 'well known,' the evidence (the blinding evidence) of politics from the 'everything is political' through which our imprisonment in the enclosure of politics can be described. But it is also to be taken in the sense of retracing the political, remarking it – that is, making appear what is for us a new question, the question of its essence. This could in no way constitute . . . a withdrawal into 'apoliticism.' . . . This is to say that the activity of retreat is itself a political activity – by which it is undoubtedly a question of exceeding something of the political, but absolutely not in the form of an 'escape from the political.'[8]

The move governed by the *Ent-zug* [*re-trait*] is decidedly Heideggerian, though to our knowledge Heidegger never made it or marked it politically. What is called the political? These people were submitting 'the political' to a most watchful examination, trying to sort out ways in which the politics of horror might be retrieved from the domains of the unthinkable or unanalyzable. Lyotard phrased it somewhat differently but appears to have shared similar assumptions. His aim, at the time, was to 'destroy narrative monopolies.'[9]

~

The *différend* as defined by Lyotard is an unlitigable injustice. Presented nonetheless like a philosophical brief, *The Differend: Phrases in Dispute*, argues where argument as such has been suspended. *The Differend* takes up the problematics of defense against Faurisson's outrageous claims concerning the unproven existence of gas chambers which situate him as plaintiff. It is henceforth up to the victims of extermination to prove that extermination, an impossible convening of a court of ghosts.

> As distinguished from a litigation, a differend *(différend)* would be a case of conflict, between (at least) two parties, that cannot be equitably resolved for lack of a rule of judgment applicable to both arguments. One side's legitimacy does not imply the other's lack of legitimacy. However, applying a single rule of judgment to both in order to settle their differend as though it were merely a litigation would wrong (at least) one of them (and both of them if neither side admits the rule). . . . The title of this book suggests (through the generic value of the definite article) that a universal rule of judgment between heterogeneous genres is lacking in general.[10]

What follows assumes some familiarity with the further contents of *The Differend*. In a looser sense, *differend* has come to mean unresolved differences between two parties who do not share the same rules of cognition. Thus philosophers can be seen to exhibit differends, often with the aim of undermining the legitimacy of the discourse of the other. When Jürgen Habermas, for instance, makes such outlandish claims as (1) 'All denials notwithstanding, Derrida remains close to mysticism' (a curious and symptomatic statement, for Derrida nowhere denies his affinities with Hebraic thought); (2) as a Jewish mystic, Derrida 'degrades politics and contemporary history . . . so as to romp all the more freely, and with a greater wealth of associations, in the sphere of the ontological';[11] or (3) '[a] return to the Greeks, whenever it was attempted by Jews, always had about it something of a lack of power,'[12] these utterances (to put it politely) indicate, through the effects of irresponsible indictment, a differend.

The suspicious split between Hellenism and Judaism indicates, as Michael MacDonald has argued, an act of delegitimation toward the party identified – surprise – as Jewish. The question of lining up and identifying the Jew must remain undecided, MacDonald argues, and we should read this 'must' as an effect of moral law: 'Is Derrida Greek or Jew? This must remain undecided. What should now be evident, however, is that Habermas characterizes Derrida as a Jewish mystic in order to disqualify deconstruction as a legitimate philosophical enterprise.'

The Jewish station identification is, in fact, beamed back from Hegel, whom Lyotard will set against Kant precisely owing to Hegel's anti-Judaic swallowing machines, that is, to his reduction of the other to a stage in self-consciousness. One might graft onto Lyotard's passage on Hegel in *Heidegger et 'les juifs'* a similar one from *Glas*, for the two together form a stereophonic blast. In this passage, Derrida locates the figure of the Jew within a dialectic, which is, as MacDonald has shown, above all a dialectic of master and slave 'that secures the sovereignty of the Christian by exiling Judaism from the realm of Spirit. For Hegel, the Jew represents a moment of negativity or "diseconomy" in the dialectic that ensures the transcendence of Christianity over Judaism.'[13] Derrida puts it this way: 'The Jew falls back again. He signifies that which does not let itself be raised up . . . to the level of the *Begriff.* He retains, draws down the *Aufhebung* toward the earth.'[14] MacDonald's reading of the passage is crucial here, for it shows how the reduction of difference and heterology to identity that characterizes Hegel's speculative logic persists, for Levinas, in Heidegger's fundamental ontology. This is where 'il faut enchaîner' with Lyotard's reading of *Heidegger et 'les juifs,'* where Heidegger is seen to subordinate structures governing the relation with the Other to the relation with Being. The Hegelian infection is what the etiologists of philosophy's persistent anti-Semitic agency are rightly going after. Getting back to Hegel and Derrida, where the Jew falls back again, unable to be elevated to the level of concept, we discover a regressive coherency:

> This remains true for Habermas, who determines Judaic philosophy as an irrationalism in order to exclude it from the order of philosophy; the order of the *Begriff.* In forsaking the Spirit and Logos in favor of the dead letter of writing and inscription, the Jew, for Hegel as for Habermas, falls back into the irrationalism of mystical inspiration and frenzied cryptology.[15]

I think we have sufficiently brought into focus the injustice of Habermas's position – masked as it is by the pseudocoding of legitimate argumentation – to warrant the classification of differend. Differend carves out an abyss within interlocution; cables have not been set up to hear the other without static, warping, and constant interruption. Of course, the problem is not static, parasitism, and random noise, but the published refusal, precisely, to show the minimal decency that consists in making a connection: *il faut enchaîner.* In this particular case, which has been metonymized by Habermas into the negativity of philosophical grandeur (to the extent that philosophy has kept its reputation for bludgeoning a persecuted other, call it woman or Jew, call it South Africa, if you will), one can repeat and show, cite and argue that Derrida has said this or that; one can offer evidence of injustice and wrongdoing or probe the resistance, on the part of Habermas, to discerning the phantasm and violence of 'the Jew' (Joyce, for his part, worked through to the Jewgreek). But there is something like a broken connection dominating the thinking fields.

### CERISY-LA-SALLE: TAKE TWO

Yet another form of the *différend* exists, one that strains beyond the politics of *ressentimental* phrasing. This version talks and negotiates; it listens and articulates itself responsively rather than reactively. In fact, to the extent that it explores the limits of *différend* in the mode of positivity, it is questionable whether it constitutes the differend as such, or whether the differend can indeed guarantee the conditions of colegitimacy that it promises. What I would call the 'affirmative differend' has been brought to bear by Lacoue-Labarthe in his address to Lyotard at a subsequent Cerisy colloquium, organized around the theme 'Comment juger?' Lacoue-Labarthe launches the 'Différend dans le judicieux' with the quasi-performative injunction, 'Let's talk.' But one of the differends that he puts in place as he begins negotiations with Lyotard is Lyotard's willingness to negotiate with Habermas: 'Why take seriously a kind of dinosaur from the *Aufklärung?* And why go after him?' In other words, why encourage the degradation of differend into gang wars?

Two years after the debate cited in Cerisy I, then, Lacoue-Labarthe shows up to name 'a real differend.' 'Let's talk,' he begins, because 'that's why we are here, at least in principle. But let's talk also, and above all, because two years ago, right here, you came with this motive and on these grounds, not to claim this as your theme, but to respond to an address or to an injunction that already occupied us a great deal at the time.' As I see it, Lacoue-Labarthe has come to the point where a summit meeting of sorts needs to be called. The stakes are political, as certain territorialities are going to be covered or divided up. They respond to what happened 'two years ago, right here' by repeating the inaugural gesture: you came here with this motivation which I now affirm by repetition and irony. 'In principle' we're here at Cerisy to talk. But to the extent that Lacoue-Labarthe names the motivation that he claims to be reproducing, he's calling the shots; he is the one to open talks, so to speak. He institutes the couple and draws up the contract whose terms we still have to figure.

> What does this mean: 'Let's talk?' For us (I mean for the two of us, you and me) this means, and in a way it is very simple: let's continue talking. Or: let's take up the discussion again – in the manner of: where were we now? The discussion between us is not continuous, even less is it organic in nature. But it happens that for some time now, the mode of relation properly our own, with highs and lows (there have even been some pretty low lows), sometimes also without direct exchange, from a distance and in silence, is, more than anything else, discussion. And it is discussion because despite everything, despite the esteem and friendship, despite the affection, despite the pleasure of the times we have spent together, finally we are not in agreement, we have a real differend. I emphasize: finally.

Now, the precise location of the differend creates some difficulties. Lacoue-Labarthe emphasizes 'finally,' which carries temporal implications as well as indicates the end of a logical sequence or spatial properties. Given the distance and silence, despite the times we have spent, the modulations of affect, finally, beyond a certain Kantianism, we – now that I have established us as a 'we' in our singularity ('properly our own' relation) – now find ourselves disjointed, in the predicament of a differend. My question would be addressed to both Lyotard and Lacoue-Labarthe: is the constitution of a *we* possible where there is a real differend? Or doesn't the differend precisely disarticulate the *we*, undermining the stability of the other? Sure, to get a divorce means you were really tight at one point, but when the differend finally hits does it not dissolve the very conditions binding a *we* to itself? Put differently, the differend between Faurisson and the Jews (let us hope those who feel attacked by Faurisson are not limited to the Jews), between Habermas and Derrida, essentially aims to delegitimate the other, producing through the discourse of an indictment a second annihilation that is always in communication with the first project of annihilation.

There remains another possibility. The 'finally' stressed by Lacoue-Labarthe may be referentially pointing toward the future: in the end we will have had a real *différend*. It is important to establish the precise terms of the document being drawn up here because Lacoue-Labarthe will serve in *Heidegger et 'les juifs'* as a principal target area for the installment of a real differend. The bull's-eye has Derrida's face written all over it. However, this is not news. Here, at Cerisy II, Lacoue-Labarthe appears to be constructing what Lyotard elsewhere calls the *dispositif*, the device or setup that prepares the ground for a breakdown in talks. Interestingly, when Lyotard deciphers, in a decidedly critical way, Lacoue-Labarthe's posture toward Heidegger, he reappropriates terms with which Lacoue-

Labarthe identifies himself: notably, *pious,* the word upon which he closes the address ('piety'), only to find it reanimated and transvaluated some years later. For Lyotard will find Lacoue-Labarthe, and most of deconstruction, too pious, that is to say he marks them as 'encore trop pieux, de trop respectueusement nihiliste,' a characterization that appears rhetorically to collapse and neutralize itself. The problem is, he wants to *deconstruct* what is still too pious, and so on, in deconstruction. Or rather, he wants to deconstruct 'la déconstruction derridienne.' Now, seeing as he has just rejected Heidegger's deconstruction, I personally don't figure how he's going to cut it without 'Derridean deconstruction.' (Believe me, he's not about to go for 'Paul de Man's deconstruction.') While the stakes are very high indeed, the complaint is so curious that it is difficult not to wonder whether Lyotard is proposing that we adopt some form of disrespectful nihilism to overcome the respect that still inundates deconstruction. This choice of idiom seems very odd for a Kantian.

At the same time, one understands why Lyotard would get p.o.'d at the Heidegger affair; one often shares his frustration and impatience with the slow-paced serenity that apparently rules these respectful types. The difficulty resides in the fact that the nature and feasibility of the differend are at stake.

It is Lacoue-Labarthe himself who aligns his sensibility in terms of piety. 'I do not share the hatred you have for intellectuals,' he starts.

> Reading you, my first reaction is to say to myself: there, it's very clear; I am on the side of the modern and he of the postmodern, that is what unites us (since the one does not go without the other) and what separates us (since there is a moment when the division is made, and must be made violently). And everything over which we diverge, over which we have come many times to argue, comes down to this: I regret, he experiments; I am in *melancholia,* he is in *novatio;* I am nostalgic, sad, elegiac, reactive, pious; he is affirmative, gay, satirical, active, pagan. A great separation of 'values,' and I don't exactly find myself on the best side.

While he offers the very terms of opposition around which Lyotard's critique of him years later will pivot, Lacoue-Labarthe, in a second movement of autodescription, retreats from such reactive posturing. He does not recognize himself in regret or melancholy, he now claims. What affects him, inscribes him as it were, is that the 'epoch is given to mourning, but nothing prevents us from bearing it in an easy manner, or with discretion. One can even secretly rejoice.' Lacoue-Labarthe will not sustain the oppositional logic with which the address has begun but reroutes this principle through Lyotard's modeling of tensions: 'it is the very opposition of the modern and the postmodern that bothers me and seems questionable to me. . . . It is necessary, I believe, to put into question – or rather to thwart – oppositions. But not directly, nor, above all, by attacking the opposition . . . [thus allowing] oneself to be enclosed within it.'[16]

This would be the place to spot a certain unsettling of the *différend.* The affirmative differend has come to introduce a complication into the itinerary of differences viewed as sheer oppositionality or incommensurability. 'Let's talk' at once involves a posturing of the differend *Dasein* while it challenges the unbridgeable gap imputed to the post-differend condition. 'Let's talk' figures a kind of Heideggerian *Mitsein* [Being-with] asserting the irreducible precedence of the Other to the self. Indeed, 'let's talk' means 'let's listen,' because talking always implies a prior listening. It is a mode of talking as listening that would mark our epoch – though ours is the end of epochality – as one of mourning. For listening regulates distance and alterity, the discontinuity of a dialogue with an other. It searches out the echo of freedom.[17]

~

Perhaps the way I directed Cerisy I and II as successive stagings in the launching of *Heidegger et 'les juifs'* will have seemed overly mediatic as narrative. The pervasive mood of irony and the cuts of screening are arguably incommensurate with the gravity of what is addressed when one is writing under the gun of 'Heidegger, Art and Politics.' Yet something has made itself felt, something that would turn the mechanical reproduction of the same rhetorical mood into a further instance of indecency. At times, our age of mourning unleashes a certain libidinal upsurge, the giddiness of terror. One wants to see again, according to the script of tonal modulation, Hölderlin's 'Wechsel der Töne,' which now gets fed through an entirely new technology of shredding and splicing.

Among those whose thinking has been perceptibly invaded by Auschwitz, Werner Hamacher offers a most persuasive statement:

> We do not just write 'after Auschwitz.' There is no historical or experiential 'after' to an absolute trauma. The historical continuum being disrupted, any attempt to restore it would be a vain act of denegation. The 'history' of Auschwitz, of what made it possible, supported it and still supports it in all its denials and displacements – this 'history' cannot enter into any history of development or progress of enlightenment, knowledge, reflection, or meaning. This 'history' cannot enter into history. It deranges all dates and destroys the ways to understand them.[18]

What does the disaster of a history have to do with the media? In the first place, the differend between Lyotard and 'deconstruction' unravels around the event of the Shoah. Second, Lyotard localizes the Heidegger affair as an affair of the media, underscoring, he suggests, the wholly impoverished encounter between art and politics. While the recent mediatic determination of *Shoah* is never as such submitted to critical discussion, the Heidegger story fades into an affair of the media, the single beneficiary, according to Lyotard, of philosophy's scandal. Third, the media has everything to do with the age of mourning, the pulverization of narrative monopoly, and the encrypting of unacknowledged loss. The media places us before the enigma of transference, which is to say, political hypnosis and the fascisoid *jouissance* of the sensorium. The Nazis made a number of crucial decisions concerning the media, divesting television while colonizing the air with blasts of radio and promoting Riefenstahl. Since at least the critical intervention of Kraus, Benjamin, and Adorno, the media has become a place where the clear-cut distinction between art and politics no longer abides. Call it national aestheticism, call it transference machine and body invasion, the technologies of the media are coextensive with the German disaster. This is why Lacoue-Labarthe analyzes one film, and Lyotard another; this is why Friedrich Kittler analyzes gramophone, film, and the organization of the SS in his new military histories; this is why Laurence Rickels, writing on German crypts, analyzes film, radio, and the World War II bunker; this is why Werner Hamacher analyzes journalism and the breakdown, 'after' Auschwitz, of historical narrative; this is why Alice Kaplan analyzes radio transmission and fascism; and, if you will permit me, this is why I analyze the telephone and the narcissistic blowout of the terroristic state.[19] So the media, I think, ought not to surprise us when it starts blaring the news of its being whenever the political is at stake. (The Reagan years, which have juridically regressed and morally devastated America, cannot be thought without media and the autofeeding productions of the presidency and the televisual metaphysic.) Still, Lyotard is perturbed. He names the media the principal beneficiary of the Heidegger affair.

This may not be altogether wrongheaded, but it does little to explain the inexorable relatedness to mediatic desire of Heidegger's involvement with the NSDAP, for which he momentarily became a loudspeaker. Heidegger staged himself and the university when he became an amplifier of state-*Schicksal* in the rectorate speech of 27 May 1933; while he disdained television, he likened it at one point to his thinking and did not decline an invitation to appear on it (on Sundays, he'd hang out at his neighbor's to watch soccer). He talked, finally, through the organized space of *Gerede*'s printout: the supplement to his thinking and politics appeared in his famous *Spiegel* interview, put into circulation after his death, like a black box surviving a crash. How are we to interpret the fact that Heidegger had an admission policy reserved for the press? What indeed does it mean for us that a Heidegger claims to tell the truth in a newspaper? It means, for one thing, that the media is not simply situated outside philosophy, running along parallel and aggressive tracks. Philosophy has always spilled into the streets, run diffusion campaigns, and made scratch noises on the public record. To accomplish these aims, it would travel on a different track, to be sure, at a greater speed. The media and philosophy are neither friends nor enemies; they're not even cutting it according to territorialized gang wars.

But something happened to us moderns, I think, when God got dead, and, crashing down, He slipped the microphone to Zarathustra. Zarathustra, remember, is Nietzsche's anchorman, announcing the death of God long before people were tuned in. The mediatechnic catastrophe should not be read in keeping with naive or merely technophobic command systems. What is 'the media' that it can profit from Heidegger, the Nazis, and the general administration of sensational pain? Where is it to be located, mapped out, and stabilized? These questions are circuited through the works named above.

~

The part of his book titled 'Heidegger' begins with the fifteenth chapter. Lyotard, about to put down the media, opens with the tone of an emergency broadcast. Is the interruption of media a part of it? 'Il y a urgence à penser l'affaire Heidegger.' Nietzsche – once again returning – spoke of the emergency conditions under which philosophy grows. But Lyotard urges a different temporality of urgency, even though he is himself rather fast on the trigger, 'postmodern,' and pagan. Under the circumstances, I have often found it difficult to connect. One problem, admittedly, may be that Lyotard has gone for disconnectability in his text. Even the *et* of the title names a disjunction that refuses to connect. The violence and disconnection, the surprise attacks, too, may be rooted in the fact that Lyotard has himself gone for 'tout déchainement':

> Ce n'est en effet pas 'par hasard' que 'les juifs' ont fait l'objet de la solution finale. . . . Cette absence de hasard ne signifie pas pour autant qu'on puisse 'expliquer' Auschwitz, et je ne l'explique pas plus qu'un autre. Car de la *Verdrängung* originaire il n'y a pas d'explication. Elle ne se laisse pas enchaîner. Elle est au 'principe' de tout déchainement.

> [It was not in fact by chance that 'the jews' were made the object of the final solution. This absence of chance does not however mean that one could 'explain' Auschwitz, and I no more explain it than anyone else. For there is no explanation for primal repression. It

does not let itself be linked with anything. It furnishes the 'principle' for every violent unleashing.][20]

~

It would be pointless to oppose connectability to disconnection; nowadays we are operating an entirely different switchboard. The ways in which we have been invaded by technology have only begun to affect thinking, though Heidegger saw it and called it, if only too late. *Shoah* connects the utterly disparate articulation of a Jewish person with a Nazi document that ends: 'Submitted for decision to Gruppenleiter IID, SS-Obersturmbannführer Walter Rauff. Signed: Just.' The Jewish person speaks of dreaming, survival, and the soul: 'But I dreamed too that if I survive, I'll be the only one left in the world, not another soul.' The Nazi document speaks that late spasm of metaphysics – technology:

> *Berlin, June 5, 1942*. Since December 1941, ninety-seven thousand have been processed by the three vehicles in service, with no major incidents. In the light of observations made so far, however, the following technical changes are needed: The vans' normal load is usually nine per square yard. In Saurer vehicles, which are very spacious. . . .[21]

The rhetorical disjunction between a dreaming self and the technological breach leaves the film speechless. Still, when film loses its voice, it's still on the job. The van has not vanished into this memo. On the contrary, Claude Lanzmann shows the metaphysical metaphor rolling down the Autobahn.

~

*Post Scriptum*. Lacoue-Labarthe has in the meantime alerted me to the existence of a forthcoming text by Lyotard that appears to constitute a partial retraction of some of the reflections advanced in *Heidegger et 'les juifs.'* It would be a mistake not to acknowledge this considered and welcome elaboration, the proofs of which I have just read. A reading of the installation of forgetting that has overlooked the forgotten, the pages relocate Lyotard's keen insight into Heidegger's manipulation of Kant, where Heidegger is seen to pass over the Judaic Kant (Hölderlin's 'Moses of our nation'), the Kant who affirms the Law. In addition, Christopher Fynsk has sent me a remarkable Lyotard manuscript on Kafka and the Law, which I hope will soon see publication, as it throws new light on this debate.

# SUPPORT OUR TROPES

*Reading Desert Storm*

GOING DOWN IN HISTORY: According to one version, there was a telephone call that did not take place. This is the version of Saddam Hussein. If the Iraqi troops were remarkably immobilized when they were ordered by George Bush to withdraw from Kuwait, this was because Saddam (so the version goes) was stationed at the reception desk of international politics, waiting for Bush's call. Had that call been completed, claimed Saddam on several occasions, he would have honored the demand of the community of nations for which Bush was the principal operator. But George Bush never placed that call, and Saddam Hussein refused to budge. Instead, Bush called in the tropes – or the armies of metaphors and metonymies, as Nietzsche would say, that were to justify war.

If we begin by establishing the story of a disconnected telephone line, this is for a number of reasons. None of these has much to do with the question of credibility on either side because that line of questioning has been scrambled by all parties concerned: the war was less a matter of truth than of rhetorical maneuvers that were dominated by unconscious transmission systems and symbolic displacements but which nonetheless have produced material effects. In the first place, the missed telephone appointment that Saddam Hussein has placed at the origin of the war signals at a primary level the electronic impulses that were flowing between the powers. Whether or not the crucial telephone call was to be made – Bush was relating full on to telephonics for the duration of the war – the atopos of the telephone created a primal site of technological encounter.[1] This was going to be a war of teletopologies, presence at a distance, a war which could have been averted, according to the one version, by a telephone call. Saddam Hussein said he would have transferred the locus of power to the Other, provided the Other wasn't going to be a specular other, a mere counterpart and double. No, Saddam Hussein had to hear himself speak through the locus of the Other if he was to cooperate, or at least feign cooperation with the community of nations. This is precisely what a telephone call accomplishes: it allows transference to take place in a manner that would supercede a stand-off between two egological entities or two continuous subjects; in sum, it programs another algorithm of encounter.

Saddam Hussein, inscribed by Western teletopies and coded by our projection systems, would have answered to his name, he says: he was bound to accept the call, if not the charges. That call, which Saddam said

would have made a critical difference in the way the two parties subsequently engaged their lines, never came through. The telecommunicational cast of the Gulf War remains enigmatic (despite so much focus on the participating media technologies), and seems to admit no simple reconstitution of its vicissitudes. For its part, the United States did not put that call through, preferring instead to answer a clearer call to arms. The question is how to trace this call within the dense network of motivation, parapraxes, conscious and unconscious national maneuvers, or even international strategies. The missed call to which Saddam has pointed by no means places him as the principal agency of our inquiry. The point, since there must be one in matters of war, is to take seriously that which disrupted the possibility for communication between US and Them, and between US and US. There is something at play here that goes beyond the desire to institute international law, or even beyond our oil addiction. It has to do with compulsion in politics – something that belongs to another scene of articulation. So, in the first place, why did we refrain from including Iraq on the circuit of collective calls? In part because of the different time zones that rendered any simple connection impossible. For George Herbert Walker Bush is a haunted man, and the Middle East, a phantom territory between the West and its others.

Not that the Middle East was noiseless – ghosts always make their presence known, and sometimes they seem real enough. Except in photo shoots. The call that never came through nonetheless exists. It follows the contours of a disrupted loop or a broken circuit. It presents for us, though in a fugitive manner, an allegory of nonclosure. The Middle East marks the spot to where World War II was clandestinely displaced when its history refused to close upon itself. Political scientists and historians can fill in the blanks better than I could ever hope to, so I will restrict my contribution to pointing to certain mappings of the rhetorical unconscious. This time, when history repeated itself, it was not a joke, but the production of a haunted man to whose systems of repetition compulsion we were all assigned. There was the matter of resurrecting Hitler in the Middle East, and a felt need to control the airspace. The Patriot missile system perforated two phantasmic oppressions: the Germans had never lost air control in World War II, and George Herbert Walker Bush's was not the only one of the three planes on mission to go down day. When the Avenger plunged into the ocean, young Bush, the youngest fighter pilot in the U.S. Navy, lost two close friends. Puking from fear and endless seawater, the youngest pilot started attending a funeral whose site he would never be able to pinpoint.

SON OF SAME: Let me back up. It is not the case *empirically* that the Germans retained air control. But only a naive historicist perspective would disallow the speculative impact historicity genuinely involves. In this analysis, we feel called upon to locate the Gulf War, or the return of the figure of war as such, in the disjunction between empirical history and speculative prolepsis. If we maintain that a major phantasm bequeathed by the Second World War consists in the desire for a certain closure of air, as it were, this is because one of the dimensions of the war that was left unresolved – unmourned – was both generally, and in the particular case of George Bush, located off the map, in the air.

How is it that war has returned as the excess of plenitude and the exercise of sovereignty? To be sure, every war is about the presencing of sovereignty which modern humanism's peace plans, with their absence of grandeur or divine manifestation, have never been able to secure. There is no war – the extreme exercise of sovereign right – that does not claim to disclose a transcendental trace. In this case, technology carried the message from God. But what allowed the sudden remotivation or legitimation of war as privileged space of national sovereignty? The return of war as a sanctioned figure has everything to do with the return call that at once bypassed Saddam Hussein and destined him as proxy and stand-in for an unresolved break in world history. What was it about World War II that was called back at this time? What called scores of military phantoms back into action?

World War II invented carpet bombing, creating fire storms. After the experience of mass destruction and victory, the Allies however concluded that the air war had been ineffective, even to the point of having extended the duration of the war. The scope of destruction and random targetting would remain in holding pattern until, at the time of the Gulf War, we took recourse to nuclear and smart bombs, legitimating, that is, their usage. Not only had the air war been ineffective, but it had created immense resentment among the civilian populations to whom we henceforth owed restitution. Something else came down from the air as well. When it was decided that the atomic bomb would be deployed, this event was not expected to take on a morally ambiguous cast. The atomic bomb was to accomplish what normally, in the course of carpet bombing, would take three days. The atomic bomb was understood merely to amplify the ef-

fects of these fire storms. When WWII left the air wide open, therefore we could say that it morally gave notice of an unpaid debt, an account to be settled. For the air had to be disambiguated, rescued and reterritorialized to a just cause. If a just war were ever to be fought again, it would have to restitute to the skies a moral horizon which would communicate with a failure to close WWII. The smart bomb, which addresses itself to that failure, would outsmart the inerasable error of WWII, in other words, it would not *smart.* This is not a play on words, though our war includes playing and games. What I am trying to get at is precisely the signifying chains that the phantom of WWII keeps rattling.[2]

~

The American unconscious has everything to do with riding signifiers on the rebound which, subject as they are at times to retooling, nonetheless return to the haunts of the Same. By retooling, we mean that, while increasingly technologizing death, the fundamental idiom hearkens back to the tropes instituted in this century by modern warfare. Thus 'collateral damage,' for instance, refashions the industrial production of corpses which Martin Heidegger signaled after WWII, where 'friendly fire,' while minted by the death denial inclination of California, points to the Pacific and the suicide pact which that side of the war staged through the kamikaze. By the Same, we are indicating on another level of discourse that we are guilty of reducing everything to an order of sameness. This is why the very thing responsible for the excess of meaning or the sense of otherness which occupies the Middle East is being systematically obliterated along the same lines of arrest that has kept Mr. Bush in a forty-year daze. The incredible fact that the Iraqi leader was prompted to pose as Hitler's double (Same), in other words, as a by-product of the Western logos (it is grotesque to forget that Adolf Hitler was a *Western* production), in itself demonstrates the compulsive aspect of this war.

We are reading a case study of history that presents itself as a symptom. The symptom is that of historical nonclosure and seems in itself to be arrested within a predicament of nonclosure. This war, which masquerades as being 'over' (Joyce: 'he war,' to be read in the Anglo-Germanic space that is opening up before us),[3] has not properly begun to situate its effects: in short, everything was left in the air. This is one reason the war cannot be read according to traditional protocols of historical investigation, or even along the lines of strategic or tactical analyses. I am tracing a *phantasmic history.* This is not the result of a whim or an effect of subjective contingency. The phantasmic control systems are out of my hands just as this war left a number of us disarmed. On the eve of German reunification, Goebbels's phrase 'new world order' lept out of his diaries to be recircuited through the ventrilocating syntax of George Bush. If

Saddam Hussein was a prop, it is also the case that this concept functionally suited George Bush. Indeed, we are faced here with the projections of a somewhat more original prop who, in order mythically to fill himself out, needed to rerun through the same war that had knocked him out. This corresponds to a mythic structure of return and second chance which, in life, tends to revert either to the happy few or to the severely neurotic. George Bush was one of them – or rather, two of them. At any rate Bush had always been second and secondary. This was his nature, to be a second nature.

Too young at the advent of World War II, he was destined to be late on arrival. Known as the son of Pres Bush, vice prez to the undead Reagan, a simulating machine par excellence, he was to become the uncanny president of the near end of the millennium. Something went into suspense or responded to the clandestine command 'Freeze!', when he lost his two friends. It was as if George Bush had been arrested, which is why his iconic relation to his wife, for instance, looks as though he had struck a deal with a soul murderer, giving the couple the disjunctive look of a moment in *Dorian Gray.*

It has been suggested that George Bush had the luck of encountering the Oedipal taboo head on: he was permitted actually (symbolically) to marry his mother, thus turning back the interdictory power of the law. With paternal law falling down, crashing out of the sky, the symbolic register is exposed to the most serious effects of scrambling. In the first place, this predicament maintains him in the position of son, ever competing with an ineffectual father (this was played out with Reagan, whom he all but banished from the White House). Secondly, the prez will have experienced fusional desire and the illicit communions which will have proliferated from this 'experience' – we are referring to his special missions directed by God, represented here on earth on the eve of the Gulf War by Billy Graham, with whom Bush spent the night. Perhaps we need to take a closer look at the situation. This look will not constitute the voyeur's gaze into a privately circumscribed space, but will open out onto the unconscious mappings which we are endeavoring to retrieve.

The Bush couple is proud of the generational difference that their union appears to mark. Barbara refuses to mask or suppress the mark of difference that in fact exposes a fusional desire. I am not saying that the male subject should abstain from locating his desire in an 'older woman'; that would be absurd and out of sync with the times. I am saying rather that the first couple stages its communion within the precincts of nonhistorical difference. While Barbara Bush has grown into her age – the end of the twentieth century – George Bush will not grow, he cannot age, and this in turn reflects the ahistorical fusions which his tenure accomplishes. (The scandal of difference which the first couple inscribes is displaced on to the family pet, Millie. After Bush was elected prez, the first couple announced the ritual copulation of Millie with a pure breed, which, in dog language, means Aryan. Hence the 'Millie-Vanilli' prez who would fuse and simulate histories was to oversee pure generational evolution. Indeed, Millie was so exceptionally evolved that she wrote the autobiography ventriloquized by Barbara Bush. Millie shared not only the couples' secrets but their diseases as well. The phantasms of which Millie Bush is sole receptacle will have to be treated elsewhere.)

While Bush stands arrested, his language spinning accidentally out of control, Barbara withers. She is the figure in the couple who mourns: attributing her gray hair – an overnight job – to the grief she suffered over a deceased child (a Robin), she also took a downward plunge a week before the bombing of Iraq started. Sliding downhill on a sled, Barbara Bush breaks a hip joint. The couple is disjointed, a connection dislocated. With the guilty part and partner externalized and maternalized, George Bush can go on with his business unfeelingly. If he cried uncontrollably at the event of his crash, his language oddly obsessed on his unwillingness to shed a single tear over the dead of the Gulf War (he shared this charming attribute with General Schwarzkopf). There is a whole history of pressing tears here on which Barbara bloats and George – well, he sees, he says, he feels, no reason to grieve. With Barbara as shock absorber and Millie as totemic father or expulsed superego, GeoBush somnambulizes as he occupies uninterrogated lands of the dead. (Only after the replay, in Christian rallies, he lets drop a tear: major breakthrough for the one who could not mourn.) One thing, perhaps, has become clear for us: The way the first couple presents itself is not merely a matter for quirky pomo readability. Everything that Bush does is a matter of presencing for a dead center that keeps on replicating itself. Catching up to first place, first couple, first superpower, Bush is still running behind, fluttering and second. America is losing the races; like Bush, it is losing heart, faltering in full regression. Everything that George Bush does is intended to efface history, or to bring it back to pre-civil rights days, and so on, in other words to bring it back to the day of the crash.

With GeoBush at the helm we can only go down, crash – or turn around. This is the field of his rhetorical unconscious. Hence the strange and belated evocation of the 'line in the sand' which, presenting itself spatially as a deadline, came too late. All of Bush's politics depends on reversing the order of the 'too late,' reproducing the deadline after it has passed, going back on history.

**ON RAISING THE PARATAXES:** George Bush's couplifications appear to demonstrate the principle of nonlinkage. In other words, the other is a locus of profound connectivity which first has to be articulated in order to be disavowed. His history as vice prez is summed up in the notorious avowal of May 1988: 'For seven and a half years, I have worked along side [Reagan] and I am proud to be his partner. We have had triumphs, we have made mistakes, we have had sex.' Recovering this lapsus (he means 'we have had setbacks'), he elaborates the scene of parataxes by comparing himself to a 'javelin thrower who won the coin toss and elected to receive.'[4] Others have adequately noted the 'wimp factor' that dominated Bush's electoral anxieties – being second to the top, at the feminized receiving end, and now he has to turn things around via anal-sadistic military penetrations to equally feminized territories. Curiously, Bush's initial correction reveals the proximity of sex and setback, which is to say the backside of projected progress, the place of impasse. The substitution of 'sex' for 'setback,' which in this context refers to Bush's secondary position within a structure of the couple, reveals as well the libidinal investment in the setback – which is to say, in the reversal, postponement, delay, which must be surmounted. It further shows that setback for Bush is beyond the pleasure principle and in the service of repetition and the death drive.

On the other end of Mr. Bush's couplifications, on the receiving end, we encounter the absolute dummy both in the Lacanian and popular senses of the term. The name of the symptom: Dan Quayle. As dummy par excellence, he ventriloquizes with exceptional precision the breaches in presidential linguistics. He exists, as Bush's political double or other, as that which cannot be; he scans as a sign for the impossibility of becoming president. As ventriloquizing locus and externalization of the president's inarticulable phantasmata, Dan Quayle dramatizes the executive desire for historical effacement. He is moreover the figure that George Bush has chosen to replace and repeat himself, to fill his space and articulate its contours. Where Bush restricts his elliptical performances of linguistic nonclosure to sex/setback sets, believing also that 'comme ci, comme ça' is a popular Hispanic phrase, and other confusions that name themselves (George Bush's lapses are frequently metacommentaries: the setback names the lapsus he has just committed, comme ci comme ça designates the 'undecideds' which can go either or both ways, and so on), Dan Quayle discloses himself as if to let the prez speak through an empty body-as-megaphone; he is a broadcast system switched on by the sinister vicissitudes of Bushian desire. When George Bush says, 'Read my lips,' he means look into the gaping abyss – the yawn – and listen to Dan Quayle.

(In French, Bush is pronounced 'bouche,' mouth.) One could offer a compelling, if not compelled, reading of Bush and Quayle as a mutant breed of 'cyburban' cowboys, particularly given Bush's simulated address in and from Texas, a hotel in Houston. For our purposes, however, I am going to treat the Bush-Quayle couple as a single entity or utterance machine with the sole purpose of analyzing their dehistoricizing desire. For all its emptiness and technobody hollows, the prez-vice presidential machine targets the lack in the Other in a continual setback of friendly fire.

Of the lapses that have been noted in the repertoire of the Bush administration, one in particular puts the achronos and atopos of the war in uncanny perspective: 'The Holocaust was an obscene period in our nation's history. I mean this century's history. But we all lived in this century. I didn't live in this century.'[5] The Bush-Quayle machine has produced a rich utterance which, at first sight appears to confirm Mary McGrory's insight that 'the non sequitur is the one grammatical [sic] form Bush has mastered.'[6] Clearly, there is some irony to this assertion, for the non sequitur is precisely that which eludes mastery, marking as it does a gap, the abyss of nonlinkage. Diane Rubinstein has identified this tendency to skip a beat semantically as the binary logic that would oppose the office of presidential speech to the couch of analysand: 'For Bush's digressions, non sequiturs, lapses, repetitions recall those of an analysand rather than the narrative closure of an authorial subject (i.e., the President of the United States . . .). One of Bush's most interesting and parodied linguistic tropes is his use of the word "thing."'[7] We shall get to thingification momentarily, though we are already following a logic of the automata. First let us gloss the slippage that locates the Holocaust on our shores. In fact the (vice)presidential unconscious knows how to read, and like the essence itself of the unconscious it stakes out the timeless, refusing contradiction: the Holocaust was a moment in American history, says the (vice-)president of the United States. This general assertion is followed by a single subject's intentional inflection ('I mean this century's history'), then it reverts to the general assertion ('But we . . . ') and reverts once more to a particularized subject's predicament ('I didn't live in this century'). This subject, as pure subject of enunciation and inscription, is a dead subject who makes claims for not having lived in this century, or rather, for not having lived according to calendrial or historical time. Everyone lived in this century ('we all lived') but the speaker himself did not experience this century, which in his transmission metonymically displaces 'the Holocaust.' The (vice-)presidential unconscious knows that it does not know the Holocaust, but this unknowing is obtained only as a condition of not having lived in this nation/century. The geo- and chronopolitical map of this administration's compulsion is being disclosed here. The confusion of space and time crucially underscores the possibilization of essential analogy. But beyond the structure that permits our nation to incorporate the grotesque history of Germany or Poland – an outstanding debt for which we inheritors of nazism still have to pay – Dan Quayle speaks for an administration that will not have lived. As Bush's hologram, this total recall machine (which lives with all memory but cannot live in time or with introjection) also prints out its participation in the presidential death drive.

If his compulsive program is associated with the death drive, this by no means constitutes a way of putting down Mr. Bush or that which lip syncs him. In fact, it offers a compliment, one that possibly overestimates the presidential reserve of libido. The death drive is understood both by Freud and Lacan as a normal paradox of bioinstinctual setback for our species. The Bush-Quayle entity may well extend beyond the death drive, which is to say, at the limit of the domain of drives [*Triebe*]. Going this way or that, they have mutated into a function of thingification where they are placed under instinctual arrest. I in no way intend simply to condemn one man or one man's symptomatology. It may be the case that one has to draw the line somewhere; but, as Heidegger has suggested in another contextual milieu, let us first contemplate that line. One might easily be drawn into the reactive posturing that elicits condemnation. And yet, this is precisely the time – most 'moral' of times – to resist condemnation. Perhaps such a politics of utterance deserves some explanation. Having supplanted rigorous analysis, condemnation, as if to build a roadblock to thinking, has been expressed too often and possibly too recklessly with historically signified villains. I have no interest in attacking one man or his singular decoy – this would be too metaphysical a gesture, and would accomplish no more than locating the origin of event or History in a single (male) Subject. That would be the easy way out: to pin the blame on a proper name that is placeholder for an entire symptomatology of beings. The question has to be, rather: Why was it possible for George Bush to be president? Why was it possible, at this particular moment in history, for Saddam Hussein to pose as Adolf Hitler? Whether or not you voted, protested, freaked out, or elected one or another mode of passivity, it is a question of our history.[8] The war is what we share – even if this should be exercised in the mode of repression or according to the injunction to forget. As the (vice-)presidential utterance has disclosed, the boundaries around the place of occupation, according to spatial and temporal determinations, are difficult to fix. This is why it is necessary to resist condemning one person or even one form of substance dependency, such as oil, as having exclusive rights over catastrophic blindness, for condemnation has never brought any serious analysis to term. Thus Jean-Luc Nancy crucially observes that 'condemnation, by itself, tells us nothing about what made possible that which is condemned. . . . con-demnation keeps at a distance, along with the condemned, the question of what it is that made their guilt possible.'[9]

*$*: In an essay that resists treating but names the cases of Paul de Man and Martin Heidegger, Nancy argues that 'it is our history as such that has been put in question and in abeyance' by such 'cases':

> In any case it seems as if recent history were multiplying individual 'cases,' for all that they are very different, in order to force us to ask this question [Can our history continue simply to represent itself as History, as the general program of a certain Humanity, a Subject, a Progress – a program that would only have been, can still only be troubled by accidents, by foreign bodies, but not *in itself* and as such?]. It is surely not by chance. For thirty years, self-assurance preserved or achieved at the conclusion of the war (assurance, or the fierce will to be reassured) has caused us to misconstrue the question. In the first place, a marxist self-assurance, whatever its form or consistency. But also, a techno-scientific one; and a democratic-progressivist one. In one way or another, it was the assurance of a certain 'destination,' come from way back, able to lead us far. But these assurances have worn away, or collapsed, and our history asks how we ever came to this point. The question can no longer be avoided. We cannot be content with affirming that there were 'errors,' and 'mistakes,' nor be content with denouncing them. Fundamentally, we all know that very well. Everything that claims to escape this knowledge is only pitiful dissimulation.[10]

Our history asks how we ever got to this point. We are responsible to our history, for which we have to answer. Setback. Cutback. Finback. The call for spiritual renewal 'already had a certain history behind' it. In the West, history has always been a history of reappropriated crashing – something we still need to explain, or rather, to respond to as the desire of metaphysics.

The chain of certitudes through which it is transmitted destines

metaphysics, in its last spasm, to the objectification of world in technology. When Heidegger writes about our unshieldedness, he recruits Rilke, perhaps the last mortal to have experienced in nature the Open. In the grips of technological dominion, where no mark can be zoned outside of us to land in some circumscribed area of noncontamination, man now negotiates the mutation of metaphysics and History at the unmarked frontiers of the technosphere. Since WWII, technology – including computer technology – and the promise of spiritual renewal have been going steady. Can we take a closer look at this hypothetical assertion? **FREEZE FRAME BLOW-UP:** George Herbert Walker Bush in the open seas, the Navy will not come back for him, they were on their last mission and were moving out. Endless open sea. Leo Nadeau used to say the Avenger could fall faster than it could fly. Nothing works – even the parachute proves defective. 'By rote, he found the rip cord, and the chute opened, but it was torn. . . . He was falling fast . . . bleeding. . . . – Doug West. He'd seen the blood on Bush's face, dropped a medical kit. Bush hand-paddled for it. . . . There was no paddle. There was no fresh water. The container in the raft had broken in the fall. Bush was paddling with both hands, puking from fear and seawater, bleeding from the head. He got his med kit and with a shaky left hand swabbed at himself with iodine. He got out his .38 revolver and checked it.'[11] He is bleeding. And then it happens, something that will recur incessantly through the peculiar circuitry of the unconscious. In the Open, George Herbert Walker Bush discovers God in technology. The submarine which emerged out of nowhere, the apparition of pure delivery, rose out of the infinite sublime. When the sky crashed into the ocean, God answered the call technologically. God's name, at that moment, flashed on to the sideboard of the metallic surge; it was *Finback.*

Finback was the name of the sub that rescued George Bush. Three thousand miles of ocean. They came to get him. And they filmed him. 'And the seaman he saw was standing there, watching with this thing up to his face, a camera, a movie camera. They were filming.'[12] It was known that the men on the crew loved their job. An unconscious pilot would awaken; he'd learn that he was alive, rescued. The future would happen. But George Bush was in a sense destined to remain unconscious. When he awoke, for a brief spell, back then, he cried, he was delirious. He wanted his friends. He was young, he was *hysterical.* No matter what they did, George Bush would never learn that he was alive after that day.

Finback will be the name of this war, but also of the history of metaphysics. Read bifocally, in French and English, it refers us back to an end, the apocalyptic condition for any happening. The end will have come 'back then,' in the wake of an emerging submarine or in another version of *Finnegan's Wake,* in the endless parlor where WWII refused the movement toward its own burial. Finback is the promise of a comeback, a second coming that, like the promise of the infinite, can never as such take place in finity. Finback means that the end is behind us: 'They had behind them, perhaps, in a sense, something that derived from our entire history. Did not the West begin by being, simultaneously, the acknowledgment of its own decline and the demand for its own renewal?

Was it not Athens which longed for the time of Solon, and Plato who called for renewal?' This is a question of our own history, involving the production of our own identity, and the will to be origin and end to ourselves. 'To inaugurate a new era in order to reanimate the breath of a spirit weakened by the accidents of an itinerary that is nevertheless its own, and underneath those accidents to recover a destiny, an epic, the organic growth of the spirit or of man – that is what it means or has meant to possess the *meaning* of history. . . . It knows accidents, precipitous declines, regressions, but its meaning is forever available to it, and it can always reconvoke itself once again to the undertaking of some renewal, some setting straight, some rediscovery.'[13]

Locked into the pose of the one rescued, the guilty survivor – he had sent his boys to die – Bush was delivered to a history of denial and compulsive repetition. To be sure, death or pain or catastrophe, each in its singularity, does not possess any historicity whatsoever but can only retrospectively acquire enough velocity to constitute a narrative event. Taking refuge in submersion and repression, history was going to insinuate itself through the untapped disruption that punched a permanent hole in the real. Tight-fisted and knotted up by the near miss, George Bush would never depropriate his history enough in order to set forth those conditions which might guarantee a future-to-come. He would never be able to let go of the totalized, if lost, meaning which his 'precipitous decline' immediately acquired. Instead, he got married real fast, graduated from Yale, and went into the oil business. But oil was not nowhere. Odessa, Texas was a desert back then, a site of deprivation where George and Bar could repel the aggressive incursions of melancholia. If God and technology continued to go steady in those earth-poking days, there was no breakup in sight. In fact, they were to be engaged in the Gulf War.

EATING BROCCOLI:[14] George Bush connected the deserts in his life by a thin thread. The temporal structure of this connection was exposed when in January 1991 he drew a 'line in the sand.' What kind of figure did this gesture cut? At first glance, it seems straightforward enough. George Bush was issuing an ultimatum. Yet, what concerns us is the rhetorical dimension of this act. A rather ordinary performative speech act, it spatially meant to designate a point beyond which the Iraqis must not pass. The line was evoked, however, *after* Iraq had crossed the Kuwaiti border. The line in fact functioned less as a spatially conceived marker than as a temporally pointing one. What it was pointing at was a deadline. But what sort of contract was this line drawing up? It was a line that turned back upon itself because it was intended to designate Iraqi withdrawal, a double line of the *re-trait*. In ordinary language usage, a line in the sand does not mean that one is supposed to fall back on the other side of the line, but usually means its opposite. Figuring a deadline, expiration date, and promise, the line in the sand troped instead the time limit of an hour glass. Like an hour glass, however, it was about reversal and turning things around as a measure of time. The line in the sand, catechrestically deployed, posed an ultimatum for what already had transpired in the form of a morally inflected imperative: this boundary crossing should not have occurred. The line, as line of impasse or imperfect past, implemented the signature of reversal and repetition by means of which this war would be authorized. Still, what is a line in the sand but a sign of its own effacement, a writing of disaster that territorializes the past on the ground of shifting sands? Promised to erasure, the line in the sand figurally says the forgetting to which this war was doubly committed. A figure of immediacy, masquerading in clarity of contour, the line, as word, is that which cannot be kept. In fact, it already points to a word not kept, for the Iraqis had already been granted permission, by diplomatic channels of ambiguity, to cross the line. This in part explains why the line can only point to the suspension of any clear demarcation. Ever pointing to its obliteration in time, it is not a line capable of guaranteeing even its own future, much less *the* future. Nonetheless, it is the line that we were fed.

To the extent that this line at all invites readability, it constitutes a catechrestic metalepsis – arguably the structure itself that dominated the 'events' of the Gulf War, where nothing was new under the sky. Let us recapitulate: as a boundary not to be crossed, the line in the sand presented itself as moot, for the war was said to have originated in a crossed boundary. It therefore inscribes a boundary that ought not to have been crossed, a moral line, in fact, that says: this is where America draws the line. As Mad Maxed out as it may have seemed in the inscription of its fury and spontaneity, this line in the sand pointed us to the past in general, and to the phantom double of this line that ought not to have been crossed. George Bush, youngest fighter pilot of WWII, draws the line at this time; he comes of age. Which age?

The line in the sand is, we shall see, not drawn across an indifferently figured body. This body was named a feminine body time and again, a mother's body, and a body subject to rape. A psychology of international relations is taking shape (this is not my invention but a contribution of those who have psychologized and pornographized the 'enemy,' the invention of those who have made this a war, once again, of the sexes). Where has this land feminization (be)gotten us? Somewhere between the realignment of reunified Germany and Japan, prior to the sexual warfare that informed the Clarence Thomas hearings, George Bush drew a line in the sand. As America, a faltering empire, loses its bearings the president, an eternal son not up to the task, will also have traced out a line of castration. But I want at all costs to prevent precipitous decline and to steer us slowly over this heavily symbolized terrain. A great deal has returned to haunt us now, making it hardly surprising that we are inundated by a rhetoric of restoration and reversal. The phantomic return triangulating – once again – Germany, Japan, and America, has motivated the pathos with which this administration goes about restoring the national phallus to its proper place.

The narrative of purloined oil wells crudely illustrates the stakes of this dramatic replay. Indeed, as slippery as this may seem, the possession of oil wells marked in the 1940s a critical moment in the strategies of national desire. In the 1940s the State Department described Middle East oil as 'a stupendous source of strategic power, and one of the greatest material prizes in world history,' 'probably the richest economic prize in the world in the field of foreign investment.' After the war, Eisenhower called the Middle East the 'most strategically important area in the world.' Further, at 'the end of World War II, when immense petroleum deposits were discovered in Saudi Arabia, Secretary of the Navy James Forrestal told Secretary of State Byrnes, "I don't care which American companies develop the Arabian reserves, but I think most emphatically that it [sic] should be American."' After World War II the Americans acquired Saudi concessions for themselves, freezing out the British and French.

Regardless of the real import of oil, there is no economy that is not also a libidinal economy, or that does not resignify symbolic deposits of national desire. *Z* magazine reminds us that in the view of the *New York Times*, 'a heavy cost must be paid' when an oil-rich Third World nation 'goes berserk with fanatical nationalism.'[15] *Z* justly remarks that going 'berserk' with 'fanatical nationalism' is the *Times*'s way of describing a Third World nation expecting to benefit from its own resources. In part,

though, ownership – the values ascribed to property, propriety, the proper – has gone largely symbolic, which is why the so-called Third World slips into an altogether different space of engagement. This is not to deny the value of those discussions organized around capital motivation – but that alone is not what resurrected the respectability of warfare or created the referential indetermination of what is going on. While Japan, Germany, and America triangulate into a new phase of Oedipal self-patterning – one that does not permit genuine ambivalence but is staked on repression and obsessive replay – we must not allow ourselves to forget the fourth term, or the displacement to what is being called the Middle East – at once the most artificial and originary of historical mappings.

**'IT IS TRUE THAT TROPES ARE THE PRODUCERS OF IDEOLOGIES THAT ARE NO LONGER TRUE':**[16] We have until now considered the question from the side of war. Is there another side?

In a sense, this war declared itself, when it declared itself, as a war about forgetting war. It was as if it wanted to play itself out as impasse, something accomplished by pressing the record and erase functions at once. In any case, this reflects the way the war was 'covered' by the media, simultaneously recording and erasing its referential track. At the same time as past wars were being done with, this war opened the line of vision for the institution of future wars. A war to end War in order to begin wars, this one wanted to start from scratch (chicken scratch or turkey shoot). It is a matter of civility to declare each gruesome war the last one. Modern warfare has largely been conducted with the stated aim of ending war or of safety checking democratic roadways. Now America is chattering openly about future wars and what we learned from the test site called Iraq. Let us take a brief technological reality check: third-rate Patriot missiles encountered fifth-rate, merely *ballistic* SCUD missiles, triggering mythic defense narratives. This is like getting off on a night-stick. Obviously, there were a couple of smart bombs on the loose, promoting the fiction that a missile always reaches its destination.[17] This fiction is of course crucial: it upholds our history, our metaphysics, our appropriated meaning – all of which are about to meet their destination. But what if they've got the wrong address, and what if the future is not about restoring the phallus – or, for that matter, woman – to a 'proper' place? What is the proper place of this war in our destiny? Why have we mortals never been able to act nonteleologically? And why did destiny shift its site to the nomadic desert spaces where it is said that Moses once broke the tablets of the Law, Jesus of Nazareth was pinned to the cross, and the Sphinx asked you, What is man?

There is no discourse or act of war that can put an end to war. War offers community the image of its sovereign exposition to death. Because it stages the infinity of a finitude that encounters its end, war collectivizes and stimulates to life by its horror. Little has matched the pure excess that war draws to its occurrence, as a kind of ransom for the future. As the literature of virility and heroism, war is 'the monument, the feast, the somber and pure sign of the community expressing its sovereignty.'[18] Each time it arrives as the 'once and for all' of a promised catharsis. Except, possibly, in Vietnam, where war became shameful, and our boys, abject. A kind of *conscientious abjection* took hold, and this ran interference with the loaded circuits that coded World War II.

If war has meant so much to us, how are we to let go of its power to fascinate and entrance? There is only the imperative ideal of peace. Peace is not the opposite of war, but its absolute other – something that we have never as such experienced. This in part is because peace, to be what it is, predicates the infinite where war is finite. War in fact aligns itself with the Western appropriation of meaning. Establishing epistemic breaks, a radical possibilization of the Idea in history, exacting decision, war has functioned as the special megaphone of the Western logos. It has been, in our history, a way of achieving resolution through finitizing acts of containment. Thus even this war was waged against the nonfinite, uncontrolled effects of past wars in recent history. War has articulated a readable mode of *decision* to whose cause God, nation, and other transcendental recruits have been called. It is the way the West was won. This has everything to do with truth and the apocalyptic conditions for revealing truth in its transparency. In the history of beings and the history of Being, war is truth. At least, it has been inscribed unfailingly as the necessary road to truth or to a justice rendered beyond the suspension and constitutive blindness that justice in fact figures. The decisive truth of war locates the premises upon which justice can no longer be suspended. This has been our history's way of putting behind us the undecidables. It amounts to nothing less than the Western compulsion to 'finish with,' that is, to reach the finish line. But this finish line, and the arrogant impatience that drives us toward it, is, we have seen, nothing but a line in the sand. Still, it has been drawn by language and logos. Precisely because war feeds the truth machine, aiming for truth, destinal arrival and the clean cut of history, it is our task as thinkers to decelerate finitude's thrust and abide with the inconceivable horizon of an infinite unfinished. What would it mean *not* to close a deal with transcendence, or to desist from following a path of resurrected war aims? What would it mean to follow a politics of radical nonclosure, leaving time as well as borders open to the absolute otherness that must accompany genuine futurity? The line in the sand, as the sign of the figural deconstruction of its literal meaning, promises divisibility as well as infinite granules of pathless randomness and essential aberration which can never be simply appropriated to the sure movement of a path, whether or not it leads 'nowhere.' The desert commits itself to the abolition of path.

Just as we have to renounce 'finishing with' and dealing final notice, Western logos must learn to open its Faustian fist, indeed, to desert the explosions of otherness that the logos has always detonated. For these reasons I have relied upon psychoanalysis to help us count the losses. For psychoanalysis, besides reading war, has taught us in this century to be wary of the desire for termination and has exemplarily, if relentlessly, advocated the interminable nature of working through. While it nonetheless posits a term, psychoanalysis also knows about the production of unknown meaning and the ineluctable deviancy inflecting normal self-constitution, be this of a nation state or the human subject. In an uncharacteristically simple formula, psychoanalysis has known from the start that it may be, for us in our history, a matter of choosing either interminable or exterminable. But psychoanalysis has also met the limits of theorizing its knowledge. It reads from layerings of silence and repression, if only to slow down the inclines of the death drive, with which we'll never be finished. Like a woman, psychoanalysis's job is never done. In the future, I daresay, the prerequisites for presidential candidacy, will include, besides the restrictions pertaining to age and citizenship, a growing demand for health checks and balances, namely, in addition to doctors' reports, appropriate certificates of therapy.

The Gulf War, which was meant to put to rest other wars whose wounds would not close, resurrected the respectability of war as a moment in Western discourse or polemics. While we obviously resisted opening diplomatic channels, it is not simply the case that we refused to negotiate. Rather, quick polemological tactics supplanted negotiation as a more efficient means of finishing with the problem. Yet to the extent that the war followed, at least in stated principle, strict guidelines, United Nations discussions, telephone treaties, and the Geneva Convention, the war as it was conducted cannot be seen in simple opposition to diplomacy. Of course, as Nietzsche has said about history, it is all a matter of dosage.

**DOWNLOADING:** It was Kant who tried to teach us that peace must be rigorously established. In his uncannily timely *To Perpetual Peace: A Philosophical Sketch* (1759), Kant outlines the dangers of a progressive technologization of the troop, anticipating the rhetoric of collateral damage and surgical strike ('man is thrown into the same class as other living machines,' 'paying men to kill or be killed appears to use them as mere machines and tools,' 'subjects are used and wasted as mere objects,' and so on).[19] In its delicacy of operation and telescoping futural vision this work evokes an emphatic sense of being 'on location.' It is, when reading the *Perpetual Peace,* as if Kant had been piloting Finback that day, looking forward and back, reading a special clarity from the skies whose open-endedness ought never to have obscured our history. Among the critical interventions that his text makes on behalf of an enduring peace, he warns:

> A war of punishment [*bellum punitivum*] between nations is inconceivable (for there is no relation of superior and inferior between them). From this it follows that a war of extermination – where the destruction of both parties along with all rights is the result – would permit perpetual peace to occur only in the vast graveyard of humanity as a whole. Thus, such a war, including all means used to wage it, must be absolutely prohibited. But that the means named above inexorably lead to such war becomes clear from the following: Once they come into use, these intrinsically despicable, infernal acts cannot long be confined to war alone. This applies to the use of spies [*uti exploratoribus*], where only the dishonorableness *of others* (which can never be entirely eliminated) is exploited; but such activities will also carry over to peacetime and will thus undermine it. (109)

It is interesting to note that Kant counts the necessity for ensuring the survival of peoples along with that of rights, offering them each the same ontological peace dividend. This suggests that war exceeds rights while it nonetheless, as the prerogative of power, proceeds from a concept of the rights of sovereignty. As long as there is a national entity, war is within the realm of rights, even though it threatens the survival of individual rights or a more transcendental bill of rights. The nation enjoys a sovereign right to go to war, and thus to destabilize the rights for which it may be ostensibly fighting. This contradiction belongs to the essence of the nation state. War, according to Jean-Luc Nancy, in fact exposes the 'sovereign exception' that it institutes within the realm of rights. Clearly, what needs to be rethought is the legitimacy of national sovereignty and of everything that is implied thereby. But as long as national identity continues to assert its historical 'necessity,' what becomes of the ideal of sovereign peace?

The problem that Kant faces in the entire essay involves the deflection of perpetual peace from its semantic hole in the graveyard: could there be a movement of peace that is unhitched from the death drive? Must the duty we have toward peace necessarily have as its background music that radical tranquility which resonates with 'rest in peace'? If Kant can only draw a philosophical sketch of peace, this is because his leanings push him toward the edge of undecidability where absolute peace, like war, means you're dead. To get out of this peace cemetery, Kant will have to institute performative speech acts; in other words, he will have to declare a certain type of war on war. Kant is perfectly aware of the rhetorical difficulties that face any linguistic mobilization on behalf of peace. To preempt the inevitable strike of war (we earthlings have not known, empirically or historically, a warless time zone), he will begin parergonally with ironic deterrents. Later on, the argument will move into more transcendental fields when, for instance, Kant proposes 'the transcendental principle in publicity,' which basically opposes all forms of secrecy, saying, 'if I cannot *publicly acknowledge* it without thereby inevitably arousing everyone's opposition to my plan, then this necessary and universal, and thus *a priori* foreseeable, opposition of all to me could not have come from anything other than the injustice with which it threatens everyone' (135–36). The transcendental formula of public right comes down to this maxim: 'All actions that affect the rights of other men are wrong if their maxim is not consistent with publicity.' It is only under the transcendental concept of public right, linked to publicity, that an agreement can be reached between politics and morality. To guarantee this agreement Kant initiates 'another transcendental and affirmative principle of public right' whose explanation he however indefinitely postpones, breaking off the essay with the promise for a future unfolding of perpetual peace ('I must postpone the further development and explanation of this principle for another occasion'). The principle in question reads:

> All maxims that *require* publicity (in order not to fail of their end) agree with both politics and morality. (135)

Though unfinished, the essay nonetheless names the fulfillment of its terms, namely, the establishment of 'perpetual peace, which will follow the hitherto falsely so-called treaties of peace (which are really only a suspension of war)' (108). This replacement of the peace treaty with genuine, lasting peace, Kant assures, 'is no empty idea, but a task that, gradually completed, steadily approaches its goal.' But was not the hope for peace staked in the abandonment of goal or teleological fulfillment? The disjunction, I believe, accounts for the constitutive incompletion of the text which performs its inability to reach an end or fulfill a goal, consequently swerving in its performance from the finite repetition of war. Postponing itself perpetually, the text opens out to meet the starry sky that Kant saw above his head, granting tensed suspension. It is within this pause between the performative inauguration of peace and the postponement to which its fulfillment is subject, that Kant can make out the fragile sketch of a perpetual peace. Refusing to end, Kant sends us back to the beginning of this text which never quite gets off the ground but is all the more powerful for it.

The problem for Kant, and for us, is getting started on the peace march. Kant enumerates in the first section his war grievances and prepares the ground for the installation of a perpetual peace. The first section issues as an instituting injunction that '1. No treaty of peace that tacitly reserves issues for a future war shall be held valid' (107). Kant

explains: 'For if this were the case, it would be a mere truce, a suspension of hostilities, not *peace,* which means the end of all hostilities, so much so that even to modify it by "perpetual" smacks of pleonasm' (107). In sum, a peace treaty would be self-annulling to the extent that its raison d'être is expected to crumble. A true peace treaty would constitute the war on war par excellence, and therefore suspend its function as a mere contractual deal amongst nations. A contract, as Benjamin will later point out in his *Critique of Violence,* always implies its own suspension, or a return to violence in the event that one of the parties should fail to honor its terms.[20] A contract or treaty therefore belongs to the pervasive logic of war, offering little to effect the disinstallation of war in our history.

But if we choose to cite Kant at the unclosing end of the Gulf War, it is also in order to retrieve his frame. For who has not suffered despondency these past several months (the manic victory allowances are in fact part of the experience of despondency, though on the more unsavory side of disavowal). Who has not felt the *paradox of abortion* performed on the body of history, pregnant with the future?

Kant's frame, in any case, contains its own ironic destruction. If it is to be part of the experience of knowing peace, the essay nonetheless forces him to deliver a few punchlines. The doubling up in laughter (or in pain) marked by the initial breakthrough accompanies the mood of essential peace-making. The initial breakthrough quickly stalls, however. 'To Perpetual Peace,' the essay's dedication begins; but this beginning is also an end, shadowing as it does the death of that which has not as yet come to be. One can never be sure if we are engaged in a ceremonial performative of clinking champagne glasses or if we are not saying, rather, 'In Memorium: To PP.' Precisely because of this chasm of indecision, it is necessary to follow Kant, repeating his gesture, if only to inscribe ourselves by *affirming* castration, which is to say, by putting ourselves in the place of the destitute other without displacing or colonizing this other. Kant's question begins with the undecidable nature of PP. Is it beyond the pleasure principle, on the side of death and absolute quiescence, or can it be achieved by finite beings? 'To PP,' as it turns out, is a citation that opens up the undecidable:

> Whether this satirical inscription on a certain Dutch shopkeeper's sign, on which a graveyard was painted, holds for *men* in general, or especially for heads of state who can never get enough of war, or

> perhaps only for philosophers who dream that sweet dream, is not for us to decide. (107)

Nonetheless, or even because we cannot decide the readability of the inscription – which is generalizable to the sign of signs, the ensepulchered *seme* – thinking, as if heeding an impossible injunction, must intervene. And what it does when it is called upon to intervene at the scene of absolute undecidability, in the crossfire of life and death, the real and the dream, reading and the impossible, is to name the strength of its own impotence. Writing to peace, as if this were the true but unknown address of the philosopher's dreamwork, exposes the empty phallus:

> However, the author of this essay does set out one condition: The practical politician tends to look down with great smugness on the political theorist, regarding him as an academic whose empty ideas cannot endanger the nation [*Staat*] since the nation must proceed on principles [derived from] experience [*Erfahrungsgrundsätzen*]; consequently, the theorist is allowed to fire his entire volley, without the worldly-wise statesman becoming the least bit concerned. (107)

The theorist, then, can fire away precisely because his words are from the start diverted from a teleological path or aim. But if Kant seems to be launching a war of the worlds between politician and theorist, it is in order strategically to avert the assaults which theorizing peace ineluctably attracts. In fact, Kant's project in the set up of his essay is to ensure the immunocompetence of his text, which is to say, he is sending out antibodies to neutralize the war utterance of the political body. For, in times of trouble – and thinking's business concerns making trouble by responding authentically to trouble – the political body always sends in troops to subdue the critical intervention that true philosophical mobilization must contemplate. Kant allows himself to 'fire his entire volley' because they are blanks; they are the stuff of dreams and address themselves to that which does not exist in the present. Kant's army of metaphors and metonymies, while participating in the structure of destination, cannot touch the statesman and therefore arrives, if it arrives, as a blank flag of surrender.

It is a surrender that protects by establishing the terms of an absolute *différend:*

> Now if he is to be consistent – and this is the condition I set out – the practical politician must not claim, in the event of a dispute with a theorist, to detect some danger to the nations in those views that the political theorist expresses openly and without ulterior

> motive. By this *clausula salvatoria,* the author of this essay will regard himself to be expressly protected in the best way possible from all malicious interpretation. (107)

Theorists, behold! In German, Kant writes that the theorist will know [*wissen*] protection. Where does this knowledge come from? In order to pass beyond the limits of the peace treaty, Kant must initially draw up this legally articulated contract with the politician. Its detachability from the body of the text – the threat of beheading or castration – always attends this essay which in fact sets out to abolish the conditions for instituting a peace treaty. Because the theorist is fundamentally disarmed by the state, and barred by the nature of philosophizing from producing a referential dent in policy, the politician will have to desist from waging war or polemics on theoretical activity. Nonetheless, what this essay makes clear from the start is that the state practices the duplicitous policy of remaining at once unconcerned with theoretical reflection while menacing it with reprisal for betraying the interests of national security. What is sad for us today, is that institutions of learning, linked as they are to the state and other corporate configurations, have tended to internalize this threatened and threatening posture. Hence the myth or, depending on which side you find yourself, the wish fulfillment of 'tenured radicals.'

Well, at any rate, Kant, in order to protect his text from malicious interpretation, heads up his essay with a joke, a dream, castration, and contract. The detachable introduction, which nonetheless enables reflection on a lasting peace to occur at all, ends with a kind of proxy signing. For, as we know, the politician will not then and not now cosign this contract which Kant, in his own and our defense, draws up. That is why I, Immanuel Kant, 'the author of this essay,' will regard myself to be 'expressly protected' by my performative declaration which, alas, may only be a decoy. From what is he performatively protecting himself? From that part of war that politicians have consistently waged on reflection ('in the event of a dispute'). But this is not merely a professional suit that he brings to bear. What politics may justly deem threatening is the interminable, morally anxious, and genuinely ambivalent cast of speculative analysis.

Perhaps the most serious challenge that Kant poses to us today does not so much concern a regional or local disturbance (wherever that may be) but one that requires us to reflect upon the repressed disjunction of freedom and democracy:

> Among the three forms of government, *democracy,* in the proper sense of the term, is necessarily a *despotism,* because it sets up an executive power in which all citizens make decisions about and,

> if need be, against one (who therefore does not agree); consequently, all, who are not quite all, decide, so that the general will contradicts both itself and freedom. (114)

Whether standing alone to mark the cleave in which freedom breaks off from itself, or drawing up an unabating contract with the political statesman, the theorist constitutes that figure which cuts into the idealized imaginary of state politics. Indeed, the theoretical imperative consists principally in making the state back off from its disavowal systems – particularly in moments when a nation's predicament reflects a mode of psychotic disassociation.

# ACTIVIST SUPPLEMENT

## *Papers on the Gulf War*

### BRING HOME THE TROPES I*

I shall assume that your opinions, evaluations, and feelings concerning this war have been formed. I shall also assume that we are in San Francisco, and therefore my aim will not be to persuade you of anything but to do my job, which essentially consists in raising questions. If I can only tentatively advance the assumption that we are in San Francisco, this is in part because the war in the Persian Gulf has destabilized our understanding of location, and has instituted a teletopical logic: a logic of spaces aligned according to technological mappings, where the near is far and vice versa. Among other things, this means that what seems to be outside our borders is in fact occurring on the inside, which is to say that crucial projections are taking place and that what we understand by boundaries will have to be entirely rethought. This means especially what constitutes national boundaries and systems of bordering. It will never again be the case that the crude materiality of territorial divisions will sufficiently constitute a national entity. But we'll get to that momentarily.

When, in the hour of its primal triumph, the United States of America first constituted itself as a nation, the first country from among the nations of the Old World to recognize the emergent republic in the New World and to lend it legitimacy was a Moslem, Arab country, Morocco. 'The American nation will remain indebted,' wrote the founding fathers over and again. On some level of consciousness there is a matter of national debt to be settled here, one which has sought refuge in the regions of a national unconscious. This line of thought has been taken up, in an unpublished essay, by Mona M. Abul-Fadl of the International Institute of Islamic Thought. In the time that has been allotted to me, I can only produce a kind of discursive sampler and make little more than scratch noises on the public record. However, it may well be the case that one can do little more than make scratch noises, scatter stray shots at a monolithic regime, because, as friends from the so-called Third World, and France, and elsewhere remind us, there are no clear transmission systems that would allow us to be heard here. The disappearance of the

*Ubik Gallery, San Francisco, May 17, 1991

public sphere is a catastrophe of historical dimension. The public sphere – the polis – is where we once located politics. What we have to come to terms with is the vanishing of politics. One of the things that the Gulf War has shown us is our own mutism. It is from this place of silence that I am trying to speak today.

Now, John Muse has titled this conference 'Reading Desert Storm.' A lot can be said about this title, but I will limit myself to a few observations. Among other things, the necessity of reading implies, against the classical grain, that war is an *un*natural phenomenon. This is why war has always involved ceremonials, peace treaties, events of signing, the founding of a new law, instituting a new order. War teaches us that the violence it unleashes is not natural or physical in the first place, but that the concept of violence belongs to the symbolic order of law, politics, and morals. This is the good news. It was first broadcast, in a different tone and context, by Jacques Derrida in his essay on Benjamin's *Critique of Violence.* This is good news because to the extent that war is not natural but waged in the name of transcendental inscriptions – justice, God, truth, country, freedom, the white metaphysical subject's autonomy – the extent to which war is waged in the name of certain readings, whether perverted or not, indicates that it is susceptible to a critique. You cannot criticize nature; you cannot offer a critique of the earthquake as such, but you can and must criticize, that is, *read* Desert Storm. But there's the catch: Desert Storm masks itself as a natural catastrophe, it appears to have concealed itself in the language of natural eruption. But this naturalness in fact covers something else, which resonates as well with the lightning strike to which our fighter pilots assimilated their actions. The move to a natural idiom of calamity tries to efface the symbolic order in which modern warfare is waged. But it also points to another covert linguistic action: the storm and the lightning are not natural borrowings, but an account that America has opened with the past, referring us in this age to the storm troopers and *Blitz* – lightning – *krieg.* This rehabilitation of Nazi signifiers shows that George Bush's relation to the phantom of World War II is more complicated, haunted and difficult than one might have supposed.

Well, 'Reading Desert Storm' invites a number of reflections. My title for this paper would have been 'Support Our Tropes.' Tropes are figures of speech, metaphors, and metonymies, what Nietzsche called the *armies* of metaphors that dominate our thinking fields. What does it mean to support the troops, what kind of utterance is this, and why has it become the major indictment against anyone who has shown concern, resistance, horror? What kind of figure does 'support the troops' cut? Where to locate the tropes we are supporting? And who is 'we'? There is no doubt about it. Submitted to a rhetorical analysis, 'support our troops' institutes a moderate level of catachrestic violence, that is, an abuse of language, a perversion of metaphor. Strictly speaking, the troops are supposed to support *us*. What does this turn around, or about-face, mean? Turning around the rapport of troops to the population once again rehabilitates the ideological maneuvers of fascist Europe. The utterance 'support the troops' is a sign of the involvement of the entire populace in the war; it says that we are holding to the fascistic notion of total war as articulated by Erich Ludendorff, which means that the theater of warfare is not limited, and further that military strategy is deflected from the mobilization of troops toward the psychologistic or propagandistic control of the homefront. This in turn – tropes are about turning and twisting – brings us to yet another catachrestic maneuver which consists in resorbing the home into the theater of operations by making it into a *front*. I wish I could go on, turning this insupportable trope, but instead I'll speed ahead to other considerations of language usage and problems in controlling textual detail that have dominated the way in which this war has interpreted itself. These range from reading and misreading the Geneva Convention, which, even at the worst moments of violence and massacre, remained the stable locus of reference, to Bush's self-written declaration of war – it took him two weeks to write it, though it was well-timed to spring his son from S&L indictment and to push through a military budget. But 'Reading Desert Storm' also means reading theories of retreat, the two main texts being those of Clausewitz and Rousseau. According to one, military retreat occurs only when equipment is dropped, and according to the other, observed by the Geneva Convention, retreat essentially means recoiling from the scene of battle and nothing more. According to such a reading, the U.S. would have to be tried for war crimes on this point alone.

As you all know, America is involved in many wars, including the war on drugs, the homeless, the sick, the poor, the educated. There exist more fronts than can be simply included in the theater of operation. The need for such a theater and for extremist localization is something that ought to be reviewed, for the community has been divided, cut, and downloaded from a number of atopical zones that require an altogether new mapping of world, neighborhood, proximity. But America's wars not only involve a matter of spatial discontinuity: there is also a distortion of time, a kind of warped temporality which does not make the Gulf War easy to focus in traditional historical terms. For the war in the gulf has come to mean a phantomic blast, a blast from the past. When did this war take place? We know that Bush was reading – once again reading – the history of World War II when he decided to go to war. The signifier of gas went into recirculation, evoking that war; given the gas masks, the threat of chemical warfare, and so on, it resurrected World War I as well. In addition, we mobilized the technology that had been aimed for years at the Soviet Union. Suddenly we had no enemy, no specular other. Can America live without an enemy? That is to say, can America, for purposes of group bonding and simulated collectivization, renounce being an enemy (or 'protector,' or the world's policemen)? In any case, we are now demarcating a spectral theater of operations: so far, the phantoms of two world wars have been mobilized, as well as the war we did not have with the Russians but had planned, not to mention the invasions of fragile Third World nations. Of course, in these haunted regions of the American unconscious we were also fighting the ghosts of the so-called Vietnam syndrome. Now, the war in the Persian Gulf was supposed to be a 'healing' war, if such a monstrous misuse of language can be admitted. As a nation, with a psyche – and the national psyche has got to be deconstructed – we were suffering from an unmournable loss, or so the story goes. We were to be cured of Vietnam. Does this imply that we were finally going to be able to acknowledge the loss, let go of Vietnam? However, doesn't this mean that the cure would consist of forgetting Vietnam: would that have helped us get over the Vietnam syndrome? In other words, how can a cure depend upon uncomplicated forgetting – unless it issued from a Nietzschean injunction which our sorry-assed political body would be incapable of assimilating? Even this would require some understanding of what it was we were supposed to forget. The problem is that the Vietnam syndrome is not about the grief we might feel about the dead, or the guilt we might acknowledge for having destroyed a culture; the Vietnam syndrome is not even about the nonclosure of the war, though its duration was wearing on the American attention span. The Vietnam syndrome is about losing a war and returning home without heroization, mythologization, or the experience of total mobilization, however tropic that may be. One reason the Vietnam syndrome cannot be cured is because it is not an illness. Rather, the illness resides in the drive to cure our mature resistance to war. The war against Iraq has a peculiar symptomatology attended by all sorts of ghosts that were resurrected in the theater of operations. One of those ghosts was the idea of a just and restorative, or healing, war.

Of course this war may be readable as the spasms of a declining empire. As with the death of god, there is always stench and pollution when paternal law is falling down. Still, we have to interrogate our destructive desire, that is, the *desire* for war, for having a blast, for the apocalypse which is promised to us as the revelation of truth. We should be courageous enough to interrogate the excitement of armageddon, the fluttering hearts of those who ascribe meaning to war. There are a number of other points to be made, and these do not refer us to a concept of linkage, suppressed or not, but to exceedingly complicated configurations and complexities. (I know it is fashionable to hope for simplicity and a direct hit of 'reality' over theoretical reflection, but these matters are far from simple. It is now more necessary than ever to resist being simplistic or hardened by oppositional logic and rude calculation.) I offer a few points for our discussion. Some of these are inspired by an open letter circulated among friends and signed by philosopher Jean-Luc Nancy (I have a dossier of published responses to the war by other French writers, including Lyotard, Deleuze, and others). These are the issues which I propose we address after the panel has finished speaking: (1) We need to review the successful return of the concept of a 'just war.' This includes the prescription for a new world, that is, Western order; (2) We have to consider the police action taken by the U.S. in the name of international law. The difference between police and military action is important. The police action in which we are symbolically, that is, really inscribed, was reproduced in miniature by the Los Angeles police attack on Rodney King. The L.A. police performed a partial allegory of the war in the Persian Gulf, implicating issues of media, race, violence, law; (3) The idea of a just or legitimate war has been doubled by a just technologization of war, in other words, by the promise of bloodless, sutureless, and surgically precise targetting. Since technology is my special field of inquiry, I could talk about this for hours. Let me just say that there is a logic of the test site at work here: there is no technology that will not be tested. But once it is tested, it is no longer merely a test. This was and was not a test. The problem is that advanced technology regresses us to a belief in ideological progress: if the method of destruction is high tech, then we have made progress. We have to interrogate the relations between war and progress; (4) Along with the notion of a just war, we seem to be returning to the idea that 'war gives birth to history.' But if the virtue or fatality of war is once again to appear as the midwife to history, it is odd that this classical thought and desire (more precisely, this Hegelian desire) can come back in a context that offers nothing classical in this regard. This time, this war, does not create History or any concept of historical appropriation, except possibly the secret and compulsive sense of having taken a step in our indiscernible destiny. The only way that this return of the regressive, truth-promising values of war could make claims for a future order would be by disavowing our history: this entails the repression of those disasters which have rendered possible the Occident. In short, we do not know how to think war as something we should wage, which is why we think we can conduct warfare as if it were extraneous, momentary, simulated, and not engaging the very core of our being. This, incidentally, is no longer Hegelian, this thought of remaining outside of our own war and external to it as though one were not fundamentally marked by it. War in the Hegelian context produced History and implicated our very being; if this war, by contrast, has something to teach us, it is that we no longer have access to it.

## BRING HOME THE TROPES II (OR WHY IN CYBURBIA THERE ARE A LOT OF COWBOYS)*

This is part of an ongoing reflection on the technologically constellated state, the Gulf War, and the prosthetic subject. In 'Bring Home the Tropes I,' I explained the linguistic warping of 'support our troops,' who should be supporting us, and how this inversion, or chiasmus, implicated the entire population. This belongs to a fascistic notion of war in which the theater of warfare is deflected from the mobilization of troops toward the psychologistic or propagandistic control of the homefront. This signaled yet another deflection. What does it mean to resorb the home into the theater of operations by making it into a front? In the time allotted, I can only offer a few aphoristic statements, which I will try to present as clearly as possible, with a view to the discussion to which these papers ineluctably lead. At the same time, I do not want to renounce the complexity that thinking has to engage if it is to fulfill its contract with itself. The war is a strain on all of us; thinking accompanies the strain, reproducing genuine enervation, anxiety, and the sense of not knowing where we are. It is to this twilight zone between knowing and not knowing that I commit myself, because the upperhand (which is not yours or mine) has acted as if it knew where we were going and thus, implicitly, where we have been. This involves, among other things, the psychotopologies of everyday life.

'Now, where were we?' asks the scholar. The assignment for this evening's panel concerns virtual reality (VR), media, and the war in the Persian Gulf. I do not feel that I master the materials, or even the immaterials (VR opens the question of immateriality), I do not feel that I possess the mastery required to transmit knowledge properly or to produce linkage. Yet this assignment is about mastery and I consider myself an infomaniac. VR is philosophically complex even though it is system dependent on classical tropes of representation, imagination, the sovereign subject and negated otherness (negated otherness is what Hegel called the enemy). So it is dependent on a number of metaphysical cravings, but then who isn't? Might as well face it: there has always been a desire to transcend the body, and I have often said that I would donate my own body to science fiction. But the donation of a body in life is part of a metaphysical striving toward an indeterminate elsewhere. VR is jamming the master codes of this historical desire for transcendence and exteriority, and deserves to be heard out in all its effusions. Because VR is also

*San Francisco Art Institute: Conference on Mass Media, Virtual Reality and the Persian Gulf (June 12, 1991)

about Being-in-the-world, and liberating the location of being to non-substantial spaces, it is trying to reconfigure the possibilities for sharing the world. According to Jaron Lanier, Howard Rheingold, and others, VR practices a politics of finitude, and demands an ethics of technology.[21] At the same time, however, VR is jacking into Mattel Corporation, the military, and NASA – but it is *also* a design testing ground for architecture and the medical sciences. 'So, where were we?' asks the scholar. A rigorous study of virtual reality cannot be made to fit entirely into the frame of this event, but I will try to raise some questions to indicate the direction of my reflections on this difficult topic.

Virtual reality, artificial reality, dataspace, or cyberspace are inscriptions of a desire whose principal symptom can be seen as absence of community. Lanier's discourse has everything to do with the possibilities of constituting an ecstatic community that would refuse to be governed by a goal or a totalitarian drive toward unification. It is as if Lanier were tempted to retrieve Bataille's community of shattered egos. To a certain extent, the metaphysical subject is broken up and displaced to routes of splintering disidentification. The subject no longer finds its mooring in identification with a substantial image. Still, Lanier, like all transmitters on behalf of radio VR (VR is said to be more like a telephone or radio, disconnected from the televisual apparatus), emphasizes the ego-building prowess of VR designs. This is a double-edged claim that we need to probe with unrelenting clarity. In cyburbia there is always a risk of blurring the distinction between simulation and the operational world. I am not convinced, though others are, that this risk is very new. More seriously, perhaps, there is still a tendency to retrofit the technological prosthesis to a metaphysical subject: the sovereign subject of history, destiny's co-pilot. In other words, the technological prosthesis would merely be an amplifier and intensifier borrowed by a centered subject whose fragmentation is, as they say, a simulation – that is, a device for *disavowing* fragmentation, self-loss or, on another register, castration. This aspect of disavowal in part explains why Lanier, for his part, would have preferred to see VR called, as he asserts, 'Intentional Reality.' Now this move exposes a whole problematics of the intentional consciousness that I will address momentarily. The intentional consciousness is a philosophical construct that emerges when it is felt that we are not in control of our actions. And that is precisely where Lanier's project takes hold, in the control rooms of his majesty, the ego. In addition to arguing that VR is 'good for the ego,' he launches an assault against the contemporary subject's passivity; this assault on passivity – quite understandable at first sight – is made, however, in the dubious name of action and control.[22] The subject will take control. The argument against passivity, which I can only graze swiftly, is, I believe, false and highly problematic, though I also agree with the need to activate radical creativity. But the opposition of passive and active proffers a deluded equation. Take a look around you. Haven't we, as a culture, been *too* active, *too* action filled, even if action splits itself into representations of the traumatized spectator and manic warrior? Any uninterrogated invention made in the name of action has got to attract our deepest suspicions, girls and boys. A true ethics of community, be it located in cyberspace or among lovers, readers, artists, activists, and so on, would have to locate a passivity beyond passivity – a space of repose and reflection, a space that would let the other come. Exposing oneself to the other, or to the other's death, has nothing to do with action as such. It is because of an articulated desire for action that cyberspace is also west of the west, that is, a Memorex cowboy frontier.

One of the errors that Lanier makes is to say that 'ultimately, everything is done by people and technology is only a little game that we play.'[23] The war has shown us that people do not play little games. Nor is technology zoned outside of us, but as cybernetics and AI have shown, man-machinic hybridizations involve a refashioning of the human being, following a trajectory of altogether new alignments of self and the technobody. Now, the body, from Marvin Minsky onwards, has been devalorized into the 'bloody mess of organic matter.' I am not an essentialist feminist, but I do think that this utterance could never have been made by a woman, who takes out monthly mortgages on her body in the form of periodic bloodbaths and PMS. I am saying this too quickly, perhaps, but it is urgent to recognize that the body of a woman has a fundamental relationship to death and despair, to finitude – and life. While the woman's body produces the eternal return of the 'bloody mess of organic matter,' the cyborg soldier, located in command and control systems, exercises on the fields of denial. Intentional Reality eliminates the body as an organic, finite, damageable, eviscerable, castratable, crushable entity, thus closing off the orifices and stemming leakage and excrement. We are not very far from Deleuze and Guattari's BWO: the body without organs. Orificial shutdown and excremental control help explain why this war was conducted under the compulsive sign of cleanliness: on the American side of language usage, this was a clean war, a cleanup job accomplished according to the moral, political, and military evaluations that were represented. It was so clean, in fact, that there were blank screens assuring the protocols of propriety – the covering up of coverage –, but it was also so clean on our side of the line in the sand that the American body, if it was to be lost, was lost in an ascension of friendly fire. The point is that the other side never got to us, which I shall try to analyze briefly as the immunopathological dimension of this war.

For the duration of the war, contact with the negated other was nano-minimalist, and the language of contact was suspended. Thus, even the inevitable contaminations implied by linkage were avoided. No linkage means, among other received things, no parasitical or random eruptions on the main line of firing, but also no complexity and no ambivalence concerning this war, its aims or the aims of man (the new order is about the aims of man, and we know which way they're aiming). The dis-association of communicating parts – 'no linkage' – reflects the effects of derealization with which the war continues to bombard us.

So, where were we? If we are still in SF, which is not only a place but also a time of reflection – a site where geopolitical and chronopolitical tensions are being played out – then we are particularly sensitized to economies of justice that the war has rendered transparent. In this area of discourse that we share, certain economies have come to light, but it is the light of apparent contradiction. I shall take one crucial example.

We constitute a community of readers and speakers who have stressed time and again that the cost of this war has drained the resources of AIDS research, or at least we have noticed that our friends with AIDS are not receiving the support they urgently require. We have wondered collectively and singly about the displacement of funds from health concerns to the demands of the military. It appears that there exists a contradiction between the external and internal needs of this country. However, this is not a contradiction, nor a blindspot, nor even a fundamental displacement of a psychic investment. The war on the Gulf *is* a war on AIDS. Let me explain. The lack of AIDS support and the war investment are part of the same experience of a national desire to the extent that the war has been guided by a rhetoric of renewal and regeneration; in other words, this war was conducted entirely within the symbolic registers of fascistic health. In his essay entitled 'Our History,' Jean-Luc Nancy has argued that an 'ideology must be called "fascist" in the general sense in which themes of spiritual and national regeneration, of the vigorous recovery of health through firmness and discipline, correspond to a fascist or fascistic vision of things.'[24] In the name of symbolic health (a unity of world that sees its image in wholesomeness and the project of renewal), we have waged war on what was repeatedly represented as a degenerate, sickly *something* that carried the threat of contagion. In this regard, America has been carrying out its newly transcendentalized project of killing the unwell, the contaminated. The enemy is imagined as being disorderly, inefficient, tactically illiterate, dysfunctional, and to a certain degree, the projected solution, cybernetics, promises to overcome such instabilities.

The hygienic project has everything to do with establishing a new world order that consists in nothing less than purifying an imaginary – and real – territory, guaranteeing that it be proper and that it espouse values of propriety and property. The invisibility of the enemy inhabits this logic, which is essentially viral. Our war body has not only tested itself, but it has come out of this test site relatively intact, clean, healthy. This accounts for the other apparent contradiction: our insensible casualty rate, their massacre. Our surgical strike, their bodies, our high-tech shoots, their blood: a translation, on a world-historical scale, of the AIDS test on which we scored HIV-negative, because this was a safe war, run by the telelogic of what we are provisionally calling 'virtual reality' – which is almost an anagram of viral reality. Some of you may know that virtual comes from the Latin *virtus:* strength, manliness. The clean bill of health was, however, only temporary. After a considerable latency period, a mysterious disease showed up on the scanner: the Gulf War syndrome.

Meanwhile, back at the Gulf, we have once again instituted an autoimmune laboratory. I wish to emphasize that I am analyzing the symbolic effects of the war according to the letter of the war: I take the theater of operations, the rhetoric of surgery and other health metaphors quite seriously. I even take seriously the fact that the Bush family has its own private theater of thyroid operations, which, as if the disease had externalized itself, is called in medical terms a thyroid storm. Commander in chief of one storm, the president is internally besieged by another storm. It is difficult to locate the origin of the storm – inside the deserted presidential body, in the resurrection of Nazi terminology (storm troopers) or in the projections onto the desert.

On a less unconscious level of corporeal transmission, the desert has been conflated with woman's body. Why have we stormed the figure of a woman's body? why have we entered this mysterious legacy? I can only point to where we might go in order to explore the imaginary contours of the feminine body which our forces stormed. (Of course you know that before they went up, fighter pilots were fed attack doses of pornography, which, together with drugs, helped them to drop on the feminized body of Iraq while protecting Kuwait from rape.) If this were a seminar, and perhaps it is, I would ask you to turn your attention to Jacques Lacan's essay on 'Aggressivity and Paranoia in Psychoanalysis,' in *Écrits.* Here you will find Lacan interpreting Melanie Klein's excellent work on the coordinates of original aggressivity. Through Klein we know the function of the imaginary primordial enclosure formed by the *imago* of the mother's body; through her we have the cartography of the mother's internal empire, the historical atlas of the intestinal divisions in which the *imagos* of the fathers and brothers ('real or virtual,' says Lacan) – in which the voracious aggression of the subject himself – dispute their deleterious dominance over her sacred regions. What I would have to point out with regard to the particularity of this war, which may or may not be generalizable to other wars, is that the figure of the mother was always prominent, on both sides ('the mother of all battles'), and that it was always understood that we were in a region of some originarity: the site of primordial aggression, the sacred origin of all culture. This zone of primordial encounter was also read as a place of armageddon and apocalyptic showdown – the end that was also to designate a beginning: the *new* world order. As the original war, it encompassed all the wars in modern history: the world wars, Vietnam, and so on.

Because the war assumed status as origin – the initiator of the new world order, conducted in the womb and cradle of our civilization – it is not farfetched to follow Lacan and read this war in its rapport to the subject's paranoiac mapping of the maternal body. A splinter of evidence in support of this view could be retrieved from the compulsive focus on the mothers who went to war. This insistence names the symptom – the mother's body – but in the mode of disavowal. Mother may have gone to war but she was not the site of aggression; mother was finally on the map but she was not the map itself or a conflictual site constituted by the imaginary. I'll ask more generally: What is the battlefield? What are its boundaries and symbolic localities? Where does the battlefield take place? And how does it place us? What about the myth of the homefront? And so on. In any case, Lacan in this difficult but crucial text establishes a link between space and aggressivity: the domination of space is related to the narcissistic fear of damage to one's own body. In fact, he argues that the fear of death – the 'absolute Master' according to Hegel – is subordinate to the narcissistic fear of damage to one's own body. Aggressivity, as one of the intentional coordinates of the human ego, especially regarding the category of space – and this includes real or virtual space – allows us to conceive of its role in modern neurosis. The preeminence of aggressivity in our civilization, Lacan adds, would be already demonstrated sufficiently by the fact that it is usually confused in 'normal' morality with the virtue of strength. The glorification of strength as a social value is a sign of social devastation initiated on a planetary scale and justified by the image of a laissez faire accorded to the strongest predators. This condition should set off our psycho-alerts.

~

At first, I did not entirely see the connectedness of virtual reality and the war. The promise of VR is immense, at times liberatory, and very careful in its articulated negotiations with metaphysics, technology, and play. VR is so new that it has only begun to display its existence; the war, on the other hand, seemed like something that ought to have been obsolesced, and in fact it was, though it did happen and it did tend to make claims for high-tech breakthroughs. This war incorporated many wars and was played out in a spectral battlefield: WWI (the gas masks), WWII (the calculated resurrection of Hitler), the Vietnam syndrome. These phantom wars that participated in the Gulf War even included the war we did not have with the Russians or, for that matter, with the Martians. Can we live without an enemy?

If indeed there is something new about this war at a time of felt closure (most of us figured that the conditions for real war were vanishing, and that war games were a residual symptom of a history of battle) and if we still feel that we are in a time of closure, then we have to recognize that closure is not the same thing as the end. Closure does not simply close a domain or an epoch; by tracing the limits of its possibilities, closure also reaches the other side of its limit, exposing itself to its own exterior. In 'Our History,' Nancy has shown that there is no simple opposition or exteriority of the closure to the opening; there, perhaps, VR comes into the picture.

A question that VR poses, in its full positivity, is where to locate the community. Because we are vanishing. In the absence of the *polis,* something like VR obligates us to pose ethical questions about contact, memory, the prosthetic subject, and it teaches us to dislocate our proper place.

There is no proper place: this includes ghettoes and kitchens, and all corresponding systems of the proper place. The politics of a room of one's own has to be rethought today, however enlightened it was yesterday. The question is a hard one, surpassing as it does the video-game logic of good and evil, winner and loser, presence and absence: Can there be an atopicality of the community that nonetheless gathers, a community going nowhere, but ecstatic, a community of shattered egos, where the control towers come tumbling down, and where the other is genuinely anticipated? By this I also mean the other technologies.

# Trauma TV

*Twelve Steps Beyond the Pleasure Principle*

CHANNEL TWELVE: Ethics has been largely confined to the domains of doing, which include performative acts of a linguistic nature. While we have understood that there is no decision which has not passed through the crucible of undecidability, ethics still engages, in the largest possible terms, a reflection on doing. Now what about the wasted, condemned bodies that crumble before a television? What kinds of evaluations, political or moral, accrue to the evacuated gleam of one who is wasting time – or wasted by time? There is perhaps little that is more innocent, or more neutral, than the passivity of the telespectator. Yet, in *Dispatches*, Michael Herr writes, 'it took the war to teach it, that you were as responsible for everything you saw as you were for everything you did. The problem was that you didn't always know what you were seeing until later, maybe years later, that a lot of it never made it in at all, it just stayed stored there in your eyes.'[1] What might especially interest us here is the fact that responsibility no longer pivots on a notion of interiority. Seeing *itself,* without the assistance of cognition or memory, suffices to make the subject responsible. It is a responsibility that is neither alert, vigilant, particularly present, nor in-formed.

HEADLINE NEWS: *Testimonial video functions as the* objet petit a *for justice and the legal system within which it marks a redundancy and of which it is the remainder.*

CHANNEL ELEVEN: The defense team takedown involved approaching George Holliday's video tape by replicating the violence that had been done to Rodney King.[2] The unquestioned premise upon which the team of lawyers based their defense of the police called for an interpretation of video in terms of a 'frame-by-frame' procedure. No one questioned this act of framing, and the verdict which ensued unleashed the violence that would explode the frames set up by the court. In the blow-by-blow account, counting and recounting the event of the beating, the defense presented a slow-mo sequencing of photographs whose rhythm of articulation beat a scratchless track into the court records. The decisive moves that were made on video require us to review the way in which media technology inflects decisions of state. That would be the larger picture. The smaller picture, encapsulated by the larger one, concerns the legal ramifications of distinct interpretive maneuvers. Thus, the chilling effects of warping video into freeze-frame photography cannot be overlooked – even where *overlooking* can be said to characterize the predicament in which testimonial video places the law. For the duration of the trial, the temporization that reading video customarily entails was halted by spatial determinations that were bound to refigure the violence to which King was submitted. No one needs to read Derrida's work on framing in order to know that justice was not served in Simi Valley, California. But, possibly, if one had concerned oneself with the entire problematic of the frame, its installation and effects of violence – indeed with the *excessive force* that acts of framing always risk – then it would have been something of an imperative to understand what it means to convert in a court of law a video tape into a photograph. For the photograph, according to the works of Walter Benjamin, Roland Barthes, Jacques Derrida, and a number of others, draws upon phantomal anxieties as well as the subject's inexorable arrest. I need not stress to what extent the black body in the history of racist phantasms has been associated with the ghost or zombie. Perhaps we ought to begin, then, with the astonishing remarks of Jacques Lacan when he was on *Television:*

> – *From another direction, what gives you the confidence to prophesy the rise of racism? And why the devil do you have to speak of it?*
>
> – Because it doesn't strike me as funny and yet, it's true.
>
> With our *jouissance* going off the track, only the Other is able to mark its position, but only insofar as we are separated from this Other. Whence certain fantasies – unheard of before the melting pot.
>
> Leaving this Other to his own mode of *jouissance*, that would only be possible by not imposing our own on him, by not thinking of him as underdeveloped.[3]

It would appear that, in *Television,* the incompletion of our *jouissance* is marked with some measure of clarity only by the Other; or, at least its off-track predicament engages a boundary that exposes the Other to the projections of racist fantasies. Claiming the relative stability of a position, the Other becomes the place which failed *jouissance* targets, if only because it provides a range of separation. This separation, this *tele-*, constitutes the distance we have to travel, whether this be accomplished hand-held or alone, on the streets or *in camera.* Of the fantasies that set off the signals for mutilating the body of Rodney King, one involved precisely a kind of tele-vision that could see little more than the *jouissance* of the Other, a night vision flashing a second degree of self that emerges with destructive *jouissance:* the night blindness that operates the intricate network that is responsible for the policing of drugs. In order to get in gear, the police force had to imagine their suspect on PCP; and they fantasized, they claimed, that they were considerably threatened by the solitary figure, 'buffed out' as he was perceived to be. What does it mean to say that the police force is hallucinating drugs, or, in this case, to allow the suggestion that it was already in the projection booth as concerns Rodney King? In the first place, before the first place, they were watching the phantom of racist footage. According to black-and-white TV, Rodney King could not be merely by himself or who he was that night. In order to break Rodney King, or break the story, the phantasm of the supplemented Other – on junk, beside himself, not himself, more than himself, a technozombie of supernatural capabilities – had to be agreed upon by the police force. The police reached such a consensus on location. So, in the first place (we are reconstructing the politicotopography slowly), the Rodney King event was articulated as a metonymy of the war on drugs; this war, ever displacing its target zones, licenses acts of ethnocide by hallucinating mainstreamers. But there are other places and other types of projections that come to light here: the Rodney King event is equally that which opens the dossier of the effaced Gulf War. When television collapses into a blank stare, whiting out the Gulf War, nomadic video in turn flashes a metonymy of police action perpetrated upon a black body. I would like to argue these points with as much clarity as the blurs and the static allow. While things and connections should be encouraged to become clear, they should not perhaps hold out expectations of becoming, once and for all, 'perfectly clear' – an idiom which has all too often served as a code for the white lie.

The empirical gesture through which the violence erupted on 3 March 1991 was linked to Rodney King's legs. Did he take a step or was he charging the police? The footage seemed unclear. The defense team charged that King had in fact charged the police. 'Gehen wir darum einen Schritt weiter,' writes Freud in *Beyond the Pleasure Principle* – a text bringing together the topoi of charges, repetition compulsion, violence, and phantasms. Let us take another step, and another, and as many as it takes, in order to read the charges that are electrifying our derelict community.

HEADLINE NEWS: *Read the step digitally: crime serials/serial murders.*

CHANNEL TEN: Unlike telephony, cinema, or locomotion, television emerged as a prominent figure of our time only after the Second World War. There are many reasons for this (the Nazis voted in radio as the transferential agency par excellence; television was canceled out of the secret service of fascisoid transfixion). The mass invasion of television occurred after the war; it was served on the cold-war platter, which is to say that, in one way or another, TV is not so much the beginning of something new, but is instead the residue of an unassimilable history. Television is linked crucially to the enigma of survival. It inhabits the contiguous neighborhoods of broken experience and rerouted memory. Refusing in its discourse and values to record, but preferring instead to play out the myths of liveness, living color and being there, television will have produced a counterphobic perspective to an *interrupted history.* I hope to scan the way TV acts as a shock absorber to the incomprehensibility of survival, and views being 'live' or outliving as the critical enigma of our time.

Walter Benjamin theorized the difference between *überleben* and *fortleben* – surviving and living on. Television plays out the tensions between these modalities of being by producing narratives that compulsively turn around crime. These narratives, traveling between real and fictive reference, allow for no loose ends but suture and resolve the enigmas they name. Television produces corpses that need not be mourned because, in part, of the persistence of surviving that is shown. Still, television itself is cut up, lacerated, seriated, commercial broken, so that its heterogeneous corpus can let something other than itself leak out. I would like to explore in slow-mo, though scheduling always rushes us, the status of crime time which has saturated television, if only to name an unreadable relation to the incomprehensibility of survival and its relation to law.

CHANNEL NINE: The death of God has left us with a lot of appliances. Indeed, the historical event we call the death of God is inscribed within the last metaphysical spasm of our history as it continues to be interrogated by the question of technology. The event of the death of God, which dispersed and channeled the sacred according to altogether new protocols, is circuited through much of technology, occasionally giving rise to electric shocks. I am referring to God because, despite everything, He in part was the guarantor of absolute representability and the luminous truth of transparency. In an era of constitutive opaqueness – there is no transcendental light shining upon us; we dwell in the shadows of mediation and withdrawal; there will be no revelation, can be no manifestation as such – things have to be tuned in, adjusted, subjected to double takes and are dominated by amnesia. Without recourse to any dialectic of incarnation, something however beams through, as though the interruption itself were the thing to watch.

CHANNEL NINE: Media technology has made an irreversible incursion into the domain of American 'politics.' The anxieties which have ensued concern not so much the nature of fictioning – politics has always been subject to representation, rhetoric, artifice – as the newly intrusive effects of law. This is not to say that the law has ever been zoned outside of us, but, thanks to the media, different maps of arrest have been drawn up; the subject is being arrested according to altogether new protocols of containment. And practically everybody in homeless America is under house arrest. In this restricted space (the 'space allotted' by the conventions of an essay), it is possible to scan seriously only one episode in the relation of media to law. This episode is exemplary because it functions as an example – something that implies a generality of which it is a part; but at the same time one must not lose sight of the singularity it brings to bear upon our understanding of media and state politics. Few episodes have broken the assignments of their frames and exploded into the socius as has the Rodney King 'event.' Beyond the articulated outrage that this episode has produced, its persistent visibility has forced us to ask tough questions about American scenes of violence. When they pass into the media and graduate into 'events' are these scenes already *effects* of the media? To what extent is serial killing an *effect* of serial television or its imprinting upon a national unconscious? Or, to return to our channel: What is the relationship between mutant forms of racism (today's racism is not the same as yesterday's; it is constituted by a different transmitter) and the media, which appears to resist older types of racism? I am merely trying to pose the questions, if only to adjust the proper channels through which they may be circuited. One may wonder why it was the case that the Los Angeles Police Department, and not an equally pernicious police force, became the object of coverage by television. On some crucial level, television owns and recognizes itself in the LAPD, if only because television first produced the mythic dimension of policing by means of 'Dragnet' and the like. The LAPD is divided by referential effects of historical and televisual narration. That the one is constantly exposed by the other, flashing its badge or serial number, is something we now need to interrogate. But exposed as the LAPD appears to be, it is always covered by television. What is television covering? This seems to bring us a long way from the question of politics in America. Yet, owing to the teletopies created by television when it maps political sites, we no longer know where to locate the polis, much less 'home.' This is why we must begin with the most relentless of home fronts.

HEADLINE NEWS: *Some of you think that it is the hour of TV-guided destitution. Inside and outside the home, the time has come to think about the wasted, condemned bodies that crumble before a television.*

CHANNEL EIGHT: Among the things that TV has insisted upon, little is more prevalent than the interruption or the hiatus for which it speaks and of which it is a part. The television persists in a permanent state of urgency, whence the necessity of the series. The series, or seriature, extradites television to a mode of reading in which interruption insists, even if it does so as an interrupted discourse whose 'aim is to recapture its own rupture.'[4] If we are going to attempt to read the interruption as such, then we shall be reading something that is no longer appropriable as a phenomenon of essence. The question remains as to whether we can read the trace of interruption that is put into some sort of shape by a series or net, without having it be dominated by the logic of the cut but rather by tracking the intricacies of *destricturation;* that is, the interruptions which constitute a network where knots never land or tie up but cause traces of intervals to be indicated. Precisely such fugitive intervals – as elusive slip or trace of interruption – bind us ethically. Through its singular mode of persistence, the hiatus announces nothing other than the necessity of enhancing the moments, particularly the moments of rupture, albeit in a nondialectical fashion: it would be absurd to make claims for producing a dialectical summation of all the series, that is, interruptions, that tie up TV and its breaks. Where the effect of shock continues to jolt or to make the image jump, there is still the necessity of enchaining the moments and producing linkage.

So, in the space of interruption (an atopy or interruption that used to be called Television Land), there exists a muted injunction to read the hiatus and let oneself be marked by the hiatus – a necessity of negotiating the invisible lineage of the net.[5] To this end, it becomes necessary to displace the focus from television as totality to the seriality of derangement, a place of disturbance, something that can be designated as being 'on location' only on the condition that it remain dislocated, disarticulated, made inadequate and anterior to itself, absolutely primitive with regard to what is said about it. If TV has taught us anything – and I think it is helpful to locate it somewhere between Kansas and Oz, an internal spread of exteriority, an interruption precisely of the phantasmic difference between interiority and exteriority – the teaching principally concerns, I think, the *impossibility of staying at home.* In fact, the more local it gets, the more uncanny, not at home, it appears. Television, which Heidegger, when he was on, once associated with the essence of his thinking, chaining you and fascinating you by its neutral gleam, is about being-not-at-home, telling you that you are chained to the deracinating grid of being-in-the-world. Perhaps this explains why, during his broadcast season, Lacan spoke of *homme*-sickness.[6] We miss being-at-home in the world, which never happened anyway, and missing home, Lacan suggests, has everything to do in the age of technological dominion with being sick of *homme.* In the closing words of *The Wizard of Oz,* 'There's no place like home.' So where were we? asks the scholar.

We have no way of stabilizing or locating with certainty the 'in' of being-in-the-world, no matter how much channel surfing you are capable of enduring. Television exposes that constitutive outside that you have to let into the house of being, inundating and saturating you, even when it is 'off.' While television, regardless of its content or signified, tends toward an ontologization of its status – no matter what's on, I daresay, it is emptied of any signified; it is a site of evacuation, the hemorrhaging of meaning, ever disrupting its semantic fields and the phenomenal activities of showing – television traces an articulation of sheer uncanniness. This is what Heidegger understands as our fundamental predicament of being-not-at-home in this world (which we have yet to locate and which technology helps to map in terms of teletopies, which is of no help). While television's tendential urge guides it toward ontology, there are internal limits that, however, freeze frame the ontological urge into an ethical compulsion. One of these internal limits that is at once lodged outside *and* inside TV is a certain type of monitoring – the nomadic, aleatory, unpredictable eruption we sometimes call video.

CHANNEL SEVEN: TV has always been under surveillance. From credit attributions to ratings and censorship concessions, television consistently swerves from the ontological tendency to the establishment of legitimacy, which places it under pressure from an entirely other obligation. It is no wonder that television keeps on interrupting itself and replaying to itself the serial crime stories that establish some provisional adjudication between what can be seen and an ethicolegal position on the programs of showing. Oedipus has never stopped running through television, but I'll get to the violence of legitimation and patricidal shooting momentarily. At any rate, the crime stories that TV compulsively tells itself have been charged with possession of a mimetic trigger; in other words, as TV allegorizes its interrupted relation to law, it is charged with producing a contagion of violence. A perpetual matter of dispute, the relation of television to violence is, however, neither contingent nor arbitrary but zooms in on the absent, evacuated center of televisual seriature. At the core of a hiatus that pulses television, I am placing the mutism of video, the strategy of its silence and concealment. Though I recognize the radically different usages to which they have been put empirically and the divergent syntaxes that govern their behavior, I am more interested in the interpellation that takes place between television and video, the way the one calls the other to order, which is one way of calling the other to itself. In fact, where nomadic or testimonial video practices a strategy of silence, concealment and unrehearsed semantics, installed as it is in television as bug or parasite, watching (out) (for) television, it at times produces the **Ethical Scream** which television has massively interrupted.

This ethical scream that interrupts a discourse of effacement (even if that effacement should indeed thematize crime and its legal, moral, or police resolutions), this ethical scream – and video means for us 'I saw it' – perforates television from an inner periphery, instituting a break in the compulsive effacement to which television is in fact seriously committed (I am not speaking of the politically correct gestures that TV has produced by star trekking interracial and interspecial specials: these are on the order of thematic considerations which have been sufficiently interpreted elsewhere). When testimonial video breaks out of concealment and into the television programming that it occasionally supersedes, it is acting as the call of conscience of television. This is why, also, when television wants to simulate a call of conscience (the call of conscience [*Gewissensruf*] is the aphonic call discussed in Heidegger's *Being and Time*), it itself reverts to video. The abyssal inclusion of video as call of conscience offers no easy transparency but requires a reading; it calls for a discourse. As we have been shown with singular clarity in the Rodney King case and, in particular, with the trial, what is called for when video acts as the call of conscience is not so much a viewing of a spectacle, but a reading, and, instead of voyeurism, an exegesis. On both sides of the showing of this video, we are confronted with the image of condemned and deserted bodies – what I try in *Crack Wars* to define as the 'trash bodies,' dejected and wasted – and this is why, when you're on television, as its spectral subject on either side of the screen, you've been trashed, even if watching television is only a metonymy of being wasted in the form, for instance, of 'wasting time.' To the extent that we, like Rodney King, are shown being wasted by the deregulation of force, and are left crumpled by the wayside, we know we are dealing with a spectral experience and the screen memory of the phantom. At the same time, we also must endeavor to understand why the generative impulse of the Rodney King story was pivoted on the missappropriation of drugs – by the police. TV on drugs, policing drugs: the working-out of a hallucinogenre in which the suspect is, on the surface, viewed as being on PCP, a problem relating *alētheia* to phantomal force. The collapse of police into television is only beginning to produce a history of phenomenal proportions. As the technical medium returns to the site of its haunted origins, it shows one of the more daunting aspects of the collaboration between law enforcement and performative television to consist in the growing number of arrests that the latter has made.[7]

~

Haunted TV: the phantom of the Gulf War, bleeding through the body of King. Haunted TV: showing by not showing what lay at our feet, the step out of line. Haunted TV: focusing the limitless figure of the police, this 'index of a phantom-like violence because they are everywhere.' The police aren't just the police 'today more or less than ever,' writes Derrida; 'they are the *figure sans figure*.'[8] They cut a faceless figure, a violence without a form as Benjamin puts it: *gestaltlos*. This formless, ungraspable figure of the police, even as it is metonymized, spectralized, and even if it installs its haunting presence everywhere, remains, for Benjamin, a determinable figure inextricably linked to the concept of the civilized state. This is why we are never going to be on furlough as concerns the necessity of reading the effects of haunted TV.

The Rodney King interruption of broadcast television not only forces a reading of force and enforcement of law, but requires citation and the reading precisely of the phantom body of the police. If anything, it announces the ubiquity of the police station identification. The police become hallucinatory and spectral because they haunt everything. They are everywhere, even where they are not. They are present in a way that does not coincide with presence: *they are television*. But when they come after you and beat you, they are like those televisions that explode out of their frames and break into a heterotopy that stings. Always on, they are on your case, in your face.

What video teaches, something that television knows but cannot as such articulate, is that every medium is related in some crucial way to specters. This ghostly relationship that the image produces between phenomenal and referential effects of language is what makes ethical phrasing as precarious as it is necessary. Because of its transmission of ghostly figures, interruption, and seriature, it would be hardly sufficient to assimilate television to the Frankfurt School's subsumption of it under the regime of the visual, which is associated with mass media and the threat of a culture of fascism. This threat always exists, but I would like to consider the way television in its couple with video offers a picture of numbed resistance to the unlacerated regimes of fascist media as it mutates into forms of video and cybernetic technology, electronic reproduction, and cybervisual technologies.

HEADLINE NEWS: *The disfiguring writing on the face of Rodney King.*

CHANNEL SIX: Television is being switched on out of a number of considerations. Despite and beside itself, TV has become the atopical locus of the ethical implant. Not when it is itself, if that should ever occur or stabilize, but when it jumps up and down on the static machine, interfering as an alterity of constant disbandment.

One problem with television is that it exists in trauma, or rather, trauma is what preoccupies television: it is always on television. This presents us with considerable technical difficulty, for trauma undermines experience and yet acts as its tremendous retainer. The 'technical' difficulty consists in the fact that trauma can be experienced in at least two ways, both of which block normal channels of transmission: as a memory that one cannot integrate into one's own experience, and as a catastrophic knowledge that one cannot communicate to others. If television cannot be hooked up to what we commonly understand by experience, and if it cannot communicate, or even telecommunicate, a catastrophic knowledge but can only – perhaps – signal the transmission of a gap (at times a yawn), a dark abyss, or the black box of talking survival – then what has it been doing? Also, why does it at once induce the response of nonresponse and yet get strapped with charges of violent inducement?

CHANNEL FIVE: I have to admit that initially, when adjusting myself to technology, I was more pointedly drawn in by the umbilicus of the telephone, whose speculative logic kept me on a rather short leash. On first sight, television seemed like a corruption, as in the case of many supersessions, of the serious lineage of telephony; it seemed like a low grade transferential apparatus, and I felt television and telephone fight it out as in the battle in *Robocop* between mere robot (his majesty the ego) and the highly complex cyborg (who came equipped with memory traces, superego, id, and – ever displacing the ego – a crypt). In yet another idiom, telephony was for me linked to the Old Testament (the polite relation to God, as Nietzsche says), whereas television seemed like the image-laden New Testament (where one rudely assumes an intimacy with God and makes one of His images appear on the screen of our historical memory). Needless to say, I was on the side of the more remote, less controlled, audible sacred, to the extent that its technical mutation can be figured as telephone. The Old Testament unfolds a drama of listening and inscription of law; in contrast, the New Testament produces a kind of videodrome revision of some of the themes, topoi, and localities of its ancestral text. Now, I am not referring us to these texts in order to admit a conversion of any sort, but merely for the purpose of turning the dial and switching the ways in which our being has been modalized by a technology that works according to a different protocol of ethical attunement. If I refer us to the twin Testaments, this in part is for the purpose of exploring the site of testimony that television, despite and beside itself, has initiated. It is no accident that television, in view of the dramas we have come to associate with the names of Lacan, Elvis, Heidegger, Anita Hill, Rodney King, Lee Harvey Oswald, Vietnam – fill in the blanks – and Desert Storm, has become the locus of testimony, even if we are faced with false testimony or resolute noncoverage. In a moment I will try to show, to the extent that anything can be shown, why the Gulf War was presented to us as a discourse of effacement; in other words, why at moments of referential need, the experience of the image is left behind. This has everything to do with the interruptive status of death, but also with the problematic of thematization. In other words, there is, I believe, a concurrent mark of an invisible channel in television that *says* the problematic of thematization, which makes the rhetoricity of the televisual image collapse into a blank stare.

At moments such as these – most manifestly, during the seriated nothing that was on at the time of the Gulf War – television is not merely performing an allegory of the impossibility of reading, because this would still be a thematizing activity (the problematic activity of thematizing will have been taken up again in the Rodney King case). During the Gulf War, television, as a production system of narrative, image, information flow, and so forth, took a major commercial break as it ran interference with its semantic and thematic dimensions. The interference that television ran with itself, and continues to rerun on a secret track, points us to something like the essence of television. I would like to argue that the Rodney King event, which forced an image back on the screen, presented that which was unpresentable during the war. Rodney King, the black body under attack by a massive show of force, showed what would not be shown in its generalized form: the American police force attacking helpless brown bodies in Iraq. Now it so happens that the Rodney King trial was about force itself. Thematically, what is being measured, tested, and judged in the televised trial, is the question of force as it eventuates in the form of excessive police force. And there's the catch. We saw it blown up and cut down in the Anita Hill case – force can never be perceived as such. This is a persistent question circulating in the more or less robust corpus of philosophical inquiry. The question now is: How can philosophy talk about force?

The 'theme' par excellence in 'Cops on Trial' produced arguments concerning the regulation of force, its constitution and performance, which proved to be thematically disturbed and could be scaled only in terms of an ethics of dosage (escalation and deescalation of force). This served to demonstrate that we still do not know how to talk about force with an assured sense of its value or implications for judgment. While TV was under the covers, nomadic video captured images of brute force committed by the LAPD. Anyone who was watching the trial knows that the referential stability of the images was blown out of the water. Witnesses were reading blurs and blurring images. The status of the image as a semantic shooting range has been severely undermined as TV conducts this interrogation of force. The interrogation was forced upon TV – it involves an interrogation, I would submit, about its own textual performance in the production of force. What comes out provisionally, at least, is the fact that video, *nomadic* video – aleatory, unpredictable, vigilant, testimonial video – emerges as the call of conscience of broadcast TV, including CNN, C-SPAN, and so on.

HEADLINE NEWS: *Expenditure, wasting time. Getting wasted. A bug or virus that started spreading after the war: the endless survival of what has not been fully understood. The circuits are loaded with the enigma of survival.*

CHANNEL FOUR: What interests me provisionally, today, concerns the two eyes of television. TV is always watching, always involved in or subjected to monitoring and surveillance when it has two eyes, one of which can be the eye donated by video. I am not saying that video is the truth of television, nor its essence. Rather, it is what is watching television; it is the place of the testimonial that cannot speak with referential assurance but does assert the truth of what it says. This is why I want to focus it as the call of conscience, which is to say that video responds in some crucial sense to the call of television. Now, you have seen me play with the contrast and wave TV into the realm, or rather logic, of telephony. How can TV make a call, or more precisely, respond to a call? The way we call it is critical. (At the same time as TV is being watched by video and called to order, football has decided to dispense with instant replay. This decision, while made by team owners and not by media technologists, theorists, or media activists, nonetheless asserts that when it comes to calling it, TV withdraws its bid for claims made on behalf of referential stability.)

Let me try to unfold some of these points, and indicate where I think I'm going. On one level, television calls for a theory of distraction which appears to be rooted in the trauma that it is always telling, yet unable to fix. This suggests a complicated economy of visual playback and shock absorption, for trauma essentially involves an image without internalization. Recently, Cathy Caruth has argued that trauma does not 'simply serve as a record of the past but precisely registers the force of an experience that is not yet fully owned. . . . this paradoxical experience . . . both urgently demands historical awareness and yet denies our usual modes of access to it. . . . while the images of traumatic reenactment remain absolutely accurate and precise, they are largely inaccessible to conscious recall and control.'[9]

HEADLINE NEWS: *The relatedness of television to the end of history. Codes for such a reading were punched in when Benjamin and Freud discovered the experience of shock and the steps beyond the pleasure principle. This leads us to ask: What does it mean precisely for history to be the history of trauma?*[10] *It becomes necessary to translate the possibility of history by means of technology's flashback programming or the prerecorded logic of* TV.

Let me bring some of these strands into contact with one another. TV is irremissible; it is always on, even when it is off. Its voice of conscience is that internal alterity which runs interference with television in order to bring it closer to itself, but this closed-circuit surveillance can be experienced only in the mode of an estrangement. Television presents itself as being there only when it is other than itself: when it mimes police work or when, during the Gulf War, blanking out in a phobic response to the call of reference, it becomes a radio. And yet, it's not that simple: in this case it *showed* itself not showing, and *became* the closed, knotted eye of blindness. Within this act of showing itself not showing, posing itself as exposed, which is to say, showing that its rapport to the promise of reference is essentially one of phobia, it produces a dead gaze – what Blanchot would call 'a gaze become the ghost of eternal vision.' There is something in and from television that allows sight to be blinded into a neutral, directionless gleam. Yet, 'blindness is vision still,' 'a vision which is no longer the possibility of seeing.'[11]

In a sense, TV doubled for our blindness and in fact performed the rhetoric of blindness that guided the Gulf War. Television entered us into the realm of the eternal diurnal, night vision and twenty-four-hour operational engagement; its unseeing gaze was figured by the hypervision responsible for flaring TV-guided missiles that exploded sight at the point of contact. Television showed precisely a *tele*-vision, that is, a vision which is no longer the possibility of seeing what is at hand, and if it taught us anything, it was this: What fascinates us robs us of our power to give sense; drawing back from the world at the moment of contact, it draws us along, fascinated, blinded, exploded. Despite the propaganda contracts which it had taken out, television produced a neutral gleam that told us the relation between fascination and not seeing. If it showed anything, television showed a television without image, a site of trauma in which the experience of immediate proximity involved absolute distance. But it was through video, intervening as the call of conscience of TV, as foreign body and parasitical inclusion in broadcast television, that a rhetoricity of televisual blindness emerged. Marking the incommensurate proximity of the same, testimonial video split television from its willed blindness and forced it to see what it would not show. Something was apprehended.

There was the undisclosed Gulf War. Earlier I tried to read this according to Lacanian protocols of mapping the maternal body. The imaginary mapping of the primordial aggression of the subject reproduces the cartography of the mother's internal empire, marking the origin of all aggression, according to Lacan and, before him, Melanie Klein. This in part explains why mothers became such prominent figures in this war that refused to figure itself materially. Mother ('mother of all battles,' 'mothers go to war,' and so on) was not only put on the map by this war; she *was* the map. Can't get into her now, though it can be said that all forms of (paranoiac) aggression are perpetrated upon a displaced cartography of the maternal or, in the case of white on black, upon a body mangled by the rage through which the Other is marked with lacerations in the feminine.[12] As crude as it may seem to recognize this – and yet who doesn't know it? – Rodney King was put upon and sodomized ('Saddamized' in the metonymic citation) by brutal hets.

CHANNEL THREE: So, as I was saying, the Gulf War was blanked out, put into a position of latency. As with all unsuccessful attempts at repression, the symptoms were bound to come rocketing from a displaced area of the vast televisual corpus. The Rodney King event of 3 March 1991 stages the survival of the Gulf War in its displaced form. Indeed, on his last day in office, on television, Chief of Police Gates blamed the media for precisely this type of displacement: 'You made it [the Rodney King beating] into something bigger than the Gulf War' (broadcast news reports, 27 June 1992). This holds for the beating, but when the troops were sent into L.A. to subdue the targeted population, the media reverted to their failure to show, recovering in essence their rerunning away, or the structural relation to the whited-out war.

What we call 'Rodney King' has brought the question of force, or, officially, that of excessive use of force, to a hearing; it has placed police action on trial. Desert Storm was time and again understood as police action. Whether or not this represents a conceptually correct assessment in terms of strategy, buildup, tactical maneuvers, declarations of intent, and so on, it remains the case that at this instance the national unconscious inscribed the collapse of police action and military intervention. 'Rodney King' (who in fact never presented himself in the first trial that refers us to him) names the hearings which never took place for war crimes committed in the Persian Gulf War. Condensed and displaced to the beating of Rodney King, the televised trial, subtitled 'Cops on Trial,' thematized unthematizable force fields of intensity, while studying the problem of impact and the incitement to brutality with which TV has always been, in one form or another, associated. What is the relation between TV and violence? Hasn't this been television's only question when you get down to it?

COMMERCIAL BREAK: 'That's not the way force is studied,' retorted use of force expert Robert Michaels several weeks into the trial. Bringing to the fore a study of force impact involving the difference between incapacitating strikes and pain compliance impact devices (in particular the electric Taser gun), upper-body control holds, theories of escalation and deescalation of force, the trial induced by Rodney King showed how television, forced by video, was hearing out arguments organized around its own essence. This essence was shown to be critically linked to questions concerning trauma control and the administration of force. As the use of force expert tells it, on the first level the 'empirical' force spectrum entails evaluations of verbal communication and effects of presence, while the second level involves responsiveness to pain compliance impact devices, including upper-body control holds and the chokehold (whose routinely racist applications the police recognizes and hence avoids using when beating King). Resolutely uninterrogated, the force spectrum however fails to provide a reliable grid for evaluating force because it has not been tapped by theoretically sound means that would throw some light on what constitutes 'effects of presence,' 'responsiveness,' 'communication,' and the like. I am not so foolish as to prescribe a mandatory reading list of Heidegger, Wittgenstein, Deleuze, Foucault, and Derrida for police training, though it would not hurt (their victims). But once the police started reading or knowing what they were doing, or whom they were representing and why, they would no longer be the police, the phantom index to which Benjamin's argument pointed us. At the very least they would be, as readers, essentially detectives (and only *esse*ntially): those loners who, resisting group formation, sometimes have to turn in their badges or cross an ethicolegal line in order to investigate, piece together, read, and scour unconscious densities of meaning. It's not a pretty job, and it's generally managed according to a different time clock than that which the police regularly punches. To the extent that pedagogy was blamed for the failure of the police to understand the scene of arrest or to control the usage of brute force, and teachers were asked to speak about teaching, certain questions of how to read, or, at least, how to produce effects of learning, were emphatically focused in the trial. While the introduction of the 'force spectrum' was never in itself reflected upon or theorized, it nonetheless serves to circumscribe such levels of responsiveness as law enforcement and television, each in the idiom peculiar to it, attempt to elicit and regulate. Working over the arrested body, each inscribes and wastes it, making it do time, sometimes along the lines of teaching a lesson.

HEADLINE NEWS: *If television and the police are experiencing some kind of shared predicament of being on call, it is necessary that we understand how these calls are circuited through the transmission systems of police force. The circuits are loaded: they range from the call of duty, to which an officer is likely to respond with violence, to highly suspect considerations of what constitutes responsiveness. (The defense's refusal to interpret King's calls as cries of pain was maintained throughout the trial.) Yet, the motif of the call ambiguates the scene of violence, for the possibility of appeal and the call of conscience are logged on to the same systems.*

One would have to bring to bear a critique of violence in the manner of Benjamin, if it were not that TV was itself trying to tell us something about the status of legal and social fictions. TV does not know what it knows. In the idiom of Heideggerian insight, TV cannot think the essence of TV which it is however constantly marking and remarking. Television's principal compulsion and major attraction comes to us as the relation to law. As that which is thematized compulsively, the relation to law is at once there and not there, cancelling its program by producing it. (Hence the proliferation of police shows, from 'Dragnet' to 'Perry Mason,' '911,' 'Hard Copy,' 'Top Cops,' 'FBI,' 'Law and Order,' and courtroom dramas; even westerns with their lone law enforcer and inevitable sheriff belong to this topos.) This relation to law which television compulsively repeats as its theme is simultaneously presented as the unthematizable par excellence – that is to say, this is a relation that cannot be presented as such but can only be appealed to or offered up as metonymic citation. Television is summoned before the law, but every attempt to produce the relation to law on a merely thematic level produces instead a narrative which is itself metonymic; the narrative is metonymic not because it is narrative, but because it depends on metonymic substitution from the start.[13] In other words, television cannot say the continuity of its relation to itself or its premier 'object', which can be understood as force. This is why Rodney King's show, 'Cops on Trial,' is about television watching the law watching video, its call to order, a figure of order that tries to find the language by which to measure out an ethical dosage of force. At no point do television or policing delude themselves into assuming they can do without force, but they do not question this essential supplement. (Concerning supplement and dosage, Television, as a drug, is also a tranquilizing force, regularly absorbing and administering hits of violence. After a hard day's work on *Psycho,* Alfred Hitchcock used to doze off in front of TV, claiming that TV, unlike film, was soporiferous.) Alternately stimulating and tranquilizing, ever anxiety producing, television belongs to the domain of the internalized *Ge-Stell* or 'posure' of drugs, which is why, once again, the Rodney King event has to start its narrative engine with a false start acknowledged by all – everyone involved in the chase had to start by assuming that they were pursuing a PCP suspect. Without technology's relation to the asserted effects of drugs, hallucination and supernatural force, there would be no act of television reading itself, which is to say reading images of a phenomenal 'self' pumped up on the supposition of drugs but without any substance behind it.[14]

HEADLINE NEWS: *Implicit difference between tele-vision and video according to chapter seven of* Sein und Zeit. *Heidegger comments that the* scheinen *of semblance, in its various forms, 'is founded upon pure* phainesthai, *in the sense of phenomenal presencing. The Greek sense of phainetai,' he notes, 'differs from that of the Latin* vidētur, *even where mere semblance is denoted, for the Latin term is offered from the perspective of the observer, rather than from out of the unconstrained spontaneity of presencing.'*[15]

HEADLINE NEWS: *The disruption of experience and comprehension that trauma involves.*

What, then, were the charges made in the Rodney King trial? The defense has tried to show that, following the car chase, King took a step which in fact was a charge – he was said to be charging the LAPD. The countercharges, made by the defense in this case, pivot on the difference between a subject who is taking a step and one who is charging. If King was charging, then the force used to subdue him would have been justified. The distinction between taking a step and charging could not be determined with certainty by the footage provided in the George Holliday video tape. There seems to be an impasse, even though a phenomenal imaging of this scene exists. Repeated several hundred times in court, the frame-by-frame analyses explicitly raise questions about the relation between video recording and human memory. When witness David Love relies on his own memory of the beating he feels the violence to have been entirely justified; however, when he is asked to interpret the video he finds the 'same' scene to display an excessive and altogether inexplicable use of force. Throughout the testimony it is asked of this witness to express 'what the video does and does not say.' The entire problematic of witnessing comes into play. An assertive if provisional conclusion nominates the video as 'the best witness'; but video, it is further argued, 'doesn't tell the whole story' because it cannot reveal 'state of mind.' There were no strong readers around, at least none were called in. Superior Court Judge Weisberg rules out the expert testimony even of psychologists (who perhaps should not be confused with strong readers).

Is there a whole story, a totality of a story that eludes the video scope but can be located elsewhere? Is there a state of mind, a clarity of intention, an interpretation with its totalizing impulses, upon which the LAPD can confidently count?[16] We know that a 'strong reading' (one should measure how much force strong reading requires) of the tapes would need first to account for these metaphysical ploys and rhetorical deceits, if only to discern the axiology upon which the constitution of force could be thought. What the video cannot in any case show, states the court, concerns an interiority which it cannot inscribe; the video is pure surface without depth, running a mystifying release precisely because it fails to record inner perceptions. Unfueled by metaphysics, video is running on empty. Without access to interiority, the videotape deflects the scene from its locus in truth. This is why the court rules in favor of human memory of violence, the flaws and gaps in recall notwithstanding. Precisely where human memory of experience fails to achieve cognition – so the logic seems to go – it captures the 'whole story.' The court depends upon this evacuated site in order to retrieve a sense of the totality of the scene. This explains how the videotape's excess weighs in as deficiency in court. A mere machine, simply present while at the same time devoid of presence, it originates in a place without truth. As pure surface, the videotape effaces interiority as a condition of running. This is why the police give it chase – but they are also chased down by this suprapolice tape; on and off the streets, in your face and behind your back, the tape indifferently keeps running.

But let us keep in line with the first step of this process. Did Rodney King charge or step? The video that records this moment does not tell. The phenomenal instability of the image is staggering; there is no assured way to read the syntax of the move on a literal level. This step, which is out of line with all the certitudes we think we have about documenting the real, is in sync with Lacan's assertion that our encounter with the real is a missed appointment. In terms of the reading protocols that make up our legacy, the step that hesitates referentially between a step and a charge, tripping up the case as it does, is also a Freudian slip, a lapsus and collapse in the grammar of conscious imaging. So the television watches as the video is on compulsive replay, tripping over this unreadable scene that it has witnessed. 'Gehen wir darum einen Schritt weiter,' writes Freud in *Beyond the Pleasure Principle.* Freud, like the video on compulsive instant replay, reruns this step throughout the text that goes beyond the pleasure principle. Let us take another step.

HEADLINE NEWS: *Implications for memory: the difference between internalized memory and Memorex clips that run along the lines of flashback and other intrusive phenomena.*

It is as if Freud is watching us watching this scene that returns incessantly. Running through psychoanalysis, we learn that vectorizing our thoughts toward 'current events' means that we are in fact looking at recurrent events whose eventuation cannot as such be easily located. Trauma reduces us to scanning external stimuli whose signals beam out a density of materials for historical reconstitution: 'Solche Erregungen von aussen, die stark genug sind, den Reizschutz zu durchbrechen, heissen wir traumatische. . . . Ein Vorkommnis wie das äußere Trauma wird gewiß eine großartige Störung im Energiebetrieb des Organismus hervorrufen und alle Abwehrmittel in Bewegung setzen [We describe as 'traumatic' any external stimuli which are powerful enough to break through the protective shield [layering]. . . . The occurrence of a trauma externally induced is bound to create a major disturbance in the functioning of the organism's energy and to set in motion every possible defensive measure].'[17] What I would like to suggest is that the Rodney King trial in its particularity constitutes a moment when television reads itself, and, staging itself reading itself, it is prompted by the interpretation of force set out in *Beyond the Pleasure Principle,* where the death drive kicks in by taking repetitive steps toward a beyond. It was Derrida who first noted, in *La Carte postale,* how Freud keeps on trying rhetorically to take another step in an attempt to get beyond a textual impasse. But going nowhere on a fast and invisible track, Freud steps up the momentum of external force, eventually achieving what he sees as the phenomenon of 'breaking into the psychic layer that protects against excessive force.' The dramatic incursion of excessive force peels down this protective layering, radically exposing the subject to the domain of the traumatic. In the realm of media technology, such a structure of protective layering has been historically provided by television which, up to a point, manages the scenography of external stimuli. The excess of the Rodney King intrusion upon broadcast television dramatized the rupturing of the protective film with which television habitually covers itself by showing and producing the traumatic scene of 'excessive force.' Broken in upon by testimonial video, television ceased to protect against that very thing which it is intended to regulate. Formally on par with television, what Freud calls the domain of the traumatic is not as such a domain according to classical calculations of space and time but that which opens up a site of tremendous disturbances ('wird gewiß eine großartige Störung . . . in Bewegung setzen') whose limits are difficult to discern. Like television, the 'domain' of the traumatic, while producing historical effects of reference, cannot be located in the world, but points instead to paradoxes of temporal complexities. We are on location, dislocated to the site of a provocation from the past that stammers over the 'pas au delà' – that Blanchotian space where the step can and cannot go beyond, restricted by a prohibitory injunction that points us backward as we attempt to trace the future of a step. The step beyond also involves the tripping that made it possible for the taped brutalization of King to blow out of teleproportion and into the streets.

HEADLINE NEWS: *'The historical power of trauma is not just that the experience is repeated after its forgetting, but that it is only in and through its inherent forgetting that it is first experienced at all.'*[18]

What urges us on, and motivates linkage between the Freud text and Rodney King event text and with the discourse underlying the war on drugs, and all the steps we have been impelled to take beyond the pleasure principle, involves the same break in consciousness. We now encounter the fact of fundamental disruption in traditional modes of consciousness and understanding, a disruption that occurs traumatically in the very experience of our history. This invasion of consciousness, a type of break in the possibilities traditionally allowed for experiencing experience, is what Benjamin called the *Chockerlebnis* – a jolt which occurs when an event is dissociated from the understanding that might attach itself to it; shock produces a split of memory from consciousness, often triggering technologically morphed mechanisms on the order of flashback or hallucination.

CHANNEL TWO: The trial has produced a number of maps, photographs, and flowcharts of chronological time sequences; yet these common devices for capturing empirical parameters of events have failed to prove much of anything. Except, possibly, that we are dealing here with a type of experience that eludes temporal and spatial determinations altogether – something that can bust into a scene at any time, any place, miming the experience of the police. If the Rodney King beating figures the survival of the effaced Persian Gulf War, then its principal 'object' of projection would involve the phantom text of a trauma. Precisely because the trauma is hidden from televised view – the Rodney King beating is a metonymy of a hidden atrocity, be this the unshown war or the atrocities to which African-Americans are routinely subjected – it is accessible only by reading. The spectral trauma remains hidden even to the hidden camera that blindly captures it. Yet, capturing the hidden trauma – and not the suspect called Rodney King or even the police out of line – is the way that video has participated in focusing the disruption of experience and comprehension that TRAUMATV involves. Under nocturnal cover, nomadic, guerrilla video captures no more than the debilitating discrepancy, always screened by television, between experience and meaning which Freud associates with trauma. This is why it could prove nothing but this discrepancy in a court of law. 'Gehen wir darum einen Schritt weiter.'

When the trial tries to number the blows, count the strikes and determine the velocity of force, all it can do is attempt to parry the shock that 'in modernity dissociates once and for all the traditional cohesion of experience and cognition.'[19] The repeat performance of a frame-by-frame blow shows how this text became nothing more than the compulsive unfolding of a blank citation. In this instance, video intervened as a distance that separates the witness's knowledge of the traumatic occurrence from the sheer repetitiveness which marks the experience of its telling.

CHANNEL ONE: Is it accidental if one refers to the function of witness repeatedly by using the masculine pronoun? Or is it perhaps an 'accident' of such magnitude that its enigmatic character has been somewhat effaced? Testimony, as Freud knew, reverts to the privilege of testicles, engendering truth within the seminal flow of testimonial utterance. Let's take this a few steps further. Standing as witness, in step with Freudian logic, and bearing testimony [*Zeug, zeugen*], swearing in the truth of one's testimony upon one's testicles, implies that the subject before the law comes under the threat of castration. The truth is related to this threat. Oedipus the video, lagging behind, limping out of step and out of line, plucking his eyes out when he sees the truth – this is the truth of video, the site of the neutral gleam that knows something which cannot be shown. When Freud traces testimony back to testicles he is also severing truth from any security net that might underlie cognition. Testimony, and that which it begets, is linked not so much to perception but to speculation. When Roman jurists swore upon their testicles they were swearing upon a truth that could never be known for sure, to whose resolution no amount of evidence could do more than swear. Swearing, bearing witness, producing the testimonial – these constitute acts of language that, unfounded (that is, neither 'founded' as in poetic speech nor 'grounded' as in philosophical speech nor even secured by 'ordinary language' usage), rely upon the vagaries of speculation, displacing the *testimony* to the fragility of the eyes: the two eyes of television and video, which are committed to the uncertain rigors of reading. Whether you are making sense or semen, you can never know for sure whether you are indeed the father of truth. Thus, in its essence and logic, testimonial is fragile, uncertain, performative, speculative. (In this regard, the one who is feminized, on the side of sense certainty, penetrated by force, the figure of excluded negativity, is bound to lose out to the symbolic inscription of the testimonial.) The legal mode of the trial 'dramatizes . . . a contained and culturally channelled, institutionalized crisis of truth. The trial both derives from and proceeds by a crisis of evidence, which the verdict must resolve.'[20] As a sentence, the verdict is a force of law performatively enacted as a defensive gesture for not knowing.

FACE THE NATION: To this end, the Clarence Thomas hearings say more about that which cannot be presented, the relation between phallus and castration, the unrelenting crisis of evidence, and the nature of the testimonial as the drama by which the symbolicity of testicles come to be marked. These hearings bore witness to the powerful but empty phallus that could not be summoned to appear but around which the hearing was organized. This was not a negligible testimonial but one addressing itself to the essence of a supreme organ of state, namely, the Supreme Court of the United States. In this case, which tested the case of the case – the essence of testimony and the rectitude of justice – race, I daresay, initially disguised the sexual difference upon which legal testimony is erected and judgment based. It will not do to simplify the case by stating that Justice Thomas is a black man; identified as such, the African-American nominee carried with him phantasms of the *jouissance* of the Other and effects of the phallus. In this regard, race aggravated the demand for presenting the phallus; but, like the phantom it is when presentation is beckoning, the phallus was shown for what it is: *in camera* as on camera, it can only be nothing.

CHANNEL ZERO: My contention is (and others have argued this according to different impulses and grammars) that television has always been related to the law, which it locates at the site of crucial trauma. When it is not performing metonymies of law, it is still producing some cognition around its traumatic diffusions; thus even the laugh track, programming the traumatic experience of laughter, can be understood to function as a shock absorber. It signals the obsessive distraction that links laughter to a concept of history within which Baudelaire located the loss of balance and, indeed, 'mankind's universal fallen condition' ('On the Essence of Laughter'). With the loss of balance and the condition of falling, we are back to that unreadable blur that is said to project the step – or the charge – taken by Rodney King on 3 March 1991.

'Trauma stops the chronological clock,' writes Lawrence Langer in 1991. This stopwatch configures, in fact, what makes television, despite the insistence of its '60 Minutes'-like ticking or the breathless schedule that it runs, freeze. Still, television stops the chronological clock which it also parallels in a fugitive, clandestine way and according to two modes of temporal assignment. Television stops time by interrupting its simulated chronology in the event of an 'event' which is neither of time nor in time but something that depends upon repetition for its occurrence. The 'event' usually enters television from a place of exteriority in which the witness is figured by an untrained video operator (consider here the footage of the collapsed Bay Bridge in the 17 October 1989 San Francisco earthquake). Television also stops the chronological clock by miming its regularity and predictability around the clock, running and rerunning the familiar foreignness of traumatic repetition. Indeed, one would be hard pressed to prove that the effectivity of TV was not a symptom of the traumatic stress which it also works to perpetuate. In their article on trauma entitled 'The Intrusive Past,' B. A. van der Kolk and Otto van der Hart describe trauma as if it were linked to the very functioning of the television apparatus, or, at least, as if the traumatized subject were caught in a perpetual state of internalized channel surfing: 'He switches from one [existence] to the other without synchronization because he is reporting not on a sequence but a simultaneity. . . . A different state consists of a continuous switching from one internal world to another.'[21] A monument to that which cannot be stabilized, television captures disruption, seriature, the effraction of cognition, and internal breaks – whether commercial or constitutive – and is scripted by a need to play out the difference between reference and phenomenality. On this score, there remains one more thing to be said about the relation of television to trauma. This has everything to do with the essential character of traumatism as a nonsymbolizable wound that comes before any other effraction: *this* would be TV's guide – how to symbolize the wound that will not be shown.

Of the symptoms that television most indelibly remarks, one is the alternation marked between hypermnesia and amnesia. What is the relation between amnesia and the image? We have observed in films such as *Total Recall* that, in order to discover the limits of any possible reality, acts of remembering are prompted by mnemonic devices along the lines of video implants. In fact, video has tracked considerable thematizations of internalized, commemorative memory (*Erinnerung*, in Hegel's vocabulary) that are nothing if not the literalization of *Gedächtnis*, an external memory prompter, a cue, or memo padding. While these video implants are often accompanied by nightmarish hues, they somehow remain external to the subject who needs these prompters to supplement an absence of memory. The image comes to infuse an amnesiac subject. 'Total recall' is not the same as memory or recollection, and it is only total to the extent that it names the need for a prosthetic technology that would produce a memory track. In such films, the video transport – always pointing to a modality of transport, they constantly neurotransmit highs, crashes, incessant repetition or fuzzing, they combine the idioms of drugs and electronics – the technochip induces some sort of trip, a condition of memory seen as lapsus, stimulating the transmission of the slip. The video transport coexists with a condition of stated amnesia. It is to such intractable amnesia, channel surfing through blank zones of trauma, that television, sponsored by screen memories and forgetting, responds, secretly measuring the force of an unbearable history.

# NOTES

INTRODUCTION

1 Maurice Blanchot, citing Georges Bataille, *The Unavowable Community,* trans. Pierre Joris (Barrytown, NY: Station Hill Press, 1988), 44.

2 The gift and the offering as a relation to time beyond the economy of owing have been explored by Hélène Cixous in her seminar 'Le Don' (Paris VIII, 1985–86), Jacques Derrida (*Donner le temps* [Paris: Galilée, 1991]), and Jean-Luc Nancy ('L'offrande sublime,' *Du sublime* [Paris: Belin, 1988]). I am also accompanying the movement set forth in Blanchot's *The Unavowable Community,* which itself accompanies the community of Jean-Luc Nancy and Marguerite Duras.

3 Georges Bataille, 'La Limite de l'utile,' in *Oeuvres complètes,* 12 vols. (Paris: Gallimard, 1970), 7:245–46; my trans. All subsequent translations are my own unless otherwise noted.

4 Derrida discussed the modalities of questioning and the difference between *Neugier* [curiosity] and *Sorge* [care] in Heidegger's *Being and Time* in the seminar entitled 'The Secret,' University of California, Irvine, March–May 1992. In *Spirit in Ashes: Hegel, Heidegger, and Man-Made Mass Death* (New Haven, CT: Yale University Press, 1985), Edith Wyschogrod comments on Heidegger's thinking of death as the 'shrine of Nothing,' the relation between man and animal, thus: 'Man is not different from animals by way of reason; instead the purely human task of man is to *become* mortal. This analysis is similar to Hegel's view of death in the *Philosophy of Nature,* in which man transcends animal existence by foreclosing his own death' (185).

5 See Nancy, *Une Pensée finie* (Paris: Galilée, 1992), 19ff., for a discussion of finity, exteriority, and extermination. I would also refer the reader to his exposition of the 'here-and-now' in the lead essay of the volume.

6 Alexander García-Düttmann has analysed Derrida's thinking of *différance* in 'The Violence of Destruction,' a paper given at the symposium organized by David Ferris, 'Walter Benjamin and Literary Theory,' Yale University, 18 October 1991.

7 Christopher Fynsk, *Heidegger: Thought and Historicity* (Ithaca, NY: Cornell University Press, 1986), 157.

8 Gérard Granel, 'Et Tu, qui es?' *Critique: La Philosophie malgré tout* 369 (Feb. 1978): 179.

9 *Moderato Cantabile,* in *Four Novels by Marguerite Duras* (New York: Grove Press, 1965), 63.

10 Emmanuel Levinas, 'Reality and Its Shadow,' *Collected Philosophical Papers,* trans. Alphonso Lingis (Dordrecht: Martinus Nijhoff Publishers, 1987), 5.

11 *Moderato cantabile* (Paris: Éditions du Minuit, 1958), 7. In the appended review by Claude Roy (*Libération,* 1 Mar. 1958), it is said: 'Le nouveau roman de Marguerite Duras, *Moderato cantabile,* pourrait se définir: *Madame Bovary* réécrite par Bela Bartok' (97).

12 Jacques Lacan, 'Homage to Marguerite Duras,' trans. Peter Connor, in *Duras by Duras* (San Francisco: City Lights Books, 1987), 122–30.

FINITUDE'S SCORE

1 Friedrich Nietzsche, *The Genealogy of Morals,* in *The Basic Writings of Friedrich Nietzsche,* trans. Walter Kaufmann (New York: Random House, 1968), 136. Follow these strains from *The Birth of Tragedy* onward, where the Dionysian figure presents itself as a space of telephonic reverberation: 'The Dionysian musician is, without any images, himself pure primordial pain and its primordial re-echoing' (trans. Kaufmann [New York: Vintage Books, 1967], 50). The negative trope of *ressentiment* covers the modes of operatic transmission. See Sarah Kofman's discussion of 'La Musique, art priviligié,' in *Nietzsche et la métaphore* (Paris: Galilée, 1972).

2 *L'Opéra ou la défaite des femmes* (Paris: Grasset, 1979), trans. Betsy Wing under the title *Opera; or, The Undoing of Women* (Minneapolis: University of Minnesota Press, 1988).

3 Ibid., 18.

4 Friedrich Kittler discusses Wagner's displacement of the orchestra to the pit in 'Weltatem: Über Wagners Medientechnologie,' in *Diskursanalysen 1,* ed. Kittler, Manfred Schneider, and Samuel Weber (Opladen: Westdeutscher Verlag, 1987), 94–107.

5 I am accompanying the score set by Derrida in 'Des Tours de Babel,' trans. Joseph F. Graham, in *Difference in Translation,* ed. Graham (Ithaca, NY: Cornell University Press, 1985).

6 The tense reopening of an aesthetics of closure is treated by David Carroll in *Paraesthetics: Foucault, Lyotard, Derrida* (New York: Methuen, 1987).

7 Ibid., 191.

8 See the logic of acquired immunodeficiency syndrome (AIDS) in the shared text of Mozart and Nietzsche in the following chapter, 'Queens of the Night: Nietzsche's Antibodies.'

9 Clément, 13.

10 Ibid., 14, 15.

11 Of course, to the extent that they are both engaged in rebabelizing the Word, Moses and Luther are compatible figures. We might recall here

Michel Foucault's assertion in *Les Mots et les choses* (1966) that the modern age began with two great hysterics: Don Quixote and Luther. The first to introduce desire, Luther deposes the Father in the name of the Other.

12 Jean-François Lyotard, 'Several Silences,' trans. Joseph Maier, in *Driftworks* (New York: Semiotext(e), 1984), 104.

13 Jean-François Lyotard, *Heidegger and 'the jews,'* trans. Andreas Michael and Mark S. Roberts (Minneapolis: University of Minnesota Press, 1990). For an astute reading of the place of Freud in Lyotard's work, see Anne Tomiche, 'Lyotard's Freud,' *Esprit Créateur* 31 (Spring 1991): 48–61.

14 See Jean-Luc Nancy, 'Vox Clamans in Deserto,' trans. Nathalia King in *The Birth to Presence,* trans. Brian Holmes et al. (Stanford, CA: Stanford University Press, 1993): 234–47.

15 Other operas fascinated by the telephone include Gian-Carlo Menotti's *The Telephone,* subtitled *L'Amour à trois,* in which interruption and scrambling are thematized, and Lee Hoiby's *Three Women: Composed for Miss Beardsley, 1988.*

16 Keith W. Daniel, *Francis Poulenc: His Artistic Development and Musical Style, Studies in Musicology* 52 (Ann Arbor, MI: UMI Research Press, 1982), 29.

17 On the links between background music and the death drive, see Philippe Lacoue-Labarthe, 'The Echo of the Subject,' *Typography: Mimesis, Philosophy, Politics,* ed. Christopher Fynsk (Cambridge, MA: Harvard University Press, 1989), 139–208.

18 Francis Poulenc, *Correspondence 1915–1963* (Paris: Éditions du Seuil, 1967), 270. All citations of [Jean Cocteau] *La Voix humaine* were taken from *The Human Voice,* trans. Carl Wildman (London: Vision Press Ltd., 1930). See also the pertinent passages in Francis Steegmuller's *Cocteau: A Biography* (Boston: Little, Brown and Company, 1970) and Pierre Bernac, *Francis Poulenc: The Man and His Songs,* trans. Winifred Radford (New York: W.W. Norton, 1977).

QUEENS OF THE NIGHT

1 In 'Ce qu'on aura pu dire du sida: Quelques propos dans le désordre,' *Poésie* 58 (Dec. 1991), Alexander García-Düttmann demonstrates how AIDS has restructured the possibilities for self-disclosure in the autobiographical narrative and the 'confessional' texts of Jean-Paul Aron (*Mon Sida*), Pierre Bachelier (*Moi et mon sida*), Renaud Camus (*Tricks*), Susan Sontag (*AIDS and Its Metaphors*), and others. A major question that García-Düttmann proposes for analysis concerns the relationship of deconstruction to AIDS, beginning with an interpretation of Heidegger and the subject of illness: 'La maladie occupe-t-elle une place dans la méditation sur l'histoire et l'historialité . . . Quelque soit l'angle depuis lequel on considère ses symptomes, la maladie reste toujours un phénomène exis-

tentiel, et cela à même titre que la mort. Or il s'agit peut-être de comprendre que la maladie affecte le *Dasein* lui-même, qu'elle touche au *Dasein* en entier, ou que le pouvoir-être-entier (*Ganzeinkönnen*) qui caractérise le *Dasein* ne se laisse penser sans penser la maladie' (10).

2 Jean-Luc Nancy, in his 'Entretien sur le mal,' *Apertura* 5 (1991): 29, argues that we now exist in absolute malignancy, which is to say that we no longer experience malignancy [*le mal:* 'evil' and 'illness'] as misfortune [*malheur*] – that is, as an irreparable rupture which still makes sense – nor as infirmity [*maladie*] – that is, a reparable rupture, because 'classical thought reasons on the basis of the disappearance or the cancellation of death.' The malignancy (or evil) in which the history of malignancy appears to culminate is neither reparable nor does it any longer make sense; it is linked to the question of technology, which designates an immanence without transcendence. *Le mal* can also consist in the positive possibility of existence which occurs (as in Schelling) when freedom is free to unleash within itself forces against itself. See Nancy, *L'Expérience de la liberté* (Paris: Galilée, 1988), 164. On the relationship between infirmity and racial markings, see the works of Sander Gilman, especially *Inscribing the Other* (Lincoln: University of Nebraska Press, 1991).

3 Michel Bounan, *Le Temps du sida* (Paris: Éditions Allia, 1990), 59.

4 Ibid., 85.

5 Ibid., 77.

6 Mirko D. Grmek, *Histoire du sida* (Paris: Payot, 1990), 187–88.

7 'The New French Retrovirus,' *The New York Native,* 19 Dec. 1983–1 Jan. 1984, 24.

8 The homogeneous if not homosexual grounding of the university is amply documented in such traditional studies of the university as, for example, Charles Homer Haskin's *The Rise of Universities* (1923; Ithaca, NY: Cornell University Press, 1957), 2–3: 'the medieval university was, in the fine old phrase of Pasquier, "built of men" – *bâtie en hommes* . . . they created the university tradition which belongs to all our institutions of higher learning, the newest as well as the oldest, and which all college and university men should know and cherish.' For recent critical readings of institution and higher learning, see Jacques Derrida, 'Unoccupied Chair: Censorship, Mastership and Magistrality,' *Recherches Sémiotiques/Semiotic Inquiry* 4 (1984): 123–39; 'Mochlos; or, The Conflict of the Faculties,' *Logomachia: The Conflict of the Faculties* (Lincoln: University of Nebraska Press, 1992); 'The Principle of Reason: The University in the Eyes of Its Pupils,' *diacritics* 13 (Spring 1983): 3–20; Jean-François Lyotard, *The Postmodern Condition: A Report on Knowledge,* trans. Geoffrey Bennington and Brian Massumi (Minneapolis: University of Minnesota Press, 1984); Samuel Weber, *Institution and Interpretation* (Minneapolis: University of Minnesota Press, 1987).

9 'The New French Retrovirus,' 24.

10 Jacques Derrida, *Art contre/against Apartheid,* trans. Peggy Kamuf: Antonio Saura, Chairman (New York: UNESCO Publications, 1983), 28.

11 Friedrich Nietzsche, *Genealogy of Morals,* ed. Walter Kaufmann (New York: Vintage Press, 1969), 72.

12 Hazard S. Adams, in *Profession '83* (New York: Modern Language Association, 1983), 34.

13 Gilles Deleuze, *Nietzsche et la philosophie* (Paris: PUF, 1967). Consider also in this context Deleuze's understanding of the Nietzschean body: 'ce qui définit un corps est ce rapport entre des forces dominantes et des forces dominées . . . Dans un corps, les force supérieures ou dominantes sont dites *actives,* les forces inférieures ou dominées sont dites *réactives.* Actif et réactif sont précisément les qualités originelles, qui expriment le rapport de la force avec la force' (45).

14 *The Portable Nietzsche,* ed. Walter Kaufmann (New York: The Viking Press, 1968), no.25, 470. The preface to the *Twilight,* written in 1888, Nietzsche's last productive year, rhymes with a thematic cord that will be pursued in Mozart's last work. Before writing of the 'tuning fork,' Nietzsche argues that 'even in a wound, there is the power to heal. A maxim, the origin of which I withhold from scholarly curiosity, has long been my motto:

*Increscunt animi, virescit volnere virtus.*
[The spirits increase, vigor grows through a wound.]

Another mode of convalescing – under certain circumstances, even more to my liking – is *sounding out idols*' (465).

15 Thomas De Quincey, 'The Last Days of Kant,' *Miscellanies: Chiefly Narrative* (Edinburgh: James Hogg, 1854). ('The author of this work notifies that it is his intention to reserve the right to translating it.')

16 For an impressive study of the hypothetical causes of Mozart's death, see Carl Bär, *Mozart: Krankheit – Tod – Begräbnis* (Salzburg: Salzburger Druckerei, 1966), and Michael Levey, *The Life and Death of Mozart* (London: Weidenfeld and Nicolson, 1971).

17 R. B. Moberly, *Three Mozart Operas* (London: Victor Gollancz Ltd., 1967), 230.

18 See *Viral Immunology and Immunopathology,* ed. Abner Louis Notkins (Bethesda, MD: National Institutes of Health, 1975); *Immunological Aspects of Infectious Diseases,* ed. George Dick (Baltimore: University Park Press, 1979), esp. E.H. Nauta's 'Infection in the Compromised Host'; and *Current Topics in Immunology: Immunodeficiency,* ed. Anthony R. Hayward (Chicago: Yearbook Medical Publishers, 1977).

19 *Nietzsche: A Self-Portrait from His Letters,* ed. Peter Fuss and Henry Shapiro (Cambridge, MA: Harvard University Press, 1971), 12, 18. A letter to

Erwin Rohde (29 Mar. 1871) suggests that Nietzsche's rapport with the university is linked to the question of health. In the same letter announcing 'a new principle of education utterly repudiating our high schools and universities,' Nietzsche writes, without transition, 'Oh how I long for good health! . . . As it is, some of my lower internal organs seem to be ruined.' At the same time, however, he warns against the implications of an endnote such as this: 'But do not be kind enough to trace the aforementioned state of mind to my ganglial condition, or I'll fear for my immortality' (17–18).

20 We might recall here Nietzsche's discussion of the philosopher's 'maternal instinct.' Regarding *Die Zauberflöte*'s thematization of host susceptibility, remember that Tamino had no arrows when he entered the queen's domain.

21 *Immunological Aspects of Infectious Diseases*, 101.

22 *Viral Immunology and Immunopathology*, 1.

23 In *Advances in Psychosomatic Medicine*, ed. Arthur Jores and Hellmuth Freyberger (New York: Robert Brunner, Inc., 1961), 312ff.

24 For a provocative reading of asceticism and obsessional neurosis, see Sarah Kofman, *Nietzsche et la scène philosophique* (Paris: Union Générale d'Éditions, 1979). Also see her 'La musique, art priviligié,' in *Nietzsche et la métaphore* (Paris: Galilée, 1972).

HITTING THE STREETS

1 Walter Benjamin, 'Karl Kraus,' *Reflections*, trans. Edmund Jephcott (New York: Schocken, 1986), 261, 241.

2 Martin Heidegger, 'Tragedy, Satyr-Play, and Telling Silence in Nietzsche's Thought of Eternal Recurrence,' trans. David Farrell Krell, *Boundary 2* 9 (Spring 1981): 36.

3 Heidegger, *What Is Called Thinking?* trans. J. Glenn Gray (New York: Harper and Row, 1968), 49, 48.

4 A reading of the nonarticulation of the eternal return has been promoted by Bernard Pautrat. See 'Nietzsche Medused,' trans. Peter T. Connor, in *Looking After Nietzsche*, ed. Laurence Rickels (Albany: SUNY Press, 1990).

5 Benjamin, 'The Destructive Character,' *Reflections*, 301–3. The German text is in the *Gesammelte Schriften* (Frankfurt am Main: Suhrkamp, 1980), 4:396–98.

6 The translation has led us astray. Heidegger actually writes of the difference between a Mercedes and an Adler, translated as a *bug* in English.

7 Benjamin, 'Karl Kraus,' 247.

8 Friedrich Nietzsche, *The Gay Science*, trans. Walter Kaufmann (New York: Random House, 1974), §312.

9 This is unfolded in the work of Philippe Lacoue-Labarthe, particularly

in 'L'Oblitération,' *Le Sujet de la philosophie* (Paris: Aubier-Flammarion, 1979).

10 Margot Norris, *Beasts of the Modern Imagination: Darwin, Nietzsche, Kafka, Ernst and Lawrence* (Baltimore: Johns Hopkins University Press, 1985), 4.

11 Ronald Hayman, *Nietzsche: A Critical Life* (New York: Penguin Books, 1980), 334. For details of the collapse, see the chapter on 'Euphoria, Melancholia and Madness.' The exact location of the collapse seems to have shifted within different accounts: it took place variously at the Piazza Carlo Alberto, the Piazza San Carlo, or the Piazza Carina, leaving the 'Carl' pretty much intact.

12 Ibid., 156, 90, 93.

13 Peter Heller, *Studies on Nietzsche* (Bonn: Bouvier, 1980), 204.

14 Hélène Cixous, 'Le Bon Pied, le bon oeil,' *Cahiers Renaud Barrault* 87 (1982): 47–75.

15 Rudolf E. Kuenzli, 'Nietzsche's Zerography: *Thus Spake Zarathustra*,' *Boundary* 2 9 (Spring 1981): 110.

16 Nietzsche, *The Birth of Tragedy*, in *The Basic Writings of Nietzsche*, trans. and ed. Walter Kaufmann (New York: Random House, 1968), 173.

17 Nietzsche, *Human, All-too-Human: A Book for Free Spirits*, trans. Marian Faber (Lincoln: University of Nebraska Press, 1984), §433.

18 Nietzsche, *The Birth of Tragedy*, 82.

19 Plato, *Phaedrus* (Indianapolis: Bobbs-Merrill Educational Publishing, 1983), 28.

20 Ibid., 37–39, 39, 28.

21 Kaufmann, *Nietzsche: Philosopher, Psychologist, Antichrist* (Princeton, NJ: Princeton University Press, 1974), 4–5, 3; emphasis added.

22 In Curt Paul Janz, *Friedrich Nietzsche* (Munich: Carl Hanser Verlag, 1979), 351. *Gerücht*, the word for *fama*, related as it is to the barely material sense of smell, constitutes a grand thematics in Nietzsche's corpus.

23 Pierre Klossowski, *Nietzsche: le cercle vicieux* (Paris: Mercure de France, 1969), 198.

STREET-TALK

1 'Nur noch ein Gott kann uns retten,' *Der Spiegel* 31 May 1976, 193–219; trans. under the title 'Only a God can save us now,' *Graduate Faculty Philosophy Journal* 6 (Winter 1977): 5–27. The translation repeats the exclusion of Husserl's name (12). Heidegger had dedicated *Sein und Zeit* to Edmund Husserl 'in friendship and admiration.' However, by the time of the fifth edition, in 1941, the dedication to his Jewish mentor had been effaced.

2 The subtitle to *Thus Spake Zarathustra* places the work in precarious circulation: 'For Everyone and No One.'

3 Hannah Arendt, introduction to Benjamin, *Illuminations* (New York: Schocken Books, 1969), 46.

4 *Reflections,* vii.

5 Martin Heidegger, *The Question of Being,* trans. Jean T. Wilde and William Kluback (New Haven: College and University Press, 1958), 41, 105 (trans. mod.).

6 The disjunctive reading of Hölderlin's *ent-stehen* originates in Paul de Man's *The Rhetoric of Romanticism* (New York: Columbia University Press, 1984).

7 Benjamin, 'Karl Kraus,' 247.

8 Sigmund Freud, *Three Case Histories,* ed. Philip Rieff (New York: Macmillan, 1963), 99.

9 Benjamin, 'Karl Kraus,' 247.

10 Benjamin, 'The Destructive Character,' *Reflections,* 301–3; the German text is in *Gesammelte Schriften* 4:1 (Frankfurt am Main: Suhrkamp, 1980), 396–98.

11 Heidegger, *What Is Called Thinking?* 72; trans. mod. Also compare Stephen Spender's poem on the stock market and rumor.

12 Heidegger, *What Is Called Thinking?* 73. The task of the translator has fallen into rumor. There is no 'Johnny' in *Was heißt denken?* but only in *What Is Called Thinking?*

13 Part of Defoe's title page to the *Journal of the Plague.*

14 Jean-Jacques Rousseau, *Les Rêveries du promeneur solitaire* (Paris: Garnier-Flammarion, 1964); trans. Peter France under the title *Reveries of the Solitary Walker* (New York: Penguin Books), 35, 32, 47, 48.

15 Acts of walking and remembering have been brilliantly linked in E.S. Burt's 'Mapping City Walks: The Topography of Memory in Rousseau's Second and Seventh Promenades,' *Yale French Studies* 74 (1988).

16 Paul de Man, *Allegories of Reading: Figural Language in Rousseau, Nietzsche, Rilke, and Proust* (New Haven, CT: Yale University Press, 1979), 161.

17 See de Man, *Allegories of Reading,* 'Part II: Rousseau.'

18 Rodolphe Gasché traces rumor to a 'long-sustained howl,' asking 'what is rumor if not a report widely disseminated with no discernible origin or source?' (Gasché, 'Self-Engendering as a Verbal Body,' *Modern Language Notes* 93 [May 1978]: 688).

19 Marie-Hélène Huet has opened up the possibility of this reading in 'Living Images: Monstrosity and Representation,' *Representations,* no.4 (Fall 1983). 'The monstrous is no longer anything but an accident' (84), and, suggesting monstrosity as a sort of publicity, she writes that 'the monster stands as a *public* rebuke' (73; emphasis added).

20 Nor should we forget that we still do not know the precise grounds of Benjamin's burial place somewhere in Port Bou. This belongs to a cryptological reading of our haunted rapport to Benjamin.

21 'Excessively present in the series relating the historical events, the virus is a poison. Turning about itself (*virer*) it becomes absent in the second series in order to make place for the desired body without organs' (Gasché, 'Self-Engendering as a Verbal Body,' 693).

22 This is cited in an old pamphlet, 'The Psychology of Rumor.'

23 Benjamin, 'Karl Kraus,' 267.

THE SUJET SUPPOSITAIRE

1 Jacques Lacan, 'The Function and Field of Speech and Language in Psychoanalysis,' *Écrits: A Selection*, trans. Alan Sheridan (New York: W.W. Norton and Company, 1977), 87. In its entirety, the title of Mr. Glover's essay reads, 'The Therapeutic Effect of Inexact Interpretation: A Contribution to the Theory of Suggestion' (*International Journal of Psychoanalysis* 12 [1947]).

2 This is James Strachey's interpretation of 'reversal' in *The Interpretation of Dreams*, in *The Standard Edition of the Complete Psychological Works of Sigmund Freud*, trans. and ed. James Strachey (London: Hogarth Press, 1953–74), hereafter abbreviated SE, vols.4 and 5. While any reading of the body reflects, at least in part, the organization of a social space and the hierarchical ordering of its representations, anal zones have tended to attract the politics of the pun. As Walter Redfern points out in *Puns* (Oxford: Oxford University Press, 1984), Swift's *Regarding the End* reminds us that eschatology and scatology are close kin, since both concern the final issue of things (Spanish uses the same word for both: *escatologico*): 'his love of inversion and reversal, his black outlook are all inspirations for his punning' (54). In regard to the about-face and the militarisms that attend the scenography of the Rat Man case, we might also refer to the example of Alphonse Allais whose poem 'Xylopages' (the title refers to woodcuts and to wood-boring insects) puns on the militaristic 'Fais ce que dois' as follows:

Un général anglais, dans une bataille,
Eut les deux fesses emportées par la mitraille.
Il en fit faire une autre paire en bois,
Mais jamais il ne les paya.
Moralité
Fesses que doit!

(The moral: Do as you must / He owes for his ass.)

3 In this regard see Jane Gallop, 'The Immoral Teachers,' and Shoshana Felman, 'Psychoanalysis and Education: Teaching Terminable and Interminable,' in *The Pedagogical Imperative: Teaching as a Literary Genre, Yale French Studies* 63 (1983).

4 Lacan, 'Function and Field,' 87.

5 Rat Man produced an abbreviated protective formula, *Glejisamen*. 'It is easy to see,' Freud writes, 'that this word is made up of

GISELA
S AMEN

and that he had united his *Samen* ["semen"] with the body of his beloved – i.e., putting it bluntly, had masturbated with her image' ('Notes Upon a Case of Obsessional Neurosis' [known as the case of Rat Man], SE, 10:281).

6 Lacan, *Feminine Sexuality: Jacques Lacan and the École Freudienne*, trans. Jacqueline Rose, ed. Juliet Mitchell and Jacqueline Rose (New York: W.W. Norton and Company, 1982), 164. The *objet petit a* is 'Lacan's formula for the lost object which underpins symbolization, cause of and stand in for desire. What man relates to is this object and "the whole of his realization in the sexual relation comes down to this fantasy"' (Rose, 'Introduction II,' 48).

7 Martin Heidegger, *Nietzsche* (Pfüllingen: Neske, 1961), 1:64.

8 The degree to which words are loaded is suggested by the brand name of this container: *Squibb* means not only a filler in journals but also a little pipe or a hollow cylinder of paper filled with powder or combustible matter. Examples stressing the explosive character of the pun are legion: 'Never point a pun at a friend. It might be loaded.' To emphasize the specificity of the suppository logic for the case of the pun, we refer to two French sources, beginning with Michel Corvin's *Petite folie collective:* 'The pun is a stretched tautology, shimmering with meaning, an explosive incantation which plays upon repetition all the better to destroy it, and drags the mind along the slope of the Same the better to leave room for the break-in of the Other' (Redfern, *Puns,* 32). Noah Jonathan Jacobs, in *Naming-Day in Eden* (London: Gollancz, 1958), offers the following gelastic formulation: 'The Janus word makes of human speech a *slippery instrument.* It is, however, the reflection of the double nature of man himself, of the contradiction that lies at the very heart of humanity. In Eden man knew no ambiguity, but when he fell, he became Janus-faced, a *parvus mundus* of opposites, perilously poised at the juncture of nature and spirit, the riddle of the crossroads, the glory and the jest of the world' (150).

9 This is taken verbatim from part 2 of the case study, entitled 'Theoretical: Some General Characteristics of Obsessional Formations,' 228.

10 See Patrick Lacoste, *Il Écrit* (Paris, 1981), and Lacan, *Écrits,* 237.

11 Redfern, *Puns,* 21; citing Michael West's study of Thoreau's scatology, Redfern documents Thoreau's 'excremental wordplay' (67).

12 Lacan, 'Function and Field,' 88–89.

13 Freud, *Three Case Histories*, ed. Philip Rieff (New York: Macmillan Publishing Co., 1963), 265.

14 Leonard Shengold, 'More About Rats and Rat People,' *Journal of the American Psychological Association* 36 (1982): 462, 483.

15 Lou Andreas-Salomé, 'Anal und Sexuell,' *Imago* 4 (1916): 259.

16 See Samuel Weber, *The Legend of Freud* (Minneapolis: University of Minnesota Press, 1982).

17 Freud, *Three Case Histories*, 265, 208, 266.

18 'Our patient used to employ as a defensive formula a rapidly pronounced "*aber*" ("*but*") . . . He told me on one occasion that this formula had become altered recently; he no longer said "*áber*" but "*abér*." When he was asked to give a reason for this new departure, he declared that the mute *e* of the second syllable gave him no sense of security against the intrusion, which he so much dreaded, of some foreign and contradictory element, and that he had therefore decided to accent the *e*' (224–25).

TAKING IT PHILOSOPHICALLY

1 Julia Gauss has stressed Goethe's interest in the monstrous in 'Entsagung, Bildung und Freiheit,' *Goethe-Studien* (Göttingen: Vandenhoeck and Ruprecht, 1961).

2 G. W. F. Hegel, *Vorlesungen über die Ästhetik* (Stuttgart: Reclam, 1977), 72. These remarks are intended for Schiller as well. (The 'Goethe-*and*-Schiller' reading of German letters remains as inevitable as it is problematic. In addition to objecting to Hegel in general, Nietzsche of course objected to the G.-and-S. strategy, which is still being practiced today.)

3 In fact, a reading of *Faust* nurtured the conception of the great monster narrative, Mary Wollstonecraft Shelley's *Frankenstein; or, The Modern Prometheus* (1831).

4 On the relationship of accident and chance to literature and psychoanalysis see Jacques Derrida's 'My Chances/*Mes Chances:* A Rendezvous with Some Epicurean Stereophonies,' trans. Irene Harvey and Avital Ronell, in *Taking Chances: Derrida, Psychoanalysis, and Literature*, ed. Joseph H. Smith and William Kerrigan (Baltimore: Johns Hopkins University Press, 1984).

5 *Hamburger Ausgabe* (Munich: C.H. Beck, 1975), 13:14–15.

6 Madame de Staël, *De L'Allemagne* (Bielefield: Velhagen und Klasing, 1916), 120. Paul de Man's reading of Tasso's place in Rousseau suggests the extent to which Goethe's originary rapport to a devastating Tasso in *Dichtung und Wahrheit* might in fact be a repetition of Rousseau's autobiography: 'The omission and surreptitious replacement of the Sophronie passage is at most a symptom, all the more so since "Tasso," in Rousseau, implies a threat as well as a wound' (Paul de Man, 'Excuses (*Confessions*),' *Allegories*

*of Reading: Figural Language in Rousseau, Nietzsche, Rilke, and Proust* [New Haven, CT: Yale University Press, 1979], 296).

7 See in particular Eugenio Donadoni's discussion of Tasso and the passage devoted to 'how he longed to be considered a philosopher,' in *A History of Italian Literature,* trans. Richard Monges (New York: New York University Press, 1969), 256ff. Goethe's commitment to discursive androgyny turns on an incestuous liaison between prose and poetry that he locates in a figure who simultaneously traverses Italy, France, and Germany. She/he, poetry/prose, and so on, collapses under the pressure of *Bildung*'s phallic discourse in *Wilhelm Meisters Lehrjahre.* Mignon eventually becomes a sign of herself when monumentalized, after its impossible existence, in the form of androgyny's angel.

8 Cited in Richard Friedenthal, *Goethe: Sein Leben und seine Zeit* (Munich: DTV, 1963), 345ff.

9 When arguing the difference between Goethe and Nietzsche in *Faux Pas* (Paris: Gallimard, 1943), 346, Maurice Blanchot offers the image of the shipwreck that would suggest a reference to the Tasso-Antonio couple. I have pursued this issue in 'Namely, Eckermann' (infra).

10 See Jacques Derrida, *La Vérité en peinture* (Paris: Flammarion, 1978), for his now famous discussion of the parergon and Kantian aesthetics.

11 Another version and another translation as well. 'Vorspiel auf dem Theatre' has been translated variously as 'Prologue for the Theatre' (Boyesen), 'Prelude at the Theater' (Jarvell), 'Prelude in the Theatre' (Kaufmann), and 'Prologue on the Stage' (Prudhoe), thus inventing a supplementary prologue for *Faust.*

12 Hegel, *Vorlesungen über die Ästhetik,* 48–49.

13 Hegel, *Phenomenology of Mind,* ed. Jacob Loewenberg (New York: Charles Scribner, 1957), 31. I shall also be citing from the German version (Frankfurt am Main: Suhrkamp, 1970).

14 See Shoshana Felman, 'Psychoanalysis and Education: Teaching Terminable and Interminable,' in *The Pedagogical Imperative: Teaching as Literary Genre, Yale French Studies* 63 (1982): 21–44.

15 Cited in *Immanuel Kant,* ed. Claussen and Bosse (Reinbek bei Hamburg: Rowohlt, 1965), 55.

16 *Dokumente zu Hegels Entwicklung,* ed. Johannes Hoffmeister (Stuttgart: Frommann, 1936), 430.

17 Kant, *Kritik der Urteilskraft* (Wiesbaden: Insel, 1977), 17, 'Vom Ideale der Schönheit,' 153. I have consulted but modified James Creed Meredith's translation (Oxford University Press, 1978).

18 Kant, *Anthropologie in pragmatischer Hinsicht* (Königsberg: Fr. Nicolovius, 1800), 212.

19 Derrida, 'L'âge de Hegel,' *Qui a peur de la philosophie?* (Paris: Flammarion, 1977), 88.

20 Kant, *Anthropologie,* 249.

21 Leonore's itinerary is a complicated one; she switches tracks after the foreplay is over, guided principally by Alfons's aesthetic politics of 'interestedness.'

22 Kant, *Anthropologie,* 249; Kant's emphasis.

23 Hegel, *Phenomenology,* 252.

NAMELY, ECKERMANN

1 In H.H. Houben, *J.P. Eckermann: Sein Leben für Goethe* (Leipzig: H. Haessel, 1925–28), 1:45.

2 See Jean-Luc Nancy, 'Exscription,' trans. Katherine Lydon in *The Birth to Presence,* trans. Brian Holmes et al. (Stanford, CA: Stanford University Press, 1993): 319–40.

3 See Bernard Pautrat, 'Nietzsche Medused,' trans. Peter Connor, in *Looking After Nietzsche,* ed. Laurence Rickels (Buffalo: SUNY Press, 1990), and Gilles Deleuze, *Nietzsche and Philosophy,* trans. Hugh Tomlinson (New York: Columbia University Press, 1983).

4 Maurice Blanchot, *Faux Pas* (Paris: Gallimard, 1943), 316.

5 This, of course, is a translation of the opening lines of *Ecce Homo,* which in turn reads as a translation, of sorts, of the name 'Ecke(r)-mann.' I thank Werner Hamacher for pointing out the syntonic qualities linking *Ecker*mann to Nietzsche within the concept of another recess or depression of the Nietzsche family, namely as 'niche.'

6 For a discussion of name and credit, see Jacques Derrida, 'Otobiographies: The Teaching of Nietzsche and the Politics of the Proper Name,' trans. Ronell in *The Ear of the Other: Otobiography, Transference, Translation,* ed. Christie V. McDonald (New York: Schocken, 1985).

7 Richard Friedenthal, *Goethe: Sein Leben und seine Zeit* (Munich: R. Piper, 1968), 143.

8 *Gespräche mit Goethe* (Berlin: Aufbau Verlag, 1982), 2.

9 Ibid.

10 I am grateful to Rainer Nägele for having discerned a peculiarly Nietzschean moment in this dream narration in terms of the second tractatus, sixteenth section of the *Genealogy,* which addresses the origin of humanity or the becoming-of-humanity of water animals [*Wassertiere*] as they first step onto land: 'als es den Wassertieren ergangen sein muß, als sie gezwungen wurden, endweder Landtiere zu werden oder zugrunde zu gehen, so ging es diesen . . . glücklich angepassten Halbtieren – mit einem Male warren alle ihre Instinkte entwertet und "ausgehängt." ' In the same section Nietzsche traces the becoming of the human soul not as something that grows inside the body but rather *onto* the body; thus 'dies ist das, was ich die *Verinnerlichung* des Menchen nenne: damit wächst erst das an den Menschen heran, was man später [seine] "Seele" nennt.' In a

way, Nietzsche describes the becoming of the soul almost as Goethe describes Eckermann's growing onto him, Nägele suggests, as the enabling fiction of immortality – a belated supplement to the concept of the specifically human.

DOING KAFKA IN THE CASTLE

1 Franz Kafka, *Tagebücher*, ed. Max Brod (Frankfurt a.M.: Fischer, 1951), 99. In his discussion of Derrida's *Glas*, Geoffrey Hartman (in 'Psychoanalysis: The French Connection,' in *Psychoanalysis and the Question of the Text*, ed. Hartman [Baltimore: Johns Hopkins University Press, 1978], 93), argues along similar lines that 'the wounding of a name is too much like the wounding of the body not to be significant. . . . There may be such a thing as a specular name or "imago du nom propre" in the fantasy development of the individual, *a name more genuinely one's own than a signature or proper name*' (emphasis added). This is taken up in John Leavey's and Gregory Ulmer's essays in *Glassary* (Lincoln: University of Nebraska Press, 1986).
2 The view of K. as an impostor is set forth in Marthe Robert's *Sur le papier* (Paris: Grasset, 1967), 25; in Erwin R. Steinberg's 'K. of *The Castle:* Ostensible Land-Surveyor,' *College English* 32 (Dec. 1965): 185–89; and, less convincingly, in Walter Sokel's *Franz Kafka* (New York: Columbia University Press, 1966), 39.
3 For an excellent discussion of title, reference, and impostorship considered from a juridical-philosophical perspective, see Denis Kambouchner's 'Le Régime de la turbulence: La Question du titre' in *Imposture ou pas, cahiers confrontation* 1 (Spring 1979): 19–41.
4 See Robert, *Sur le papier* and *L'Ancien et nouveau* (Paris: Grasset, 1963); Maurice Blanchot, *L'Entretien infini* (Paris: Gallimard, 1965) and *L'Espace littéraire* (Paris: Gallimard, 1955); and Charles Bernheimer, 'Symbolic Bond and Textual Play: Structure of *The Castle*,' in *The Kafka Debate*, ed. Angel Flores (New York: Gordian Press, 1977).
5 Bernheimer, 'Symbolic Bond,' 367, 371.
6 Derrida, 'Devant la Loi,' trans. Ronell, in *Kafka and the Contemporary Critical Performance: Centenary Readings*, ed. Alan Udoff (Bloomington: Indiana University Press, 1987), 128–49.
7 The Kafkan text, then, takes no narcotic relief from some comforting notion of the transcendental signified on any level, whether it be God, political authority, the literary work, or merely meaning itself. For a broad discussion of the relationship between the 'transcendental signifier and an ultimate substantialized dimension of meaning,' and for an equally broad consideration of the structure of language in relation to the subject, consult Frederic Jameson, *The Prison-House of Language* (Princeton, NJ:

Princeton University Press, 1972), 182–86. See also Derrida, *Positions* (Paris: Les Éditions du Minuit, 1972), 88–98.

8 The measure of this distance has been determined in an original and suggestive way through the citational rapport that Udoff discovers among Goethe, Rosenzweig, and Kafka. See his 'Before the Question of the Laws: Kafkan Reflections,' in *Kafka and the Contemporary Critical Performance*, 178–213.

9 Stanley Corngold, *The Commentator's Despair* (New York: Kennikat Press, 1973), 12, 27.

10 Kafka, *Gesammelte Werke*, ed. Max Brod, *Briefe 1902–1924* (Frankfurt am Main: Schocken Books, 1958), 385. See also Corngold, *The Commentator's Despair*, 26.

11 *Dysfunctionality* is meant to designate the way in which *The Castle* stages the *technē*, or in Paul de Man's sense of textual technology, the machine of its performance and constitution. This word should not be made to coincide with *nonfunctionality*, for the text, while never as such fully technologizable or merely implementary, appears to 'function,' but as a rather complicated engine that short-circuits in its performance, possibly pointing to a three-pronged metamorphosis of critical paradigms from the rhetoric of organicity to machinal structures well on the road to cybernetics (Kafka has always been credited with futural vision). In the most general outline, dysfunctionality refers to the system of signification operative in the text which, however, shares physiological and technological properties. Thus a nervous 'breakdown' or the implicit normativity of a healthy 'functioning' human being may be viewed as the effect of *Dasein*'s technological turn. The electrical charges which have simultaneous currency in the body and with tools will have to be read elsewhere, however, beginning precisely with the telephone hookup to the castle. While notions of the text qua machine need to be used guardedly, our usage is derived from the novel's central paradigm for textual production, the bureaucratic apparatus, which enjoins us to read it as a manifesto against literature. For a different perspective, see Allen Thiher, 'Kafka's Legacy,' *Modern Fiction Studies* (Winter 1981).

12 Jacques Lacan, *Écrits* (Paris: Éditions du Seuil, 1966), proposes this view of language as a kind of *béance* or opening onto the Other. I return to this discussion of desire and narration, which makes K. a kind of hero of *béance*.

13 A thorough treatment of the 'subject as locus' can be found in Anthony Wilden, *The Language of the Self* (Baltimore: Johns Hopkins University Press, 1976), 191–95.

14 Martin Walser, *Beschreibung einer Form* (Munich: Carl Hanser Verlag, 1961), 35. Walser's views, as those of his mentor, Beissner, have been taken to task by Jörgen Kobs, *Kafka: Untersuchungen zu Bewußtsein und Sprache*

*seiner Gestalten*, ed. Ursula Brech (Bad Homburg V.D.H.: Athenäum Verlag, 1970), 144–45, and Judith Ryan in the *Schiller-Jahrbuch* (1970), 569.

15 Kafka, *Das Schloß* (Berlin: Fischer Taschenbuch Verlag, 1968), 11.

16 See Paul de Man's discussion of this process of substitution in 'Action and Identity in Nietzsche,' *Yale French Studies* 52 (1975): 16–19.

17 See Terence Hawkes, *Structuralism and Semiotics* (Berkeley: University of California Press), esp.145–50.

18 The reference is to Kafka's statement that 'in addition it is imposed on us to do the negative' (*Hochzeitsvorbereitungen auf dem Lande une andere Prosa aus dem Nachlaß*, ed. Brod [Frankfurt am Main: Fischer, 1953], 42).

19 The term *asignificatory* is borrowed from Deleuze and Guattari, *Kafka: Toward a Minor Literature*, trans. Dana Polan (Minneapolis: University of Minnesota Press, 1986). It is perhaps interesting to note in this context that Deleuze and Guattari never place a period after 'K' – their misreading of the protagonist's 'name' suggests, I believe, a view of a protagonist who has achieved a certain completion. In Kafka's text, however, K. always appears as an abbreviation of something unknown, something cut off from the possibility of self-completion.

20 Thus making K. very Derridean indeed. See for example Derrida, 'Me – Psychoanalysis: An Introduction to the Translation of "The Shell and the Kernel" by Nicolas Abraham,' *Diacritics* 9 (Spring 1979), esp.10.

21 On 19 and 20 November 1913, Kafka writes in his diary that 'everything appears to me constructed. . . . I am chasing after constructions' (*Gesammelte Schriften*, 6:108). Nine years later his protagonist chases after a construction Kafka calls the castle.

22 The concept of desire as a consent to time, or the disorders of desire as resulting from an attempt to keep alive the delusion of the ultimate satisfaction, is developed in Lacan's *Écrits*, 46–53. Jameson draws the following conclusions: 'Lacan's stoicism is thus the antithesis of the sexual optimism of Wilhelm Reich, whose doctrine of orgasm amounts to what the Structuralists would no doubt think of as a myth of total satisfaction, analogous to the myth of total presence denounced by Derrida' (*The Prison-House of Language*, 72).

23 Lacan, *Écrits*, 691.

24 The very next chapter rewards K. with the repetition of this moment. Chapter 4 reinstitutes the intricate configuration of eros, estrangement, and search when, for example, the 'raging embraces' of their 'searching' bodies 'did not let them forget but rather reminded [Frieda and K.] of their duty to search' (60). This is just one instance of Kafka's eroticization of despair; the lovers' search leads them through a region whose only 'ground' is furnished by their bodies and not the castle or Klamm. For 'just as dogs claw desperately at the ground, so they clawed at each other's body; and helplessly, disappointedly over the other's face' (60).

25 Lacan, *Écrits,* 691.

26 See especially the interpretations of Maria Torok, 'Histoire de Peur,' *Études freudiennes* (Paris: Denöel, 1975), nos.9–10, and Anthony Wilden, *The Language of the Self,* 182–85, regarding the rapport between 'Professor' Freud and Little Hans. It is perhaps not entirely fortuitous that Kafka sets this scene in a schoolroom, with K. occupying the professor's chair.

27 Derrida extends this notion of an ontological shortcoming within a text to include all texts [*archi-écriture*]. At issue here, however, is the self-deflecting thematization of this lack in the Kafkan text.

28 Kafka, 'The Silence of the Sirens,' in *The Great Wall of China: Stories and Reflections,* trans. Willa and Edwin Muir (New York: Schocken Books, 1970), 143; trans. mod.

29 Kafka, *Tagebücher,* 99, 343.

30 Walser, *Beschreibung einer Form,* 107.

31 See for instance page 194, where K. suggests that had he not been caught by Schwarzer, *The Castle* might well have been a different novel and K. a different type of protagonist, a simple wanderer. He speculates that without Schwarzer his dealings with the castle would have been immediate and only provisional. On page 36, K. muses that 'once he had become undifferentiated [*ununterschiedbar*] from Gerstäcker or Lasemann – and this had to come about quickly, everything depended on this – then all avenues would, with one stroke, surely open up [*sich erschlossen*] for him.'

### STARTING FROM SCRATCH

1 *Being and Time,* trans. John Macquarrie and Edward Robinson (New York: Harper and Row, 1962), 212–13.

### THE WORST NEIGHBORHOODS OF THE REAL

1 Jacques Leibowitch, *A Strange Virus of the Unknown,* trans. Richard Howard (New York: Ballantine Books, 1985), 97.

2 Michael Bernstein, 'On Foucault,' *University Press: An International Quarterly Review of Books* 13 (1984): 14.

3 Michel Foucault, 'Language to Infinity,' *Language, Counter-Memory, Practice: Selected Essays and Interviews,* ed. Donald F. Burchard (Ithaca, NY: Cornell University Press, 1977), 65.

4 Foucault, *History of the Present,* ed. Keith Gandal, Stephen Kitkin, and Paul Rabinow, University of California – Berkeley Publications, Department of Anthropology, 1 (1985).

5 Jean-Luc Nancy, *L'Oubli de la philosophie* (Paris: Galilée, 1986), 56.

6 See Jean-Luc Nancy, 'Exscription,' trans. Katherine Lydon in *The Birth to Presence,* trans. Brian Holmes et al. (Stanford, CA: Stanford University Press, 1993): 319–40.

7 The age of nerves, while no doubt beginning to stir in the corpus of Nietzsche's works, has acquired its peculiar heuristic value through Walter Benjamin who, citing Robert Scheu, has introduced the 'rights of nerves' as a principle of reading and valuation in his essay 'Karl Kraus,' *Reflections,* trans. Edmund Jephcott (New York: Schocken, 1986), 246.

8 Martin Heidegger, 'Nur noch ein Gott kann uns Retten,' *Der Spiegel* 31 (May 1976): 193; trans. Macquarrie and Robinson under the title 'Only a God Can Save Us Now: An Interview with Martin Heidegger,' *Graduate Faculty Philosophical Journal* 6 (1977): 12.

9 Rüdiger Campe, in his 'Pronto! Telefonate und Telefonstimmen,' *Diskursanalysien 1: Medien,* ed. F. A. Kittler, Manfred Schneider, and Weber (Opladen: Westdeutscher, 1987), produces evidence for Husserl's telephobic strain: 'It was publicly known that Edmund Husserl had no love for telephoning. This professor of philosophy in Göttingen (1900–1916) did not own a hookup; this Ordinarius in Freiburg had a number between 1916 and 1920, but then disconnected it for nearly the entire remainder of his tenure. If the thesis can be maintained that there exists an implicit telephone theme in Husserl, this points to an "insidious relationship" of phenomenology not to the "empirical analyses of a person," but rather to the quotidian media-technical life of the philosopher' (87).

10 Derrida, *Ulysse gramophone: Deux mots pour Joyce* (Paris: Galilée, 1987), 108.

11 See Derrida, 'Otobiographies: The Teaching of Nietzsche and the Politics of the Proper Name,' trans. Ronell in *The Ear of the Other: Otobiography, Transference, Translation,* ed. Christie V. McDonald (New York: Schocken Books, 1985), esp.21–22.

12 Friedrich Nietzsche, *Thus Spake Zarathustra* in *The Basic Writings of Friedrich Nietzsche,* trans. Walter Kaufmann (New York: Random, 1968), 250.

13 Nietzsche evokes the telephone, a kind of transcendental Sprint to the beyond, in *The Genealogy of Morals;* but already in the stages of foreplay that figure 'the seduction of the ear,' he starts wiring his texts telephonically in *The Birth of Tragedy.* In the competition between phenomenal image and the sonic blaze, who would be so petty as to deny the possibility that Dionysus is a telephone? 'The Dionysian musician is, without any images, himself pure primordial pain and its primordial reechoing,' (*Basic Writings,* 50).

14 James Joyce, *Ulysses* (New York: Vintage Books, 1961), 414.

15 This was first emitted in Hélène Cixous's lecture of 15 November 1982 at the Colloquium pour James Joyce at the Centre Georges Pompidou, and can now be read as 'Joyce: The (R)use of Writing,' in *Post-Structuralist Joyce: Essays from the French,* ed. Derek Attridge and Daniel Ferrier (Cambridge: Cambridge University Press, 1984), 15–30. Derrida's commentary

runs: 'pour relancer ce qu'Hélène Cixous vient de nous dire: la scène primitive, le père complet, la loi, la jouissance par l'oreille, *by the ear* plus littéralement, par le mot d'"oreille," selon le mode "oreille," par exemple en anglais, et à supposer que jouir par l'oreille soit plutôt féminin' ['To bring up again what Hélène Cixous has just said to us: the primal scene, the complete father, law, coming through the ear, more literally *by the ear* through the word "ear," as in English for example, and which leads one to suppose that the ear's coming is more or less feminine'] (*Ulysse,* 16).

17 Ernest Jones, 'The Madonna's Conception through the Ear,' in *Essays in Applied Psycho-Analysis* (London: The Hogarth Press, 1951); originally in *Jahrbuch der Psychoanalyse* 6 (1914). No attempt will be made to paraphrase this richly connoted essay. Jones addresses the ear and its position of privilege as receptive organ (273); treating, among other elements, the pneuma that generates thought and semen (298); noise; Christian logos, and 'an old German picture which was very popular at the end of the fifteenth century' (reproduced by Pierre Charles Cahier, *Caractéristiques des saints dans l'art populaire,* 1867): 'In this the Annunciation is represented in the form of a hunt. Gabriel blows the angelic greeting on a hunting horn. A unicorn flees (or is blown) to the Virgin Mary. . . . a second example is even less ambiguous, for in it the passage of God's breath is actually imagined as proceeding through a tube; over a portal of the Marienkappelle at Würzburg is a relief-representation of the Annunciation in which the Heavenly Father is blowing along a tube that extends from his lips to the Virgin's ears, and down which the infant Jesus is descending' (reproduced by Fuchs, *Illustrierte Sittengeschichte; Renaissance; Ergänzungsband,* 1909) [330–31]). Further along we read, 'We are not told whether Jesus was actually born, like Rabelais' Gargantua, through his mother's ear, as well as being conceived through it. . . . That the danger of this form of conception is regarded by the Catholics as not having entirely passed is shown by the custom with which all nuns still comply of protecting their chastity against assault by keeping their ears constantly covered, a custom which stands in a direct historical relation to the legend forming the subject of this essay (see Tertullian, *De Virginibus Velandis*)' (345).

18 Blanchot, *The Space of Literature,* trans. Ann Smock (Lincoln: University of Nebraska Press, 1982), 32.

19 Ibid., 32, 33.

20 Philippe Lacoue-Labarthe, 'L'Imprésentable,' *Poétique* 21 (1975): 53–95.

21 Martin Heidegger, *Being and Time,* trans. John Macquarrie and Edward Robinson (New York: Harper and Row, 1962), 127, 177.

22 See Derrida, 'Otobiographies': 'Forcing himself to say who he is, he goes against his natural *habitus* that prompts him to dissimulate behind masks' (10).

THE WALKING SWITCHBOARD

1 The reading of transference as effigy is Lacan's. It reminds us that the telephone can be plugged into the paradoxical dialectic of love, which is split between the expected and the utterly unexpected, the unforeseen (that thing which is *attendu/inattendu*). The telephone as installation plays this structure for keeps; hence its terroristic effect, which also means that, to the extent that you are always expecting it to summon you, the call comes from you. Still, this doesn't prevent it from happening 'suddenly.' The questions of originary nonpresence, the technical and mechanical death drives have been made possible by the thinking of Jacques Derrida. For a detour through the Other, see Rodolphe Gasché, *The Tain of the Mirror: Derrida and the Philosophy of Reflection* (Cambridge, MA: Harvard University Press, 1986), and Christopher Fynsk, *Heidegger: Thought and Historicity* (Ithaca, NY: Cornell University Press, 1986).

2 See Jacques Derrida, 'Freud and the Scene of Writing,' in *Writing and Difference,* trans. Alan Bass (Chicago: University of Chicago Press, 1978).

3 Thomas A. Watson, *Exploring Life: The Autobiography of Thomas A. Watson* (Boston: D. Appleton and Company, 1926), 123.

4 The sudden death of Bell's brothers seems to call for an interpretation of telephonics in terms of the 'cryptonomy' elaborated by Maria Torok and Nicolas Abraham. Bell signed a contract with his second brother promising that communication superior to that of spiritualism would be attempted. Nowadays many grave sites in California maintain open telephone lines.

5 A grammatology of the deaf would have to show the resistance posed by the hearing subject to signing and to a general writing that seems to bypass vocality. The legal history of the deaf would provide an abundant space of reference for this sort of study, recalling, for example, the controversies surrounding citizen status, marital and property rights of the deaf evidenced in Congressional records of the nineteenth century in the United States. It's not a pretty sight. This is what prompted me to consider both ears separately in order to deconstruct, in this place at least, the guarantees we might think we have about being entirely hearing: one of the ears plunges into deafness. In our Congress, Bell fought to have the deaf officially listed under a category separate from that reserved for the 'feeble-minded.'

6 To my knowledge, no study has yet been written on *Frankenstein* and electric circuitry. The novel follows the lines of a felt split between art and science, sexual difference and the mother's unmournable death. (When he takes leave of the city, Victor visits the graveyard – everybody's resting there, but no mention is made of mother.) Electricity always turns on the phantasm of reanimation. See Peter Haining, *The Man Who Was Frankenstein* (London: Frederick Muller, Limited, 1979), which focuses on An-

drew Crosse, the electrician who turned Mary Shelley on. On electricity and melancholia, for instance: 'To a degree, this company lifted Andrew Crosse out of the mood of melancholia brought on by his mother's death, and there are indications that he began to start playing jokes again with electrical machines' (37). Moreover, the monsterized figure, often going under the name of 'the frame,' may be read as a material frame in the sense of *Ge-stell.*

7 The line – "Kein Ding sei wo das Wort gebricht" – comes from Stephan George's poem "Das Wort."

8 Martin Heidegger, 'The Origin of the Work of Art,' trans. Albert Hofstadter, in *Poetry, Language, Thought* (New York: Harper and Row, 1971).

9 *The Question Concerning Technology and Other Essays,* trans. William Lovitt (New York: Harper and Row, 1977), 13. When Heidegger became disenchanted with the destinal promise of the national socialist revolution, he began to assimilate its movement to a reading of error and technology. In his introduction to 'The Origin of the Work of Art,' Hofstadter evokes the hollow of the technological age when consulting the task of the poet. For Heidegger, he writes, citing Hölderlin, this 'time of technology is a destitute time, the time of the world's night, in which man has even forgotten the true nature of being . . . a dark and deprived time' (xv). This is why we are traveling the path of technological light, for however nuanced and 'deep' Heidegger's encounter with technology may be, its effects, as well as the context of its expression, often propose peculiar acts of self-blinding which the telephone writes out for us.

10 In Woody Allen's film of collapsed media, *The Purple Rose of Cairo,* the single object that traverses both asserted worlds is a white telephone which engages inner and outer dimensions simultaneously, the real and the fictive. Cinema went for the telephone without reservation, at times assigning lines to it of an enigmatic theatre of visible speech. It is a rare thing on camera, particularly in the case of television, for anyone, when hanging up the phone, to utter 'good-bye.' The call normally interrupts narrative without granting itself closure. The telephone inevitably tends to participate in a scene metonymically in order to call up a death sentence; it is a commanding machine of terroristic performative competence. For example, Bob Cummings says in Alfred Hitchcock's *Dial M for Murder:* 'That has a pretty guilty ring to it' and 'It's delayed action.' Or the hanging phone culminates in having the character juridically declared to hang. See also John Auerbach's *The Phone Call,* wherein the one who picks up the phone finds herself under orders to kill. She fulfills the command. Turns out to have been a wrong number. In this light consider also, *Lady in a Cage, Pennsylvania 6-5000, The Man Who Envied Women,* and Kurosawa's *High and Low,* as well as the entire gamut of the *Poltergeist* series and spin-offs. For the sheerly electric conjunction, *Cell 2455: Death Row*

furnishes a good example imaging two pieces of technology together: the electric chair and the telephone. At the scheduled moment of execution, the electrocutee is intended to receive a pardon, but the governor's secretary does not get through in time, having dialed a wrong number.

THE DIFFERENDS OF MAN

1 Jacques Derrida's immense reading of the Holocaust and the metaphysics of race includes: 'White Mythology: Metaphor in the Text of Philosophy,' *Margins of Philosophy,* trans. Alan Bass (Chicago: University of Chicago Press, 1982): 207–72; 'On a Newly Arisen Apocalyptic Tone in Philosophy,' *Raising the Tone of Philosophy: Late Essays by Immanuel Kant, Transformative Critique by Jacques Derrida,* trans. and ed. Peter Fenves (Baltimore: Johns Hopkins University Press, 1993): 117–71; 'Racism's Last Word,' trans. Peggy Kamuf, in *'Race,' Writing, and Difference,* ed. Henry Louis Gates, Jr. (Chicago: University of Chicago Press, 1985): 329–38; 'Geschlecht I: Sexual Difference, Ontological Difference,' trans. Ruben Berezdivin, *Research in Phenomenology* 13 (1983): 65–83; 'Geschlecht II: Heidegger's Hand,' trans. John P. Leavey, Jr., in *Deconstruction in Philosophy: The Texts of Jacques Derrida,* ed. John Sallis (Chicago: University of Chicago Press, 1987): 161–96; *The Post Card: From Socrates to Freud and Beyond,* trans. Bass (Chicago: University of Chicago Press, 1987); 'Two Words for Joyce,' trans. Geoffrey Bennington, in *Post-Structuralist Joyce: Essays from the French,* ed. Derrick Attridge and Daniel Ferrer (Cambridge: Cambridge University Press, 1984); *Of Spirit: Heidegger and the Question,* trans. Bennington and Rachel Bowlby (Chicago: University of Chicago Press, 1989); *Glas,* trans. Leavey, and Richard Rand (Lincoln: University of Nebraska Press, 1986); 'Otobiographies: The Teaching of Nietzsche and the Politics of the Proper Name,' trans. Ronell, in *The Ear of the Other: Otobiography, Transference, Translation,* ed. Christie V. McDonald (New York: Schocken Books, 1985): 1–38; *Cinders,* trans. and ed. Ned Lukacher (Lincoln: University of Nebraska Press, 1991); 'Restitutions,' *Truth in Painting,* trans. Bennington and Ian McLeod (Chicago: University of Chicago Press, 1987); ' "Eating Well"; or, The Calculation of the Subject: Jacques Derrida Interviewed by Jean-Luc Nancy,' in *Who Comes after the Subject?* ed. Eduardo Cadava, Peter Connor, and Nancy (New York: Routledge, 1991): 96–119; *Schibboleth: Pour Paul Celan* (Paris: Galilée, 1986).

2 Jean-François Lyotard, *Heidegger et 'les juifs'* (Paris: Galilée, 1988) 16; trans. Andreas Michael and Mark S. Roberts under the title *Heidegger and 'the jews'* (Minneapolis: University of Minnesota Press, 1990), 4.

3 In what follows, I translate and cite from the 'débat' following 'Discussions: Ou, Phraser "après Auschwitz" ' in *Les Fins de l'homme: À partir du travail de Jacques Derrida, colloque de Cerisy, 1980* (Paris: Galilée, 1981), 312–13.

4 Lyotard, *Heidegger et 'les juifs,'* 152.

5 Lyotard, *Just Gaming*, trans. Wlad Godzich (Minneapolis: University of Minnesota Press, 1985), 52–53.

6 See David Carroll, *Paraesthetics: Foucault, Lyotard, Derrida* (New York: Methuen, 1987); Geoffrey Bennington, *Lyotard: Writing the Event* (New York: Columbia University Press, 1988), and 'August: Double Justice,' *Diacritics* 14 (Fall 1984): 69.

7 Carroll, 'Rephrasing the Political with Kant and Lyotard: From Aesthetic to Political Judgments,' *Diacritics* 14 (Fall 1984): 80.

8 Jean-Luc Nancy and Philippe Lacoue-Labarthe, *Rejouer le politique* (Paris: Galilée, 1981), 18.

9 See Cecile Lindsay's discussion of *Au Juste* in 'Experiments in Postmodern Dialogue,' *diacritics* 14 (Fall 1984): 52–62, esp.59.

10 Jean-François Lyotard, *The Differend: Phrases in Dispute*, trans. Georges Van Den Abbeele (Minneapolis: University of Minnesota Press, 1988), xi.

11 Jürgen Habermas, *The Philosophical Discourse of Modernity*, trans. Frederick G. Lawrence (Cambridge: MIT Press, 1987), 182, 181.

12 Jürgen Habermas, *Philosophical-Political Profiles*, trans. Frederick G. Lawrence (Cambridge, MA: MIT Press, 1983), 33. Consider also the waste-product metaphors with which Habermas insults deconstruction, for example, deconstruction lets the 'refuse heap of interpretations, which it wants to clear away in order to get at the buried foundations, mount even higher' (*The Philosophical Discourse of Modernity*, 183). Beyond the indecency of metaphorical selection, the statement makes little sense.

I would like to take the opportunity to correct a technical error I made in the first printed version of this essay, when I attributed this last citation to the *Philosophical-Political Profiles*. In fact, it occurs, as cited above, in *The Philosophical Discourse of Modernity*. In the interest of clarity, I should say, again, that Habermas is not being associated with anti-Semitism. Rather, the essay addresses here the peculiar logic according to which Derrida is excluded from the domain of serious philosophy. The logic dividing philosophy and Jewish mysticism produces genuinely disconcerting effects. For further discussion, see the excellent book by Alexander García-Düttmann, *Das Gedächtnis des Denkens: Versuch über Heidegger und Adorno* (Frankfurt am Main: Suhrkamp Verlag, 1991), 254ff., where several pages are devoted to Habermas's assimilation of Derrida to Jewish mysticism.

13 Michael J. MacDonald, '"Jewgreek and Greekjew": The Concept of the Trace in Derrida and Levinas,' *Philosophy Today* 35 (Fall 1991): 218, 219.

14 Derrida, *Glas*, trans. John P. Leavey, Jr., and Richard Rand (Lincoln: University of Nebraska Press, 1986), 55; trans. mod. See also Werner Hamacher's work on Hegel and Christianity, 'Pleroma – Zu Genesis und Struktur einer dialektischen Hermeneutik bei Hegel,' which appeared as

the introduction to Hegel's 'Der Geist des Christentums,' *Schriften 1796–1800* (Frankfurt: Ullstien, 1978).

15 MacDonald, '"Jewgreek and Greekjew,"' 219.

16 Philippe Lacoue-Labarthe, 'Talks,' trans. Christopher Fynsk, *diacritics* 14 (Fall 1984), 24–25. The talk was originally delivered on 1 August 1982, at Cerisy-la-Salle during the colloquium honoring the works of Lyotard.

17 See Jean-Luc Nancy, 'La Liberté est l'in-fini de la pensée,' *L'Expérience de la liberté* (Paris: Galilée, 1988).

18 Werner Hamacher, 'Journals, Politics: Notes on Paul de Man's Wartime Journalism,' trans. Susan Bernstein et al., *Responses: On Paul de Man's Wartime Journalism*, ed. Werner Hamacher, Neil Hertz, and Thomas Keenan (Lincoln: University of Nebraska Press, 1989), 459.

19 See Lacoue-Labarthe, *La Fiction du politique (Heidegger, l'art et politique)* (Paris: Bourgois, 1989); Friedrich Kittler, *Gramaphon, Film, Typewriter* (Berlin: Brickmann und Bose, 1987), and *Lectures on the SS, Computers, Military Strategies* in Siegen, Kassel, and Bochum (1989); Laurence A. Rickels, *Aberrations of Mourning: Writing on German Crypts* (Detroit: Wayne State University, 1988); Werner Hamacher, 'Journals, Politics'; Alice Yaeger Kaplan, *Reproductions of Banality: Fascism, Literature and French Intellectual Life* (Minneapolis: University of Minnesota Press, 1986), 135–37; Avital Ronell, *The Telephone Book: Technology – Schizophrenia – Electric Speech* (Lincoln: University of Nebraska Press, 1989).

20 Lyotard, *Heidegger et 'les juifs,'* 130.

21 *Shoah: An Oral History of the Holocaust (The Complete Text of the Film)* (New York: Pantheon, 1985), 103.

SUPPORT OUR TROPES

1 I have treated the technologically constellated state and the telephone in *The Telephone Book: Technology – Schizophrenia – Electric Speech* (Lincoln: University of Nebraska Press, 1989). Consider George Bush's departure from the White House. His stoicism collapses only when he has to separate from the telephone operators: 'He thought he could handle the farewell to the White House operators. But, as he put it, "I overflowed." They had been for so long, so diligent, so patient. John Kennedy had said, "they could raise Lazarus." They had hooked Bush up to the far world's leaders like no other president' (Hugh Sidey, 'Bush's Flight into the Sunset,' *Time*, 1 Feb. 1993, 47). One might also consider, in the context of the telephone and the technologically constellated state, the terror of Stalin's nocturnal phone calls.

2 In 'The *Differends* of Man' (infra), an essay on Lyotard, deconstruction and Heidegger, I have tried to reveal historical woundings that will not heal.

3 Derrida has explored the polysemous aspects of James Joyce's 'he war' in 'Two Words for Joyce,' in *Acts of Literature: Jacques Derrida,* ed. Derek Attridge (New York: Routledge, 1992).

4 On Bush's discourse, see the challenging readings produced in Diane Rubinstein's essay, 'This Is Not a President: Baudrillard, Bush and Enchanted Simulation,' in *The Hysterical Male: New Feminist Theory,* ed. Arthur and Marilouise Kroker (New York: St. Martin's Press, 1991), 259ff. The principle of nonlinkage belongs to psychoanalytical investigations. Consider in this regard the definition of 'isolation' in J. Laplanche and J.-B. Pontalis, *The Language of Psycho-Analysis,* trans. Donald Nicholson-Smith (New York: W.W. Norton and Company, 1973).

5 Cited in Paul Simms, 'How to Become President,' *Spy,* Nov. 1988, 128.

6 Mary McGrory, *Washington Post,* 29 Sept. 1988, A2.

7 Rubinstein, 'This Is Not a President,' 264.

8 See Jean-Luc Nancy, 'Our History,' trans. Cynthia Chase, Richard Klein, and A. Mitchell Brown in *diacritics* 20 (Fall 1990). I am also following the protocols established by Nancy for considering this war. See 'Guerre, Droit, Souvraineté – Techné,' *Les Temps modernes* 539 (June 1991).

9 Nancy, 'Our History,' 107.

10 Ibid., 101.

11 Richard Ben Kramer, 'How Bush Made It: A Portrait of the President as a Young Man,' *Esquire,* June 1991, 82.

12 Ibid., 83.

13 Nancy, 'Our History,' 108.

14 When George Bush proudly proclaimed that he could now abandon the odious burden, imposed by his mother, of eating broccoli, he signaled the decline of the superegoical function for him. As prez nothing would be forced down his throat any longer; he could expulse the law without remorse. Elsewhere I have shown what it means for Freud 'to learn to love spinach' – an unbearable internalization of mucosity. For Freud's table of laws, this turn toward the totemized spinach meant he had successfully integrated the superego and lawgiver. I analyze the utterance 'Eat your spinach!' – a once common injunction issued by parents to their children – in *Dictations: On Haunted Writing* (Lincoln, NE: University of Nebraska Press, 1993). The spinach episode in Freud's oeuvre functions as an exemplary passage through Oedipus. The more phallically organized broccoli, which Bush has graduated into not eating, suggests rather a refusal of castration: the classical Freudian condition of disavowal, which forms his major character traits.

15 Cited in Joel Beinin, 'Origins of the Gulf War,' *Open Pamphlet Magazine Series* 3 (February 1991): 32.

16 Paul de Man, *Allegories of Reading: Figural Language in Rousseau, Nietzsche, Rilke, and Proust* (New Haven, CT: Yale University Press, 1979), 157.

17 This argument implies some familiarity with the debates figured by Derrida and Lacan in the case of Edgar Allan Poe's 'The Purloined Letter.' For this discussion, see Lacan's 'Le Séminaire sur "La Lettre volée,"' *Écrits* (Paris: Éditions du Seuil, 1966); an English translation is available in *The Purloined Poe: Lacan, Derrida and Psychoanalytic Readings,* trans. Jeffrey Mehlman, ed. John P. Muller and William J. Richardson (Baltimore: Johns Hopkins University Press, 1988); and Derrida's 'Le Facteur de la vérité,' in *The Post Card: From Socrates to Freud and Beyond,* trans. Alan Bass (Chicago: University of Chicago Press, 1987) and also his 'My Chances/ *Mes Chances:* A Rendezvous with Some Epicurean Stereophonies,' trans. I. Harvey and A. Ronell, in *Taking Chances: Derrida, Psychoanalysis, and Literature,* ed. Joseph H. Smith and William Kerrigan (Baltimore: Johns Hopkins University Press, 1984).

18 See Nancy's work on Georges Bataille and community in *The Inoperative Community and Other Essays,* trans. and ed. Peter T. Connor (Minneapolis: University of Minnesota Press, 1991), 17–23.

19 Immanuel Kant, *Perpetual Peace and Other Essays,* trans. Ted Humphrey (Indianapolis: Hackett, 1983).

20 Derrida has evoked some of these motifs in his treatment of Benjamin's essay in 'Force of Law: "The Mystical Foundation of Authority,"' trans. Mary Quaintance, *Deconstruction and the Possibility of Justice,* special issue of *Cardozo Law Review* 2 (July–Aug. 1990).

21 See Timothy Druckrey, 'Revenge of the Nerds: An Interview with Jaron Lanier,' *Afterimage* 18 (May 1991). Some utterances that invite interpretation include: 'This technology has the promise of transcending the body, depending on what you think the body is.' 'There's no object that could be less biological or messy. It doesn't have blood, it doesn't fart, it doesn't have eczema. The slick blackness of technology is a way of avoiding the messiness of the body. I think that's why sometimes you see more men associated with this technology than women. Men find themselves in a more desperate situation with the flight from death.' 'From a political point of view the clear precedent for virtual reality is the telephone.' 'I view VR as a fancy telephone in many ways.' 'The young generation who saw the political stakes in struggles over representation . . . now they have to face up to its indeterminacy. Is there something like an ethics of technology?' 'What I'm hoping the virtual reality technology will do is sensitize people to these subjective or experiential aspects of life and help them notice what a marvelous, mystical thing it is to communicate with another person.'

22 John Barlow, 'Life in the Data Cloud: Scratching Your Eyes Back In,' interview with Jaron Lanier, *Mondo 2000* (Summer 1990): 2. 'The computer is a map you can inhabit. Which is very seductive. It's mostly seductive because it makes you seem very powerful. So it's good for the ego, . . . a way

for people to get ecstatic and be with each other.' While the ego remains a problem, I do wish to signal that being with [*Mitsein*], ecstatic temporality, and being called are crucial issues in the philosophy of Martin Heidegger. Lanier is also inclined to plug the telephone: 'My favorite story is the telephone. The telephone is a total win.' If Lanier is unwilling to count the losses, and keeps tallying technology according to egological scoreboards, this *may* be traceable to the fact that his mother was a victim of destructive technologies and suffered the dehumanizing effects of the Nazi camps. While I do not feel that it is necessarily appropriate in this case to psychoanalyze VR's unconscious genesis, I have tried to configure these relations – the maternal function, technology, and the terroristic state – in *The Telephone Book.*

23 Barlow, 'Life in the Data Cloud,' 49. Also see, Adam Heilbrun, 'Virtual Reality: An Interview with Jaron Lanier,' *Whole Earth Review* (Fall 1989).

24 Nancy, 'Our History,' 98.

TRAUMATV

1 Cited in Cathy Caruth, 'Unclaimed Experience: Trauma and the Possibility of History,' in *Literature and the Ethical Question,* ed. Claire Nouvet, *Yale French Studies* 79 (1991): 181.

2 This essay was written while 'Cops on Trial' was being aired on Fox Television, prior to the announcement of the Simi Valley's jury's verdict of not guilty. The logic of the ethical scream by which testimonial video is here understood appears to have stood its test: when the verdict of nonreading came out, the video produced effects of insurrection on the streets. It will not do to go with the unassailed diction of 'burning down one's *own* neighborhood' when in fact it is a matter of radical expropriation and being not at home, which is the subject of this paper. Delivered in New York City, Oakland, Berkeley, and Los Angeles before and during the 'riots,' this paper retains stylistic traces of the circumstances in which it was first presented. (I am not as opposed to the usage of the word *riots* as others have been, no doubt because I am not seriously susceptible to supporting the order or logic of reason to which the riot addresses itself. As a type of noise and disturbance, *riot* belongs to the field of the ethical scream.) I have benefited greatly from the papers and discussions of Fred Moten, Peter Connor, and Shireen Patell.

3 Jacques Lacan, 'Television,' in a special issue, ed. Joan Copjec, of *October,* no.40 (Spring 1987): 36.

4 On interruption and the logic of destricturation, I am following Jacques Derrida's argument in his discussion of Levinas in 'En ce moment même dans cet ouvrage me voici,' *Psyché: Inventions de l'autre* (Paris: Galilée, 1987), 159–202.

5 A number of works have provided the frame within which to cast the catastrophic topicalities of television/video. I have benefited from discussions with and papers by a community of media scholars, which includes Mary Anne Doane, Gregory Ulmer, Meghan Morris, Maggie Morse, John Hanhardt, Jonathan Crary, Mark Taylor, Patricia Mellencamp, David Levi Strauss, Gilles Deleuze, and others. I would also like to acknowledge a paper given by Deborah Esch, 'No Time Like the Present: The "Fact" of Television' at the University of California Humanities Research Institute, Irvine, March 1992. It was there, while participating in the 'Future Deconstructions' conference, that I had the opportunity to watch intensive television and follow the Rodney King trial in detail.

6 I am implicitly networking through the signifying chain of home-*homme* and homophobia. The technical media has thrown into relief an unreadable line between sexual marking and racial identification. On the law and its relation to sodomy in Freud, see my 'The *Sujet Suppositaire:* Freud and Rat Man' (infra). In this essay I begin to develop a reading of the difference between detective and police work in terms of their relation to truth.

7 Television has made an increasing number of arrests in recent years; one show has recently celebrated its two-hundredth arrest.

8 See Jacques Derrida's remarkable discussion of Walter Benjamin's 'Critique of Violence' in 'Force of Law: The "Mystical Foundation of Authority,"' trans. Mary Quaintance, *Deconstruction and the Possibility of Justice,* spec. issue of *Cardozo Law Review* 2:5–6 (July/August 1990): 1009.

9 Caruth, introduction to *Psychoanalysis, Culture, Trauma II,* ed. Caruth, special issue of *American Imago* 48 (Winter 1991): 417. On the relation of atopy and flashback, Caruth writes that what the 'history of flashback tells – as psychiatry, psychoanalysis and neurobiology equally suggest – is, therefore, a history that literally *has no place,* neither in the past, in which it was not fully experienced, nor in the present, in which its precise images and enactments are not fully understood. In its repeated imposition as both image and amnesia, the trauma thus seems to evoke the difficult truth of a history that is constituted by the very incomprehensibility of its occurrence' (418).

10 On an urgent inflection of this question, see also Caruth and Thomas Keenan, '"The AIDS Crisis Is Not Over": A Conversation with Gregg Bordowitz, Douglas Crimp, and Laura Pinsky,' in *Psychoanalysis, Culture, Trauma II,* 539–56.

11 Maurice Blanchot, 'The Essential Solitude,' *The Space of Literature,* trans. Ann Smock (Lincoln: University of Nebraska Press, 1982), 32.

12 See 'Support Our Tropes (Reading Desert Storm),' esp. the 'Activist Supplement' (infra).

13 Consider Paul de Man's demonstration of metonymic substitution in 'Time and History in Wordsworth,' *Diacritics* 17 (Winter 1987): 4–17.

14 For two relatively new readings of technicity and *Ge-stell* in Heidegger, I would suggest Véronique Foti's *Heidegger and the Poets: Poiēsis/Sophia/Technē* (Atlantic Highlands, NJ: Humanities Press International, 1992), and, especially, Jean-Luc Nancy's title essay in *Une Pensée finie* (Paris: Galilée, 1990).

15 Foti, *Heidegger and the Poets,* 4.

16 The tensional relationship between interpretation and reading is drawn from Andrzej Warminski, *Readings in Interpretation: Hölderlin, Hegel, Heidegger* (Minneapolis: University of Minnesota Press, 1987).

17 Sigmund Freud, 'Jenseits des Lustprinzips,' *Psychologie des Unbewußten* (Frankfurt: Fischer Taschenbuch Verlag, 1975), 239. For the English translation see *Beyond the Pleasure Principle, Complete Psychological Works,* ed. James Strachey, 18:29 (trans. mod.).

18 Caruth, introduction to *Psychoanalysis, Culture and Trauma I,* ed. Caruth, special issue of *American Imago* 48 (Spring 1991): 7.

19 Kevin Newmark, 'Traumatic Poetry: Charles Baudelaire and the Shock of Laughter,' in *Psychoanalysis, Culture, Trauma II,* 534.

20 Shoshana Felman and Dori Laub, *Testimony: Crises of Witnessing in Literature, Psychoanalysis, and History* (New York: Routledge, 1991), 18.

21 B.A. van der Kolk and Otto van der Hart, 'The Intrusive Past,' in *Psychoanalysis, Culture, Trauma I,* 448, 449.

# INDEX

In the *Texts and Contexts* series:

*Affective Genealogies:*
*Psychoanalysis, Postmodernism,*
*and the "Jewish Question"*
*after Auschwitz*
By Elizabeth J. Bellamy

*Sojourners:*
*The Return of German Jews*
*and the Question of Identity*
By John Borneman and Jeffrey M. Peck

*Serenity in Crisis:*
*A Preface to Paul de Man,*
*1939–1960*
By Ortwin de Graef

*Titanic Light:*
*Paul de Man's Post-Romanticism,*
*1960–1969*
By Ortwin de Graef

*The Future of a Negation:*
*Reflections on the Question of Genocide*
By Alain Finkielkraut
Translated by Mary Byrd Kelly

*The Imaginary Jew*
By Alain Finkielkraut
Translated by Kevin O'Neill
and David Suchoff

*The Wisdom of Love*
By Alain Finkielkraut
Translated by Kevin O'Neill
and David Suchoff

*The House of Joshua:*
*Meditations on Family and Place*
By Mindy Thompson Fullilove

*Inscribing the Other*
By Sander L. Gilman

*Antisemitism, Misogyny, and the Logic of Cultural Difference: Cesare Lombroso and Matilde Serao*
By Nancy A. Harrowitz

*Opera: Desire, Disease, Death*
By Linda Hutcheon and Michael Hutcheon

*Between Redemption and Doom: The Strains of German-Jewish Modernism*
By Noah Isenberg

*Poetic Process*
By W. G. Kudszus

*Keepers of the Motherland: German Texts by Jewish Women Writers*
By Dagmar C. G. Lorenz

*Madness and Art: The Life and Works of Adolf Wölfli*
By Walter Morgenthaler
Translated and with an introduction by Aaron H. Esman in collaboration with Elka Spoerri

*Organic Memory: History and the Body in the Late Nineteenth and Early Twentieth Centuries*
by Laura Otis

*Crack Wars: Literature, Addiction, Mania*
By Avital Ronell

*Finitude's Score: Essays for the End of the Millennium*
By Avital Ronell

*Herbarium/Verbarium:*
*The Discourse of Flowers*
By Claudette Sartiliot

*Budapest Diary:*
*In Search of the Motherbook*
By Susan Rubin Suleiman

*Rahel Levin Varnhagen:*
*The Life and Work of a*
*German Jewish Intellectual*
By Heidi Thomann Tewarson

*The Jews and Germany:*
*From the "Judeo-German Symbiosis"*
*to the Memory of Auschwitz*
By Enzo Traverso
Translated by Daniel Weissbort

*Richard Wagner and the*
*Anti-Semitic Imagination*
By Marc A. Weiner

*Undertones of Insurrection:*
*Music, Politics, and the*
*Social Sphere in the Modern*
*German Narrative*
By Marc A. Weiner

*The Mirror and the Word:*
*Modernism, Literary Theory,*
*and Georg Trakl*
By Eric B. Williams